entertaining

entertaining

FRANCES BISSELL

MACMILLAN

To Tom, always, and to the Daughters of Britannia

First published 2002 by Macmillan
an imprint of Pan Macmillan Ltd
Pan Macmillan, 20 New Wharf Road, London N1 9RR
Basingstoke and Oxford
Associated companies throughout the world
www.panmacmillan.com

ISBN 0 333 74129 3

9 8 7 6 5 4 3 2 1

A CIP catalogue record for this book is available from
the British Library.

Typeset in Helvetica and Minion by
SX Composing DTP, Rayleigh, Essex
Printed and bound in Great Britain by
Mackays of Chatham plc, Chatham, Kent

contents

introduction

I started writing this book about thirty years ago. Well, perhaps it is more accurate to say that that is how long I have been accumulating the experience on which the book is based. It is all about entertaining, not only how to do it, but how to enjoy it.

I have friends who say they never give dinner parties any more. They 'invite people for supper'. But when you go to their house for supper, a glass of bubbly is pressed into your hand before you have a chance to take your coat off. When the time comes to eat, the dining table sparkles with the best silver, china and crystal. The candles are lit, the white wine is brought out, properly chilled, and something red and glorious is served with the main course, as well as something delicious with the pud, or rather puds. Before that, there will be carefully chosen cheeses, and sometimes, even homemade bread. I call this a dinner party. Why all this inverted snobbery about a name?

Over the years much has been written in the style pages about the demise and resurgence of the dinner party; friends now meet for supper at each other's homes, eating informally at the kitchen table, dining off dishes bought from the local M&S. Or they meet at the latest fashionable restaurant. Perhaps it is this that gives the game away. These anti-dinner party souls live in the big city, where there is a 'latest fashionable restaurant' to which they can go.

But not all metropolitans are anti-dinner party, and not all kitchen suppers are dressed up convenience food. Once, staying overnight with friends, we were told that Saturday evening was to be a kitchen supper for the four of us, Saturday lunch having been for sixteen people. The food was simple and delicious and yes, convenient, in its way – figs and prosciutto, a creamy fish pie and leftover summer pudding. But the vintage Bollinger was followed by 1986 Bâtard Montrachet, from two different growers.

At home, I have been cooking for friends and family for many years, more than twenty-five of them documented in a series of food diaries. At the end of each year, I buy a French household 'Agenda', and use it to make a note of what I cook every day, what is in season, how much it costs, and an occasional shopping list. I started doing this long before I became a food writer, and it has proved useful many times. I like, for instance, to check that I am not planning to give friends the same main course they ate the last time, and Tom, my husband, always wants to know what wines he served.

Food and wine, though an essential element in any dinner party, soirée, supper or call it what you will, are not the only consideration. There is also, for want of a better word, etiquette. Life is too short, and we are all too busy to spend three or four hours in uncongenial company. In the days of casual telephone invitations, pitfalls await the unwary. 'Are you free Friday evening?' You say yes, and then you hear, 'and we thought we would invite X and Y.' You can't stand X and Y, but it is too late to back out. A better approach might be, 'We are inviting X and Y for dinner next Friday, and we wondered if you would be free to come too.' There is now enough time for an inventive and face-saving excuse to be proffered on the other end of the phone.

I cannot commend this ploy too highly. A friend told me that she was once left sitting at a dinner party in the realization that her husband was never going to return from a visit to the loo. It was summer, and he had been overwhelmed by the sight of the open front door and the garden gate, a much more attractive prospect, he later told her, than returning to the table to sit down again beside a particularly difficult guest.

Tom says that two expatriates should never be seated next to each other at a dinner party. If they wanted to talk to their countrymen, they would return home. Expats are not tourists; they secretly want to belong.

'Is there anything you can't eat or drink?' is a question I always ask if someone is coming to dinner for the first time. When people answer on behalf of others, they do not always get it right. Who would have thought melon would be a problem? Once I served melon sorbet to some friends and, after smelling it, one of our guests turned quite funny and had to leave the room. His companion had told me earlier in the day that he could eat anything. On another occasion, a food writer friend was bringing a well-known television cook from America for dinner. Do ask her if there is anything she can't eat, I said. 'Oh, don't worry darling; she's a foodie, and can eat anything', he replied. But one look at her face, when I served a heaped tureen of mussels, told me otherwise. Smoked salmon came to the rescue though. I wish I could claim always to be so organized.

It is as well to stay relaxed and flexible so that, when disaster occurs, you are not so tightly wound that you snap. I will never forget inviting two serious and important food people for dinner one evening when I was a fledgling cookery writer. As a main course, I had planned roasted veal kidneys with a Roquefort sauce, an idea developed from a dish that I once ate at Le Cochon d'Or in Paris. I thought I would get a little *mise-en-place* out of the way and, having made the sauce, I decided to half roast the kidneys, and finish them off at the last minute. But I cooked them beyond that point of perfect pinkness. What to do? It was already after 6.30. I didn't have a freezer, from which to pull out a delectable little standby, and the late-night corner shop had only miserable looking steaks and chops. Tom, who is always looking for a new pasta creation, suggested I chop the kidneys and, with the addition of herbs and spice and a little ricotta, make tortelloni, which I did, serving it with the Roquefort sauce. I do not recommend making fresh pasta an hour before your guests appear, but in this instance it proved a good solution.

When calamity strikes, as it inevitably does, even to cooks and cookery writers, even after years of experience, and even on occasions that have been planned with military precision, the first, and only, rule is don't complain, don't explain.

Assuming that it happens after your guests have arrived, you have about ten seconds to assess the damage, and two or three minutes to put it right before your guests cotton on and become embarrassed.

Almost worse is having it happen about five minutes before the doorbell rings. At 7.55 one winter evening I was taking my mincemeat and almond tart out of the oven, ready to place it on a rack by the sink to cool. It was quite heavy and I could feel the baking tray tilt, starting the tart's inexorable slide. I tried to clutch it and arrest its fall, hot tart against tummy, then it hit my shoes and the floor. I slid what I could back on to the baking tray, scooping up as much filling as possible, binned the broken bits, managed to clean the sticky mess from the floor and my shoes, and was just changing my blouse when the door bell rang. I was catatonic for the first half hour. When it was time to serve the dessert, I neatened the edges, cut the remains into four elegant triangles, and liberally dusted them with icing sugar. Icing sugar is quite indispensable, especially for disguising pies, clafoutis and tarts that have been left in the oven a few minutes more than was good for them. For this reason I keep a small sieve permanently in the same bag as my icing sugar.

Some common problems – to do with size of oven or fish kettle not matching turkey or salmon – are inexcusable, however, and can easily be avoided. For goodness' sake, use your brain and measure before you order.

With other, less predictable disasters, inventiveness can often save the day. Once my tomato pudding wouldn't turn out of the basin. I forked it up, served it in small bowls garnished with mint or basil, and called it Tuscan bread and tomato salad. Similarly, when I had a panna cotta that refused to slip out of its mould, I whizzed it with a stick blender until smooth, and spooned it over raspberries. You could call on other fruity emergency rations and serve it perhaps with a layer of crushed amaretti between cream and fruit, and a splash of fruit or almond liqueur. No emergency rations? Fold in grated lemon zest, add a dash of sweet white wine when whizzing, and spoon into elegant glasses. With a generous grating of nutmeg on top, you have a perfect syllabub.

Many years ago, at a charity dinner for the Académie Culinaire, I offered, as a prize in the raffle, to cook dinner for the highest bidder and five friends. It was both gratifying, and somewhat overwhelming at the end of the bidding, to realize that I would be cooking dinner for Anton and Kathrin Mosimann and their guests, including, I later discovered, Nico Ladenis and his wife, Dinah Jane. I had decided on oriental salmon wontons for appetizers, followed by fennel and champagne risotto, and then pot-roast quail stuffed with black pudding as the main course, farmhouse cheeses next, and to finish, a version of summer pudding, using tropical fruit, which I thought a very clever idea. Ha! There is such a thing as trying to be too clever.

The dinner was for a Sunday night, and on Sunday morning, I had a peek at the individual puddings I had made the night before. Bread slices had been replaced with sponge cake, tart summer berries with diced mango, guava and papaya with passion fruit juice. The puddings tasted dull and bland; they were also, since tropical fruit has no pectin to hold it together, falling to pieces. Still with no freezer to fall back on, I had to look to the local shops for the solution. New season's Spanish strawberries, yoghurt, ricotta and cream, and just enough time, enabled me to make coeurs à la crème, macerate some strawberries, and turn some into a coulis. That experience taught me a couple of lessons. Some recipes are so perfect that they cannot be improved upon, and certainly not changed with impunity. And dinner parties do not have to be complicated to be successful.

Since then, I have cooked often for chefs, and I have to say that they are among my favourite guests, as they are the most appreciative and undemanding. For them, I usually cook the simplest, homeliest food. In winter, for instance, it might be a game cobbler, a meatloaf or a shoulder of lamb, slowly braised on a bed of sliced onions and potatoes, in preference to 'noisettes d'agneau en robe de soir', as it were.

The cellar master in our house has reminded me to include wine etiquette in this introductory note. Do you take a bottle when you are invited for dinner? If you know your hosts, then you will know the answer to that question. If you do not know them, you risk upstaging the host with a better bottle, or worse, offending him or her by implying that they might serve inferior wine. The cellar master once got his comeuppance, when asked by a guest what he should bring. 'Oh, something dry and white,' was Tom's response. A bag of flour was what he got. On the other hand, a bottle from a fine cellar is more than welcome, especially when it is given, not to be drunk that evening, but to be put away for a rainy day.

But this book is not just about dinner parties. It's about the many other opportunities for entertaining that occur, including friends and family for a lazy breakfast, a parents' golden wedding anniversary or a working lunch for business acquaintances. Here you will find ideas, menus and recipes for barbecues and cocktail parties, for breakfast, lunch and supper. Suggestions on what to cook for friends who visit on Burn's Night. How to plan a Black & White dinner, a Glyndebourne Picnic, a traditional Afternoon Tea and a fuss-free Christmas? It is all here, and much more besides.

If I had indeed written this book years ago, it would have been based solely on my experiences of entertaining family and friends at home, or in their home, as I have always loved cooking in other people's kitchens. When my mother-in-law, Edith, first let me help her make the nut rolls she baked at Christmas, I felt I had been accepted into the family, and was the recipient of the lessons Edith had learned from her mother in the art of eastern European baking. Shopping and cooking with my sister-in-law in Hong Kong, I learned how to plan and cook an authentic Cantonese meal. In the early seventies, I cooked for the members of a country rock band, The Ozark Mountain Daredevils, when they came to Britain on tour, and played at the Rainbow and on the *Old Grey Whistle Test*. These suppers, often cooked in the very fancy accommodation rented for them by their record company, would go on to the early hours as Tom opened splendid bottles of wine and I introduced them to dishes they had never tasted before, trying out recipes that I had only just learned after travelling in France and Portugal. They loved the stuffed squid.

From the early eighties, when I began my second career, as a cookery writer, I also started to cook professionally. British food was just beginning to be recognized as worthy of a place at the world's table, and I began to receive invitations from hotels and restaurants, first abroad and then in Britain, to spend time in their kitchen as guest chef. Sometimes it would be for a week or two, sometimes for a one-off gala dinner.

The relevance to this book is that I learned how to cook on a large scale, and how to adapt my recipes from domestic circumstances to the professional kitchen. I learned about planning, the chef's *mise-en-place*, where before each service, lunch and dinner, every ingredient you might possibly need is washed, trimmed, sliced, filleted, sieved or kneaded – whatever is required to get it to the point of final readiness before cooking. I cannot emphasize enough how useful this technique is in both a professional and domestic kitchen.

More recently, I have found myself in diplomatic kitchens. I have been lucky enough to cook in Residences in cities as diverse as Paris and Cairo, and have learned about the many constraints under which British Embassy households operate. In a series of seminars that I gave at the Foreign Office we examined how to make do and adapt. How do you make apple pie without apples? You will find the answer in Appendix 2. I have incorporated some of this material, because many people have assured me that this book will also be useful for those who entertain abroad, whether in the diplomatic service or in multinational corporations. My work in this field has also informed much of what I have written in the chapter on buffets. In fact, I have learned so much while doing this work, had so many memorable experiences and made so many good friends amongst diplomatic wives, that it seemed only right to dedicate the book to them – the Daughters of Britannia.

a note on ingredients

I buy organic food whenever I can, so you can take it as read that when I refer to eggs in a recipe, I mean organic eggs, when I refer to beef or pork, I mean organic beef or pork. Similarly with cheese, milk, cream, butter, fruit, vegetables, flour and other groceries. The recipes can all be made, however, using ingredients that are not organic.

a note on measurements

I find metric straightforward to use, but appreciate that there are those who object to using metric on practical grounds and on principle. I have, therefore, included imperial measurements as well, but do not look for symmetry. Some recipes will show 125g as 4oz, others will show 100g as 4oz. What is important is to follow one system of measurement in each recipe, and ignore the other, and you will find that the proportions of the ingredients in that system work in relation to each other. Quite often, the imperial version of a dish will be slightly smaller than the metric version, since I use logical measurements, 500g/1lb, 250g/8oz, when in fact 450 grams is closer to a pound in weight, and 225g closer to 8oz. Fractions of ounces have been avoided where possible, since scales and measuring jugs are not usually so finely calibrated, and metric measurements are given in multiples of 25g for the same reason.

Where possible, I have dispensed with measurement altogether in favour of units, i.e. 4 carrots, rather than 250g/8oz carrots. With the exception of baking, recipes do not need to be exact down to the last gram (or fraction of an ounce). And for baking, of course, the ingredients we use, flour, butter, sugar, are all sold by metric weight.

breakfasts, lunches and suppers

This is not such a strange combination as it might at first seem. Much, although not all, of the food that we serve at breakfast is suitable for lunch or supper. Kedgeree, ham and eggs, Finnan haddock, corned beef hash, scrambled eggs and smoked salmon – all of these are perfect at any time of the day. In Western cultures soup is not served at the breakfast table, so the soup recipes that follow are more suitable for lunch or supper. Similarly, cheese is more usual at the end of lunch. However, cold meat and cheese platters feature strongly on the northern European and Scandinavian breakfast table, and it is a good idea for a late breakfast or a breakfast buffet.

For me, breakfast, lunch and supper have roughly the same weight and importance; more than a snack, less than a dinner. And more casual than formal. But not all breakfasts are the same.

Breakfast is one of those unique gastronomic idiosyncracies which all add to the rich cultural fabric of culinary practices, such as eating pasta twice a day in Italy; Portugal's 365 recipes for salt cod; feta cheese, olives, radishes and pickled peppers for the Turkish breakfast; hoppers and potato curry for a Sri Lankan breakfast; a predilection for snails with garlic butter in France; a fondness for guinea pigs in Colombia.

Food habits are evolutionary, rather than revolutionary, present practices owing much to what has gone before. The same is true of breakfast. It is, in most cultures, the least changed of any meal. We tend to eat similar food to that which our parents ate. And, as with much else in Britain, we can attribute what we eat at breakfast today to various events of the Victorian period.

Records show (and these generally only exist from well-to-do households), that until the 16th century breakfast consisted of bread, fish (which was usually salted) and ale. During the 17th and 18th centuries, chocolate and coffee, then later tea, became the breakfast beverages of choice, and as a result the accompanying food altered to what we would today describe as a continental breakfast – fancy breads, buttered toast and baked goods.

By the middle of the 19th century, modern working patterns began to be established, with the head of the household going to the bank, the office or other place of work, rather than to the estate office, and this brought with it an earlier and more substantial meal for breakfast. With the Industrial Revolution came more intensive farming methods. The influx of cheap wheat from America to Europe meant that European wheat farmers had to diversify, which they did to spectacular effect in Denmark, producing bacon which was exactly to the British taste.

At the same time, a new breed of hen, the Cochin, a good layer, was introduced to Britain, initially as a pet, but then the commercial possibilities were realized, and eggs became even more popular at breakfast time. With more efficient forms of transport, and with factory farming, it became possible not only to produce cheap sausages and other pork products, such as black pudding, on a large scale, but to distribute them to towns and cities.

Today's British breakfast is but a pale copy of the Victorian one, which consisted not only of bacon and eggs and porridge (dried and toasted breakfast cereals were not introduced to this country from America until the 1920s), but cold joints, potted meat, game pies and cold tongue or ham, supplemented by hot dishes such as cutlets, devilled kidneys, grilled fish and sausages, as well as all the trimmings – toast, muffins, marmalade, coffee and tea.

The first reference to the English partiality for bacon and eggs may well be Andrew Borde's writing in *A Compendyous Regyment, or a Dyetary of Health* in 1542:

'. . . Bacon is good for carters and plowmen, the whiche be ever labouring the earth . . . I do say that collopes [slices of bacon] and egges is as holsome for them as a tallow candle is good for a blereyed mare.'

In 1711, the year in which the *Spectator* was first published, an early issue of the magazine noted that good London households were now serving tea in the morning, instead of breakfast beer and that dinner had been pushed forward to well past noon. The English breakfast had begun to come into its own. Breakfast parties, given at noon, became the custom later in the century.

In 1840, London entrepreneur Thomas Wall inherited a business in Jermyn Street which became the country's leading producer of sausages and meat pies, as well as bacon curing. During the Second World War, the company developed ways to produce heavy pigs efficiently, essentially through intensive rearing practices.

Food historian Alan Davidson, author of the compendious *Oxford Companion to Food*, confirms that the fry-up probably dates back to the last century, in a sense a plebeian down-grading of the copious country house breakfast. However, he has evidence, too, that this was the food that farmers ate mid-morning, as their second breakfast, their first early breakfast being much lighter.

One element of the fry-up – baked beans – probably did not appear on the British breakfast plate until the 1920s. Heinz test-marketed them in the north of England in 1905, without great success, but when they opened their north London plant in Harlesden in 1928, the head of the British division is said to have vowed, 'I'm going to manufacture baked beans in England, and they're going to like it.'

It was Somerset Maugham who said that anyone who came to this country from abroad and who wanted three first-class meals a day should order three breakfasts. One might surmise that the French and Italians do not indulge in a British-style breakfast because they are supremely confident that they will get a good lunch. I suspect that, as we become more and more sure of getting a good lunch and dinner, we, too, will entirely adopt the Continental habit of having coffee and baked goods at breakfast time, rather than anything more substantial.

However, breakfast, and its weekend counterpart, brunch, can sometimes be a suitable occasion for entertaining, whether it is a working breakfast around a boardroom table during the early part of the day, or a midday meal for friends on Sunday. Brunch is certainly one of my favourite meals for a long holiday weekend.

My breakfast recipes in this chapter can be adapted to either occasion, can be served buffet style or plated, or indeed can be served at lunchtime or supper time.

dill and onion baps

These baps, or soft rolls, are the perfect accompaniment to kippers, poached Finnan haddock, undyed smoked haddock, smoked salmon and fresh or marinated salmon, all of which can be accompanied by scrambled eggs.

makes 6

300g (10oz) plain wholemeal flour

200g (7oz) strong plain flour

1 tsp salt

2 tsps fast-action, easy-blend dried yeast

1 tbsp dried dill weed, or dill seeds

1 onion, peeled, chopped and fried gently

250–275ml (8–9fl oz) hand-hot water

Mix together the dry ingredients, by hand or in a food processor, then stir in the onions. Gradually add the water. Turn out the mixture on to a lightly floured surface and knead to an elastic dough. Divide this into six, and shape into flat cakes. Place the baps on a greased baking sheet and allow to rise in a warm place for 40 to 60 minutes until doubled in size.

Bake at 200°C/400°F/gas mark 6 for about 20 minutes. Cool on a rack before splitting open and filling them.

To make dill and lemon butter, crush some fresh dill with sea salt, then mix with unsalted butter, grated lemon zest, lemon juice and pepper.

devilled mushrooms

serves 4 to 6

750g (1½lb) button or cap mushrooms, sliced

75g (3oz) butter

chilli or Tabasco

salt

freshly ground black pepper

2 tbsps medium paprika

2 tbsps mango chutney, chopped

soured cream (optional)

Fry the mushrooms in the butter until soft. Season with chilli (or Tabasco), salt and pepper to taste, then stir in the paprika and mango chutney. Cook for 3–4 minutes, and spoon into a serving bowl. Soured cream can be stirred in, or served separately, if you wish.

eggs en cocotte

This dish is versatile enough to serve at lunch or dinner, as well as breakfast.

serves 2

small nut of butter or extra virgin olive oil

2 ripe tomatoes, seeded and chopped (peeled too, if you can be bothered)

half a dozen basil or tarragon leaves, shredded or finely chopped

salt

freshly ground black pepper

2 large eggs

2–3 tsps of cream per ramekin or extra virgin olive oil

Lightly grease two ovenproof ramekins with either the butter or olive oil and put in the tomatoes. Add the herbs and seasoning, then crack an egg on top. Season that too, and spoon the cream or oil over it. Place the ramekins on a baking sheet and bake in a preheated oven at 180°C/350°F/ gas mark 4 until the egg white is just set, about 7–8 minutes.

If you do not wish to use the oven, place the ramekins on a rack in a sauté pan with a couple of centimetres (an inch or so) of water, cover with a lid and steam. You will need to blot off excess water from condensation before serving them.

the perfect kedgeree

Kedgeree started life in India as a dish of rice and lentils under the name of *kitchri*. During the time of the Raj, the Victorians took a fancy to it and dressed it up for their breakfast table, adding fish and eggs. It is versatile enough to serve at lunch or dinner, as well as breakfast. You can also vary the composition of the kedgeree, using salmon or a mixture of salmon and scallops in place of the smoked haddock, and serve a creamy lemon and dill sauce rather than a curry sauce. Wild rice or red rice can be added to the basmati rice if you like.

Kedgeree can also be adapted to cocktail parties. On p.223 I recommend serving it in Chinese soup spoons, but you can also use the tartlet recipe on p.251. In fact, these tartlets are perfect for miniature breakfast food servings of scrambled eggs and caviar or smoked salmon, black pudding topped with a quail's egg and the salmon hash described on p.21.

serves 2

2 tbsps olive oil

1 small onion, thinly sliced

a few whole spices, such as crushed cardamom, cloves, coriander,
  peppercorns, cumin and a splinter of cinnamon

150–200g (5–7oz) basmati rice

575–700ml (1–1¼ pints) water or fish stock

250g (8oz) undyed smoked haddock fillet, skinned

2 eggs

Fry the onion and spices in the oil until the onion is wilted and golden, stir in the rice, then add just under twice its volume of water. Bring to the boil, stir, cover, lower the heat and cook for 15 minutes.

Place the fish on top of the rice, cover again, and cook for a further 5–8 minutes. Meanwhile, boil the eggs for 5 minutes, and shell when cool enough to handle. Cut up the fish and eggs into the rice and serve.

To make a delicious sauce to serve with it, cook 2 tbsps medium curry paste in a non-stick pan, and then add 100ml (4fl oz) water, 100ml (4fl oz) coconut cream and 1 tbsp chopped mango chutney. Bring to the boil, simmer for 5 minutes, then add half a fresh mango, diced, and some chopped fresh coriander leaves.

breakfast fruit compote

This is delicious served with homemade muesli and thick Greek yoghurt. The quantity given here should ensure plenty of leftovers which can be kept in the refrigerator.

serves 6 to 8

> 200g (7oz) each of dried apricots, peaches, prunes and figs
> 200g (7oz) each of dried cherries, cranberries, moscatels and raisins (optional)
> 3 fresh, hard pears, peeled, cored and quartered
> 3 apples, peeled, cored and quartered
> 6 plums, halved and stoned
> 600ml (1 pint) pear, grape or apple juice
> 2 cinnamon sticks
> sugar to taste

Soak the dried fruit overnight in 575ml (1 pint) water. The following day, put the soaked fruit into a saucepan with the fresh fruit, together with the fruit juice and cinnamon. Bring slowly to the boil, and simmer for 10–15 minutes. Add sugar at this stage if you think it needs it. Remove from the heat and allow to cool. You might also like to add a couple of star anise, some cloves and crushed cardamom to the fruit.

the american breakfast

I like American breakfasts, and feel they adapt well to occasions for entertaining. One of the most welcome signs in any café window is, 'Breakfast served all day'. In Pittsburgh's Strip District, not too far from the Andy Warhol museum, is De Luca's Restaurant, on Penn Avenue. It has been there since the mid 1940s and is little changed, according to the photographs. A long bar, with chrome and red leatherette stools on one side and the short order cooks on the other, is the focal point. Small, uncomfortable booths line the opposite wall, and this is where a mixed bag of people come for their breakfast, a particularly mixed bag on Sunday mornings. Cops from the precinct going off duty coincide with those coming on duty; joggers disturb the warm greasy fug when they open the door wide and enter with their bright and white gear. But they, too, succumb like the rest of us Sunday morning layabouts, as we munch hot cakes, home fries and country sausage, and wade through the papers. 'More cawfee, hon?', asks the waitress, and we decline our fifth cup. From 6 am to 3 pm, breakfast is served all day.

Whilst breakfast food does require short order cooking skills, it is very simple, and you can rope in willing guests to help. Someone can mix and make the muffins, someone else the salmon hash. Those who want fried eggs might be persuaded to cook their own; that way they can have them sunny-side up, over-light, or over-easy, without troubling host or hostess. Fresh, chewy bagels, warm croissants split and filled with scrambled eggs, made with butter not milk, and plenty of wholewheat toast play an important supporting role, together with a plentiful supply of homemade jams and jellies, not to mention the cream cheese.

Sweet baked goods also feature on the American breakfast table, so I have included a couple of muffin recipes, as well as some for my favourite hot cakes. A large-scale all-day breakfast needs more than just comfort food and morning food, and I suggest plenty of fruit, perhaps a fresh compote of seasonal fruit, or a compote of dried fruit, cooked in tea, and enlivened with a few lightly toasted nuts. Thick plain yoghurt will probably accompany these better than cream.

Steak for breakfast does not appeal. Grilled kidneys do, as do devilled kidneys and grilled bacon. Sausages are much easier to deal with when you slip them out of their skins, flatten them into patties, and bake in the oven. Under a grill or in a frying pan, they need too much watching and often cook unevenly. Even simpler than buying, and then dismantling, sausages, is to buy loose sausage meat. Sausage cakes go very well with the bacon-wrapped tomatoes below.

Everyone has different views on what should be drunk with breakfast food. It is as well to cater for all tastes, and to offer fresh orange or grapefruit juice, a jug of Bloody Mary, some chilled bottles of bubbly, as well as the usual hot drinks. I would also serve a jug of vegetable juice, as I love its flavour first thing in the morning, and the juicer attachment on my food-processor makes short work of it. The blender can also be brought out to make fruit smoothies

breakfast vegetable juice

serves 6 to 8

4 carrots

2 red peppers

1 bunch watercress

2 celery sticks

1 fennel bulb

6 tomatoes

small piece of ginger

Scrub and trim the vegetables as appropriate, and feed into the juicer gradually. Rather than chill with ice cubes, which dilute the juice, I prefer to keep the vegetables in the refrigerator overnight.

fruit smoothies

For these, allow one 150g carton plain yoghurt per person, a handful of crushed ice, one piece of prepared fruit weighing about 150g (4–5oz), and something to sweeten the mixture if necessary. Put everything in the blender, blend until smooth, pour into a chilled jug and thence into chilled glasses. The addition of banana in any of the mixtures produces an even creamier result. Yoghurt can be low fat or extra rich, as you prefer, and you can use soya milk in its place for an excellent non-dairy version. Here are some ideas to get you started:

- Blueberries, banana and lemon juice
- Cranberry and apple juice and bananas
- Pears and fresh ginger with a little honey
- Apple, banana and honey
- Fresh peaches or nectarines and elderflower syrup
- Papaya, demerara sugar and fresh lime juice
- Canteloupe or charentais melon and apricots

compote of summer fruit

serves 2, plus leftovers

1 ripe galia, piel de sapo, honeydew or other sweet melon

2 peaches or nectarines

4 golden plums

250g (8oz) large muscat grapes

Scoop the melon into balls, or cut it into wedges, and then slice thinly. Slice the peaches or nectarines, and halve or quarter the plums. Halve the grapes, and remove the seeds. Mix gently, and put in a bowl. Chill until required. Freshly squeezed orange juice can be added for a more juicy compote.

curried chicken hash

serves 4 to 6

- 1 onion, peeled and finely chopped
- 2 celery sticks, trimmed and finely sliced
- 25g (1oz) butter or chicken fat
- 1 tbsp curry paste, or more to taste
- 25g (1oz) flour
- 300ml (½ pint) chicken stock
- 150ml (¼ pint) cream or coconut cream
- 350g (12oz) cooked chicken
- 50g (2oz) cashew nuts
- fresh coriander leaves

Fry the onion and celery in the butter or chicken fat until soft, then stir in the curry paste and the flour. Cook for a few minutes, then gradually stir in the stock, and cook until the sauce thickens. Add the cream or coconut cream, the chicken and nuts. Simmer for 5 minutes, then stir in the coriander leaves and serve.

salmon hash

The same recipe can be adapted to smoked haddock and kippers. If you prefer, you can also use shredded ham or smoked trout.

1kg (2lb) large new potatoes

1 onion, peeled and finely chopped

25g (1oz) butter

1 tbsp olive oil

750g (1½lb) salmon fillet, skinned and diced

1 tbsp chopped chives or dill

2–3 tbsps soured cream or crème fraîche

100g (4oz) smoked salmon pieces, shredded

Scrub the potatoes, then parboil them in their skins. When cool enough to handle, peel the potatoes and either coarsely grate or finely dice them. Meanwhile, gently fry the onion in the butter and oil until soft, then add the potatoes and the diced salmon. Partially cover for 4–5 minutes, to let the salmon cook, then remove the lid, stir in the herbs and cream, and, just before serving, scatter shreds of smoked salmon on top.

breakfast smoked fish

serves 2

2 thick slices wholemeal bread or 2 bagels

75g (3oz) cream cheese

1 tbsp capers, chopped

2 tbsps mild onion, finely chopped

250g (8oz) thinly sliced smoked salmon, flaked smoked mackerel
    or smoked trout

Toast the bread or warm and split the bagels. Mix together the cream cheese, capers and onion and spread over the toast or bagels. Top with a generous helping of smoked fish.

filled croissants

I came across one of my best breakfast suggestions years ago when I was the *Sunday Times* cookery writer, researching and writing a series about people entertaining at home. My hosts on this occasion had persuaded their baker to make them a giant croissant, which they filled with smoked salmon, cream cheese and watercress. It made a fabulous centrepiece for a brunch party. I used the idea the following year when I was guest cook at the Intercontinental. I had rashly agreed to do the breakfast buffet as well as lunch and dinner. The giant croissant became quite a feature. If you have a friendly local baker, it is something you can easily incorporate into your own entertaining.

You can also make traditional-sized croissants and fill them yourself. Buy the small cylindrical containers of pre-rolled and cut croissant dough. Unroll them and separate them. Wrap a piece of cheese or some pre-cooked bacon in the dough, or make your own *pain au chocolat* by wrapping a piece of chocolate in the dough before rolling and baking it.

For cocktail parties, try cutting the croissant shapes into miniatures, before filling and baking them.

bacon baked tomatoes

serves 12

12 firm, ripe tomatoes

12 rashers smoked streaky bacon (rind removed),
    blanched in boiling water for 30 seconds

freshly ground black pepper

Make a nick in the skin of each tomato, to stop it splitting, and encircle with a rasher of bacon. Place, join side down, on a baking sheet, and bake in a hot oven at 200°C/400°F/ gas mark 6 for 10–12 minutes. For miniatures, wrap cherry tomatoes in half rashers, and bake for 8–10 minutes.

cream cheese hotcakes with maple and pecan syrup

makes 4 to 6 large or 12 small cakes

100g (4oz) cream cheese

1 egg

1 tbsp plain yoghurt

150g (5oz) plain flour, sifted together with 1 tsp baking powder

150ml (¼ pint) skimmed milk

3 tbsps pecan nuts, shelled and roughly crushed

150ml (¼ pint) maple syrup

Soften the cream cheese, then beat in the egg and yoghurt. Gradually add the flour and baking powder, and the milk, and beat to a thick dropping consistency. Allow the batter to stand for 20 minutes or so while you heat up a griddle or non-stick pan. Meanwhile, mix the nuts and maple syrup, and pour into a jug.

Spoon or pour the batter on to the hot surface and, when it bubbles and then dries on top, flip the cakes over and cook for a further 3–4 minutes. Serve warm with the maple syrup. (Honey or golden syrup can replace the maple syrup, but the latter is best.) The cakes can be kept warm while you are cooking the rest by putting them on a plate, set over a saucepan of simmering water.

hotcakes with apple and blackberries

makes 4 to 6 hotcakes, serves 2

    250g (8oz) plain flour

    5 tsps baking powder

    pinch of salt

    1 tbsp each porridge oats, oat bran and wheatgerm

    1 tbsp each sunflower and melon seeds

    1 large egg

    200ml (7fl oz) skimmed milk

    1 tsp lemon juice

Sift together the flour, baking powder and salt, then mix in the remaining dry ingredients. Beat together the egg, milk and lemon juice, then blend into the dry ingredients until you have a smooth, thick – but not stiff – batter. The mixture should be of pouring consistency. Allow to stand until it starts to bubble.

Heat a griddle, or frying pan, oil lightly, then pour on enough of the mixture to give you a hot cake about 12cm (5 inches) in diameter. Cook until the surface is matt and pitted with holes. Flip over, and cook the other side. Serve with thinly sliced apples and fresh blackberries, tossed in lemon juice and honey.

entertaining

mandarin ricotta hotcakes

A compote of mandarins and poached dried apricots or mixed dried fruit is very good with these, as is an extra helping of ricotta.

makes 12

6 large eggs, separated
175g (6oz) ricotta cheese
juice of a mandarin orange
50g (2oz) butter, melted
100g (3½oz) plain flour
2–4 tbsps unrefined sugar
pinch of salt
3 or 4 tbsps mandarin zest
icing sugar

In a large bowl, mix together the egg yolks, cheese, mandarin juice and butter. In a separate bowl, combine all the dry ingredients, except for the mandarin zest. Gradually mix the dry ingredients into the egg mixture, then fold in half the zest. Whisk the egg whites until they hold firm peaks, then fold into the batter.

Heat an oiled griddle (or use a non-stick pan) and, when hot, ladle the batter on to the griddle in batches – you should be able to cook the cakes in three batches of four. Cook the cakes until golden, then turn them over, flattening the cooked side with a spatula, and continue to cook until they are golden brown on the second side.

Stack the cakes on a plate set over a pan of simmering water until finished. Serve dusted with icing sugar, sprinkled with the remaining mandarin zest.

golden fruit muffins

makes 24

350g (12oz) self-raising flour

100g (4oz) cornmeal

2 tsps baking powder

2 tbsps golden caster sugar

pinch of salt

75g (3oz) butter, melted, or sunflower oil

2 eggs, lightly beaten

225ml (8fl oz) buttermilk

1 tbsp each chopped dried mango, apricot, peaches and gold sultanas

Sift the dry ingredients into a bowl. Stir in the butter or oil and eggs, and enough buttermilk to produce a soft, quite wet, mixture. Stir in the fruit and spoon the mixture into greased muffin tins, deep bun tins or paper cases, arranged on a baking sheet, filling them about two thirds full. Bake in a preheated oven at 200°C/400°F/gas mark 6 for 18–20 minutes. Serve warm.

bacon, courgette and cheese muffins

makes about 12

350g (12oz) plain flour

1 tbsp baking powder

½ tsp bicarbonate of soda

½ tsp salt

3 smoked or green streaky bacon rashers, without the rind, finely chopped

3 courgettes, grated

75g (3oz) cheese, grated

3 eggs

225 ml (8fl oz) buttermilk

5 tbsps melted butter or sunflower oil

In a large bowl, sift together the flour, baking powder, bicarbonate of soda and salt, then stir in the bacon, courgettes and cheese. Beat together the eggs and buttermilk, then quickly stir into other ingredients. Spoon into greased muffin tins or paper cases, arranged on a baking sheet, and bake in a preheated oven at 200°C/400°F/gas mark 6 for 20–25 minutes. Serve hot or warm. These also freeze and reheat well.

carrot cake

serves 10

5 eggs, separated

300g (10oz) light muscovado sugar

grated zest of 2 lemons and juice of 1 lemon

300g (10oz) ground almonds

300g (10oz) carrot, finely grated

¼ tsp each salt, ground cloves, ground cinnamon and ground cardamom

2 tsps baking powder

75g (3oz) cornflour or potato starch

4 tbsps kirsch or other eau de vie

to decorate

water icing or sweetened cream cheese

marzipan carrots

Beat together the egg yolks, sugar, lemon juice and zest until you have a pale, foamy mixture. Fold in the almonds, carrots, spices, baking powder and corn-flour, and finally the kirsch.

Whisk the egg whites to firm peaks, then gently fold into the cake mixture. Spoon into a 5cm (2 inch) deep, greased and floured cake tin measuring 20 × 25cm (10 × 12 inch). Bake for about an hour in a preheated oven at 180°C/350°F/gas mark 4. Remove from the oven, and allow to cool slightly before removing from the tin and placing on a rack to cool.

Either make a thin glaze with icing sugar and lemon juice, and spread over the cake while still warm or, when the cake is cool, spread with cream cheese. Decorate with small marzipan carrots.

entertaining

almond, lemon and yoghurt cake

After I have made almond soup, I am left with a residue of ground almonds that I am loath to discard, as they still have some flavour and, of course, their unique texture. I use them in this moist, fairly plain cake, which is very good with coffee. You can, of course, use ground almonds straight from the packet.

Spices can be added to the cake mixture – cloves, in particular, go well with the lemon. Orange juice and zest can also replace the lemon, in which case cardamom is the perfect matching spice.

serves 8

125g (4oz) unsalted butter, softened, or sunflower margarine

125g (4oz) light muscovado sugar

juice and finely grated zest of 2 lemons

175g (6oz) ground almonds

50g (2oz) self-raising flour

3 eggs, separated

3 tbsps plain yoghurt

Cream the butter and sugar until pale and light. Stir in the lemon juice and zest with half the ground almonds, then add the remaining almonds and flour alternately with the lightly beaten egg yolks, and then the yoghurt. Whisk the egg whites and fold the two mixtures together. Spoon into a 1kg (2lb) loaf tin, smooth the top and bake in a preheated oven at 180°C/350°F/gas mark 4 for about 50–60 minutes. The cake is cooked when a skewer inserted in the middle comes out clean. Turn out and cool on a wire rack before slicing.

luncheon

Lunch is a useful meal for entertaining, as it can be as flexible or as rigid as you like when it comes to timing. Its starting point is usually fixed, but thereafter it is up to you to decide when it ends. If you keep the courses moving at a smart pace, guests generally do not linger long after they have finished coffee. If it is a more languorous, lazy affair, you may not say goodbye to your guests until nearly bedtime. For the purposes of entertaining close friends and family, I favour the latter approach. Conversely, acquaintances and larger groups of people may feel more comfortable with a more structured luncheon.

an english summer lunch

There are many tastes and smells of summer. A sharp *citron pressé* at a pavement café mingled with Paris traffic fumes. Charcoal-grilled sardines, which you wait for in an Algarve restaurant whilst drinking tongue-prickling vinho verde. Onions, hot dogs and beer outside the baseball stadium in a Midwestern American city. Frying olive oil wafting its aroma across the beach bar in Chipiona, as you sip chilled fino and treat yourself to a plate of jamon serrano. An achingly cold granita as you walk through the shady colonnades to some Tuscan piazza. Just to imagine them makes me want to be there, everywhere.

To these should be added the delight of English summer food eaten in an English garden. And should the weather be unpredictable, sit near an open window and enjoy the fragrance of roses as you eat juicy crab salads, delicate chilled soups and ripe fruit desserts.

I was treated to a memorable lunch one summer, where our hostess, Fiona, had transferred some of the delights of her considerable garden to our plates. One dessert was a mound of creamy, sweetened fromage frais, whose slopes were strewn with fragrant rose petals, which she had crystallized and then served with slivers of mangoes; it was a brilliant and unusual combination. Try it, too, with home-grown raspberries.

A moist and flavoursome terrine of chicken was studded with pistachios and served with a salad of lettuce hearts and avocados. As *bonnes bouches* to accompany these, were the crispest, shortest tartlets imaginable, filled with egg mayonnaise and topped with a quail's egg. Quite delicious. Our host, Desmond, greeted us with magnums of Krug, perfectly chilled, which he followed with Le Montrachet and other treats, ending on a joyous top note of 1934 Château d'Yquem.

I have included many of my favourite English summertime ingredients in this chapter, although some of them are combined with oriental flavours, many of which are readily available in the high street multiple, and, if not, the nearest oriental provisions shop.

Walking through Fiona's garden under the linden tree reminded me, by association, of how I used to love bottled lime juice cordial, diluted to make a long drink, and now I make my own for nostalgic summer drinks. Whilst it is very good with fizzy water, my memory tells me I used to drink it diluted with tap water, for who used to buy bottled water, for heaven's sake? A few dried linden flowers added to the saucepan will give a new meaning to lime cordial, as well as a subtle fragrance. The cordial also provides the base for an exquisite sorbet.

The first pair of recipes make use of the two very different parts of the crab, the creamy meat from the shell and the strands of white flesh from the claws and body. Patience is required to dig out this part, but is well rewarded.

crab, courgette and fennel soup

serves 4

1 large, freshly boiled crab

1 onion, peeled and sliced

500g (1lb) courgettes

1 small fennel bulb, thinly sliced

50g (2oz) butter

1 tbsp flour

300ml (½ pint) crab cooking liquor, plus juices from the claws and body

300ml (½ pint) full cream milk

150ml (¼ pint) single cream

seasoning, including a pinch of mace

175g (6oz) soft crab meat

fennel tops, chopped

Pick over the crab, keeping the white meat for another dish, such as the crab salad with oriental flavours, on p.33. Gently cook the onion, courgettes and fennel in the butter until soft. Stir in the flour, and add a little crab liquor to blend it in.

Gradually add the milk, and cook until smooth. Remove from the heat, and allow to cool before blending until smooth. Pour back into a saucepan, stir in the cream, bring to the boil, then add the seasoning, the crab meat and the fennel tops.

crab, cucumber and ginger salad with salted black bean dressing

This salad is also very good with cold noodles, or eaten wrapped in lettuce leaves.

serves 4

bunch of spring onions, peeled, trimmed and sliced obliquely

3 thin slices ginger, cut into fine strips

1 tbsp groundnut oil

1–3 tsps lime juice

grated zest of a lime

1 cucumber, plus additional slices for serving

250g (8oz) white crab meat

for the dressing

1 tbsp fermented (salted) black soya beans

½ tsp freshly ground black pepper

1 tbsp sherry or rice vinegar

2 tbsps toasted sesame oil

4 tbsps water

1 tsp unrefined sugar

2 garlic cloves, peeled and crushed

Mix together the spring onions, ginger, oil, juice and zest, and crab meat. Peel and halve the cucumber, and discard the seeds. Grate the cucumber, salt lightly, and let it drain for half an hour or so. Wring it dry in a clean tea towel, then arrange on top of the slices of cucumber on plates, and heap the crab salad on top. Make the dressing by crushing together the beans and pepper, and then stirring in the rest of the ingredients. Spoon it around the salad.

cauliflower and broccoli with lime, ginger and soy vinaigrette

serves 6 to 8

approx 500g (1lb) cauliflower and broccoli, broken into florets

3 tbsps groundnut oil

1 tbsp toasted sesame oil

2 tbsps soy sauce

1 tbsp lime juice

2 tsps freshly grated ginger

½ tsp freshly ground black pepper

pinch of dried chilli flakes (optional)

nasturtium flowers, to decorate

Steam, or boil, the vegetables until just tender. Mix together the remaining ingredients (including the chilli, if using), and use some to brush the inside of a pudding bowl. Arrange the vegetable florets in the bowl, flower side out, stalks to the middle, so that the tangle of stalks in the centre will hold the vegetables together. Pour on the vinaigrette, and leave for 30–40 minutes. Turn out on to a plate, and decorate with nasturtium flowers, if you have them. And if the heap collapses, no matter, you still have an extraordinarily good salad.

entertaining

new potato and samphire salad

serves 6

750g (1½lb) new potatoes, scrubbed

250g (6–8oz) samphire shoots, trimmed

extra virgin olive oil

lemon juice

coarse sea salt

freshly ground black pepper

Boil the potatoes in plenty of water until almost tender. Put in the samphire, bring back to the boil, and then drain. Toss in olive oil and lemon juice to taste, with a little seasoning. Serve warm or just cool.

tarragon grilled chicken with kitchen garden salad

serves 6

6 chicken breasts

several sprigs of tarragon

½ tsp coarse sea salt

1–2 tbsps mild mustard

1 tbsp Greek yoghurt

freshly ground black pepper

splash each of Worcestershire sauce, Tabasco and Angostura bitters

Remove the skin from the chicken breasts. Grind the tarragon leaves with the sea salt in a mortar, then blend in the mustard, yoghurt and other seasonings.

Halve the chicken breasts horizontally, and cover with the paste. Heat the grill and, when hot, grill the chicken on both sides until cooked through.

Serve on a bed of salad made up of whatever you have available of small, crisp, peppery, flavoursome leaves of rocket, watercress, purslane, mizuna, lamb's lettuce, herbs and edible flowers.

Balsamic vinegar sprinkled on the warm chicken and salad is delicious.

lime cordial

makes about 500ml (18fl oz)

 juice and thinly peeled rind of about 8 limes, enough to give 200ml (7fl oz) juice

 300g (10oz) granulated sugar

 300ml (½ pint) water

Put all the ingredients in a saucepan set over a low heat. Heat gently, stirring from time to time, until the sugar has dissolved completely. Bring to the boil, and simmer for a minute or so. Remove from the heat and let the lime rind infuse overnight. Strain, bottle and label.

Keep in the refrigerator, and dilute a tablespoon of cordial with a glass of chilled still table water. With rum and fizz, you have the makings of a good punch.

the perfect elderflower syllabub

This is the quintessential taste of June in England. You can flavour the syllabub with other aromatics and herbs as the season advances, even rose petals or lavender flowers.

serves 8 to 10

 several elderflower heads

 300ml (½ pint) each white wine and white grape juice

 grated rind and juice of 2 lemons

 generous grating of nutmeg

 200g (7oz) golden caster sugar

 1 litre (35fl oz) whipping or double cream

Put all the ingredients, except the cream, in a non-reactive saucepan. Bring to the boil, remove from the heat and steep overnight. Whip the cream in a large bowl, then gradually whisk in the strained liquid. Spoon into wine glasses and serve chilled, with sponge fingers.

---

entertaining

more lunchtime pleasures

mint juleps for derby day

Frozen mint juleps clutched in our hands, we watched Real Quiet come up from behind to win the 124th Kentucky Derby at Churchill Downs, his Cajun jockey, Kent Desormeaux, yelling, 'Go baby, go'. It was an exciting two minutes. Then thoughts turned to food. It inspired me, too, to think about food for our own Derby Day. We may not have the glossy tall magnolias, the soft winds, the chattering cardinals and blue jays that I came to enjoy during my visit to Georgia and Alabama, but we can, at least, buy the ingredients.

Just as our famous sporting occasions have particular food and drink associations (think Pimms at Henley, strawberries and cream at Wimbledon, and picnics at Glyndebourne), America's Derby Day is for ever associated with mint juleps. But strawberries usually feature too, and almost certainly a whole cold ham (see p.112), served with hot biscuits, rather like our scones, and plenty of relishes. An oyster stew, or shrimp puffs, might be served to begin with, or some marinated asparagus, or even, with a nod to the Spanish heritage of parts of the Deep South, gazpacho tarts.

The important ingredient, however, is fresh mint. When we went shopping on the morning of the race, we noticed the mint was selling like, well, like mint on Kentucky Derby Day. The way I made the juleps was to put half a dozen fresh mint leaves in the bottom of each tumbler with a teaspoon of sugar. The mint leaves are crushed or 'muddled' with the spoon against the side of the glass, the sugar helping to crush the mint. A teaspoon or so of water is then added to dissolve the sugar. Each tumbler is packed to the brim with crushed ice, and bourbon is then poured over the ice until the tumbler is full. I didn't have time to carry out the next stage, as the horses were being led from the ring to the strains of 'My Old Kentucky Home'. The tumblers should be put in the refrigerator for 15 minutes to get a nice frost on them. Some of the ice will begin to melt, and you should then, apparently, put a tablespoon of bourbon on top so that your first sip is a good strong one. (Each glass should also be decorated with a sprig of fresh mint.)

For a non-native, the first mint julep is described as a 'sensation', the second as a 'rhythmic benefaction', and the third 'a grievous error'. We found one mint julep to be an 'elegant sufficiency', as they say in the South.

The next day, I studied my friend, Carolyn's, library of southern cookbooks, to discover that whilst my mint julep recipe was fine in its rough and ready way, it was by no means the only one. I found at least as many versions as there were horses in the Derby. There is clearly no authorized version. Some make a sugar syrup, others let the mixture steep with the mint and bourbon for hours before the ice is added. I disagree. Freshness in mint is all. My method, outlined above, works well for up to half a dozen glasses. If I were making a large quantity, I would use the recipe below, preparing a mint syrup. Have the ice crushed in advance, and put it back in the freezer; it is surprising how long it takes to crush enough ice to fill four tumblers.

Use some more bourbon in a rich butterscotch sauce to go with a peach and almond tart, as an alternative to strawberries and cream.

mint julep

makes 6 to 8 (depending on how strong you like them)

½ bottle bourbon

generous handful of mint leaves

6 tbsps granulated sugar

12 tbsps water

crushed ice, sufficient to fill all the tumblers

6–10 sprigs of fresh mint

Put your tumblers and bourbon in the freezer. Tear up the mint leaves, then crush in a mortar with the sugar. Transfer to a saucepan, using some of the measured water to rinse the mortar of mint, and put that, too, in the saucepan.

Bring the mint, sugar and water to the boil. Remove from the heat, and steep until the syrup is cool. Strain into a glass jug, and refrigerate.

When you are ready to make the juleps, put a generous teaspoon of syrup into each chilled tumbler and fill with crushed ice. Stir. Divide the bourbon amongst the glasses. Stir again, stick in a mint sprig, and serve.

shrimp puffs

makes 18

150ml (¼ pint) water

65g (2½oz) butter

pinch of salt

75g (3oz) plain flour

2 eggs, lightly beaten

125g (4 oz) cooked and peeled shrimps or prawns, roughly chopped

2 tbsps crème fraîche, mayonnaise or thick Greek yoghurt

2 spring onions, trimmed and finely chopped

2–3 sprigs fresh dill, finely chopped

freshly ground black pepper

First make a choux paste by bringing to the boil the water, butter and salt. Tip in the flour and stir vigorously with a wooden spoon, until the mixture becomes smooth and begins to leave the side of the pan. Remove from the heat and beat in the eggs, a little at a time, making sure each addition is thoroughly incorporated. Keep beating until you have a smooth paste.

Spoon or pipe the mixture into 18 heaps on a lightly buttered baking sheet. Bake in a preheated oven at 220°C/425°F/gas mark 7 for 15 minutes, until puffy and golden.

Remove from the oven and cool on a wire rack, first making a slit in the bottom to let the steam escape.

Meanwhile, mix the shrimps with the remaining ingredients. When the choux puffs are cool, split them and spoon in the shrimp mixture. Pile on a platter and serve.

gazpacho tarts in spiced pastry

makes about 2 to 3 dozen, depending on the size of the tart tins

250g (8oz) plain flour

125g (i.e. half a pack) salted butter, chilled and diced

1 tsp each ground cumin, cardamom, coriander and paprika

iced water

for the filling

5 or 6 ripe tomatoes

1 cucumber

1 green and 1 red pepper

salt

freshly ground black pepper

1 tsp sherry vinegar

1 sheet leaf gelatine or 1 tsp gelatine granules

1 or 2 shallots or spring onions, chopped

Rub together the flour and butter until the mixture resembles fine breadcrumbs. Stir in the spices and enough iced water to bind. Knead briefly and lightly on a floured worktop. Cover the pastry, and let it rest in a cool place.

Place a sieve over a bowl. Peel the tomatoes, then halve them, and scoop the seeds and pulp into the sieve. Thinly peel most of the skin from the cucumber, halve it, and scoop the seeds into the sieve.

Peel the peppers, cut off the caps, and discard the seeds. Finely chop all the vegetables, place in a bowl, season lightly, and mix in the vinegar. If you like, you can add chopped shallots or spring onions.

Rub the pulp in the sieve to obtain as much liquid as possible. Measure 150ml (¼ pint) into a Pyrex jug, adding water or vegetable stock to make up the amount, if necessary. In it soften the gelatine, and then put the jug in a pan of hot water to let it dissolve.

Meanwhile, line tartlet tins with the pastry, prick all over, and bake blind in a preheated oven at 180°C/350°F/gas mark 4 for 12–15 minutes. Remove the tart shells from the oven and cool on wire racks. Spoon in the vegetable mixture, draining any excess liquid, if necessary, flatten slightly, and add a teaspoon of the gelatin liquid. Allow to set in a cool place. Serve.

peach and almond tart
with bourbon butterscotch sauce

The bourbon butterscotch sauce is also very good with vanilla ice cream.

serves 6 to 8

    250g (8oz) sweet short pastry

    200g (7oz) almond paste

    6–8 peaches

    2 tbsps demerara sugar

for the bourbon butterscotch sauce

    250g (8oz) granulated sugar

    100ml (3fl oz) water

    300ml (½ pint) double cream

    2–3 tbsps bourbon

Line a 25cm (10 inch) loose-bottomed tart ring with the pastry. Flatten the almond paste, or roll it out, and use to line the bottom of the pastry case. Slice the peaches, then arrange them over the almond paste. Sprinkle with sugar, and bake in a preheated oven at 180°C/350°F/gas mark 4 for about 35 minutes. Serve warm, with the sauce.

To make the sauce, boil the sugar and water for 2–3 minutes until it caramelizes, and then stir in the cream and bourbon. Cook for a further 2–3 minutes to amalgamate the flavours and evaporate the alcohol.

sunday lunch

For a Sunday lunch or an all-day holiday table, I like to serve a grand centrepiece, such as a large roast, a cold ham or a platter of stuffed chicken breasts. These major meat main courses are perhaps best served after a composed vegetable salad or a vegetable soup, chilled or hot, as the weather dictates. In season, freshly cooked English asparagus, served with melted butter, enlivened with a spark of lime juice, or with homemade mayonnaise or with a sauce mousseline, would be a perfect starter for all these meals. As would a salad of grilled vegetables.

What I am trying to get away from is the feeling that I ought always to serve a fish course before a meat course. There is, however, a good reason why fish is followed by meat. Two good reasons, in fact, white burgundy followed by claret or, occasionally, red burgundy. To Tom, my husband, it is not a proper occasion without the full works, and hang the expense; we can live on pasta and vegetables for the rest of the week.

I am conscious of this, too, in restaurants with a fixed price menu. Even the best restaurants seem to feel it is important to offer a substantial protein-rich starter, followed by another large helping of protein for the main course. But vegetables are not cheap second-class citizens of the culinary world. A serving of prime asparagus, a perfect globe artichoke, a salad of grilled aubergine and pepper, will cost as much as many fish courses. And, if I want a celebratory meal, but do not want to serve meat or fish, I will make a colourful vegetable terrine, serve it with a comforting mix of grains and pulses, and garnish it with mushroom tartlets.

grilled vegetable terrine

serves 6 to 8

2 large aubergines

4 courgettes

4 red peppers

2 yellow peppers

extra virgin olive oil

1 sheet leaf gelatine

150ml (¼ pint) well-seasoned vegetable stock

Slice the aubergines and courgettes lengthways. Quarter the peppers, and remove the seeds and pith. Brush the vegetables lightly with oil, then either bake in the oven at 200°C/400°F/gas mark 6 until tender, or cook on a griddle or under a grill. The peppers should be charred and will need, when cool enough to handle, to be skinned. Meanwhile, soften the gelatine in cold water, then dissolve it in the stock.

Layer the vegetables in a loaf tin or terrine. Pour on the vegetable stock, and let the vegetables absorb it for 20–30 minutes. Then cover the terrine with cling film, and drain off most of the excess liquid. Refrigerate overnight, turn out, slice, and serve with a herb vinaigrette or a mint, yoghurt, shallot and cucumber sauce.

hot mushroom tartlets

makes 6 to 8

    250g (8oz) button mushrooms, wiped and sliced

    25g (1oz) unsalted butter

    2 tbsps dry oloroso or amontillado sherry

    freshly ground black pepper

    salt

    2 pickled walnuts, chopped (optional)

    good pinch of mace

    2 tbsps soft white breadcrumbs

    grated zest of ½ lemon, and a little juice

    250g (8oz) flaky pastry

    egg yolk, lightly beaten with water, to glaze (optional)

Fry the mushrooms in the butter over a high heat, then add the sherry and let it evaporate. Season, then mix in the walnuts, mace, breadcrumbs, zest and lemon juice.

Roll out the pastry, and use to line tart tins, reserving some of the pastry for lids. Spoon the mushroom mixture into the tart shells and top with pastry lids. Brush with an egg yolk and water glaze if you wish, and bake in a preheated oven at 200°C/400°F/gas mark 6 for 15–20 minutes. Serve either hot or warm.

warm quinoa and lentil salad
with mint and sherry vinaigrette

serves 6 to 8

250g (8oz) Puy or other small 'blue' lentils

125g (4oz) quinoa

extra virgin olive oil

sherry vinegar

fresh mint leaves, shredded or chopped

fresh basil leaves, shredded or chopped

6–8 spring onions, trimmed and chopped, or 3 shallots,
   peeled and chopped (optional)

salt

freshly ground black pepper

Cook the pulses and grains separately in water; the lentils in at least twice their volume; the quinoa in two to three times its volume. Drain, then mix them together. Stir in olive oil and vinegar to taste, then add the herbs (as much, or as little, as you like), the onion, if using, and some seasoning. Serve warm.

summer vegetable soup

serves 6 to 8

50g (2oz) butter

500g (1lb) asparagus

4 lettuce hearts, chopped

2 leeks, trimmed and sliced

500g (1lb) courgettes

small bunch chervil, parsley and mint, finely chopped

1.5–2 litres (3–4 pints) vegetable or chicken stock

salt

freshly ground black pepper

2 egg yolks

150ml (¼ pint) whipping or double cream

for the garnish

freshly cooked peas, asparagus tips, herbs, peeled and diced tomatoes,
as available

Melt the butter in a large pan, and sweat the vegetables for about 10 minutes without colouring. Add the herbs and the stock, and simmer until the vegetables are tender. The soup may then be rubbed through a sieve or blended in a liquidizer, although this is not obligatory. Return the soup to the pan, and season with salt and pepper. Blend the egg yolks with the cream, and add to the soup. Heat through without boiling. Serve garnished with herbs or cooked vegetables.

cucumber cream soup

serves 6 to 8

4 cucumbers

1 onion, peeled and chopped

1 medium potato, peeled and chopped

850ml (1½ pints) vegetable or chicken stock

850ml (1½ pints) milk, hot

50g (2oz) butter

50g (2oz) flour

salt

freshly ground black pepper

200ml (7fl oz) double cream

2 tbsps finely chopped chives or dill

Halve the cucumber, discard the seeds and chop. Place the prepared cucumber in a saucepan with the onion, potato and stock. Cook for 20 minutes, or until the vegetables are tender.

Make a white roux with the butter, flour and milk, then gradually stir in the cucumber mixture. Season with salt and pepper, and simmer for a further 10 minutes, stirring frequently. Rub the soup through a sieve or blend in a liquidizer. Return the soup to the pan, add the cream and herbs, and reheat gently before serving.

roast breast of veal
stuffed with mushrooms and kidney

If you plan to ask your butcher to prepare the joint for you, make sure he gives you the bones, as you will need them. In winter, I also add oysters to the stuffing, about 8 or 10, and add the liquid to the pan juices for gravy.

New potatoes can be roasted alongside the veal for the last hour or so.

serves 6 to 8

1kg (2lb) prepared breast of veal, boned (but keep the bones for later) and
    trimmed to a neat rectangular shape, about 20 × 30cm (8 × 12 inches)

500g (1lb) veal kidneys

salt

freshly ground black pepper

250g (8oz) button mushrooms

1 tbsp chopped fresh chives

½ tbsp chopped fresh tarragon

2 tbsps fromage blanc or 1 petit suisse

15g (½ oz) softened butter

1 clove of garlic, crushed and finely chopped

2 tbsps olive oil

Lay the veal on a flat surface. Trim most of the fat from the kidney, and snip out the core. Lightly season both with salt and pepper.

Fry the mushrooms in butter on a high heat for 4–5 minutes. Mix together the rest of the ingredients, except for the olive oil, and add the mushrooms. Spread the mixture over the meat, lay the kidney on top, roll up and tie with string at 1cm ($\frac{1}{2}$ inch) intervals.

Place the veal roll in a roasting tin on top of the veal bones. Place in a preheated oven at 150°C/300°F/gas mark 2, and roast for about 3–3½ hours, brushing with olive oil every 40 minutes.

Remove the meat from the oven, and keep it warm while you make the gravy from the pan juices.

baked stuffed pork tenderloins
with oriental flavours

serves 6 to 8

>   4 × 300g (10oz) pork tenderloins

for the marinade

>   4 tbsps groundnut oil
>
>   4 tbsps soy sauce
>
>   3 tbsps toasted sesame oil
>
>   2 tbsps rice or sherry vinegar
>
>   2 tbsps light or dark muscovado sugar
>
>   1 tsp five spice powder

The tenderloins need to be prepared the day before they are required. Split them down the middle, but do not cut right through, and open up like a book. Mix together the ingredients for the marinade, brush over the tenderloins and leave overnight.

stuffings

>   250g (8oz) good-quality pork sausage meat

1st stuffing

>   125g (4oz) button mushrooms, wiped and sliced and fried in 2 tbsps
>   groundnut oil
>
>   50g (2oz) beanshoots, blanched, dried and chopped
>
>   50g (2oz) shelled prawns, finely chopped
>
>   pinch of five spice powder

2nd stuffing

>   8 stoned ready-to-eat prunes, chopped
>
>   75g (3oz) cashew nuts, chopped
>
>   1 tsp freshly grated ginger

3rd stuffing

    2 apples, peeled, cored and grated

    1 green chilli, seeded and finely chopped

    2 spring onions, trimmed and finely chopped

4th stuffing

    6–8 smoked oysters, chopped

    2 shallots, peeled and finely chopped

    pinch of Szechuan peppercorns

    1 tsp finely chopped lemon grass

    cornflour

Divide the sausage meat between four bowls, and mix the rest of the stuffing ingredients as indicated in each bowl.

When ready to cook, remove the meat from the marinade, letting any excess marinade drip back. Open up the meat and sprinkle the surface very lightly with cornflour. Spread each tenderloin with one of the stuffings, and place in an oiled, ovenproof dish. Cover with foil, and bake in a preheated oven at 180°C/350°F/gas mark 4 for 20 minutes. Remove the foil, and baste the stuffed meats with the marinade. Bake for a further 15–20 minutes until the meat is tender.

Serve with steamed rice, baby bok choi and a chilled bottle or two of Tokay d'Alsace.

chicken breasts stuffed
with chorizo and dried figs

serves 6

6 chicken breasts, with bones to make stock

200g (7oz) dried figs, stalks removed and cut into quarters

75ml (3fl oz) anis liqueur or spirit

100g (3oz) lard – *see* recipe

1 large mild onion, peeled and thinly sliced

2 or 3 sprigs of parsley, finely chopped

2 garlic cloves, peeled and crushed

250g (8oz) chorizo, diced

6 large Swiss chard or cabbage leaves

flour

salt

freshly ground black pepper

150ml (5fl oz) dry amontillado or oloroso sherry

1 bay leaf

Chop the chicken bones, and put in a saucepan of water. Bring to the boil, skim the foam from the surface, and simmer. Reduce until you have about 500ml (18fl oz) stock. This can be prepared the day before, as can the figs.

Place half the figs in a bowl, cover with the anis, and leave to macerate for six hours. Remove the figs from the liquor and dry with paper towels.

When ready to prepare the dish, melt the lard and in it gently cook the onions until soft and golden. (If you wish to cut down on the amount of lard, which is, nevertheless, important for the authentic flavour of the dish, which I learnt to cook in Majorca, reduce it to 25g (1oz) and use a non-stick frying pan.) Add the soaked figs, parsley, garlic and 200g (7oz) of the chorizo, and mix well.

Make a pocket in the chicken breasts, and fill with the mixture. Wrap in the chard or cabbage leaves, and tie with thread. Dust with flour, and fry on all sides in lard. Season and place in a shallow earthenware casserole dish.

Pour in the sherry and the stock, and add the bay leaf. Tuck in the remaining figs and chorizo, and cook in a preheated oven at 180°C/350°F/gas mark 4 for about 20–25 minutes.

---

entertaining

tea cream

As a change from crème caramel and crème brûlée, try this elegant, pale, creamy dessert flavoured with tea. Good quality Earl Grey, green tea with jasmine flowers or a single estate Darjeeling are all much better than a nondescript blend.

serves 6

600ml (1 pint) full cream milk

1 level tbsp tea leaves of your favourite variety

2 large eggs and 3 egg yolks

100–125g (generous 4oz) caster sugar

150ml (5fl oz) double cream

for decoration

candied angelica and toasted, flaked or halved almonds

Put the milk and tea leaves in a saucepan and bring to the boil. Remove from the heat and allow to infuse for 5–6 minutes. Put the eggs, sugar and cream in a bowl and beat thoroughly. Strain the milk over the beaten egg mixture, and mix thoroughly. Strain into individual ramekins, and place in a roasting tin containing hot water that reaches halfway up the sides.

Bake in a preheated oven at 170°C/325°F/gas mark 3 for 25–30 minutes, depending on the depth of the custard. When cooked, a knife inserted into the centre should come out clean. Cool, then chill until required. Decorate with toasted almonds and angelica.

summer sunday lunches

I once took part in a discussion on *Woman's Hour* about how to do Sunday lunch in summer. Can it be a proper Sunday lunch without a roast, two veg and a steamed pud? Who wants to eat that in high summer? And how can you get the whole family to sit down together? I sympathize with the last question. As a child, I used to dislike the Sunday lunch ritual, and preferred to opt out. I'd have my roast beef sliced, then I'd make a sandwich, take it off to another part of the house and read my book.

There are many strategies for making a summer Sunday lunch, or its equivalent, a special occasion, different enough from weekday meals to tempt even the most reluctant person to sit down and join in. My colleague Marie-Pierre Moine, who writes for *House & Garden*, decided her lunch would be light and elegant, set on a table with white cloth under the trees. Salads, chicken or salmon, and a delicious bowl of strawberries in cassis and raspberry purée were her choices. Jenni Murray, the presenter, opted for a barbecue. I suggested something hot and spicy – refreshing if the weather turns sultry, comforting if the weather is cool.

Sunday lunch should indeed look attractive and appetizing, but it should not give the impression of being too formal. Food that is easy to assemble and easy to eat – perhaps using fingers – is, for me, particularly appealing. I also like dishes that do not need to be eaten as soon as they come out of the oven. I would not ban the barbecue, but instead use it as an alternative cooking method. Chargrill the meat or fish outside and bring it in to the table, rather than barbecue everything and stand around eating off plastic plates and drinking from plastic tumblers.

The main course in the following menu, a rack of lamb, can be cooked on the barbecue, as well as conventionally roasted in the oven as described in the recipe. The well-trimmed rack is a very small joint, with the meat evenly distributed along the rib, which will ensure uniform and relatively quick cooking. This particular version is good served hot, cold or room temperature. Naturally, as with any cooked meat, you will not want to let it sit around for hours and hours, but a couple of hours or so will be fine.

Rack of lamb is one of the best roasts to tackle for those who do not often cook a joint. It is so much more manageable than a large pork or beef roast, and is very adaptable to a range of flavourings and accompaniments. With it I would serve freshly cooked new potatoes tossed in olive oil, coarse sea salt and a generous snipping of chives.

Fresh goat's cheese seems the right thing to serve as the third course, and for dessert, I have chosen something easy, yet delicious, a fruit fool. Use this recipe as a blueprint for all your summer fruit fools. Raspberries, blueberries, plums, dessert gooseberries, peaches and greengages can all be cooked in the same way. You can replace the yoghurt or custard with crème fraîche or whipped double cream. I rather like the tartness of the yoghurt as a foil against the honey. Naturally, though, this can be replaced with sugar if you prefer. And if lavender is not to your taste, try cooking the fruit with rosemary, angelica or sweet cicely, or simply a few shavings of lemon zest and cardamom seeds.

However, if you have not tried using lavender as a herb, I commend it to you. Every year I place three or four fresh lavender spikes in a bottle of white vinegar, which I keep topping up as I use it, in vinaigrettes for both summer and winter salads. You might also try a spike or two tucked into a rack or leg of lamb when you roast it; not the one with pesto as this is too many conflicting flavours and scents.

That summer quartet of vegetables – tomatoes, peppers, courgettes and aubergines – appears in many guises. Ratatouille would be perfect with the lamb, for example. But they also make a very good first course, a salad or a vegetable tart perhaps. Or try this variation on a pudding. It looks handsome when you turn it out of its mould, and tastes very good.

pressed summer vegetable pudding

This is best made the day before. Slices of goat's cheese and crusty bread accompany the pudding very well, if you want to serve something more substantial. It can be served hot, cold or, best of all, at room temperature.

serves 6

    3 medium size aubergines, 1 sliced lengthways, the others in rounds

    2 red and 2 yellow peppers, quartered

    4 courgettes, sliced into rounds

    extra virgin olive oil

    salt

    freshly ground black pepper

    18 pieces semi-dried tomatoes – *see* recipe

as an accompaniment

    fresh basil or mint leaves

    miniature plum tomatoes

Place all the vegetables, except for the tomatoes, on oiled baking sheets, and brush with oil. Roast them in an oven preheated to 200°C/400°F/gas mark 6 until just tender, but not falling apart. The skin of the peppers should be blistered and loose; once they are cool enough to handle, this can be peeled off. Alternatively, the courgettes can be blanched in boiling water and the peppers charred under a grill until you can peel off the skin. Once all the vegetables are cool, season them lightly with salt and pepper.

Line a 1 litre (2 pint) pudding basin with cling film, to make unmoulding easier. Arrange five long slices of aubergine petal-fashion in the bottom and up the sides of the pudding basin, then layer the rest of the vegetables in it, interspersing each layer with some pieces of tomato. If you can only get very dried tomatoes, soak them first in boiling water for 20 minutes.

When you have assembled the pudding, cover it with cling film and weight it down heavily, so that when you come to unmould it and cut into it, the pudding will retain its shape. Stand it in a soup plate, as the juices may overflow. These should be poured back over the pudding, as they contain pectin, which will also help the pudding keep its shape.

When ready to serve, turn out the pudding on to a large plate. Top with a sprig of mint or basil, and surround with more herbs and small tomatoes.

baked sardines, mediterranean-style

serves 4

8–12 sardines, scaled and gutted, with backbone and head removed

salt

freshly ground black pepper

75g (3oz) prepared couscous

4 tbsps ground almonds

handful of raisins or sultanas

12 mint leaves, plus extra for garnish

2 onions, peeled and thinly sliced

4 red peppers, peeled and thinly sliced into strips

2 tbsps extra virgin olive oil

Trim the sardines to a neat shape and remove any large bones and fins. Open out and season each sardine lightly with salt and pepper, then place a teaspoon of couscous on top. Sprinkle on about the same quantity of ground almonds, and add a few raisins and a mint leaf. Fold over the sardines, end to end, not side to side, and secure with cocktail sticks. Put to one side while you prepare the vegetables.

Gently fry the onion and peppers until soft and wilted, the onion golden and the peppers just beginning to caramelize at the edges. Spoon into an ovenproof dish and lay the folded sardine fillets on top.

Bake in a preheated oven at 180°C/350°F/gas mark 4 for 15–20 minutes. Tear up the remaining mint leaves and scatter over the fish before serving. Or if you prefer to use basil all the way through, put a basil leaf inside the folded sardine and scatter shredded basil leaves on top. You can also add a scattering of pine nuts or flaked almonds, which will toast nicely in the oven. A couple of handfuls of miniature plum tomatoes and olives, well, actually might just be overdoing the whole thing.

pesto-crusted rack of lamb

serves 6

>3 racks of new season's lamb – *see* recipe
>
>3 generous tbsps pesto
>
>3 tbsps fine dry breadcrumbs

Ask your butcher to French-trim the lamb racks for you. This means cutting away all the fat and flesh from the ribs, chining it, i.e. removing the back bone, leaving you with just the 'eye' or fillet of meat. This is also a very easy joint to carve. You can either divide it into its separate cutlets, or simply cut each rack in half, as one rack serves two people.

If there is still too thick a layer of fat on the rack, remove it. Spread the pesto all over the top surface, and sprinkle with breadcrumbs. Roast in a preheated oven at 200°C/400°F/gas mark 6 for 20 minutes, 25 if you prefer your lamb to have no more than a hint of pink. Remove from the oven and let the meat rest for 5 minutes before carving.

Note If you are using lamb from an older animal, the rack will be larger, and you will need to adjust the cooking time.

lavender apricot fool

serves 6

750g (1½lb) apricots, stones removed

2 tbsps lavender honey

8 sprigs lavender

golden caster sugar

300–400ml (10–14fl oz) thick Greek yoghurt or custard

Rinse the apricots and put them in a saucepan with the honey and two sprigs of lavender. Cover with a lid and simmer very gently until the apricots are soft. Rub the pulp through a sieve and allow to cool for 20 minutes or so. Fold the mixture into the yoghurt or custard, spoon into glasses and chill for a couple of hours.

Meanwhile, rinse the remaining sprigs of lavender, shake them dry and roll in the sugar. Put somewhere very dry (even the bottom of the oven once it has been switched off) and allow to become crisp. Serve the glasses of fool on saucers, with a sprig of lavender for an edible decoration.

a boardroom lunch

With more and more people running their businesses from home, the question of boardroom lunches needs to be addressed in quite a different way. The cook may well be the director's spouse, or even you, the director, the boardroom a corner of the kitchen, and the boardroom table the dining or kitchen table.

When I have meetings at home, I generally have them not in our office, but in the bright airy roof-top room that is mainly kitchen, but also dining and living room. At some point, the meeting and lunch overlap, so I try to plan to prepare some of the food in advance, even if I do usually serve one hot dish.

A casserole might send everyone to sleep afterwards. And a grill or pan-fry needs an eagle eye kept on it, as well as some fast work with the spatula and plates. Not everyone likes the smell of fish cooking, so I leave the fish lasagne for when I know what my guests really like. The hot dish I really favour is a potato-topped pie, whether a shepherd's pie, a cottage pie or something with a more exotic name and filling. How about a *Parmentier de crabe*? Or even lobster? Venison diced small and cooked in a rich sauce makes a delicious version, as does black pudding. And, fish cooking smells notwithstanding, a potato and smoked haddock pie is wonderful, especially with a layer of spinach hidden in the middle.

These dishes are easy to eat, with a fork only, if papers are still being passed around. A really well-made potato-topped pie is a treat, and it is not difficult to achieve. You can assemble it in advance, and put it in the oven just 30–40 minutes before you want to serve it, perhaps as the meeting ends and you serve drinks.

A terrine that you can prepare a day or two in advance is perfect for this type of entertaining, as it looks extremely elegant and professional, but is not difficult to make. You will find plenty of recipes for these in the Buffet chapter.

I like to use potato in both fish and vegetable terrines, as the flavour and texture is highly satisfying. In the following recipe I combine potato with aubergine, and use pesto as a flavouring, with a piquant dressing of lime or lemon juice mixed with the rich nutty flavour of pumpkin seed oil. You might vary the terrine with cooked leeks and slices of celeriac in place of the potatoes. Or perhaps try a red pesto, using soaked dried tomatoes and a little chilli and garlic.

I also strongly recommend the smoked salmon and potato terrine, on p.119, although not if you are serving a smoked haddock pie for your main course. Or you might consider potted smoked fish, another recipe that you can prepare in advance. I have also suggested variations on the same theme for main courses, which you can mix and match into several menus, following the hot dishes with a peppery, crisp green salad. My recommended dessert is a universal favourite, the authentic English trifle, for which you will find the recipe on p.140. I have never known anyone to refuse it, but if you prefer, a cheese board and apples provides a more sober course. Or, as an alternative dessert, consider a grape jelly. Chocolate mousse, too, is a good bet, especially if you serve it in tiny ramekins with small spoons, then it seems not like dessert, but just a *bonne bouche* with the coffee. It can be made a day or two before it is required.

I always keep long-life cartons of grape juice on hand, both red and white. Not only are they good and refreshing juices when chilled, they are the basis of some excellent desserts, whether a jelly, a sorbet or a syrup. And they provide a starting point for non-alcoholic drinks. Try red grape juice, the juice of a Seville orange or half a lemon, and a topping up of soda or sparkling mineral water. White grape juice is similarly good with fresh lime.

With these blueprint recipes and menus, you can be sure of playing safe, but entertaining with style. Boardroom lunches are not the only occasions when this can be an advantage, it can also be important when meeting the in-laws for the first time, for example, or entertaining the boss.

grilled aubergine, potato and pesto terrine with pumpkin seed vinaigrette

serves 8

2 large, long aubergines, sliced not too thinly

2–3 red peppers, quartered and seeded

extra virgin olive oil

2 large Romano or other firm potatoes

1 sheet leaf gelatine or 1 tsp gelatine granules

100ml (3½fl oz) well-seasoned vegetable stock

150–200ml (5–7fl oz) pesto

sea salt

freshly ground black pepper

100ml (3½fl oz) pumpkin seed oil

juice of a lemon or lime

4 tbsps pumpkin seeds, lightly toasted

Line a long, narrow 1kg (2lb) terrine with cling film. Brush the aubergine slices and pieces of pepper with olive oil and grill or bake until the aubergine is tender and the pepper skin loose enough to peel off. Boil the potatoes in their skin until tender and, when cool enough to handle, peel and slice. Meanwhile, soften the gelatine in cold water, then dissolve in the vegetable stock.

Assemble the terrine by first lining the long sides and base, but not the two ends, with slightly overlapping slices of aubergine. Then build up layers of potato slices, pesto and any remaining aubergine slices and red pepper, lightly seasoning each layer, and finishing with a layer of aubergine. Pour on the vegetable stock, and let the vegetables absorb it for 20–30 minutes. Cover with cling film and weight the terrine with cans of tomato. Any vegetables left over that do not fit the terrine can be diced and used as a very fine omelette filling.

To serve, turn out and slice the terrine, not too thinly, and serve with a dressing made by simply whisking together the oil and citrus juice and a little seasoning. Scatter a few pumpkin seeds over each plate and serve.

entertaining

potted smoked trout
with cucumber and horseradish relish

serves 8 to 10

> 3 smoked trout
>
> 170g (6oz) unsalted butter at room temperature
>
> zest and juice of ½ lemon
>
> pinch of ground mace or freshly grated nutmeg
>
> freshly ground black pepper
>
> 4 anchovy fillets
>
> 75g (3oz) clarified butter, for keeping

for the relish

> 1 cucumber
>
> 1 tsp sea salt
>
> 4 spring onions
>
> 2–3 sprigs fresh mint
>
> 1 tbsp grated horseradish
>
> 150ml (¼ pint) thick Greek yoghurt
>
> freshly ground black pepper
>
> small wedge of honeydew melon

Flake the fish into a bowl, removing as many of the fine bones as possible. Beat in the butter with a fork. Grate in the lemon zest, add the lemon juice, and season with mace or nutmeg and pepper. Pound the anchovy fillets, and stir into the mixture, which should be smooth before you pack it into ramekins or a china dish. If you wish to keep the fish for a day or two, pour clarified butter over the top, and refrigerate until required. Serve with hot toast and the chilled cucumber relish. This is simply made by dicing all the vegetables and melon, then mixing them with the seasoning, yoghurt and mint.

shepherd's pie

serves 6 to 8

1 large onion, peeled and finely chopped

2 tbsps olive oil

1kg (2lb) rare or medium-rare cooked lamb, minced or finely chopped

300ml (½ pint) lamb stock or gravy

3 tbsps port

2 tsps Worcestershire sauce

pinch of grated nutmeg

pinch of ground allspice

pinch of chopped fresh rosemary

1 tbsp finely chopped parsley

salt

freshly ground black pepper

1kg (2lb) mashed potatoes

Lightly brown the onion in the olive oil. Mix with the rest of the ingredients, except for the potatoes. Line an ovenproof dish with a layer of potatoes, spreading them up the sides, and spoon in the lamb mixture. Spread the remaining mashed potato over the top and score with the tines of a fork.

Bake in the top of a preheated oven at 180°C/350°F/gas mark 4 for about 45 minutes.

chocolate mousse

Note that this recipe uses raw eggs.

serves 8

250g (8oz) chocolate, 70 per cent or more cocoa solids

50g (2oz) unsalted butter, at room temperature

1 tbsp orange, almond or raspberry liqueur, or rum

5 eggs, separated

Break up the chocolate and melt it in a bowl over hot water. Remove, and allow to cool slightly before beating in the butter, liqueur or spirit and egg yolks. The mixture will thicken. Whisk the egg whites, then fold them into the chocolate. Spoon into small ramekins or espresso cups. Cover and chill until firm.

a winter lunch menu

November is surprisingly rich in saints' days, to which particular foods can be attributed, starting with the feast of St Martin, or Martinmas on the 11th, followed by those of St Clement, St Catherine and St Andrew.

This is a good time of year to lay in stocks of dried fruits and nuts, to replenish your jars of spices, and to make sure you have plenty of varieties of sugar on hand for winter baking. None of these will be wasted in the coming weeks.

Spiced beef is often suggested for Martinmas, a suitably robust, autumnal and festive dish as befits one of the quarter days, when hirings were made and debts repaid. A steaming and fragrant steak and kidney pudding, complete with a feather-light suet crust is a good alternative.

Instead of cooking oysters in the pudding, serve them as a first course, chilled and on a bed of ice, with accompaniments of lemon, brown bread and butter, red and green Tabasco and the classic shallot vinaigrette. This is made by peeling and chopping a few shallots very finely, putting them in a bowl and covering with red wine vinegar. Keep it long enough for the flavour to develop.

A carefully chosen side of Scottish smoked salmon also makes a good first course, especially if there is someone on hand who can slice it at the table. Otherwise, buy it ready sliced and interleaved, and make up the plates in the kitchen, together with lemon wedges and brown bread and butter, and freshly ground black pepper. To help with larger gatherings, I find plate stacking rings invaluable as they allow you to stack plates, once made up, in the refrigerator or larder; Lakeland Ltd (015394 88100) sells them in packs of two. They are particularly useful over the holidays.

An alternative first course is a spinach and bacon salad; fry plenty of lardons until the fat runs and the bacon crisps, then mix with baby spinach, rocket and watercress and, if you like, top with a poached or fried egg, even a quail's egg.

To follow such a substantial main course, I suggest a crisp salad, if you have not served salad as a first course. If you have, then serve grapes or celery with a piece of Montgomery Cheddar, then a fruit dessert. I have suggested a selection of easy fruit-based ones, any one of which would be excellent after the steak and kidney pudding, though perhaps the pineapple one would be best of all, for its digestive qualities.

If you do not have time to prepare any of the desserts I describe below, you could try the following exceedingly quick, delicious and unusual idea. Pour a trickle of acacia honey over scoops of cinnamon ice cream and dot with ancient, thirty-year-old *aceto balsamico tradizionale di Modena*, then dust the whole plate with icing sugar before serving. A cheap balsamico will not have the sweet, rich concentration you need for this dish, merely acidity. Instead use Nocino, a walnut liqueur, or Pedro Ximenez sherry.

In Victorian times, when fresh oysters were inexpensive, they were a traditional ingredient in steak and kidney pudding, placed on top of the filling, just under the suet crust. In this recipe I have used mushrooms, but this does not mean that you cannot also add the oysters.

steak and kidney pudding

serves 6

1 large onion, peeled and sliced

25g (1oz) butter

1kg (2lb) rump, chuck or blade steak, trimmed and cubed

250g (8oz) veal kidney, trimmed and cubed

250g (8oz) button or cap mushrooms, wiped and sliced

250ml (8fl oz) beef stock or ale

salt

freshly ground black pepper

for the crust

250g (8oz) self-raising flour

pinch of salt

125g (4oz) suet, grated

iced water

Lightly brown the onion in the butter in a frying pan, remove and put to one side, then brown the steak and kidney. Put the meat with the onion and quickly fry the mushrooms. Remove them, too, then deglaze the pan with the stock or ale. Strain the liquid into a bowl or jug.

Sift the flour and salt into a bowl, add the suet, and lightly rub into the flour until you have the texture of breadcrumbs. Gradually add a little iced water. This amount of fat and flour will take about 100ml (3½fl oz). With your hands or a knife, work the mixture together, just until you have a soft, pliable, but not wet dough. Lightly, and briefly, knead the dough on a floured work surface until just smooth, then roll it out into a circle with light, quick strokes to a diameter of about 30cm (12 inches). Flour the dough, if necessary, but sparingly, to stop it sticking.

Grease a 1.75 litre (3 pint) pudding basin. Fold the dough in four and, with the broad edge outwards, fit the pastry into the basin, pressing it to the sides. It should overhang the edges of the basin. Remove some of the overhanging pastry, but leave enough for a pastry rim around the lip of the basin, to which you can anchor the pastry lid.

Pile the steak, kidney, onions and mushrooms into the lined pudding basin. Add about 200ml (7fl oz) of the cooking liquid, and season lightly.

Gather together all the remaining pastry trimmings and roll out a round of pastry to generously fit the top of the basin. Pinch together where the lid joins the pastry walls to seal it well. Cover with a round of greased, greaseproof paper, pleated down the middle to allow for the pudding to rise, and tie a pudding cloth over it. Place on a steamer rack in a saucepan, and pour in enough boiling water to come a quarter of the way up the basin. Cover with a lid and steam for 2–2½ hours, adding more boiling water if there is a danger of the pan drying out.

Turn the pudding out on to a heated serving plate. Serve by cutting into wedges and transferring to hot dinner plates. Or wrap the pudding basin in a large clean cloth and serve straight from it. The pudding should be eaten hot.

winter fruit desserts

baked pears stuffed with gingerbread

serves 6

    6 Conference or other English pears, peeled and cored

    6 tbsps crumbled ginger cake or parkin

    1 tbsp softened butter

    1 tbsp ginger wine

    1 tbsp melted butter

    2–3 tbsps light muscovado sugar

Mix together the crumbs, softened butter and ginger wine, and stuff into the pear cavities. Brush all over with the melted butter, dust with the sugar and bake in a preheated oven at 180°C/350°F/gas mark 4 for 30 minutes or so until the pears are soft, but not collapsing.

entertaining

frances bissell's pear and chocolate crumble

Crumbles have moved beyond the sugar, butter and flour topping. Chopped and flaked nuts are added for flavour and texture, as are spices. Crumbled ginger biscuits added to the basic mixture, together with some spices, makes an excellent crumble, as does crumbled up leftover ginger cake. But I had never come across a chocolate crumble. Until now. I had some leftover chocolate cake, to which I added chopped chocolate, cocoa and the traditional crumble mixture of flour, sugar and butter. I have not combined it with anything other than pears, its classic partner.

serves 6

50g (2oz) plain flour

1 tbsp cocoa powder

50g (2oz) butter, plus extra for greasing

75g (3oz) light muscovado sugar, plus 1 tbsp

50g (2oz) crumbled chocolate cake

50g (2oz) chocolate, chopped, or use chocolate chips

8 ripe pears

Sift together the flour and cocoa, rub in the butter, then stir in the sugar, cake crumbs and chocolate.

Peel, core and thinly slice the pears. (If the pears are of the harder Conference variety, then poach the slices first in a little sugar and water.) Butter an ovenproof dish and put in the pears. Sprinkle with the tablespoon of sugar, spoon the crumble over the fruit, and bake in a preheated oven at 180°C/ 350°F/gas mark 4 for 25–30 minutes.

grape ice cream with caramelized grapes

This is a particularly attractive dessert to make when you can get a variety of grapes.

It is wonderful accompanied by a Muscat de Frontignan or St Jean Minervois, or even better, a black Muscat wine from California.

serves 6

1 litre (1¾ pints) white or red grape juice

4 egg yolks, lightly beaten

250ml (8fl oz) double cream

200g (7oz) granulated sugar

grapes

1 egg white, lightly beaten

icing sugar

Put the grape juice in a saucepan, bring to the boil and reduce by half. Off the heat, pour the grape juice over the egg yolks, stirring continuously. Add the cream, then strain the mixture back into the saucepan. Cook gently until it thickens slightly. Remove from the heat, allow to cool, then freeze until required.

Put the sugar in a saucepan and cook to a pale caramel. Dip little bunches of grapes into the caramel. Allow these to dry on a marble or non-stick sheet. Other bunches can be frosted by dipping in lightly beaten egg white and dusting with icing sugar. Yet more bunches can be left plain.

roasted pineapple

serves 6

1 large ripe pineapple, peeled
100ml (3½fl oz) rum
100g (3½oz) unsalted butter
75g (3oz) light muscovado sugar
juice of ½ lemon
2 vanilla pods, split and halved

Stand the pineapple in a roasting tin. Make a syrup of the rum, butter, sugar and lemon juice and pour it all over the pineapple. Spike it with the vanilla. Roast in a preheated oven at 200°C/400°F/gas mark 6 for about an hour, basting from time to time. Flame in extra rum when you take it to the table, and serve with Hill Station's rum and coconut ice cream.

suppers

Late-night entertaining need not mean dial-a-pizza, chicken-tikka-take-away, or a surreptitious little number from the supermarket. With just a modicum of planning and preparation, you can produce a feast of homemade food as easily as if you had spent the whole evening cooking.

There are several ways of organizing late suppers. The easiest is to plan on having cold food, all of which can be prepared in advance – pâté, a plate of crudités and hummus, or potted smoked fish to start, for example. Move on to a platter of cold roast beef, a jellied fish terrine, *boeuf à la mode* or cold barbecued chicken joints. Serve with a bowl of salad leaves, again prepared in advance, and finish with a fruit flan, chocolate mousse, trifle or other cold pud. Not entirely welcoming is it, unless it's a breathless tropical night outside? The plan can be transformed, however, with one or two warm notes, such as hot toast or pitta bread with the starter, a hot consommé after it, and perhaps warm potato salad with the main course, or a hot custard sauce or sabayon with the fruit flan.

Another way of feeding your friends and family late in the evening, after the theatre for example, is to stick to cold food to top and tail the meal, but have a hot pot cooking at the lowest oven setting. Chilli con carne, beef in Beaujolais, lamb tagine or an Italian *stracotta* of beef are all favourites for such an occasion because they mean I can use the tougher, less expensive cuts of meat which positively demand long slow cooking.

Let this main dish dictate the rest of the meal and the wines. If you choose to cook a spicy lamb tagine, for example, continue the theme with yoghurt and cucumber salad, olives and salted almonds and hummus served with hot pitta bread. Sliced oranges, mint leaves and chopped dates make a refreshing fruit salad to finish the meal, and a crisp rosé wine will accompany it perfectly.

A *stracotta* can be preceded by Parma ham served with wedges of fennel, and followed with a creamy tiramisu. A chunky Barolo or Chianti will drink well with it, depending on what you have cooked the beef in.

On balance, I think the slow-cooked pot that is just ready to take out of the oven when you get home is a better bet than the precooked casserole that you reheat, but that is just because I like the welcoming smell of good food cooking when I open the door.

There is, however, yet another way of feeding hungry theatre-goers. Again, I have the starter and pud made in advance, but then I turn to fast food for the main course. Having done my *mise-en-place* or preparation earlier in the day, such as peeling potatoes, dicing, slicing or skewering meat or fish and preparing vegetables, there are a number of dishes I can have ready in little more than twenty minutes. Top of my list is fried or grilled calves' liver with sage, for which creamy mashed potatoes is the best accompaniment. As it is with bangers. I fry the sausages gently to get rid of excess fat, then raise the heat and finish them off in white wine. Rice is the best accompaniment to two other long-time Bissell favourites, one a dish of lamb's liver quickly cooked in white wine and olive oil, which we first came across many years ago in Lisbon, and the other grilled skewers of fish and apple. But first, something to spread on crostini.

ricotta and dried tomato crostini

This cream is also very good spooned into chicory and radicchio leaves. I have also made a version using a combination of tofu and cottage cheese when I could not get ricotta.

serves 6 to 8

6–8 pieces dried tomato, chopped

250g (8oz) fresh ricotta

freshly ground black pepper

If the tomato is very leathery, first soak for 15 minutes in hot water, then drain and dry.

Put the ricotta and tomato in a food processor and process until smooth. Alternatively, by hand, cream the ricotta, finely chop the tomato, and mix. Season with black pepper. If sun-dried, the tomato will probably add enough salt, if not, season as appropriate. You can add chopped chives, garlic, basil, spring onions and so on, but I really think this is nicer as plain as possible. Spread on hot toast or grilled polenta, and serve immediately.

smoked salmon, avocado and cream cheese

serves 4

1–2 ripe avocados

100g (4oz) smoked salmon, off-cuts will do

100g (4oz) cream or curd cheese

2–3 tbsps soured cream

1–2 tsps finely chopped chives or coriander

freshly ground black pepper

Line ramekins with cling film. Peel the avocado and finely dice the flesh. Cut up the salmon into small pieces. In a large bowl, blend together the cheese and soured cream, then fold in all the other ingredients. Spoon into the ramekin dishes, smooth, cover, and chill until required. To serve, turn out on to plates, discard the cling film and accompany either with salad leaves or simply a wedge of lime or lemon, and warm bread or toast.

grilled skewers of fish with apple

serves 4

500g (1lb) firm-fleshed fish, off the bone, such as monkfish or cod

2 crisp dessert apples

4 tbsps unsweetened apple juice

2 tsps toasted sesame oil

salt

freshly ground black pepper

1 tbsp toasted sesame seeds

Cut the fish into bite-sized chunks. Core and quarter the apple, then cut each quarter into two or three pieces, horizontally. Mix together the apple juice and sesame oil in a bowl. Add the fish and apple, coating the pieces well with the marinade. Season lightly, then thread the fish and apple alternately on small skewers. Place under a moderate to hot grill for about 8 minutes, turning them and basting them occasionally with the marinade. When done, arrange the skewers on one large dish or on individual serving plates on a bed of rice. Sprinkle with toasted sesame seeds.

iscas (lamb's liver in white wine)

This is based on a traditional Lisbon recipe and, as you can see from the method, a traditional Portuguese *cataplana* would be the ideal cooking pot. It can be prepared and marinated the day before.

serves 6

750g (1½lb) lamb's liver

75ml (3fl oz) dry white wine

4 tbsps extra virgin olive oil

1 mild onion, peeled and thinly sliced

salt

freshly ground black pepper

to garnish

fresh coriander leaves, chopped

Remove any piping from the liver, then cut first into slices and then into strips about the size and thickness of your little finger. Place in a bowl with the wine, olive oil and sliced onion. Mix well to thoroughly coat the liver. Leave to marinate overnight, or for at least several hours.

Heat a heavy casserole with a lid, and preferably handles, on top of the stove. Drain the liver, reserving the marinade. Sear the liver in the hot casserole, perhaps doing it in two or three batches so as not to crowd the pan, which would lower the temperature and cause the meat to steam rather than sear. Cover with the lid, and shake the casserole vigorously. Return it to the heat to cook for no more than 3–4 minutes. Remove the liver, and keep it warm. Repeat until all the liver is cooked. When you have removed the last of the liver from the casserole, pour in the marinade, boil until reduced by half, then pour over the liver. Season lightly, stir in the coriander leaves, if using, and serve immediately.

spiced braised shoulder of lamb

I cook this in a round earthenware dish from which I also serve it.

serves 4 to 6

1.5kg (3lb) shoulder of lamb

1 tbsp olive oil

1 onion, peeled and thinly sliced

3 cloves

piece of cinnamon

1 tsp coriander seeds

1 tsp ground cumin

150ml (¼ pint) red wine

150ml (¼ pint) lamb or other meat stock

salt

freshly ground black pepper

Remove the skin from the lamb and cut off the shank if it will not fit your cooking pot. Heat the olive oil in a frying pan and lightly brown the onion. Transfer to a casserole. Brown the meat and put it on top of the onion. Lightly fry the spices and add to the meat. Deglaze the pan with the wine, add the stock, bring to the boil and pour over the meat. Cover the casserole with a lid or foil and place in the bottom half of a preheated oven at 125°C/275°F/gas mark 1 and cook for about 4 hours. The meat will be tender enough to eat with a spoon and will have yielded a wonderfully perfumed broth. I serve this dish in soup plates, with rice, couscous, bulgar wheat or potatoes to accompany. Sometimes I add a few blanched vegetables, such as beans and asparagus, for the last 20–30 minutes' cooking time.

st emilion au chocolat

I first tasted *St Emilion au chocolat* twenty-five years ago in a very good, small restaurant called Randall's, on the quayside in Brixham, where it was part of the £1.75 set lunch. I still have the bill and see that a modest £3.50 for two, turned into an extravagant £13.73, with Riesling at £2.50 a bottle, and framboise and armagnac 50p a glass. Randall's St Emilion recipe came from Elizabeth David. It is essentially a charlotte, using macaroons, for which the town of St Emilion is famous, instead of sponge fingers. Ratafias or amaretti can be used in their place. Note that this recipe uses raw eggs.

serves 6 to 8

   2 egg yolks, lightly beaten
   150ml (¼ pint) single cream
   100g (4oz) unsalted butter
   100g (4oz) icing sugar, sifted
   250g (8oz) best quality dark chocolate, minimum 70 per cent cocoa solids
   12 amaretti or 18 ratafias
   brandy, rum, coffee or orange liqueur

Put the egg yolks in a bowl. Bring the cream just to the boil, and whisk it with the egg. Leave to cool. Cream the butter and icing sugar until light. Break up the chocolate, and melt in a bowl set over hot water. Remove from the heat and allow to cool. Beat the custard mixture into the melted chocolate, and then the creamed butter and sugar, mixing until smooth.

Dip the biscuits in the brandy, rum or liqueur, and place in the bottom of small ramekins. Spoon the chocolate cream over the top, and smooth the surface. Chill overnight or for at least 12 hours for the flavours to ripen. Alternatively, a deep, rather narrow glass bowl or soufflé dish can be used in which you layer the biscuits and chocolate cream alternately.

chilli flavours for summer

This menu illustrates perfectly the point I made in my introduction about certain foods and recipes being right for any time of day. The following dishes are suitable not only for a summer brunch, but also lunch or supper.

Food with chillies is perfect for a British summer. It cheers you up if the weather lets you down, and if it does turn really hot and sultry, then nothing is more refreshing. One can look to Thai food with its chilli heat tempered by the fragrance of basil, mint, lemon grass and lime leaves. Or consider a southern Indian meal with its selection of vegetable curries, dosas and rice. All the accompaniments – naans and chapatis, pickles, sambals and chutneys – make for an appetizing yet casual array, liable to tempt to the table even those who normally find Sunday lunch too formal.

Moroccan, North African and Middle Eastern flavours are appropriate too. Make a spicy mixed vegetable stew, grilled lamb kebabs and *merguez* and a heap of steaming, fragrant couscous. Prepare some vegetable salads and richly flavoured dips to start with, one made with grilled aubergines, one with chickpeas, and a cucumber, yoghurt and chilli salad, and serve these with warm pitta bread.

But my favourite would be a meal with soft tortillas and flavours of chilli, coriander, limes and fruit, the kind of food you'd get in Arizona, California and Texas, where the Mexican influences are strong and the sun is hot. It's lively, appetizing, flavoursome food, fun to assemble and easy to eat.

I'd start with a piece of skirt or rump steak, marinate it with onions and pineapple juice and, while that was marinating, I would gently fry some sliced onions and red and green peppers. I would grill the meat on an iron griddle or barbecue. While it was cooking, I would warm up the tortillas, prepare some guacamole and have shredded lettuce to hand. When the meat is cooked, it is sliced thinly, piled on a platter with the onion and pepper to one side, and everyone assembles their own tortillas, not forgetting the final element, a spoonful of homemade salsa. This dish of grilled sliced meat, *fajitas*, is also extremely good when made with duck breasts. Cook them with the skin on, but remove the skin before you slice and serve the meat.

Once you've made salsa yourself, you'll never buy a jar again. It is incredibly easy and absolutely delicious, much better than the commercial versions which are mainly tomato and peppers, with far too much stabilizing gum and thickeners. You can vary your salsa ingredients, but the structure should be: fruit – a sharp one such as underripe mango, pineapple, kiwi fruit or tomato; hot – red or green chillies; sour – lime or lemon juice; savoury – onion, red onion, spring onions, shallots or leeks; and sweet – a little unrefined sugar, to bring out the juices. Then you need some salt and some herbs, in particular chopped coriander and mint.

I like to make a green salsa with kiwi fruit, with little red warning lights of chilli, but for a confetti effect, add some seeded diced tomatoes and peeled mango. In fact, this is, for me, one of the very best things to do with kiwi fruit. The salsa is a perfect accompaniment to grilled meats, especially duck, and fish, goes well with tortilla wraps of various kinds, and is also good as a dip with crisp tortilla chips.

The best guacamole I have tasted, and it was as much a texture as a taste, was at Rosa Mexicana in New York, where the waiter mixed it expertly at the table. He split, stoned and chopped the avocado into a lava stone mortar, having somehow got rid of the skin in the process. Then he added coriander, fresh chilli, lime juice and some chopped tomato, all of which he then crushed into a chunky mass, not a paste, with the back of wooden spoon. We ate it, not with tortilla chips, but wrapped in small, thin, soft tortillas, freshly made and still warm from the griddle.

I also commend the dish we ate after that, *taquitos de morongo*. For this you need, again, small, fresh flour tortillas and some diced, fried black pudding, still warm, chopped fresh coriander leaves and thinly sliced, mild onion. These three simple ingredients are wrapped in the tortillas, which are then served on a bed of finely shredded raw cabbage and chopped tomato.

As they make such delicious and easy first courses, I suggest, on p.82, another dish to try with tortillas. And don't forget how good they are for brunch, wrapped around a filling of scrambled egg, chillies and spring onions, together with some cooked diced chorizo. Or indeed, the fried, diced black pudding. With that, you might like my melon margarita.

However, these fresh flavours and chilli heat are well partnered in the summer by crisp German wines, high in natural acidity, with plenty of fruit, yet naturally low in alcohol, which is particularly attractive if we have some really lazy dog days, especially for the last Bank Holiday weekend in August. I recommend wines from the Mosel, and the best you can afford. A creamy, smooth, classic *flan* rounds off the meal to perfection.

melon margarita

serves 6

1 ripe and fragrant melon, such as a galia or charentais
2 limes
3 measures Cointreau
6 measures tequila
fine salt for salting the glass (optional)

Have all the ingredients ice-cold. Halve the melon, discard the seeds and scoop the flesh into a blender. Take off six thin curls of lime zest, and squeeze the juice into the blender. Add the spirits, and blend until smooth. Pour into chilled glasses, decorate with lime zest, and serve. If you like, moisten the edge of the glass with the squeezed lime skin, and then dip it into salt.

ham and corn enchiladas

serves 6

3 corn cobs

6 flour tortillas

200g (7oz) crème fraîche or cream cheese

500g (1lb) cooked ham or gammon off the bone, preferably in a piece,
    diced or shredded

6 tbsps salsa

6 tbsps grated Gouda

2–3 tbsps fresh coriander, finely chopped

Drop the corn into boiling water and cook for 2 minutes. Remove and drain. When cool enough to handle, cut off the corn kernels. Soften the tortillas in a frying pan or steam over hot water. Spread each tortilla with crème fraîche or cream cheese, then build up layers of corn, ham, salsa, cheese and herbs in a band down the middle.

Fold the tortillas in at two sides, then roll them up. Place in a well-greased baking dish, cover with foil, and bake in a preheated oven at 180°C/350°F/ gas mark 4 for 20–25 minutes.

Serve with shredded iceberg lettuce, refried beans or cooked black beans, guacamole and a wedge of lime.

entertaining

flan

serves 6

300ml (½ pint) single cream
300ml (½ pint) full cream milk
1 vanilla pod
2 eggs, plus 2 extra egg yolks
150g (5oz) sugar
2 tbsps water

Bring the cream and milk slowly to the boil in a saucepan with the vanilla pod. Meanwhile, beat the eggs and egg yolks in a bowl with two tablespoons of the sugar. Pour on the hot liquid, whisking all the time. Remove the vanilla pod, and rinse and dry it for future use. Or, for a rich vanilla flavour, after rinsing the pod, scrape some of the seeds into the custard. The pod can then still be used to flavour a jar of caster sugar.

In a small, heavy saucepan dissolve the rest of the sugar in the water. Raise the heat, and allow to caramelize. Pour the caramel quickly into a soufflé dish, swirling it around to cover the base and sides.

Pour the egg and cream mixture through a sieve into the prepared dish and stand it in a roasting tin containing a little water. Bake in a preheated oven at 180°C/350°F/gas mark 4 for about 35 minutes. It is cooked when a knife point inserted into the centre of the cream comes out clean. Allow to become completely cold before refrigerating. To serve, turn out on to a deep plate.

early spring supper

February and March usually bring the first sighting of family and friends from abroad. What to serve them? Just as I do when I'm travelling, they want to eat food from here rather than there. So I put aside the chillies and coconut, soy sauce and lemon grass and look to see what home-grown produce my local shops have in store. Well, not much, to be truthful. Most of the fruit and veg seems to come from elsewhere. But there are potatoes and greens, celery and carrots, rhubarb and baking apples, and there are always mushrooms.

Meat is not a problem. A slowly braised dish of organic pork or a beef casserole with dumplings? It might be the start of British Summer Time, but the weather is still cool enough for warming casseroles, and the dumplings are a rare treat. They are so easy to make that you will want to keep them in your repertoire, large ones for casseroles and small ones for dishes such as oxtail soup and, in season, game soups and casseroles. The recipe I have developed here is based on the traditional Exeter beef stew.

As for fish, cod, lemon sole, Dover sole, monkfish and haddock are all fabulous at this time of year. And smoked fish is always a good bet. You might serve a smoked fish salad, perhaps some lightly poached smoked haddock with baby spinach or salad leaves and a poached quail's egg. Or a smoked salmon terrine. Or try my very simple version of potted fish, using trout, salmon and mackerel. Trout and mackerel are hot smoked, which cooks the fish and makes it opaque. Sliced smoked salmon is cold smoked, giving it that lovely translucent appearance. However, you can also find hot-smoked, also called kippered, salmon, and this is what I would use for preference when making potted fish. I'm sure, in fact, that pounded fish, or even fish paste describes the dish better, since potted fish used to be packed as whole fillets sealed under a layer of butter.

Use new season's rhubarb for a pretty sorbet, and Bramleys for a baked apple dessert, to which clotted cream is the perfect accompaniment. Before that, serve some crisp celery and oatcakes with a selection of English farmhouse cheeses, some familiar, such as Stilton and

---

Cheddar, and some newer ones, such as the hard goat's milk and ewe's milk cheeses. Try an English white wine with the smoked fish, and save some for the cheese. Sharpham Estate Reserve, made from the Madeleine Angevine grape, and having spent a little time in oak, has sufficient character to support the flavour and texture of both fish and cheese.

menu planning

The recipes which follow are perfect for a supper or a late Sunday lunch. If you want to serve the baked apple and clotted cream for dessert, I suggest a plainer first course, of smoked trout fillets with the cucumber relish. The richer first course of potted fish is perhaps better matched with the rhubarb sorbet. Serve it with crisp, thin almond biscuits.

time planning

Potted fish can be made a few days in advance. The beef casserole can be made the day before it is required and reheated with the dumplings 40 minutes before you want to serve it. You can put the baked apples in the oven at the same time. The sorbet can be made the day before, but is best made on the day as it quickly loses its fresh flavour.

trio of potted smoked fish
with cucumber, dill and horseradish relish

serves 6

1 smoked trout

200g (7oz) hot or cold smoked salmon

1 smoked mackerel

250g (8oz) unsalted butter, at room temperature

zest and juice of ½ lemon

pinch of ground mace or freshly grated nutmeg

freshly ground black pepper

75ml (3fl oz) clarified butter (if keeping the potted fish)

for the relish

1 cucumber, halved, seeded and finely chopped

1 tsp sea salt

4 spring onions, trimmed and chopped

1 tbsp chopped fresh dill

1 tbsp grated horseradish

4 tbsps good mayonnaise

Flake the fish into three separate bowls, removing as many of the fine bones as possible. Into each, beat a third of the unsalted butter with a fork until the mixtures are smooth. Grate in the lemon zest, and season with lemon juice, mace or nutmeg and pepper. Pack the mixtures into containers, cover and refrigerate until required. If you wish to keep the fish for a day or two, pour clarified butter over the top first.

If you like, you can use a food processor on pulse to pound the fish and butter. And if you start with the mildest fish first, the trout, and finish with the mackerel, you can get away with not having to wash the food processor between each operation.

To make the cucumber relish, simply mix all the ingredients and serve, together with hot toast, with the potted smoked fish.

---

entertaining

beef casserole with celery, mushrooms and dumplings

serves 6

1kg (2lb) shoulder or shin beef, off the bone, or beef cheek

2 tbsps cider vinegar

3 onions, peeled and sliced

4 celery stalks, trimmed and sliced

200g (7oz) button or cap mushrooms

50g (2oz) butter

25g (1oz) flour

750ml (1¼ pints) cider

salt

freshly ground black pepper

flat-leaf parsley, chopped

for the dumplings

100g (4oz) flour

75g (3oz) soft breadcrumbs

50g (2oz) finely grated suet

1 tbsp finely chopped parsley

½ tsp fresh thyme

½ tsp fresh chives

½ tsp each salt and baking powder

freshly ground black pepper

water, milk or lightly beaten egg to bind, as required

Trim the meat and cut into a dozen or so pieces. Put in an oven-to-table casserole with the vinegar, and place in the bottom half of a preheated oven at 150°C/300°F/gas mark 3.

Gently fry the onion, celery and mushrooms in the butter, sprinkle on the flour, and let it brown all over. Stir in the cider, bring to the boil, and pour over the meat in the casserole. Season lightly, cover, put back in the oven, and cook until the meat is tender. This can take up to three hours, depending on the cut of meat you use.

---

breakfasts, lunches and suppers

About 40 minutes or so before the cooking time is finished, make the dumplings by mixing together all the ingredients and shaping the mixture into small balls, adding a little milk, water or beaten egg, if necessary. Place the dumplings on top of the meat, cover the casserole again with the lid, and return to the oven.

Serve the beef and dumplings straight from the casserole, with a good sprinkling of chopped flat leaf parsley.

rhubarb sorbet

serves 6

500g (1lb) trimmed rhubarb
500g (1lb) sugar
500ml (16fl oz) water
vanilla pod
juice of ½ lemon

Rinse the rhubarb and cook it gently until tender. Make 500ml (16fl oz) sugar syrup by dissolving the sugar in the water and infusing it with a vanilla pod. When both the rhubarb and the syrup are cool, blend them together, and add the lemon juice. Freeze in a sorbetière or ice-cream maker.

baked apple with spiced dried fruit and clotted cream

serves 6

6 slices bread or brioche, cut into rounds

75g (3oz) unsalted butter

3 vanilla pods

6 Bramley or other cooking apples, cored

6 tbsps mincemeat or mixed dried fruit

50g (2oz) light muscovado sugar

1 orange

1 lemon

6 tbsps English cider brandy, apple aperitif or mead

to serve

clotted cream

Thickly butter the bread or brioche slices, then place them in a lightly buttered ovenproof dish. Split the vanilla pods in half, lengthways. Spike pieces of vanilla into the apples, using a skewer to make holes, if necessary. Fill the centre of each apple with dried fruit or mincemeat and place one on each slice of bread. Smear the rest of the butter over the apples, and sprinkle with the sugar. Remove the citrus fruit rind in spirals, and arrange amongst the fruit. Bake in a preheated oven at 160°C/325°F/gas mark 3 for about 45 minutes. Remove from the oven, pour on the brandy, and serve warm with very cold clotted cream.

bank holiday entertaining

Crab cakes and cucumber salad, roast chicken with bread sauce and a burnt cream, or crème brûlée, if you prefer, is the perfect menu for entertaining, as quantities can easily be multiplied if you are cooking for more than six people. The cucumber salad can be made several hours in advance. The burnt cream is best started the day before, and caramelized just an hour or two before you want to serve it.

Quite often it takes a foreigner to get the best out of our dishes. Anton Mosimann's version of bread and butter pudding took that homely dessert to new heights, since when it has long enjoyed prominence on the best menus. The best bread sauce and the best crab cakes I have ever tasted came from an English kitchen run by a French chef. I went to Chewton Glen one autumn to cook one of their series of guest dinners and, as always, I picked up many new ideas to incorporate into my own repertoire, including the crab cakes. They are much better than Thai crab cakes, which can often have a rubbery and dry consistency. Maryland crab cakes, once made with 'jumbo lump' crab meat, but now more often than not made with 'colossal lump' crab meat, are just too rich. These are perfect. The consistency is that of the traditional English fish cake, with a generous helping of mashed potato.

I also acquired the accompanying cucumber salad recipe, which Pierre Chevillard in turn borrowed from Ken Hom, another guest chef at the hotel. It is crisp and refreshing, and its distinctly oriental flavour is a nice counterpoint to the plain and comforting crab cake. When I first made it, I had no fish sauce in my cupboard, and instead added a couple of pounded anchovy fillets, which I found worked very well.

It is possible to buy real free range chickens, and organic chickens, from several sources, not just supermarkets – by mail order, from farm shops, from the food halls and from the few good independent high street butchers still left. Many farmers are going back to the traditional breeds of poultry, which are slower growing than the broiler fowl, are better adapted to our climate and conditions and develop a deep, full flavour and good texture. These are the chickens to look for, and it is well worth paying extra for them.

For years I pot-roasted my birds, which produces a lovely moist meat with excellent juice, but that way you lose out on the crisp golden skin. You do also lose out on the smoke from burnt splashes of fat and a dirty oven. However, once in a while, I'm prepared to put up with cleaning the oven, because roast chicken is so delicious. I've found the most even cooking comes with spatchcocking the bird, otherwise the breast is cooked long before the thighs and, once the thigh meat is properly cooked through, the breast is overcooked and dry. To spatchcock, which you can do with any bird, cut out the back of the chicken with poultry shears and flatten it by pressing down on the breast bone.

To have enough for six or eight, you will need to cook two birds, and I have found it is best to lay them on the rack in a large roasting pan, the kind that generally comes with the oven. To stop the fat burning as it hits the bottom of the roasting pan, grease it first and then lay even, but not too thin, slices of vegetables on top. Courgettes, aubergines, onions and turnips are good candidates, though potatoes are best of all; the unburnt bits can accompany the chicken. An even crisper skin will be achieved by drying the bird. This is done with ducks in Chinese restaurants to give them their characteristically crisp skin. You can leave the spatchcocked bird uncovered overnight in the refrigerator, well isolated from any other food, for we all know how refrigeration dries out food. Or you can put it on a rack over a dish and play the hairdryer over the surface for 15 minutes. On 'blow', not on 'heat', of course.

One of my favourite sandwiches is made with leftover chicken and ripe avocado, both ingredients thinly sliced and layered in a warmed English muffin with a lemon-flavoured mayonnaise and some baby spinach leaves. I sometimes replace the avocado with the tender top portion of cooked asparagus spears.

crab cakes with cucumber salad

serves 6

2 cucumbers

1 tbsp toasted sesame oil

1 tbsp soy sauce

2 tsps oriental fish sauce

juice and grated zest of ½ lime

1 tsp demerara sugar

2 ripe tomatoes, seeded and diced

500g (1lb) white crab meat

500g (1lb) mashed potatoes

bunch of spring onions

salt

freshly ground black pepper

5 tbsps mayonnaise

breadcrumbs, for coating

olive oil or a mixture of oil and butter, for frying

First make the cucumber salad. Peel and halve the cucumbers and discard the seeds. Slice thinly, sprinkle with salt, and let drain for an hour or so. Rinse and squeeze dry in a clean tea towel. Put in a bowl. Mix together the sesame oil, soy sauce, fish sauce, lime and sugar, and pour over the cucumber. Mix well and stir in the diced tomato.

Mix together the crab, potato and spring onion in a bowl. Season lightly with salt and pepper, then carefully fold in the mayonnaise. This binds the mixture and gives a delicate texture to the crab cake. Divide the mixture into either six or twelve, depending on how large or small you like your cakes. Shape first into a ball, then flatten to a cake. Dip in breadcrumbs. Heat two tablespoons of oil, or a mixture of oil and butter, in a frying pan, then gently lower in the fish cakes. Fry until golden, then turn over carefully and fry the other sides until crusty and golden.

To serve, spoon the salad on to plates and place a crab cake on top.

roast chicken

serves 6, plus leftovers

  2 × 1.25kg (2½lb) chickens

  4 bay leaves

  4 cloves

  1 lemon

  salt

  freshly ground black pepper

  2 aubergines, courgettes, onions and turnips, or 4 potatoes, peeled as
     necessary, and sliced about 1cm (½ inch) thick

Remove and discard any excess fat from the cavities of the chickens. Using poultry shears, cut out the backs from the two birds, and press down on the breastbones to flatten them. (Use the chicken backs to make some stock while the chickens are roasting.)

Spike each bay leaf with a clove, and nail them to the underside of each half of chicken, then rub all over with the cut lemon. Lightly season on both sides and place, skin side up, on a rack in a greased roasting tin, into which you have put a layer of prepared vegetables.

Roast in a preheated oven at 220°C/425°F/gas mark 7 for 40–45 minutes. The chickens are cooked when the juices – which are released when you pierce the inner thigh with a skewer – run clear and not pink. Transfer the chicken and any usable vegetables to a serving platter, cutting each chicken into portions.

If the vegetables are too burnt and broken up, serve a watercress salad with the chicken, along with gravy and bread sauce.

gravy

Pour off any excess fat and sift a tablespoon or two of flour into the roasting tin. Scrape up any juices stuck to the bottom and work in the flour. Add a little boiling water or stock, plus a splash or two of the wine you will serve with the chicken, and stir until the mixture forms a paste, then add more liquid until you have a slightly thickened sauce. Season, if required, and strain into a small saucepan and let the gravy simmer for 5 minutes or so, before pouring into a warm jug or gravy boat.

For a cream gravy, add milk or single cream instead of water to the pan juices.

bread sauce

serves 6

1 small onion
6 cloves
1 bay leaf
600ml (1 pint) full cream milk
100g (4oz) soft white breadcrumbs
25g (1oz) butter
salt
freshly ground black pepper
generous grating of nutmeg

Stick the onion with the cloves and place, with the bay leaf and milk, in a saucepan. Bring to the boil, remove from the heat, cover, and infuse for 20–30 minutes. Stir in the breadcrumbs and butter, and cook gently for 15 minutes. Remove the onion and the bay leaf, season to taste, and add the nutmeg.

warm chocolate cakes

serves 6

butter

cocoa powder

150g (5oz) chocolate, minimum 70 per cent cocoa solids

3 eggs, plus 2 egg whites

5 scant dsps caster sugar, plus 2 tsps

icing sugar

Butter and dust with cocoa six 100ml (4fl oz) ramekins. Break up the chocolate, and melt in a bowl set over hot water. Remove from the heat.

In another bowl, also set over hot water, beat the whole eggs with the 5 dessertspoons of sugar until pale and the mixture leaves ribbons when trailed from the whisk. With a clean whisk, whisk the egg whites with the remaining caster sugar until firm.

Carefully, and gradually, fold the melted chocolate, the egg and sugar and egg white mixtures together. Spoon the mixture into the ramekins, place them in a roasting tin with a little water, and place in a preheated oven at 160°C/325°F/gas mark 3 for 15–20 minutes, or at 180°C/350°F/gas mark 4 for 12–15 minutes.

Remove from the oven and allow the cakes to cool in the ramekins for a few minutes until they begin to shrink from the edges. The cakes will have risen during cooking but will now begin to sink. Using a knife, ease round the cakes, then gently turn them out on to serving plates, and dust with icing sugar and cocoa, if you wish.

saffron and almond sauce

serves 6

200ml (7fl oz) skimmed milk

good pinch of saffron

4 tbsps skimmed milk powder

150g (5oz) marzipan, broken into pieces

Scald the milk with the saffron, then remove from the heat. Whisk in the milk powder, then stir in the marzipan. When the marzipan has dissolved, stir once more, then allow the sauce to cool. Serve either warm or cold.

burnt cream

serves 6 to 8

600ml (1 pint) double cream

1 vanilla pod

6 egg yolks

50g (2oz) golden caster sugar

100g (4oz) demerara sugar

Bring the cream and vanilla pod to the boil in a saucepan. Beat together the egg yolks and caster sugar, then pour on the scalded cream. Beat thoroughly, and strain into a double boiler. Rinse and dry the vanilla pod, split it, and scrape the seeds into the custard. Heat the custard, stirring continuously until it thickens. Remove from the heat, and stir until cool. Pour into ramekins and chill until set. Sprinkle the demerara sugar evenly over the tops of the ramekins, then put them under the grill just long enough for the sugar to melt and caramelize. Alternatively, caramelize it using a blow torch. Chill once more until required.

buffets

Writing from the experience of having cooked and prepared lunch and dinner buffets in a number of five-star hotels in Britain and in various parts of the world, I am still not sure how I feel about buffets.

I have always planned them meticulously, in the hope that guests will eat them in the order I envisage. First a small plate of cured smoked and raw fish, or perhaps some shellfish. Then a pâté or terrine with its own homemade fruit jelly or chutney. Palates will then be refreshed with cool vegetable salads, perhaps carrot and peach with hazelnuts, or melon and cucumber with flaked almonds. For main courses, I prepare fish, poultry, meat and vegetables with seasonal produce in appetizing combinations. English cheese would precede English puddings. That is the theory at least.

One Saturday night, many years ago, at the Intercontinental in London, theory flew out the window when a whole American football team descended on my buffet. I nearly cried as I saw my delicate translucent slices of Scotch salmon marinated in whisky being swamped by mounds of fish and spinach pie, vegetable gratin and duck casserole. Only lack of space prevented a scoop of summer pudding going on top.

But, nevertheless, I kept on accepting invitations to cook abroad. Another year, in the Philippines, I was, at 6 pm, putting the finishing touches to the Peninsula's Saturday evening buffet, arranging glass bowls of junkets and fruit fools, when over a hundred passengers from a much-delayed Manila to Bahrain flight were herded in for supper. Later, I discovered that this was a regular occurrence, and that 'the locusts devour everything in their path'. That it was a nice little English buffet made no difference at all.

There are two problems with buffets. One is the food itself, the other is the people who eat it. You can do little about the diner who piles his or her plate with a bit of everything, unless you stand guard, like a policeman, telling them how to do it. You might, I suppose, have one or two guests lead the way, after careful briefing, but this hardly lends itself to relaxed entertaining. Once the food is on the table or sideboard, it's open season.

The other problem is that the food quickly becomes dishevelled. After three or four servings, your trifle or summer pudding looks a mess, and the carefully garnished salmon a disaster area.

But buffets need not be like that. Friends once invited us to lunch on the 4th of July. They claimed to be nervous, inexperienced cooks, but they produced one of the best possible meals of its kind, with simplicity the keynote, underpinned by ingredients of the finest quality. The centrepiece of the buffet was a glorious, moist, flavoursome ham, cooked to perfection. There was a shrimp salad, a rice salad, some greens, excellent cheeses and a fine apple tart. The ham was partially carved, with a fan of neat slices arranged so as to be easily picked up with the serving fork. The salads were replenished before the bowls were empty, so that they never looked messy or mean. The cheese board was carefully chosen so that the cheeses were relatively easy to cut, and the correct, sharp implements were ready to hand. The apple pie was cut into wedges, but left assembled, so that slices were easy to remove.

From all this, a blueprint begins to emerge, suggesting suitable dishes and ways of serving them. Of course, reducing the number of dishes to an elegant minimum does make it imperative to find out if there is anything your guests cannot eat or drink. With a larger buffet, you can usually cater for most tastes. By offering a wide range of dishes you should be able to cater for non-meat eaters and vegetarians. Do not assume that everyone likes what you like; you may need to include items that are not your favourites. Do not put all the canapés on rounds of toast or other wheat-based products, otherwise you will exclude those who cannot eat gluten. Choose amongst the whole range of food groups, and do not include the same ingredient twice.

Similarly, cover the range of textures from soft to chewy to crisp, from mousses to crudités, and from blinis to crackers. Avoid a monochrome look, and go for vivid colours and contrasts. Beige and cream may look elegant as interiors, but are not as appealing for food. So brighten up your chicken mousse with asparagus or herbs, your *mouttabal* with coriander and lemon, and your brandade of salt cod with black olives and dried tomatoes.

Use a broad palette of tastes and flavours, but not an indiscriminate one. In the search for fusion food, take care not to introduce confusion. But do try to include sour, bitter, hot, salt, savoury and sweet notes.

food quantities for an informal fork buffet

For ten to twenty guests in summer, provide two cold dishes, a salad, two sorts of bread or rolls and two cold desserts; in winter, I suggest one hot and one cold dish, a salad, two sorts of bread, and one hot and one cold dessert.

For thirty to forty guests in summer, serve two cold dishes, two salads, two sorts of bread or rolls and two cold desserts; in winter, you need two hot dishes, one cold dish and one salad, two sorts of bread and one hot and one cold dessert.

For a large summer party, for fifty or more, you need three cold dishes, two or three salads, two breads and two or three cold desserts; in winter, provide two hot dishes and one cold, two or three salads, two or three breads and two cold and one hot dessert.

A mix of fork food and canapés can be served if you want something halfway between a buffet and a drinks party, perhaps circulating drinks and canapés, and then inviting people to the buffet, for either a seated or standing meal.

soups

Vegetable soups are perhaps the most useful, in that they will appeal to vegetarians and meat-eaters alike. A vegetable minestrone is perfect in winter, served with crusty bread and some extra virgin olive oil or homemade pesto to float on top. The simplest soups can be made using uncooked ingredients and no stock, as with gazpacho or prawn, cucumber and yoghurt soup. Creamed vegetable soups, such as vichyssoise, can be served hot or cold, according to the season and what else you are serving. Make sure the appropriate accompaniments are to hand, such as croûtons, soured cream, herbs, toast, chunky bread, butter, olive oil, pesto and whatever else you like in your soup. You will find soup recipes in the Soup and Sandwich section of Casual and Impromptu Meals on pp.191–201.

smoked and marinated fish

Gravadlax, smoked salmon, halibut, trout and swordfish are all good candidates for a buffet. As well as simply slicing them, they can also be used for smoked fish pâtés. Appropriate accompaniments are lemon and lime wedges, black pepper to grind, coarse sea salt and horseradish, as well as brown bread, toast and butter, and crispbreads.

terrines and pâtés

These are some of the most useful dishes for a buffet, as they are easy to serve, attractive to look at and can be made in advance. I have devoted considerable space to a further discussion of terrines and recipes for them on p.115.

salads

Rather than leaf salads which will wilt, except for the useful and robust Little Gem lettuces, consider those with more substance, such as wild rice salads, pasta salads, mixed bean salads, and fruit and vegetable salads, for example peach and carrot with hazelnuts and hazelnut oil dressing.

hot dishes

The dishes below are ones that I have found particularly suitable for buffets, since they lend themselves to large-scale entertaining, provided you have the space and the equipment. Crumbles, whether sweet or savoury, can be made in individual ramekins, or can be made in a large roasting dish and portioned off. You might also consider making miniatures of those dishes which are very easy to eat in the fingers, such as Cornish pasties, Glamorgan sausages, toad-in-the-hole, and bacon and egg tarts using quail's eggs.

- Glamorgan sausages
- Toad-in-the-hole
- Fricassée of chicken and mushrooms
- Spring lamb ragoût
- Shepherd's pie and its variations
- Steak and kidney pie
- Game crumble or cobbler
- Fish, spinach and potato pie
- Kedgeree
- Devilled kidneys and chicken liver
- Standing roasts for carving, plus all the trimmings

desserts

Traditional British puddings, pies, crumbles and desserts are excellent on buffets, in that they have less tendency to collapse or go soggy than delicate continental pâtisseries. The creamy ones, such as fools, mousses, syllabubs and trifles, can be served in individual glasses – wine glasses rather than sundae glasses, which are usually too big.

- Real English trifle
- Fruit fools and syllabubs
- Dried fruit compote
- Fresh fruit salad
- Summer pudding and variations
- Fruit tarts and crumbles
- Chocolate cake
- Curd tart
- Saffron, cheese and honey tart

different styles of buffet

It is worth giving some thought to exactly how you want to plan your buffet. You might choose to have all three or four courses on the buffet, with all the food laid out from the beginning. This has obvious drawbacks, not the least of which might be an invitation to salmonella and other forms of food poisoning if the event is to last for several hours in warm conditions.

If you do not have help to serve the snacks you are serving with drinks, have a buffet of hors d'oeuvres in the centre of the space, or several smaller tables; that way guests can help themselves, before sitting down to a plated meal.

Alternatively, consider plating the first and last courses, and have a carvery buffet for the main course, with accompanying vegetables also placed on the buffet. You might, for example, offer a choice of roast beef or baked ham, turkey and stuffing or poached salmon. Or you might reverse this procedure and use the buffet for the first course and puddings, and plate the main course.

If desserts are your forte, a dessert buffet (see p.140) can be absolutely splendid, a lavish treat, which at the same time is a boon to those who do not want too much more to eat. A dessert buffet should always include a simple fruit salad, not one heavily laced with liqueur, but simply bathed in fruit juice.

Once, when I cooked some dinners at the Café Royal, we served the first and main course plated, but made each table its own dessert – a delicious trifle – to serve family style. Thus tables of six had a large bowl of trifle, tables of two a smaller bowl. It is an idea I commend for formal entertaining when you have several tables. We did the same at the Academy of Culinary Arts twentieth anniversary dinner, where twenty-five tables of ten were served with a summer pudding and a bowl of trifle.

Give considerable thought to how the food is to be arranged on the buffet so that it is easy to serve, attractive to look at and fairly indestructible. It is best not to let your guests hack up a poached salmon. It should already, if possible, be divided up, or simply serve a platter of slightly overlapping pieces of poached salmon fillet.

The recipes in this chapter have all been tried and tested in much larger quantities, so you can happily multiply them to suit your own particular needs.

a quire of salmon

serves 6 to 8

24 small thin crêpes or pancakes, or 4 large ones, at room temperature

350g (12oz) each smoked salmon, gravadlax and fresh raw salmon

500g (generous 1lb) crème fraîche

1 tbsp each chives and dill, chopped

extra herbs for garnish

salt

freshly ground black pepper

grated zest of 1 lemon or lime, plus 1–2 tsps of juice

Thinly slice the smoked salmon and the gravadlax. Skin the raw salmon, chop it finely, then mix it with about a quarter of the crème fraîche, which has first been mixed with the herbs, seasoning and lemon zest and juice.

Spread the first pancake with some of the cream mixture, top with the smoked salmon, and then another pancake. Spread this with some of the salmon tartare, and top with the third pancake. Spread this with more of the cream mixture, and then add a layer of gravadlax. Top with a final pancake, and cover with some more of the cream mixture.

Decorate with whole sprigs of herbs and thinly sliced and twisted lemon or lime. Repeat for the remaining pancakes. If making a large quire rather than six smaller ones, serve it cut into wedges.

courgette and goat's cheese tart

If you like, you can add shredded ham or bacon to the filling for this tart, and a good mature Cheddar or Gouda can replace the goat's cheese. A leek flan can be made in the same way.

serves 6 to 8

for the pastry
> 200g (7oz) flour
> 4 tbsps goat's milk yoghurt
> 4 tbsps olive oil
> pinch of salt

for the filling
> 1kg (2lb) courgettes
> 1 tbsp salt
> 1 onion, peeled and finely chopped
> 2 garlic cloves, peeled, chopped and crushed
> a few sprigs each of parsley, dill, chervil and basil, or tarragon
> salt
> freshly ground black pepper
> 3 eggs, lightly beaten
> 150g (5oz) fresh goat's cheese
> 100g (3½oz) hard goat's cheese, grated, or a further 250g (9oz) fresh goat's cheese
> 200ml (7fl oz) goat's milk
>
> extra virgin olive oil
> pinch of ground mace or nutmeg

Make the pastry by mixing together all the ingredients, lightly kneading, and then gathering into a ball. Cover and refrigerate for 15–20 minutes. Roll out the pastry on a lightly floured surface and use to line a greased 25cm (10in) tart tin

entertaining

or quiche dish. Bake blind in a preheated oven at 200°C/400°C/gas mark 6 for 10 minutes.

Trim the courgettes, and thinly slice four of them. Set aside. Grate the rest, sprinkle with salt, and let drain in a colander. Put the onion and garlic in a bowl. Finely chop the herbs, and add to the bowl. Add seasoning and the eggs, cheese and milk. Mix thoroughly.

Rinse and thoroughly dry the grated courgettes, then stir them into the egg and cheese mixture. Spoon this into the prepared pastry case, and bake in a preheated oven at 180°C/350°C/gas mark 4 for 20 minutes. Remove the tart from the oven, arrange the courgette slices over the top, brush them with olive oil, and sprinkle with mace or nutmeg. Return the tart to the oven and bake for a further 5 minutes or so. Serve hot, warm or cold.

asparagus and goat's cheese pizza

makes 4 individual ones, 8 miniature ones

250g (9oz) bread flour

1 tsp fast-action yeast

1 tsp salt

1 tbsp fresh herbs, such as basil, thyme and marjoram, finely chopped

4 tbsps extra virgin olive oil

about 150ml (5fl oz) warm water

350g (12oz) green asparagus, woody stems removed

1 tbsp finely chopped parsley

200g (7oz) goat's cheese

hard cheese, for grating

Put the flour, yeast and salt in a food processor and blend together, then add the herbs and two tablespoons of the olive oil and process briefly once more. Gradually add the water (you may not need it all), until you have a soft, springy dough that is neither too wet nor too firm – it should stick to itself, rather than to your hand. Let the dough rest in the food processor while you prepare the asparagus.

Steam or boil the asparagus for 2 minutes until not quite tender, then drain.

Knead the dough for 5 minutes, then roll it into a round, or rectangle, depending on what you are baking the pizza in, or on. Brush with another tablespoon of olive oil. Slice the goat's cheese and arrange on top of the dough, along with the asparagus, then brush with the remaining olive oil.

Grate on some hard cheese, and bake in a preheated oven at 200°C/400°F/ gas mark 6 for 20 minutes.

If you prefer, you can spread a tomato sauce or good pesto on the pizza before adding the cheese and asparagus, but I rather think it is better without.

entertaining

shrimp and artichoke salad

serves 10

750g (1½lb) small artichokes, freshly cooked, or 10 artichoke hearts or bottoms

40–50 medium shrimps, fresh or frozen

5–6 tbsps extra virgin olive oil

1–2 tbsps lemon juice

2 tbsps each finely chopped chives, parsley, chervil and shallots

salt

freshly ground black pepper

for the garnish

small yellow and cherry tomatoes, halved

roasted red and yellow peppers, peeled and cut into strips

Trim the artichokes of any tough outer leaves, and quarter them. If using artichoke bottoms, quarter these too. Cook the shrimps in boiling salted water until just pink. When cool enough to handle, shell and de-vein them.

Put the shrimps and artichokes in a bowl and stir in the oil, lemon juice and herbs. Season to taste. Serve at room temperature, decorated or not, as you wish.

scallop salad with cumin, mint and honey dressing

serves 10

salad leaves, washed and dried, or thinly sliced cucumber

20–30 scallops

1 tsp sea salt

2 garlic cloves, peeled and chopped

1½ tsps ground cumin

40g (1½oz) fresh mint leaves, finely chopped

2 tbsps clear honey

4 tbsps cider vinegar

6 tbsps extra virgin olive oil

freshly ground black pepper

Arrange the salad leaves or cucumber on a serving platter. Poach, steam, grill or pan-fry the scallops. Grind the salt and garlic to a paste, then add the other ingredients, making sure that each one is well blended before adding the next. Arrange the scallops on the salad leaves. Spoon the dressing over the top, and serve immediately.

lettuce hearts with peas and spring onions

serves 10

6–8 Little Gem lettuces

4 bunches bulbed spring onions

500g (1lb) freshly shelled peas

sprig of rosemary

salt

freshly ground black pepper

mayonnaise, soured cream, crème fraîche or vinaigrette

Trim the lettuces, halve, and arrange spoke-fashion on a large platter. Trim the spring onions down to the bulb, and put in a bowl.

entertaining

Briefly cook the peas with the rosemary. Drain, remove the rosemary, and mix with the onions. Season to taste, and mix with one of the suggested dressings. Pile in the middle of the platter and serve.

rice salad

serves 10 to 12

750g (1½lb) brown rice, or mixed basmati and wild rice, freshly cooked,
    according to the directions on the packet

6 spring onions, finely chopped

2 celery sticks, finely sliced

2 tsps finely grated ginger

2 tbsps soy sauce

1–2 tbsps toasted sesame oil

4 tbsps groundnut oil

juice and grated zest of 1 lime

freshly ground black pepper

2 tbsps each toasted sesame seeds, pumpkin seeds and flaked almonds

Put the hot rice in a bowl and stir in the vegetables and seasonings. Allow the flavours to develop for at least 30–40 minutes before serving, by which time the salad will be the perfect temperature. Stir in the seeds and nuts at the last minute.

hindle wakes

This is a traditional buffet dish from the north of England, quite spectacular to look at, and worth the best organic bird you can find.

serves 8 to 10

1 chicken or turkey, boned, plus its carcass

500g (1lb) prunes, soaked overnight

250g (8oz) belly pork, minced

50g (2oz) flaked almonds or pine nuts

175g (6oz) fresh breadcrumbs

1 lemon

1 tbsp each finely chopped parsley and chervil, stalks reserved

2–3 sage leaves, finely chopped

2–3 sprigs of thyme

salt

freshly ground black pepper

parsley sprigs

1 bay leaf

handful celery leaves

Stone and chop the prunes. Crack the prune kernels and mix with the chopped prunes, belly pork, almonds (or pine nuts) and breadcrumbs. Remove thin layers of zest from the lemon, finely chop it, then mix into the stuffing, together with the chopped parsley, chopped sage, two sprigs of thyme, some seasoning and the juice of the lemon. Reserve the herb stalks and one of the thyme sprigs for the stock.

Open out the chicken, skin side down. Spoon in the filling, then wrap the boned bird into a neat parcel – an oval sausage shape is probably the best – enveloping the stuffing. Tie it at intervals with string, sew it up, or wrap it closely in muslin to hold it together.

Chop the chicken carcass. Put the stuffed chicken and the carcass in a saucepan. Just cover with water, add the herb stalks, a few more sprigs of parsley, a bay leaf and a few celery leaves. Bring to the boil, skim the surface,

entertaining

and simmer very gently for about 1½ hours. When the meat is cooked, remove from the heat, and cool as quickly as possible in the stock – a sink full of ice will speed things up. Meanwhile, you can get on with the sauce.

for the sauce
    1 sheet leaf gelatine or 1 tsp gelatine granules
    300ml (½ pint) chicken stock
    15g (½ oz) butter
    1 tbsp flour
    75ml (3fl oz) milk
    150ml (¼ pint) double or whipping cream
    grated zest and juice of 1 lemon
    salt
    freshly ground white pepper
    mace or nutmeg (optional)

Soak the gelatine in a little water. Reduce the stock by half, then stir in the soaked gelatine until dissolved. Make a roux with the butter and flour, and gradually add the hot chicken stock. Once all the liquid has been incorporated and the sauce is smooth, add the lemon zest, and cook for 5 minutes or so. Season to taste with lemon juice, salt and pepper, bearing in mind that, as the sauce will be served cold, more than usual will be needed. At this stage, I also like to add a hint of nutmeg or mace; the latter does not mar the pale creamy sauce as nutmeg does, which is also why I have suggested white pepper rather than black. Cool the sauce as quickly as possible. It will begin to thicken. If you prefer not to use a flour-based sauce, you can achieve a similar effect by leaving out the milk, doubling the quantity of cream and using two or three leaves of gelatine.

To serve the Hindle Wakes, place the cold chicken on a serving platter, removing any string or muslin. Paint on the cold sauce quite thickly. Decorate the platter with extra plumped-up prunes, lemon quarters and bunches of green herbs. It will look quite spectacular, and even more so when it is sliced to reveal the dramatic black stuffing.

bourbon-glazed ham with kumquats and peach, ginger and mint chutney

Whenever I eat good ham, I always think that I should cook it more often. We are particularly lucky that in this country we can get very good ham, often from producers who rear rare breeds of English pigs. The marvellous thing about hams is that they are actually very easy to cook, provided you keep the heat gentle. They are easy to carve, and the leftovers are not unappealing, moving from sandwiches and pickle, through potted ham to shredded ham and fresh peas in a cream sauce with tagliatelle. Diced ham baked in a batter pudding is good, and so is a baked, layered dish of ham and potatoes topped with grated cheese and breadcrumbs.

serves 10

3kg (6 lb) uncooked ham on the bone

12 kumquats

handful of cloves

Soak the ham for 4 hours or so, and then drain it and put in a roasting bag. Squeeze all the air out of the bag, and secure tightly closed. Put in a large pan, cover with water, bring to the boil, cover, and then simmer on the gentlest heat possible for 3½–4 hours. The ham is cooked when the 'mustard spoon' bone at the shank end is loose. If you have not got all the air out of the bag, the ham will float rather than remain submerged in the water.

When cool enough to handle, carefully pour out the juices, remove the skin, score through the fat in a lozenge pattern, place on a rack in a roasting tin, and rub it all over with the following, mixed together:

75ml (3fl oz) bourbon whiskey

75ml (3fl oz) Southern Comfort

175g (6oz) dark muscovado sugar

3 tbsps grain mustard

½ tsp ground cloves

1 tsp crushed juniper berries

1 tsp coarsely ground black pepper

Halve the kumquats and 'nail' to the ham at intervals with cloves. Bake in a preheated oven at 200°C/400°F/gas mark 6 for 30–40 minutes until the sugar has melted and the ham is well glazed. Allow to rest for half an hour before slicing.

Skim the fat from the pan juices, add the cooking juices from the roasting bag, thicken them with a little arrowroot, or cornflour, if you wish, boil up and serve separately.

This is good hot, warm or cold, and is ideal to serve throughout the day. New potatoes, freshly cooked, are an ideal accompaniment and will not deteriorate as they cool.

peach, ginger and mint chutney

This is a mild, fruity chutney, which keeps well and is worth making in a larger quantity than you will need for one meal.

makes about 1½kg (3lb)

1–1.5kg (2–3lb) peaches

500g (1lb) light muscovado sugar

25g (1oz) salt

1 heaped tbsp freshly chopped mint

1 tbsp freshly grated ginger

1 tbsp ground cinnamon

1 tbsp allspice

4 cloves

seeds of 6 cardamom pods

1 tbsp mustard seeds, lightly crushed

600ml (1 pint) strong wine vinegar or distilled vinegar

Stone and quarter the peaches. Put the rest of the ingredients in a saucepan, bring to the boil, then add the peaches. Simmer until the peaches are tender and the mixture begins to thicken; this will take about 45 minutes. Pot in hot clean jam jars, cover, and label.

maple mousse

Note that this recipe uses raw eggs.

serves 10
250ml (8fl oz) maple syrup
4 eggs, separated
450ml (¾ pint) double or whipping cream, whipped

for the garnish
toasted flaked almonds

Boil the maple syrup, pour it over the egg yolks in a bowl and beat thoroughly. Set the bowl over a pan of hot water, and stir until the mixture thickens. Remove from the heat, and allow to cool. Fold this custard into the whipped cream. Whisk the egg whites to firm peaks, and gently fold these into the cream. Spoon into glasses, smooth the surface, scatter the almonds on top, and chill until set. The mixture can also be frozen and served as an ice cream.

pâtés and terrines

Larousse Gastronomique has two lengthy entries under the headings of pâtés and terrines. Mme Saint-Ange is much more sensible. She deals with both in the same chapter, which she opens with: '*La composition des uns et des autres est identique. La croûte constitue la seule différence.*' Terrines, according to Mme Saint-Ange, are pâtés without the crust. However, 'pâtés en croûte' are much less frequently made than they used to be in Mme Saint-Ange's day, and the new edition of *Larousse* has it about right when it says the two terms are used interchangeably.

My own etymologically incorrect way of distinguishing between pâtés and terrines is that pâtés are soft and smooth, paste-like, in fact, and terrines have texture in the form of coarsely minced meat, diced fowl, flaked fish, slices of vegetables, nuggets of salmon fillets, what you will.

I put an asparagus terrine on the menu once when I cooked with Herbert Berger in the Café Royal Grill Room. Satisfied with all my other recipes, he rather shook his head over this one. Set only with a 'royale' or light custard, it was going to be a very fragile terrine when it came to turning out and slicing it. Instead, we made a pressed vegetable terrine, and stiffened it with a little gelatine dissolved in vegetable stock. I was glad to have that tip and now use the same method for all my vegetable terrines.

Later, I went on to develop a recipe for an asparagus terrine or loaf, encasing the asparagus, cheese and egg in a bread-lined terrine. As the buttered bread baked, it of course became firm, like a crust, which made for a fairly stable terrine. Mushrooms, I've found, are difficult in terrines. However thoroughly they have been dried after cooking, when pressed and left, they eventually release liquid and spoil the texture and appearance of the finished dish.

Extra gelatine is not required in all terrines. Some food is sticky enough to produce its own gelatine so that it will set in its cooking juices. Oxtail, for example, for a meat terrine, and skate for a fish terrine are very easy to work with and produce good results, as in the two recipes I have given here.

Fat is the binding or firming agent in many terrines and pâtés. Since game does not contain enough fat of its own, fat pork is used with it to set it as it cools. The chicken liver pâté is set with butter in a very simple recipe. Butter is also the binding agent for making simple smoked fish pâtés or pastes. Freshly cooked salmon can be combined with smoked salmon trimmings, spices and seasoning, a little sherry or Madeira, softened unsalted butter, and then packed into pots or ramekins.

The electric carving knife, I have discovered, is of the greatest help in slicing terrines, enabling you to get a smooth, intact slice.

asparagus loaf

I have tried 'improvements' to this recipe, adding slices of cheese and potatoes, and trying it with other vegetables, but the combination of bread, eggs, cheese and asparagus is perfect in its simplicity.

serves 10

50g (2oz) butter

10 slices white bread, buttered

750g (1½lb) trimmed green asparagus, blanched for 5 minutes

300g (10oz) hard cheese, grated

5 eggs

450ml (¾ pint) milk

200ml (7fl oz) double cream

generous grating of nutmeg

freshly ground black pepper

Butter a 1kg (2lb) enamelled terrine or metal loaf tin, and line it, butter side in, with the slices of bread, abutting but not overlapping them, and reserving some slices for the lid. Arrange the blanched asparagus spears in the bread case, top to tail, sprinkling some of the grated cheese on each layer.

Beat the eggs, milk and cream, then stir in the remaining cheese, a grating of nutmeg and some pepper. Pour over the asparagus and top with a lid of buttered bread.

Bake in a preheated oven at 180°C/350°F/gas mark 4 for 45–60 minutes, depending on the depth of the terrine. The terrine is cooked when a knife point inserted into the custard comes out clean.

Allow to 'set' for no more than a couple of minutes, otherwise condensation will make the bread soggy. Carefully turn out and slice either when at room temperature or somewhat warmer.

grilled aubergine, pepper and parsnip terrine

serves 10

 3 large aubergines

 3 parsnips, peeled

 4 red peppers

 2 yellow peppers

 extra virgin olive oil

 1 sheet leaf gelatine

 150ml (¼ pint) well-seasoned vegetable stock

Slice the aubergines and parsnips lengthways. Quarter the peppers, and remove the seeds and pith. Brush the vegetables lightly with the oil and bake in the oven until tender, or cook on a griddle or under a grill. The peppers should be charred and then, when cool enough to handle, skinned.

Layer the vegetables in a 1kg (2lb) loaf tin, aubergines, red peppers, parsnips, yellow peppers, parsnips, red peppers and, finally, aubergine on top. Soften the gelatine in cold water, then dissolve it in the vegetable stock by heating it gently. Pour the stock over the vegetables and allow them to absorb it for 20–30 minutes. Then cover the terrine with cling film, and drain off most of the excess liquid. Refrigerate overnight, turn out, slice, and serve with a herb vinaigrette or a mint, yoghurt, shallot and cucumber sauce.

smoked salmon and potato terrine

serves 10

- 1 × 400g pack sliced smoked salmon
- 2–3 firm-fleshed potatoes, boiled and thinly sliced
- 200g (7oz) hot smoked salmon fillet, skinned
- 3 sheets leaf gelatine or 3 tsps gelatine granules
- 100ml (3–4fl oz) fish or light chicken stock
- 200g (7oz) smoked salmon trimmings
- 250g (9oz) crème fraîche
- 25g (1oz) grated or creamed horseradish, or to taste
- 1–2 tbsps chopped dill, chervil or chives

Line a 1kg (2lb) terrine or loaf tin with cling film, then generously line it with slightly overlapping slices of cold smoked salmon, making sure that there is enough to fold over and enclose the filling. Soften the gelatine in cold water, then dissolve it in the stock by heating it gently. Set aside.

Put the smoked salmon trimmings in a food processor with the crème fraîche, herbs and horseradish, and blend until smooth, only very gradually adding the stock and gelatine mixture.

Layer the smoked salmon cream, sliced potatoes and hot smoked salmon in the terrine, tap down sharply, and smooth the surface. Envelope the terrine with the remaining, overhanging smoked salmon, cover with cling film, and chill until set. Turn out and slice. Serve with hot toast or brown bread.

terrine of salmon and pink grapefruit

In the middle of winter once, I was sent some pink Florida grapefruit. I was glad of their juicy sweetness then, and they reminded me of a starter that I used to make some years ago – smoked salmon alternated on the plate with peeled pink grapefruit segments. It was a good combination and perfectly matched by rosé champagne. Here is a more elaborate version. Because of its colour and elegance, it would also work well for a wedding buffet. I kept the grapefruit peel, crystallized it and served it as a sweetmeat. You can use just poached salmon in the terrine if you prefer, but I like the texture of the cooked, the smoked and the cured. For another dimension of flavour, you could also add a layer of cooked leeks, artichoke bottoms or peeled, seeded and blanched batons of cucumber.

serves 10

> 500ml (18fl oz) pink grapefruit juice
> 5 sheets of leaf gelatine or 5 tsps gelatine granules
> 200ml (7fl oz) fish stock
> salt
> freshly ground black pepper
> 300g (10oz) sliced smoked salmon
> 300g (10oz) salmon fillet, cured as for gravadlax
> 300g (10oz) salmon fillet, freshly poached

for the garnish
> peeled pink grapefruit segments
> bunches of dill or watercress

Make the jelly first by straining the juice into a saucepan with the gelatine. When this has softened, heat until it has dissolved. Stir in the fish stock, and season to taste.

Line a 1kg (2lb) loaf tin or terrine with cling film, and then line the sides and bottom with the smoked salmon slices, leaving the ends of the tin unlined. The slices should overhang the sides of the tin, as they will later be folded over the terrine.

Skin both the salmon fillets, and remove as many pin bones as possible. (I keep a pair of tweezers in the kitchen drawer just for this purpose.) Trim the fillets to fit the loaf tin. (Offcuts can be used to make a salmon spread or stirred into hot pasta.) Pour on the gelatine liquid; if there is some left over, pour it into a shallow container and let it set too. It can be turned out, chopped up, and used as a garnish. When the liquid in the terrine is beginning to set and has become tacky, fold over the smoked salmon. Cover with cling film and refrigerate until required.

To serve, turn out on to a long platter. With a sharp knife dipped in hot water, slice and arrange. Decorate with extra jelly, pink grapefruit segments and greenery. It is a good idea to slice the terrine when it is very cold, but allow the chill to disappear somewhat before serving.

skate, olive and garlic terrine

serves 10

2 heads garlic
20–30 black olives
1.5kg (3½lb) skate wings
freshly ground white pepper
sea salt

Separate the garlic into cloves, and peel them. Poach in about 600ml (1 pint) of water for 15 minutes or so until tender. Meanwhile, stone the olives. Remove the garlic from the pan with a slotted spoon, and put to one side. Season the skate, place in the garlic water, bring to just simmering point, cover with a lid, and cook the fish for 5–8 minutes. Remove the pan from the heat. When cool enough to handle, take the fish out of the water, and carefully remove the strands of flesh from the cartilage. Reduce the fish liquid to about 200ml (7fl oz) and cool.

Line a 1kg (2lb) terrine or loaf tin with cling film. Put a layer of fish in the bottom of the tin, followed by a layer of olives, more fish, then a layer of garlic, finishing with the rest of the fish. Lightly season each layer as you go. Pour on the reduced fish stock, and allow the whole thing to cool before covering and refrigerating until set.

Turn out, slice carefully, and serve with some salad leaves and a fresh tomato sauce, made by blending fresh tomatoes, then sieving them, and beating in extra virgin olive oil and sherry vinegar. Alternatively, a garlicky mayonnaise, rouille or alioli will go very well.

oxtail terrine

This terrine also makes a substantial main course, if served with a lentil salad and salad leaves.

serves 10

2.5kg (5lb) oxtail
2 pig's trotters
200ml (7fl oz) red wine
1 litre (1¾ pints) water
8 thin leeks
8 carrots
salt
freshly ground black pepper

Place the oxtail, together with the pig's trotter, in a saucepan with the red wine and water. Bring to the boil, then simmer for 3 hours or until the oxtail is tender. Allow to stand overnight. The following day, separate the meat and cooking liquid, and bone and degrease them. You will need at least 550g (1¼lb) cooked meat, weighed off the bone, and 575ml (1 pint) cooking juices.

Cut the meat into small dice, removing any gristle. Trim and peel the vegetables, as necessary, and steam or boil until tender. Slice the carrots in half lengthways if they are thick. Place some of the meat in the bottom of a 1kg (2lb) wetted terrine or loaf tin, and arrange half the leeks and carrots on top, then more meat, the rest of the vegetables, then a final layer of meat. Season the cooking juices quite well, and pour over the meat. Chill until set, then turn out and slice.

This terrine will also make a substantial first course, or a cold main course, if served with a lentil salad and salad leaves.

game terrine

Use pheasant, rabbit, wild duck, hare or pigeon, off the bone. If you cannot get the pork back fat to line the loaf tin, thin rindless rashers of unsmoked streaky bacon can be used, but remember that the saltpetre in the bacon will give a pink tinge to the pâté and also change its flavour. It will keep for a week, covered and unbroached, in the refrigerator.

serves 10

    350g (12oz) game meat, off the bone

    250g (8oz) lean pork or veal

    500g (1lb) fat belly of pork, rind removed

    12 crushed juniper berries

    1 tsp ground allspice

    ½ tsp ground cumin seeds

    1 tsp freshly ground black pepper

    1 tsp sea salt

    150ml (¼ pint) red or white wine, depending on whether you
        are using dark or pale game

    4 tbsps gin, grappa or *eau de vie de poire*

    250g (8oz) pork back fat, cut into thin slices or sheets

    1 tbsp potato flour or cornflour

    1 egg

    melted lard or pork fat

Chop the game into small 5mm (¼ inch) dice, removing any sinews. Mince the lean meat with the belly of pork, and mix it with the game, spices, seasonings, wine and spirits. Cover and marinate overnight in the refrigerator.

The following day, line a 1kg (2lb) loaf tin or terrine with very thin slices of pork fat. Mix the potato flour with a tablespoon of water or wine and beat in the egg until thoroughly blended. Strain this over the marinated meat. Mix thoroughly, and pack into the lined tin. Push the mixture well down, so that there are no air bubbles, and heap up the top, as the mixture will shrink down as it cooks. Cover with the pork rind, then foil and stand on a trivet or rack in a roasting tin deep enough to allow boiling water to be poured in, to come at least halfway up the loaf tin. Cook in the middle of a preheated oven at 180°C/350°F/gas mark 4 for 2 hours. Remove from the heat, weight down, and allow to cool completely. Remove the pork rind and cover the surface with melted lard or pork fat to preserve it.

This will keep for a week, covered and unbroached, in the refrigerator.

quick chicken liver pâté

serves 15

1kg (2lb) chicken livers

300ml (½ pint) milk

3 shallots or 1 onion, peeled and finely chopped

250g (8oz) unsalted butter

2 tsps crushed juniper berries

salt

freshly ground black pepper

ground mace or nutmeg

4 tbsps cognac

4 tbsps port, Madeira or amontillado sherry

Trim the chicken livers, and put them in a bowl with the milk for 15–20 minutes. Meanwhile, gently fry the shallots or onion in a little of the butter until soft. Drain, and dry, the chicken livers, and add to the frying pan with the juniper berries. Fry on a relatively high heat for 8 minutes or so. The chicken livers are nice if removed from the heat while still faintly pink inside. Season, and stir in the cognac while the livers are still hot, then add the fortified wine. The residual heat will evaporate the alcohol. When cool, place the chicken livers in a food processor with the remaining butter, and process until smooth. Pack into a pâté dish or individual ramekins. Chill until firm. Allow to come to room temperature before serving with hot toast.

pork and rabbit terrine

If you cannot get pork back fat to line the loaf tin, thin rindless rashers of unsmoked streaky bacon can be used. The terrine will keep for a week, covered and unbroached, in the refrigerator.

serves 10

400g (14oz) raw rabbit meat, off the bone, back fillets are ideal

250g (8oz) lean pork

500g (1lb) fat belly of pork, rind removed

12 crushed juniper berries

1 tsp ground allspice

½ tsp ground cumin seeds

1 tsp freshly ground black pepper

1 tsp sea salt

150ml (¼ pint) white wine

4 tbsps gin, grappa or *eau de vie de poire*

250g (8oz) pork back fat, cut into thin slices or sheets

2 tsps cornflour mixed with 1 tbsp wine

1 egg

melted lard or pork fat

Remove any sinews from the rabbit and cut into long strips, not too thin. Mince the lean pork with the belly of pork, mix it with the rabbit, spices, seasonings, wine and spirits, and marinate it overnight, covered, in the refrigerator.

The following day, line a 1kg (2lb) loaf tin or terrine with very thin slices of pork fat. Beat together the egg and cornflour mixture until thoroughly blended, then strain over the marinated meat. Mix thoroughly, and pack into the lined tin. Push the mixture well down, so there are no air bubbles, and heap up the top, as the mixture will shrink down as it cooks. Cover with foil, and stand on a trivet or rack in a roasting tin deep enough to allow boiling water to be poured in, to come at least halfway up the loaf tin. Cook in the middle of a preheated oven at 180°C/350°F/gas mark 4 for 1½–2 hours. The terrine is cooked when the juices released by a skewer inserted into the middle run clear, not pink. Remove the

---

terrine from the oven, weight down, and allow to cool completely. Cover the surface with melted lard or pork fat to preserve it.

and for dessert?

Rich, solid cakes baked in a loaf tin are as good tempered as terrines, and thus perfect for a buffet.

rich chocolate, prune and almond cake

I like to bake this cake in the enamelled, cast-iron terrine I normally use to make terrines. It is long and narrow, rather than broad, and gives small, neat slices – about twenty-five. On the whole, I find rich cakes slice better if they are loaf-shaped rather than round; with the latter the point of the wedge so often crumbles away.

Always well grease and flour any cake tins before using them. And if you use a particularly rich mix, full of fruit and sugar, it is a good idea to line the tin first with baking parchment.

The Teatime chapter also gives some cake recipes suitable for buffets. My ginger cake recipe, for example, p.456, is the perfect accompaniment to a bowl of poached pears or some pear sorbet.

serves 10 to 12

250g (8oz) unsalted butter

200g (7oz) dark muscovado sugar

275g (9oz) self-raising flour

25g (1oz) cocoa powder

pinch of salt

4 eggs, lightly beaten

200g (7oz) stoned prunes, finely chopped

100g (4oz) flaked almonds

1 tsp pure vanilla essence

75ml (3fl oz) chocolate, coffee or almond liqueur, or sloe gin

milk

Cream the butter and sugar until light and fluffy. Sift together the flour, cocoa powder and salt, then beat the eggs and flour alternately into the creamed mixture. Stir in the rest of the ingredients, adding enough milk to give a soft dropping consistency.

Grease and line a 1kg (2lb) loaf tin, spoon in the cake mixture and smooth the top. Bake in a preheated oven at 150°C/300°F/gas mark 3 for 1½–2 hours. The cake is cooked when a skewer inserted into the middle comes out clean.

Remove from the oven and allow to cool in the tin for a few minutes before turning out on to a wire rack. When completely cool, wrap the cake in greaseproof paper and foil. It will keep for several weeks and, if possible, should be kept for at least 24 hours in order for the flavours to blend and develop.

another style of buffet

The buffet has a solid tradition in the north of England, especially the curiously named but eminently sensible 'running buffet'. This is such an adaptable and movable feast that we would be foolish not to incorporate it into our entertaining.

Imagine a party that appeals to all ages, from toddlers and their parents, to teenagers and grandparents and late-night revellers. It can be done. Whether the buffet is for a wedding, for Christmas or a summer garden party, start at teatime, around 4 pm, and plan to finish about 9.30 or 10 pm. Serve both teatime delicacies and cocktails with intriguing savouries.

When luxury hotels give glamorous parties, the food is often served from 'food stations', with a chef preparing and serving food at a small stall or booth – perhaps sushi, or caviar and blinis, or fish and chips, or a selection of desserts. You can copy this idea for entertaining at home. Aim for several 'food stations' or buffets, either in one large room, or strategically placed, perhaps in the kitchen, hall and living room. In summer, you can use the garden for your food stations. In our small, converted two-storey flat at the top of a Victorian house, food stations are out of the question; I use the dining table and the worktop and, in summer, the small roof terrace. But it is a nice idea for those who have the space, which is why I pass it on.

Plan, for example, on a tea table, laden with exquisite sandwiches, scones, biscuits, beautiful miniature sponge cakes and, of course, a cake: The Cake, if you are arranging a Christmas or a wedding party. You will find suitable recipes in the Christmas chapter and also in the Teatime chapter.

Arrange another table with 'high tea' food, buying in cold cuts, a handsome pork pie, a ham for carving (as described earlier in this chapter), a whole Cheddar, Stilton or other favourite cheese, and some smoked salmon, supplementing this with a few homemade salads and bowls of raw vegetables.

Glitzy cocktails and delicious savouries should be on another table to sustain those who arrive later for an hour or so on their way somewhere else.

And before saying goodbye at the end of the evening, offer, in the winter, mulled cider and wine, fruit cake and spiced bread, or perhaps an ice-cream cornet or fruit punch in the summer.

The sample menu below is, I think, ideally suited to autumn and winter entertaining, perhaps a Christmas party or a winter wedding. Although the food sounds very elaborate it is, in fact, very easy to make. For example, the chocolate gâteau and miniature cream cakes rely on the simple classic fatless sponge recipe.

afternoon tea table

Sandwiches
- potted ham with kumquat butter and lettuce
- potted game with pickled walnut butter and mustard and cress
- Stilton with pears and walnut butter
- hot smoked salmon with horseradish butter and cucumber

Scones, clotted cream and homemade preserves

Miniature cream cakes, including
- toffee and date

- prune, cinnamon and Armagnac
- coffee and walnut
- chocolate and kirsch

Bake in advance cakes, such as
- Frances Bissell's ginger cake
- sloe gin cake
- chocolate Jonathan

Mix in advance biscuits, such as
- petticoat tails
- chocolate and almond

Christmas cake, or other suitably decorated rich fruit cake

high tea table

- side of smoked salmon, sliced
- standing pork pie or game pie
- whole Stilton
- lettuce heart salad
- whole cooked ham or cold cuts
- Cornish pasties
- Glamorgan sausages
- rolls, bread and butter
- pickles, chutneys and pickled onions

cocktail table

Cocktails and all the appurtenances; ice, shakers, chilled glasses, lemon and lime

- savouries
- cheese and almond crisps
- devilled quail's eggs
- hot anchovy toast
- miniature venison burgers in homemade buns

farewell table

- spiced apple loaf
- Welsh fruit cake
- mulled wine and cider

tea table

miniature sponge cakes

makes 6 two-layer cakes

    115g (4oz) caster sugar

    4 eggs, separated

    1 tbsp rosewater or 1 tsp pure vanilla essence or 1 tsp orange oil

    115g (4oz) self-raising flour, sifted

Preheat the oven to 180°C/350°F/gas mark 4. Grease a 23 × 33cm (9 × 13 inch) Swiss roll tin and line with greaseproof paper.

Put half the sugar in a bowl, set over a saucepan of hot water, add the egg yolks, and whisk until pale and thick (about 5 minutes). At the same time whisk in the rosewater, vanilla essence or orange oil.

Whisk the egg whites, together with half the remaining sugar, until peaks form. Fold in the rest of the sugar, and whisk until firm and glossy. Fold the sifted flour into the egg yolk mixture, and then fold in the egg whites. Spoon into the Swiss roll tin, shaking to fill it evenly.

Bake for 10–12 minutes, until just firm to the touch. Turn out on to a clean tea towel, peel off the paper, and trim the edges. When cool, cut into rounds with a plain scone cutter, then cut in half across the middle and either ice or dust with icing sugar or fill and decorate with one of the following:

- *caramel and dates* mix luxury caramel spread (Dulce de Leche) and whipped cream, fold in stoned, chopped Medjool dates and use for the filling. Dust with sifted icing sugar.

- *prune, cinnamon and Armagnac* mix soaked, stoned prunes and a dash of

Armagnac with whipped cream and use for the filling. Dust with a mixture of sifted icing sugar and cinnamon.

- *coffee and walnut* add coffee essence or freshly made espresso to whipped cream, sweeten to taste, stir in some finely chopped walnuts and use for the filling. Mix coffee and icing sugar to a thin glaze, spread on top of the cakes and decorate with half a walnut.

- *chocolate, cherries in liqueur and kirsch* melt chocolate (70 per cent cocoa solids) and spread on the top layer of the cake. Sweeten whipped cream, add a little kirsch and chopped stoned cherries and use for the filling. To make a chocolate sponge, replace 25g (1oz) of the flour with 25g (1oz) sifted cocoa.

chocolate jonathan

serves 10
3 eggs, separated
100g (3½ oz) light muscovado or golden caster sugar
25g (1oz) cocoa powder
85g (3½ oz) self-raising flour
1 tbsp strong coffee, rum, or Tia Maria

for the chocolate filling
300g (10oz) good-quality dark chocolate, of at least 70 per cent cocoa solids
1 tbsp strong coffee, rum, or Tia Maria
100g (3½oz) unsalted butter, softened
3 eggs, separated
25g (1oz) golden caster sugar
pinch of salt

Preheat the oven to 180°C/350°F/gas mark 4. Grease a 25 × 35cm (9 × 13 inch) Swiss roll tin and line with greaseproof paper.

Put the egg yolks and three quarters of the sugar in a bowl, set over a saucepan of barely simmering water. Whisk together until pale, foamy and much increased in volume.

Sift together the cocoa powder and flour, then fold gently into the egg and sugar mixture. Stir in the coffee, rum or liqueur. Whisk the egg whites until soft

---

entertaining

and glossy with the remaining sugar and fold into the cake mixture. Pour into the Swiss roll tin, shaking it to fill it evenly, and bake in the top half of the oven for about 10 minutes. Remove, turn out on to a wire rack, peel off the paper, and leave to cool.

To prepare the filling, put the chocolate and liqueur in a clean bowl set over hot water, and melt the chocolate. Remove from the heat, cool slightly, and mix in the softened butter. Whisk the egg yolks and sugar until pale and ribbon-like. Whisk the egg whites with a pinch of salt until stiff, then fold both egg mixtures into the chocolate.

Cut the sponge into pieces, and use to line a 750g (1½lb) loaf tin, ensuring that the 'shiny' surface of the cake appears towards the centre. Make sure, also, that you retain a large enough slice of cake to fit over the top. Pour in the filling and cover with the final piece of sponge.

Cover with cling film, or foil, and refrigerate for several hours until set. Turn out on to a board, slice, place on individual plates, dust with icing sugar, and serve with a spoonful of crème fraîche.

high tea table

The pork pie is, without doubt, a production. You cannot rush it, but it is well worth the time and effort, and is far superior to almost anything you can buy. You may not appreciate this, but my mother uses this recipe all the time when she gives lunch parties, and there is no sterner critic than my mother.

I varied my standard recipe a couple of years ago when I produced a version for a Bramley apple recipe leaflet. The Yorkshire pork pie can, of course, be amended to take account of regional sensibilities. Cheddar, Lancashire, Gloucester (single or double) or any of the traditional farm-house cheeses can replace the Wensleydale. You could also try it with chopped prunes or dried apricots in place of the apple.

An alternative to the pork pie is one with chicken and veal. Choose breast of veal to replace belly pork, as this will keep the pie moist. And use butter or vegetable shortening to replace the lard, but make a classic shortcrust pastry, as only lard has the properties to make a hot water crust.

yorkshire pork pie

serves 10

for the filling

500g (1lb) fat belly of pork

125g (4–5 oz) streaky bacon

500g (1lb) lean pork meat, such as tenderloin, off the bone

¼ tsp salt

1 tsp freshly ground black pepper

¼ tsp freshly grated nutmeg

1 tbsp finely chopped parsley

½ tbsp finely chopped sage

1 Bramley apple, peeled, quartered, cored and diced small

200g (7oz) Wensleydale cheese

for the pastry

up to 750g (1½lb) plain flour

1 tsp salt

250g (8oz) lard

200ml (7fl oz) water

for the jelly

300ml (½ pint) well-flavoured chicken or pork stock

2 sheets leaf gelatine or 2 tsps gelatine granules

Discard the rind from the belly pork and bacon, and mince the two together. Fry quickly, in batches if necessary, just enough to remove the raw look. Put in a bowl. Dice the lean pork and fry it lightly all over, draining off any cooking liquid into the stock. Mix the meats together, and add the spices, seasoning, herbs and apple. Cover, and stand in a cool place.

Make the pastry either by hand or in a food processor. Sift together the flour and salt, keeping back about 5 tablespoons of flour. Put the lard and water in a saucepan, and bring them to the boil. Stirring continuously, slowly add the flour.

When thoroughly blended together into a hot, smooth (rather than sticky) dough, turnout on to a worktop, and knead, adding more flour, as necessary, to form a workable pastry.

Cut off a quarter of the pastry to use as a lid, and press, or roll, out the rest to line a 1.5kg (3lb) loaf tin, pie mould, spring-form mould or cake tin, leaving about 1cm (⅜ inch) pastry hanging over the rim of the tin. Wet this. Fill with the pork mixture, moulding it to a mound in the centre. Shave the cheese into thin slices and use to cover the pork.

Roll out the remaining pastry and use to cover the pie. Press the edges together, and roll them over inside the rim of the loaf tin (that way, it will be an easy matter, when cold, to slide a palette knife all the way round the pie to ease it out of the tin), and make a fluted edge by pinching together at intervals.

Roll out the pastry trimmings to make decorations, if you wish. Make a pencil-diameter hole in the lid, and keep it open with a small roll of greaseproof paper. Brush the pie with milk, or beaten egg, to glaze it, and lay two or three layers of greaseproof paper, or foil, on top so that the crust does not become too brown. Bake in the centre of a preheated oven at 170°C/325°F/gas mark 3 for 1¼ hours. Remove the paper for the last 15 minutes. Let the pie cool in the tin for 2–3 hours.

After you have taken the pie out of the oven to cool, prepare the jelly. Soften the gelatine in cold water. Boil the stock, remove from the heat and stir in the drained gelatine. Once the pie is cool, slowly pour in, through the hole in the lid, as much of the stock as you can. Allow the pie to cool completely, ease out of the tin, then wrap in foil, or greaseproof paper, to store. Do not keep the pie for more than two or three days in the refrigerator before eating.

cornish pasties

See p.239.

glamorgan sausages

See p.245.

hot tomato, grape and cardamom chutney

makes about 1kg (2lb)
- 1 red onion, peeled and chopped
- 1kg (2¼lb) tomatoes
- 250g (8oz) seedless black grapes
- 2–3 red chillies, seeded and finely sliced
- seeds of about 15 cardamom pods
- 1 tsp salt
- 300g (10oz) dark muscovado sugar
- 250ml (8fl oz) cider vinegar

Wash, rinse, dry and heat the jars. Put the onion in a saucepan with a little water and simmer until almost tender. Meanwhile, skin and roughly chop the tomatoes. (If left on, the skin will come loose and roll into tough, thin, cellulose spindles that will spoil the texture of the chutney.) Add the tomatoes and rest of the ingredients, except for the vinegar, to the pan, and cook for 20–30 minutes. Add the vinegar and continue to cook gently until the chutney thickens. This will probably take another 30 minutes or so. Spoon the chutney into the prepared jars, cover with waxed discs, lids or cellophane covers and label.

cocktail table

devilled quail's eggs

See p.247.

hot anchovy toast

Drain the oil from a couple of cans of anchovies and mash them with 250g (9oz) softened, unsalted butter. Spread on toast and cut into fingers.

miniature venison burgers

See p.237.

cheese and almond crisps

You need 100g (3½oz) each butter, flour, ground almonds and grated hard cheese, plus 1 egg white, whisked. Rub the butter and flour together, stir in the almonds and cheese, then fold in the egg white to bind. Spread 5cm (2½ inch) discs on baking sheets, and bake for 8–10 minutes at 180°C/350°F/ gas mark 4. Alternatively, roll the mixture into a long sausage, freeze, and cut off thin slices to bake as you need them.

For cocktail recipes and more food ideas see pp.226, 255 in the Drinks Parties and Cocktail Time chapter.

farewell table

spiced apple loaf

makes 1 × 900 g (2 lb) loaf

350g (12oz) plain flour

½ tsp each ground allspice, cloves, cinnamon, cardamom,
   freshly grated nutmeg and ground ginger

pinch of salt

200g (7oz) unsalted butter

200g (7oz) light muscovado sugar

2 tsps baking powder

2 tsps dried yeast

350g (12oz) mixed dried fruit

1 Bramley apple, peeled, cored and grated

3 eggs, lightly beaten

200ml (7fl oz) dry or medium cider, warmed

Sift together the dry ingredients into a bowl. Cut in the butter, and then rub it in. Add the sugar, baking powder and yeast, and then the dried fruit and apple. Mix in the eggs and cider. Spoon the mixture into a lined and greased loaf tin, set aside in a warm place and allow to rise till double in volume. Bake in a pre-heated oven at 180°C/350°F/gas mark 4 for about 1½ hours, covering the tin with a piece of foil if the top shows signs of burning. The loaf is cooked when a skewer inserted into the centre comes out clean. Allow to cool in the tin before removing, then wrap and store. Serve sliced and buttered with a mug of mulled wine or cider.

mulled cider

The same recipe can be used to make mulled wine – simply replace the cider, apple juice and cider brandy with red wine, red grape juice and grape brandy or cognac.

makes 1.5 litres (2½ pints)

1 litre (2 pints) cider, dry or medium dry, as you prefer

300ml (½ pint) clear apple juice

1 cinnamon stick

1–2 tbsps light muscovado sugar

freshly grated nutmeg

Somerset or Herefordshire cider brandy

Warm the cider and apple juice in a saucepan with the cinnamon, sugar and nutmeg. When the sugar has dissolved, and the cider is very hot, remove from the heat and stir in the cider brandy.

some recipes for a dessert buffet

a traditional english trifle

serves 8

for the sponge base
   4 eggs, separated
   125g (4oz) icing sugar
   125g (4oz) self-raising flour, sifted

for the filling
   9 egg yolks
   75g (3oz) golden caster sugar
   1 tbsp flour, sifted
   400ml (14fl oz) full cream milk
   200ml (7fl oz) single cream
   1 vanilla pod
   500ml (16fl oz) whipping cream
   apricot glaze or redcurrant jelly
   12 amaretti or ratafia biscuits
   150ml (¼ pint) cream sherry, such as Valdespino Cream
      or Harvey's Bristol Cream
   toasted, flaked almonds

Grease a standard Swiss roll tin, and line with greaseproof paper. Whisk the egg yolks with half the icing sugar in a bowl set over hot water until pale and thick enough to leave a ribbon. Using a clean whisk, whisk the egg whites with the remaining icing sugar until stiff and glossy. Fold the flour into the egg yolk mixture, and then gently fold in the egg whites. Spoon into the prepared Swiss roll tin, shaking it to spread the mixture evenly. Bake in a preheated oven at 180°C/350°F/gas mark 4 for 10–12 minutes.Turn out on to a damp tea towel. Trim off the crisp edges, roll loosely, lengthways, and put to one side.

Put the six egg yolks, caster sugar and flour in a large bowl and whisk until

---

well blended. Scald the milk, cream and vanilla pod in a saucepan and pour it in a thin stream on to the eggs, whisking all the time. Return the mixture to the saucepan and heat very gentlly, stirring all the time, until it thickens. (If you cook it on too high a heat the egg will set as if scrambled.) Strain the custard into a bowl, split the vanilla pod with a sharp knife down its length and scrape the tiny seeds into the custard. Cover with cling film and, when cool, refrigerate until required.

Carefully unroll the sponge, spread it with the apricot glaze or jelly; roll up and slice it. Line the bottom of a glass bowl with the sponge slices. Place the amaretti on top, and pour over the sherry. Spoon on the custard and chill until set. Spread or pipe the whipped cream on top and garnish with toasted flaked almonds.

pears in red wine

Vanilla ice cream, crème fraîche or a warm sabayon are all good accompaniments, but the fruit is also very good on its own. Garnish the platter with grapes and lightly toasted split almonds, if you wish.

serves 10

200g (7oz) sugar
1 cinnamon stick
300ml (½ pint) dry red wine
6 firm pears
2 navel oranges
1 small lemon
small knob of butter

Gently heat the sugar, cinnamon and wine in a large saucepan until the sugar has dissolved. Peel, halve and core the pears. Scrub the oranges and lemon and slice them. Put the fruit in the syrup, and simmer until the pears are tender (the length of time will depend upon their degree of ripeness). Transfer the fruit to a serving dish, and reduce the syrup slightly, stirring in a nut of butter to give the sauce a nice gloss. Pour it over the fruit and serve warm.

lemon meringue pie

250g (8oz) shortcrust pastry

3 level tbsps cornflour

300ml (½ pint) boiling water

125g (4oz) golden granulated sugar

grated zest and juice of 3 lemons

50g (2oz) butter

3 eggs, separated

75g (3oz) caster sugar

Line a 20cm (8 inch) flan ring or quiche dish with the pastry and bake blind in a preheated oven at 200°C/400°F/gas mark 6 for 15 minutes.

Mix the cornflour with a couple of tablespoons of cold water, then stir it into the boiling water in a saucepan. Add the granulated sugar, lemon zest and juice, and cook until the mixture thickens. Remove from the heat and allow to cool for 20 minutes or so. Beat in the butter and egg yolks. Whisk the egg whites and, as they begin to firm up, add half the caster sugar. Continue whisking, fold in the remaining caster sugar, and whisk again until the meringue is stiff and glossy.

Pour the lemon filling into the pastry case, spoon the meringue over it, making sure it reaches the pastry edges and is heaped up in the centre. Bake in a preheated oven at 180°C/350°F/gas mark 4 for 20 minutes until the meringue is golden brown. Like many pies, this is best served warm or at room temperature. It is not pleasant at all served straight from the refrigerator.

golden fruit salad

Use some or all of the following fruits in appropriate quantities:

mango, papaya, kumquats, kaki or sharon fruit, mandarin oranges or other easily peeled oranges, golden russet apples, ripe starfruit, pineapple, golden muscat grapes, passion fruit, physalis, fresh dates, ripe galia or charentais melon, soaked dried apricots

plus 2–3 sheets gold leaf
sweet wine, such as Muscat de Rivesaltes or Moscatel de Valencia

Prepare the fruit as appropriate, but keep it in distinctive shapes rather than dice it all; for example, slices of starfruit, long curving slivers of mango, orange segments, melon balls. Leave smaller fruit whole, and be prepared to put up with kumquat pips and grape seeds. Peel any fruit that needs it over a bowl to catch the juice. Mix this with the sweet wine, and crumble in the gold leaf, if you have any. Put the fruit into a large bowl, preferably glass, and pour the gold-flecked wine over it. Serve chilled. Red fruit salad and green fruit salad are made in the same way.

plum and hazelnut crumble

Whole hazelnuts that you grind yourself to an uneven texture are very good in a crumble. This recipe can be adapted to any number of fruits and a variety of toppings, and you can use butter instead of hazelnut oil.

serves 6 to 8

750g (1½lb) plums
6–7 tbsps hazelnut oil
85g (3oz) dark muscovado sugar
125g (4oz) wholemeal flour
75g (3oz) ground hazelnuts

Stone the plums, then poach until just tender in a couple of tablespoons of water. Spoon into an ovenproof dish brushed with a tablespoon of the hazelnut oil.

Mix the sugar, flour and hazelnuts, and then gently work in the remaining oil, rubbing and lifting until the mixture resembles breadcrumbs. (Although the nuts, flour and sugar can be mixed in the food processor, it is best to add the oil and work by hand, since using oil, in any kind of baking, in place of 'dry' fat produces a heavier texture.) Spoon over the plums and bake in a preheated oven at 180°C/350°F/gas mark 4 for 25 minutes.

spiced rhubarb sorbet with ginger ice cream and brandy snap wafers

serves 10

500g (1lb) trimmed rhubarb

2 tbsps water

500g (1lb) sugar

500ml (16fl oz) water

green cardamom seeds, cinnamon sticks or cloves

juice of ½ lemon

Put the rhubarb in a saucepan, add the two tablespoons of water, and cook gently until tender. Make a flavoured syrup by dissolving the sugar in the 500ml (16fl oz) of water and adding cardamom seeds, cinnamon sticks or cloves according to preference. When both the rhubarb and syrup have cooled, blend together and add the lemon juice. Freeze in a sorbetière or ice-cream maker.

ginger ice cream

Note that this recipe uses raw eggs.

makes 1 litre (1¾ pints)

75g (3oz) fresh ginger, peeled and finely chopped

250ml (8fl oz) sugar syrup

375ml (12fl oz) full cream milk

5 egg yolks, beaten

250ml (8fl oz) whipping cream, whipped

Simmer the ginger in the syrup for 5 minutes. Remove the pan from the heat. Scald the milk in a separate saucepan, remove from the heat, and stir in the ginger syrup. Infuse for about an hour and do not strain at this stage.

Proceed with the ice-cream making in the usual way, reheating the milk and syrup mixture before pouring it on to the beaten egg yolks to make a custard. Return the custard to a saucepan and stir over a very low heat until it thickens just enough to coat the back of a spoon, but without letting it curdle. Strain the custard into a large bowl and fold in the whipped cream. For a more intense flavour, press the ginger in the sieve as you strain the custard. Freeze in a greased and lined Swiss roll tin, so as to be able to cut out rounds or rectangles for the brandy snap wafers.

brandy snap wafers

These will keep for up to a week in an airtight container.

makes about 50

75g (3oz) golden syrup

75g (3oz) demerara sugar

75g (3oz) butter

2 tsps ground ginger

1–2 tbsps brandy

75g (3oz) plain flour, sifted

In a heavy saucepan, combine the syrup, sugar and butter and heat gently, stirring until the sugar has dissolved and butter melted. Remove from the heat and cool slightly before stirring in the ground ginger, brandy and flour.

Spread the mixture on greased baking sheets and bake in a preheated oven at 160°C/325°F/gas mark 3 for about 8 minutes. Trim into neat circles or rectangles and cool on wire racks.

Cut out the ice cream to the same shape as the brandy snaps and sandwich together. For each serving, place a quenelle or scoop of sorbet on the plate, together with an ice-cream sandwich. Garnish with shredded preserved stem ginger, preserved angelica and frosted mint leaves.

summer pudding

serves 8

125g (4oz) gooseberries

75ml (3fl oz) water

125g (4oz) blackcurrants

250g (8oz) redcurrants

350g (12oz) raspberries

125–175g (4–6oz) golden caster sugar

8 slices good white bread, crusts removed

Top, tail and hull the fruit as appropriate. If necessary, rinse in a colander under running water. Put the gooseberries and water in a saucepan, and cook gently for 4–5 minutes. Add the blackcurrants and redcurrants, and cook for a further minute or so before adding the raspberries – these require the least cooking and really just need heating through. Stir in the sugar and, when this has dissolved and the juices have run from the fruit to make a well-coloured syrup, remove from the heat.

Line a 1.1 litre (2 pint) pudding basin with the bread, cut into a round for the bottom and wedges for the side, reserving one of the slices and the trimmings to cover the top. Ladle a little of the juice into the lined basin, then spoon in the fruit and the rest of the juice. Arrange the remaining bread on top, and cover with foil. Place a saucer and a weight on top, and refrigerate overnight.

When ready to serve, turn out the pudding on to a plate. It can be decorated with sprigs and leaves of the same fruit that you have used in the pudding. Whipped cream, clotted cream, yoghurt, crème fraîche will all go with it very well.

saffron, honey and cream cheese tart

serves 8

pinch of saffron threads
250g (8oz) shortcrust pastry
375g (12oz) cream cheese
4 tbsps honey
3 tbsps water
3 eggs

Soak the saffron threads for 20 minutes in a tablespoon of hot water. Roll out the pastry, and use to line a 25cm (10 inch) quiche dish, tart ring or pie plate. Use the trimmings to decorate the edges with pastry leaves or a plait. Bake blind in a preheated oven at 180°C/350°F/gas mark 4 for 10 minutes, then remove from the oven and allow to cool.

Put the cream cheese in a bowl. Melt the honey with two tablespoons of water. Mix the honey and saffron liquid with the cheese, then beat in the eggs. Carefully pour the mixture into the pastry case, and bake in a preheated oven at 190°C/375°F/gas mark 5 for 15 minutes, then reduce the temperature to 170°C/325°F/gas mark 3 and bake for a further 20 minutes or so. Serve either warm or cold.

bread and butter pudding

If you wish, sultanas, raspberries or other fruit can be added; the authentic pudding is very plain.

serves 8 to 10

> 75g (3oz) unsalted butter
>
> about 15 slices white bread, buttered and cut into triangles
>
> 125g (4oz) light muscovado sugar
>
> 4 eggs
>
> 250ml (8fl oz) full cream milk
>
> 300ml (½ pint) single cream

Liberally butter a large, rectangular ovenproof dish, and lay in it the pieces of bread, slightly overlapping each other, sprinkling each layer with sugar. Dot with butter. Beat together the eggs, milk and cream, pour over the bread, and leave to stand for 20 minutes or so before baking in a preheated oven at 180°C/350°F/gas mark 4 for 35–40 minutes. Serve warm, dusted with icing sugar and accompanied by clotted cream or double cream.

I also recommend treacle tart, Bakewell pudding and crème brûlée or burnt cream, the recipes for which you will find on pp.253–4 and 96 respectively.

casual and impromptu meals

Much of the food in this chapter has an American flavour, largely because they do casual better than we do, and it has been a source of inspiration in my cooking and menu planning for thirty years. During that time, Tom and I have travelled widely in America, and have experienced all manner of casual eating, from fast food in roadside diners to barbecues with Texas ranchers. I have cooked all over America with friends and family, and collected many recipes which I still cook in my London kitchen.

chilli and all its fixin's

Chilli is one of the best dishes I learned in America, and one of my favourite times to cook it is in January, when budgets are a little tight and the weather calls for something hot and cheering.

After rich holiday food, a plain old chilli goes down well, and with plenty of inexpensive cuts of meat available, this can be an especially economical meal.

For beef chilli, which I like to cook for a long time, I usually use meat taken from the shoulder or leg, which has plenty of flavour and lends itself to stewing. And, indeed, this is the cut I would choose for lamb, pork or venison chilli. For this version, I have chosen to use a mixture of meats, but the recipe can be used for a single meat or any combination. I prefer to dice the meat quite small, rather than mince it.

Some put beans in chilli, others do not, and each claims their chilli to be authentic. Pressure on the budget is sufficient reason to make the meat go further with the addition of pulses. I generally cook my chilli in a casserole in the oven. But if it is more convenient, you can cook it quickly in a pressure cooker, or alternatively let it cook all day in a slow cooker; in either case, carefully follow the manufacturer's directions.

How hot to make the chilli is a matter of personal taste. I do not like food that is crammed full of chilli, for two reasons. One is that the rest of the flavours are masked, and the other is that very hot chilli ruins your palate for the wine you plan to serve. My advice is to taste as you go. You can use dried, ground chilli in place of the fresh I have suggested. Of course, you may consider beer or cider a more suitable drink with chilli than wine, and there are plenty of imported beers to choose from, as well as good English ales, widely available in supermarkets and high street stores.

Chillies need to be treated with respect. If in doubt as to what kind of chilli you are using, assume it is a hot one until it proves otherwise. Remove all the seeds and veins, which are the hottest part of the plant. Do not touch the eyes or mouth after you have touched a chilli, and thoroughly wash hands and utensils after use. Capsaicin, the essential oil in chilli, is very volatile and induces powerful burning sensations when it comes into contact with soft or broken tissue. However, do not let all that put you off experimenting with these colourful and explosive fruits, more and more varieties of which are available in greengrocers, specialist shops and supermarkets.

Cornbread and polenta are not very different: both are made with ground yellow cornmeal. I have given a recipe for cornbread, as it is the more appropriate accompaniment to chilli, but you might like to serve polenta instead.

At this point, a large bowl of cool, crunchy salad will go down well, with contrasting sweet and bitter flavours; celery, chicory, radicchio, fennel, kohlrabi and Chinese leaves are all good for eating raw. Alternatively, serve the salad as a first course, as the main course is fairly robust.

In fact, this is an easy meal to stretch in both directions. It would not be impossible to serve it as a buffet for a dozen or so by doubling up quantities and making plenty of salad and cornbread. I would add a dish of coleslaw, a recipe for which is given on p.170, as it provides a nice cool contrast to the chilli.

---

mixed meat chilli

serves 6 to 8

    500g (1lb) red kidney beans, washed and soaked overnight

    1kg (2lb) pork shoulder, lamb shoulder and beef flank steak, mixed

    2 tbsps olive or groundnut oil

    1 medium onion, peeled and sliced

    3–4 garlic cloves, peeled and sliced

    1–3 fresh green or red chillies, seeded and sliced

    1 tbsp paprika

    1 tbsp cumin seeds

    1 level tbsp fresh marjoram or oregano, or ½ tsp dried

    2 bay leaves

    400g can peeled plum tomatoes or 50g (2oz) sundried tomatoes, soaked in
        150ml (¼ pint) boiling water, and cut into pieces

    salt

    freshly ground black pepper

Put the beans in a saucepan with plenty of water. Bring to the boil, and boil briskly for 15 minutes. Drain and rinse the beans, put back in the pan, cover with the same volume of water, bring to the boil, and simmer for 30 minutes.

Meanwhile, trim and dice the meat into very small cubes, which gives a better finish to the dish than mince. Brown the meat in a heavy frying pan, then place in a casserole. Heat the oil, and fry the onions until golden. Add the garlic, spices and herbs, and fry gently for 5 minutes. Add the tomatoes, and their liquid, and cook for a few minutes, scraping up any bits stuck to the bottom of the frying pan. Pour into the casserole, together with the beans and their cooking liquor. Bring to the boil and simmer, uncovered, for about 1½ hours. Taste, and season, as necessary. Serve with polenta or cornbread.

cornbread

serves 6 to 8

225g (8oz) plain flour

175g (6oz) cornmeal or polenta

4 tsps baking powder

1 level tsp salt

1 egg, lightly beaten

150ml (¼ pint) milk

3 tbsps melted butter

Mix together the flour, cornmeal, baking powder and salt in a bowl, then stir in the egg, milk and butter until blended, but do not over-mix. Butter a 20cm (8 inch) square roasting tin or cake tin, and pour in the mixture. Bake in a pre-heated oven at 220°C/425°F/gas mark 7 for 20–25 minutes.

the perfect banana split

Appealing to the child in all of us, the banana split is one of the easiest ways to finish a casual meal. And good ingredients make it into a real treat.

serves 1

1 ripe, but not over-ripe, banana

2 scoops of the best and strongest vanilla ice cream – I recommend
    Hill Station's Strong Vanilla Bean

whipped cream (optional)

hot chocolate sauce, which you can make yourself by melting Valrhona
    chocolate in 2 tbsps cream

toasted flaked almonds, for decoration

In a shallow glass dish, arrange the banana, split down the middle, and the ice cream. Top with whipped cream, then pour over the hot chocolate sauce. Scatter with toasted almonds.

Alternatively, serve the chocolate sauce separately, and for those who do not like their chocolate ration this way, heat some luxury caramel spread (such as Dulce de Leche) and offer that instead.

peanut butter biscuits

These biscuits make a delicious accompaniment to any ice cream, especially the banana splits. If you like the crunch, you can stir in some crushed toasted peanuts, or simply use crunchy peanut butter. I am informed that they may be even better with the addition of a few chocolate chips.

makes about 30 large biscuits

100g (4oz) unsalted butter, at room temperature

250g (8oz) golden caster sugar

200g (7oz) peanut butter

2 eggs

250g (8oz) plain flour, sifted with 1 tsp baking powder

You can make this in a food processor, first creaming the butter and sugar, then adding the peanut butter. Once you have a smooth mixture, add the eggs and flour alternately, and process briefly until well mixed.

On greased and lined baking sheets, place heaped tablespoons of the mixture, about 5cm (2 inches) apart, spread them into thick circles and bake in a preheated oven at 180°C/350°F/gas mark 4 for about 12–15 minutes. Remove from the oven when pale golden brown, and carefully transfer with a spatula to wire racks. They will still be pliable when you remove them from the baking sheets, but will become crisp as they cool.

good food for good friends

A hearty sauce for chunky pasta, a melting truffled potato and wild mushroom tart in a crisp feta pastry, and a richly flavoured fennel and saffron crumble are some of the dishes that I suggest for feeding a crowd, whether for a late winter supper, a party buffet or any special occasion that does not demand too great a formality.

There is no theme here, just good food for good friends, much of which will appeal to vegetarians and those who would like some more ideas for non-meat or fish recipes. These are easy, good-tempered dishes to make, and equally easy on the pocket. Yet with the addition of saffron, and perhaps truffle oil, they are lifted into the realms of more glamorous party food.

The pasta makes an easy first course, the sauce benefiting from being made in advance, and the other dishes can be served at room temperature or warm, so that the cook will not need to spend too much time in the kitchen once the party is under way. I watched this being prepared in our friends', the Lancellottis', kitchen one autumn day, and remember thinking then that it would make a good, inexpensive party dish. Unlike much of the food that comes out of their kitchen near Modena, this is not a regional or traditional dish, but a pan-Italian invention, using, as its name suggests, ingredients from both north and south. If, for a vegetarian dish, you were to replace the sausage with chunks of aubergine, cooked in the same way and at the same point in the recipe, you would have a dish very Sicilian in flavour.

salsa padana mediterranea da lancellotti

serves 15

5 onions, medium to large, peeled and sliced

6 tbsps extra virgin olive oil

300g (10oz) pancetta, chopped small

750g (1½ lb) Italian sausages, skinned and crumbled

100g (3½oz) unsalted butter

1 large green and 1 large red pepper, seeded

200ml (7fl oz) white wine

salt

3 × 800g cans crushed tomatoes

1 tbsp flaked chillies

Put the sliced onions in a large shallow pan with a generous splash of olive oil, and cook over a moderate heat to lightly brown them. Then add the pancetta and crumbled sausage meat and let it all brown nicely. At this stage, Camillo Lancellotti adds the butter, for flavour; otherwise, one would use extra pancetta. (I asked then if one could use this sauce for a baked pasta, but Il Primio says no, a lasagne is *tutto un altra cosa*, quite another thing.)

By now the onions should be browning nicely. It takes a long time to do it properly, but the end result is worth it. Chop the seeded peppers into thumbnail-size pieces, and add when the onions are soft and transparent.

The white wine is added, and the lid is put on, not too tightly, for the mixture to simmer. Add salt to taste, then the tomatoes and chillies. The sauce is ready when the peppers are cooked but not too soft.

This is a very good sauce for gnocchi, or to serve over grilled polenta slices. It keeps for about a week.

truffled potato and wild mushroom tart in feta pastry

serves 8 to 10

1.5kg (3lb) waxy potatoes, scrubbed, but not peeled

200g (7oz) unsalted butter

salt

freshly ground black pepper

500 g (1lb) fresh wild mushrooms, well brushed and cleaned

3 shallots, peeled and finely chopped

1 tsp fresh thyme, chopped

1 garlic clove, peeled and crushed

for the feta pastry

250g (8oz) plain flour

75g (3oz) butter, chilled and diced

50g (2oz) feta cheese, chilled and crumbled

white truffle oil (optional)

iced water

1–2 tsps chopped fresh thyme

Boil the potatoes until almost tender and, when cool enough to handle, peel off the skins. Heat half the butter in a saucepan, and put in the potatoes. Crush them roughly with a fork, but do not mash them, season with salt and pepper, and leave over a low heat to finish cooking.

Slice the larger mushrooms. Melt the remaining butter in a saucepan or frying pan, and fry the mushrooms with the shallots, thyme and garlic. Season to taste.

Make the pastry in the usual way, rubbing the butter and feta into the flour, then adding the chopped thyme and enough iced water to bind. Gather into a ball, knead lightly, and let the pastry relax for 30 minutes.

Line a 20–25cm (8–10 inch) tart tin with the pastry and bake blind in a pre-heated oven at 180°C/350°F/gas mark 4 for about 20 minutes until crisp.

Combine the crushed potatoes and mushrooms, together with any cooking

---

juices, spoon into the pastry case, and return to the oven for 5–10 minutes.

Serve hot or warm, with, if you like, a thread of truffle oil trickled over the top. You can also place a few thin shavings of feta on top of the potato before you return the tart to the oven or, even better, a few thin shavings of truffle when you remove it from the oven.

florentine muffins

You can make miniature versions of this dish to serve as hot canapés. Use toasted sliced baguette in place of the muffin, and quail's eggs instead of hen's eggs.

serves 8

1kg (2lb) young spinach

approx 200g (7oz) butter

8 eggs

4 English muffins, split

400ml (14fl oz) hollandaise sauce

grated white truffle or truffle oil (optional)

Thoroughly rinse and shake dry the spinach. Steam it and, as it softens, gradually stir in the butter, a bit at a time. Spinach will absorb an enormous quantity, so stop when you think you've added sufficient for your taste. Poach the eggs, trim them and keep warm in a bowl of hot water. Toast the muffins on the split side, and put in individual shallow dishes. Spoon on the spinach, making a depression in the centre. Place an egg on top, spoon over the hollandaise and just glaze under a hot grill. Just before serving, add a drop of truffle oil, or a shaving of white truffle.

hollandaise sauce

You can change the flavour of the hollandaise by using different vinegars. Chopped shallots cooked with the vinegar and water, but using an extra tablespoon of tarragon vinegar, will give you bearnaise sauce, which is wonderful with grills. Finely chopped mint added to the hollandaise will give you *sauce paloise*, a classic French sauce from Pau.

makes about 600 ml (1 pint)

6 tbsps white wine vinegar

2 tbsps water

2 blades of mace

1 scant tsp peppercorns

6 egg yolks

250g (8oz) unsalted butter, very soft

salt

freshly ground black pepper

Put the vinegar, water, mace and peppercorns in a saucepan and boil to reduce to one tablespoon. Put the egg yolks in a bowl set over a pan of simmering water and beat them with a teaspoon of the butter, a pinch of salt and grinding of pepper. Strain in the vinegar, remove the pan from the heat but keep the bowl over the hot water. Gradually whisk in the butter, a small amount at a time, until you have a smooth, glossy sauce. As with mayonnaise, you can make this in the blender, first blending the eggs, hot vinegar liquid and seasoning, and then adding the butter, piece by piece. The blender is particularly useful if you are making double quantities or more.

fennel, saffron and almond crumble

serves 8

1–1.5kg (2–3lb) fennel, trimmed and cut into slender wedges

600ml (1 pint) vegetable stock

2 bay leaves

4 cloves

blade of mace or piece of nutmeg

500ml (16fl oz) thick béchamel sauce

300g (10oz) hard goat's cheese

6 tbsps each ground almonds and rolled oats

6 tbsps flaked almonds

good pinch of saffron threads, dry roasted

Bring the stock, bay leaf and spices to the boil, add the fennel and cook for 8–10 minutes. Transfer the fennel to a lightly oiled or buttered baking dish, and reduce the stock by about two thirds, first removing the spices and bay leaf. Stir in the béchamel sauce, and cook for 2–3 minutes before pouring over the fennel. Mix together the cheese, ground almonds, rolled oats and flaked almonds, and scatter over the top. Bake in a preheated oven at 180°C/350°F/ gas mark 4 for about 25 minutes.

béchamel sauce

makes about 600 ml (1 pint)

 50g (2oz) unsalted butter

 50g (2oz) flour

 600ml (1 pint) milk, hot

 salt

 freshly ground white pepper

 nutmeg (optional)

In a heavy saucepan, melt the butter, stir in the flour, and cook for a few minutes. Remove from the heat, and stir in about a quarter of the milk until smooth. Return to the heat, stirring continuously, and, as the mixture begins to thicken, remove again from the heat. Gradually add another quarter of the milk, stirring until smooth, thickening it again over the heat, and so on, until you have a smooth thick sauce. Season lightly with salt and white pepper. If you do not mind the darker flecks, a grating of nutmeg is good too. Cook gently for 10 minutes. This is important. Even though the sauce looks finished before then, it is important to fully cook the flour.

Variations

To make a cheese sauce, to the above quantity of sauce, stir in about 100g (4oz) of your chosen grated cheese. To make parsley sauce, remove the stalks and any damaged parts from a generous bunch of parsley. Rinse well, roughly chop and put in a blender with about 200ml (7fl oz) boiling water. Blitz until smooth. Stir as much of this purée as you need into the béchamel sauce. To make egg sauce, add two or three finely chopped hard-boiled eggs.

For a richer or sweet sauce, substitute single cream for the milk. Sweet sauces can be flavoured with grated lemon or orange zest, and sweetened with sugar or honey.

fruit compote in spiced wine

serves 15

for the spiced wine
   1 bottle full-bodied red wine
   500ml (18fl oz) red grape juice
   thinly peeled zest of 2 tangerines
   1 cinnamon stick
   6 crushed cardamom pods
   freshly grated nutmeg
   1–2 measures orange liqueur

Put all the ingredients except the liqueur in a saucepan and bring just to the boil. Immediately remove from the heat and stir in the orange liqueur.

fruit
   250g (8oz) small dried figs
   250g (8oz) dried apricots
   250g (8oz) stoned prunes
   large bunch seedless black or red grapes
   250g (8oz) ripe lychees
   6–8 mandarin oranges

Use a very large bowl for this, or several smaller ones. Put the dried fruit in the bowl, and pour on the hot spiced wine. Once the liquid has begun to cool, add the remaining fruit; remove the grapes from the bunch, peel the lychees, and slice the oranges horizontally before doing so.

The compote is ready to serve when the dried fruit is as soft and juicy as fresh fruit. Serve chilled, or at room temperature, as you prefer, with or without cream, custard, vanilla, cinnamon or nutmeg ice cream.

trick or treat for hallowe'en

I have selected some of my favourite casual dishes for entertaining with an autumnal theme, together with some recipes that you can turn into treats for unexpected visitors, large or small. October and November bring fireworks parties, Diwali and Hallowe'en. Some of these ideas can be saved for later if you are planning on a Thanksgiving party.

Many children in our part of north London have taken up the American tradition of 'trick or treating' on Hallowe'en. My husband, Tom, remembers it from his childhood, when neighbours took care to hand out small treats, in the form of sweets and biscuits, in order to avoid the noisy, or messy, trick likely to be played on defaulters; dustbin lids tied together, treacle on car door handles, and other mischief.

This is food you can cook indoors, and serve outside, if you are having a bonfire party, and some of it can be eaten on the move. The potatoes are especially good this way because they act as your own personal handwarmer.

The beef, full of sweet, spicy flavours, can be cooked in advance, and then sliced, and served with its various accompaniments and a pile of warm tortillas. Serve a pineapple and chilli salsa, some avocado and tomato salad, shredded lettuce, soured cream, and some hot mashed-up cooked beans – kidney or borlotti – for a Tex-Mex meal.

For those who prefer a more formal meal, serve the beef pot-roast with jacket potatoes, or a mash of potato and sweet potato. A large bowl of coleslaw, one of green salad, and, as well as the cinnamon toast, a compote of grapes in mulled wine make this an autumnal feast.

Small guests will enjoy their pumpkins made into lanterns. Adult guests will, I suspect, prefer their pumpkin to eat. If you have the time and the energy, a baked pumpkin, filled with a richly flavoured, fragrant soup put on the table, as a first course, is a most welcoming sight on a cold night. Remember, too, that large, hollowed-out baked potatoes make excellent containers for hot soup.

If you serve pumpkin pie, you will not want a pumpkin soup for starters. But if you choose a different pudding, rather than use the pumpkin shell for a lantern, scoop out the filling and seeds, after slicing across the top, then put some of the pumpkin flesh back with spices, herbs, stock, cream, wine, aromatics, cheese, what you will, cover, and bake in the oven until you have a soft, soupy filling. Alternatively, make the soup in the conventional fashion.

stuffed baked potato

serves 1

> 1 baking potato
> 1 good quality sausage

Parboil the potato. When cool enough to handle, use an apple corer to take out the middle. Stuff the sausage meat, which you will probably have to take out of its skin first and roll more thinly, into the hole. Bake the potato in the oven for about an hour, and serve with a thick napkin.

pumpkin soup

serves 6 to 8

> 1 large mild onion, peeled and thinly sliced
> 3 trimmed celery sticks
> 2–3 tbsps olive oil
> 1.5kg (3lb) piece of pumpkin, roasted
> 2 bay leaves
> sprig of sage
> 2 cloves
> salt
> freshly ground black pepper
> freshly grated nutmeg
> 2 litres (3½ pints) chicken, ham or vegetable stock
> 200g (7oz) farmhouse Lancashire, Gruyère or Parmesan, grated
> 1–2 tbsps finely chopped parsley or chives (optional)
> rashers of streaky bacon, fried until crisp and crumbled (optional)

entertaining

Fry the onion and celery in the olive oil until just beginning to caramelize but not burn. Cut the rind from the pumpkin, dice the flesh and add to the pan. Add all the seasonings and half the stock. Cover, and cook for about 10 minutes or until the vegetables are completely soft. Take out the sage and bay leaves. Remove the soup from the heat, add the rest of the cold stock, then blend until smooth. Return to the heat, and stir in the cheeses and parsley or chives, if using. Serve scattered with the bacon pieces, which nicely complement the sage and cheese flavours.

corn fritters

makes 12 to 18 fritters
   6 fresh corn cobs
   50ml (2fl oz) milk
   75g (3oz) flour
   ½ tsp baking powder
   pinch of salt
   2 large eggs, separated
   oil or butter for frying

Cut the kernels off the cobs and lightly crush them in the milk. Sift the flour, baking powder and salt together into a bowl. Beat the egg yolks and separately whisk the egg whites to firm peaks. Mix the corn into the egg yolks, and then stir in the flour until well mixed. Fold in the egg whites.

Meanwhile, heat a heavy frying pan or griddle, grease it, and spoon on large dollops of batter; I use a ladle or serving spoon. When cooked golden brown, turn the fritters and cook the other sides. Grease the pan between each batch.

grilled devilled chicken livers and mushrooms

Shelled prawns or scallops, pieces of lamb's kidney, and meatballs made from sausage meat can all be cooked in the same way. And, of course, this will also make a very good main course for four people, if you leave all the food on the skewers and serve with rice or mashed potatoes and salad.

makes 4

6 whole chicken livers

12 mushrooms, wiped

1 tsp each thyme and oregano, chopped

cayenne pepper

freshly ground black pepper

salt

1 tbsp extra virgin olive oil

2 tbsps Dijon mustard

12 rashers streaky bacon, rinds removed

4 wooden skewers, soaked in water for 30 minutes

Separate the lobes of liver, and discard any threads and discoloured parts. Mix together the herbs, seasoning, oil and mustard, and marinate the livers and mushrooms for 30 minutes or so.

Halve the bacon, and use each piece to wrap a mushroom, or a piece of chicken liver. Thread six on each skewer, and grill for about 10–15 minutes, turning frequently to cook through.

Remove the morsels from the skewers before serving, and spear each piece with a cocktail stick for easy handling.

sweet and spicy beef pot-roast

serves 6 to 8

1.5kg (3lb) beef blade, feather steak or topside, in one piece

2 onions, peeled and grated

1 tsp crushed allspice

1 tsp salt

2 tsps freshly ground black pepper

2 tbsps wine vinegar

4 tbsps molasses sugar

4 tbsps each water, rum and dry red wine

4 whole cloves

1 bay leaf

Rub the meat all over with all the ingredients apart from the cloves and bay leaf. Stick the cloves and bay leaf into the meat. Cover, and marinate for several hours or overnight.

Heat a well-seasoned or non-stick frying pan and brown the meat all over. Transfer it, and the marinade, to a casserole and cook in a preheated oven at 160°C/325°F/gas mark 3 for about 2 hours until very tender. Transfer to a serving platter, and pour the cooking juices into a jug. Serve a heap of warm tortillas, some refried beans, soured cream, avocado and tomato salad, shredded iceberg lettuce and a fruity hot salsa, perhaps using pineapple or papaya, both of which are good with beef. Let everyone assemble their own tortillas to eat, using their fingers. As an alternative, accompany the beef with a mash of sweet potatoes, some wild rice and a bowl of mustardy coleslaw. In fact, I would include the coleslaw anyway. Quite unauthentic with tortillas, but very good with them, nevertheless.

coleslaw

2 carrots, peeled

1 kohlrabi

½ white cabbage

1 mild onion

¼ tsp sea salt

¼ tsp freshly ground black pepper

2 tsps light muscovado sugar

1 lime

1 tbsp mustard

2 tbsps thick Greek yoghurt

Using a mandolin, julienne or slicing disc, finely slice the carrots, kohlrabi and cabbage. Put in a bowl of water with ice cubes and a little salt to crisp them while you make the dressing.

Peel and chop the onion by hand, and put in a bowl. Mix the salt, pepper, sugar, lime zest, mustard and yoghurt with the juice of half the lime. Drain the vegetables, and fold them into the dressing and onions.

Note This is best made an hour or so before serving to let the flavours mature. If you prefer, mayonnaise can replace the yoghurt. When using raw onions, it is always better to chop or slice by hand. The high speed of a food processor, and the blades, seem to react with the compounds in the onion, turning it bitter.

pineapple salsa

This can be made the day before it is required. Cover and keep in the refrigerator.

serves 6 to 8

- 1 pineapple, peeled and chopped
- 2–3 garlic cloves, peeled and chopped
- ½ tsp coarse sea salt
- 1–2 green chillies, seeded and chopped
- handful of fresh mint leaves, chopped
- juice and grated zest of a lime
- 2 shallots, peeled and finely chopped
- 2 carrots, peeled and grated

Mix together all the ingredients and leave to stand for 30 minutes or so before serving to let the flavours mature.

pumpkin pie

serves 6 to 8

250g (8oz) shortcrust pastry

300g (10oz) cooked pumpkin purée or canned pumpkin

100g (3½oz) golden syrup

50g (2oz) light muscovado sugar

¼ tsp freshly ground black pepper

¼ tsp salt

½ tsp ground ginger

1 tsp ground cinnamon

1 tsp ground mixed spice

3 eggs, lightly beaten

300ml (½ pint) full cream milk or mixture of half milk and half single cream

Roll out the pastry and use to line a 22cm (9 inch) diameter pie dish.

Mix the pumpkin, syrup and sugar until thoroughly blended. Stir in the seasoning and spices, then beat in the eggs. Pour in the milk, and blend thoroughly before pouring into the pastry case.

Bake in a preheated oven at 220°C/425°F/gas mark 7 for 15 minutes, then reduce the temperature to 180°C/350°F/gas mark 4 and bake for a further 35 minutes or so until set or when a skewer inserted into the centre comes out clean.

entertaining

spices to enhance your summer entertaining

It takes just a few hot days in an English summer to make me think I am back in the tropics, and I start cooking the dishes I learned to make in kitchens in Sri Lanka and Thailand.

Thai food is amongst the most subtle and complex of all cuisines. Within one dish, all five taste sensations might be found; sweet, sour, salt, bitter and hot. It is colourful and fragrant food, drawing on the citrus notes of lime leaves and lemon grass, as well as pandanus leaves, coriander and mint. Chilli heat is tempered by coconut milk, and by the accompanying noodles or rice.

In Sri Lanka, many of the same ingredients are used, albeit with different names; rampe is the pandanus leaf, and curry leaves, too, are used. Souring ingredients, whether vinegar, lime juice, tamarind or goraka, produce a sharply refreshing note to the curries and *sambals* which are traditionally served with rice. The island's vegetable markets, in Kandy for example, are so well-stocked with both tropical and temperate climate produce, that it is easy to eat vegetarian, surrounding the platter of rice with a dozen vegetable curries, pickles, *sambals* and *mallungs*, which are shredded green leaves, quickly stir-fried with coconut.

There are several cookery books which provide a good introduction to Thai cooking, and many of the recipes can be done at home without too much difficulty, such as the classic *yam nua*, or Thai beef salad. The delicate salmon and mint salad originally relied on shredded green, that is, unripe, mango, which has a wonderful astringency lacking in the ripe fruit. I hesitate to suggest this, but using the logic that unripe mango can be substituted for cooking apples if you are desperate to make an apple pie in the tropics, peeled, thinly sliced Bramley, cut into julienne and tossed in lime juice to stop it browning, can be used to replace green mango. Green mangoes are often available in Asian markets, and occasionally in some supermarkets, but not widely so.

Maldive fish and *goraka* add important flavours to Sri Lankan cooking, where they are readily available ingredients. In their absence, I use oriental fish sauce or anchovies to add an underlying rich but not particularly fishy note, instead of the dried, pounded tuna-like fish from the Maldives, and vinegar, tamarind paste or lime juice instead of the *goraka*, which is the dried and blackened segments of an orange fruit, *garcinia cambogia*.

For dessert I have used lemon grass in partnership with our own lemon-flavoured herbs to make a syrup to accompany summer fruit. Choose peaches and nectarines from Italy and Spain, although it is quite nice with fully ripe strawberries.

salad of cured salmon and mint

serves 2 as a first course

200g (7oz) very fresh salmon fillet, skinned, and pin bones removed

3 tbsps traditionally brewed Japanese soy sauce

generous pinch sugar

sunflower or groundnut oil for frying

2 tbsps freshly squeezed lime juice

1 tbsp fish sauce

1 tsp chilli powder

3 shallots, peeled and thinly sliced

handful of mint and coriander leaves

1 small green mango, peeled and shredded – or see introduction

1–2 tbsps salmon roe for garnish (optional)

Marinate the salmon overnight in the soy and sugar. Remove the fish from the marinade, and leave to dry on a rack in the refrigerator for a day.

Deep fry or shallow fry the salmon for 2 minutes, then let it rest for 10 minutes. In a bowl combine the lime juice, fish sauce and chilli, and flake in the salmon. Carefully fold in the shallots and herbs, and serve with steamed rice, with or without salmon roe for decoration. I also like the fish mixture spooned over chilled noodles.

yam nua (beef salad)

serves 2

2–3 bird's eye chillies

1 red chilli

3 garlic cloves, peeled

4 tbsps lemon juice

3 tbsps fish sauce

1 tsp sugar

300g (10oz) grilled steak, thinly sliced

½ cucumber, quartered lengthways and sliced

75g (3oz) cherry tomatoes, halved

1 red onion, peeled and thinly sliced

2 spring onions, sliced into oblique pieces

2 tsps chopped coriander leaves

2 tsps chopped Thai parsley, if available

salad leaves, for serving

First make the dressing by pounding the chillies and garlic in a mortar, then mixing them with the lemon juice, fish sauce and sugar in a salad bowl. Add the beef and all the remaining ingredients. Line a serving bowl or platter with salad leaves and spoon the beef salad on top.

isso ambul thiyal (dry prawn curry)

An unorthodox, but very appealing, alternative way to eat this is to serve the prawns with rice as a cold dish, garnished with chopped coriander leaves.

serves 4 as part of an Asian meal

4 green chillies, seeded

3 garlic cloves, peeled and crushed

½ thumb-sized piece of ginger

½ tsp ground cinnamon

½ tbsp freshly ground black pepper

1 tsp chilli powder (optional)

½ tsp salt

1 tbsp tamarind paste or lime juice

500g (1lb) raw prawns, shelled weight

Grind the chillies, garlic and ginger in a mortar, then mix with the remaining seasoning ingredients. Stir in about 100ml (4fl oz) water and transfer to a saucepan. Add the prawns and stir to coat them with the mixture. Simmer, uncovered, until the prawns are done and the liquid almost evaporated. Transfer to a serving plate and accompany with steamed rice.

fruit salad with verbena, lemon grass and lemon balm syrup

serves 4 to 6

    2 lemon grass sticks, split

    handful each of lemon balm and verbena

    500g (1lb) sugar

    750ml (1¼ pints) water

    6 peaches or nectarines or 600g (1¼lb) strawberries

    juice and zest of 1 lemon

Put the lemon grass, herbs, sugar and water in a saucepan. Heat slowly until the sugar has dissolved, then boil until reduced by a third. Remove from the heat and steep for several hours or overnight.

Prepare the fruit as appropriate (stoning and slicing the peaches or nectarines, hulling the strawberries and slicing if large) and put in a bowl. Grate on the lemon zest and squeeze over the juice. Stir in enough syrup to flavour it, then store the rest in the refrigerator. Use it over ice cream or to make a refreshing drink with sparkling water, some lemon juice and a slice of lemon.

an alternative thanksgiving menu

Those who plan to celebrate a traditional Thanksgiving with roast turkey and all the trimmings will not need me to tell them how to do it. Those who had not given it a thought might take advantage of the fact that there are turkeys in the shops from November onwards. The main recipe that follows is far removed from classic turkey dishes and is fun to serve at a casual, eat-with-your fingers meal. Enhance the south-of-the-border flavours with a large jug of pomegranate margarita, a large bowl of chunky guacamole, plenty more tortillas and a hot and fruity salsa. Make the most of cranberries too, readily available in the winter, and give an entirely new meaning to turkey and cranberry sauce.

Cranberries keep well for two or three weeks in the crisper drawer of the refrigerator, and they freeze well, so it is always worth buying extra. These tart berries are full of pectin and 'jell' very readily, which makes them useful to add in jam-making to those red fruit which contain little pectin. I keep some in the freezer so I can add a handful when making strawberry jam in the summer. Use them in a combination with kumquats or tangerines to make a lovely winter preserve, a cross between jam and marmalade.

Commercial cranberry juice makes rather good cocktails too, although I have it on good authority that the cranberry juice and vodka combination was discovered for its medicinal properties by ladies of a certain age in suburban America long before the Cosmopolitan was created in a New York bar.

cranberry salsa

serves 8 to 10

500g (1lb) cranberries

juice of 2 clementines

3 tbsps light muscovado sugar, or more to taste

1 red onion, peeled and finely chopped

1 red or green chilli, seeded and finely chopped, or more to taste

segments of 2 clementines, as much pith and skin as possible removed

lime juice to taste

salt

Put the cranberries in a saucepan with the clementine juice, and cook until they pop. Stir in the sugar, adding more if necessary. When the cranberries have cooled somewhat, stir in the rest of the ingredients and add lime juice and salt to taste. It is important that the cranberries are not too hot, or they will cook the rest of the ingredients. These should, in fact, remain raw and crisp. In place of clementines, you might like to use pineapple juice and diced pineapple, or mango and mango juice.

chunky guacamole

serves 8 to 10

4–5 ripe avocados

1 green chilli, seeded, or more to taste

2–3 tomatoes, peeled and seeded (optional)

4 spring onions, trimmed

lime juice to taste

salt

fresh coriander leaves

Halve the avocados, scoop the flesh into a bowl and roughly crush with a wooden fork or spoon. Traditionally this is done in a stone mortar which grips the avocado, making it easier to crush. A food processor is likely to blitz the mixture too much, unless you want a smooth guacamole. Finely chop the chilli, dice the tomato quite small and finely slice the spring onion. Stir all these into the mashed avocado, then season with lime juice and salt. Just before serving, chop and stir in the coriander leaves.

turkey fajitas

serves 8 to 10

    1 turkey breast, weighing about 1.5kg (3lb)

    4 green or red chilli peppers

    fresh coriander leaves

for the marinade

    2 tbsps soy sauce

    juice of 1–2 limes

    1 tsp each Angostura bitters and Worcestershire sauce

    100ml (4fl oz) tequila

    3 tbsps extra virgin olive oil

    2–3 garlic cloves, peeled and crushed

    1–2 ripe tomatoes, peeled, seeded and chopped

    ½ tsp freshly ground black pepper

    ½ tsp sea salt

    ½ tsp dried chilli flakes

to serve

    flour tortillas

Mix together all the ingredients for the marinade. Slice the turkey breasts horizontally into two or three pieces. Slash the meat two or three times on each side, and put it in a shallow bowl with the marinade. Leave for 2–4 hours.

Heat the grill or griddle. Remove the meat from the marinade and pat it dry. Pour the marinade into a small saucepan. Grill the turkey on both sides, until it is cooked through and the juices run clear. Grill the peppers until charred. When cool enough to handle, skin them, cut in half, remove the seeds, and shred the flesh finely. (You might like to wear thin rubber gloves when doing this.) Slice the meat thinly across the grain, mix with some of the chillies and with a little of the reserved marinade, which has first been boiled for 5 minutes, and transfer to a serving platter, garnished with fresh coriander and the rest of the peppers. Serve with warm flour tortillas.

---

quick caramel dessert

A jar of Dulce de Leche, caramelized milk or caramel spread, is an indispensable store cupboard standby. In Mexico, *cuajada* is made from caramelized goat's milk, but the Argentine version we get in Britain is made from cow's milk.

300g (10oz) ricotta
icing sugar
6 large pancakes
1 jar Dulce de Leche

Beat the ricotta with the sugar until smooth, and sweetened to your taste. Spread a pancake with some of the ricotta, then with some Dulce de Leche. Place another pancake on top. Continue to build up the layers, finishing with a pancake. Wrap in foil and warm through in the oven. Dust the top thickly with icing sugar, and caramelize it with a blow torch or hot skewers. Cut into wedges.

autumn outdoor eats

Walking the dog, football matches, Hallowe'en trick or treating, Bonfire Night and foraging for wild food are all activities likely to generate a good appetite, as are late autumn spectator sports. October and November offer plenty of opportunity for casual entertaining, either in the back garden or in the kitchen. You might even consider a neighbourhood street party.

The first time I came across a street party in New York, I was astonished to see as many as fifteen blocks of main Manhattan arteries, Third Avenue one day, Lexington Avenue the next, closed off for the purpose of street festivals. Traditional New York street food and drink played an important part, homemade lemonade, egg creams, smoothies, roasted corn, pretzels, hot dogs, devilled turkey drums looking like small hams, funnel cakes and doughnuts. In fact, food seemed to be the main reason for these Indian summer festivities.

In my book, though, autumn is very much meat and potatoes weather. But try meat and potatoes with a difference. The main course below, a pot-roast, is inspired by the barbecue supper we have on our first night when we visit our friends in Auburn, Alabama. The meat, collected from one of the local barbecue pits, is cooked over a fire so long that it falls to pieces. The thin vinegary accompanying sauce took some getting used to, but is authentic and whilst the meat is very good served with vegetables and mashed potatoes, as an alternative serve the meat thinly sliced, accompanied by coleslaw, baked beans, cornbread, relish and the muscular barbecue sauce. You can also use the same cooking method for a shoulder of pork.

I have included a few ideas for recipes where potatoes are the main feature, and could indeed stand on their own. The first two are perfect for those parties where everyone brings a dish.

Peel some medium-sized potatoes, hollow them out, stuff with sausage meat, wrap in bacon, or pancetta, and roast for an hour or so until tender. Or parboil some medium potatoes, hollow them out, brush with melted butter, and bake until golden brown. Fill the potatoes with mussels, briefly steamed and taken out of their shell, mixed with butter, a little grated lemon zest, finely chopped shallots, perhaps some garlic or horseradish, and plenty of parsley. Return the potatoes to a hot oven for a few minutes for the juices to mingle and serve immediately. An extra sumptuous version is made with oysters. If you think shellfish might be a problem, then cook some mushrooms for the filling.

One of my favourite potato dishes is to cook them in their jackets, slice off the top, hollow out the soft part and use the potato as a hand-warming container for homemade soup.

And to accompany any, or all, of this food, cider or beer suggests itself rather than wine. Instead of a table of cocktail fixings, have a selection of ales and lagers, or a collection of English and French ciders.

pot-roast pork with barbecue sauce

A piece of beef, from the blade bone, can be cooked with the same ingredients, until it just falls off the bone.

serves 12

3kg (6lb) shoulder or leg of pork

4 tbsps flour

½ tsp each ground mace, freshly ground black pepper, cloves, cinnamon and cardamom

3 tbsps olive oil or lard

2 large onions, peeled and thickly sliced

4 celery sticks, trimmed and cut into 4 pieces

2 carrots and leeks, peeled, trimmed and sliced

2 small turnips, peeled and diced

500ml (18fl oz) beer, cider or good dry red wine

2–3 sprigs of thyme

2 bay leaves

Have the skin removed from the joint, and have it scored as well.

Mix the flour and spices, and lightly coat the meat with it. Heat the olive oil or lard in a heavy casserole, and brown the meat all over. Remove, and put to one side while you brown the vegetables all over. Put these to one side while you deglaze the pan with some of the beer, cider or wine, scraping up any residues that have stuck to the bottom.

Put the vegetables back in the casserole and place the pork on top, covering it with its skin. Tuck in the herbs, add the de-glazing liquid, cover, and cook very slowly on top of the stove, or in a preheated oven at about 150°C/300°F/ gas mark 3, or even lower, for 3–3½ hours. This should result in a juicily tender piece of meat, but longer will not hurt it. Add a little of the remaining beer, cider or wine liquid from time to time or, if you are letting the meat cook in your absence, add half of it before you go out, and then, when ready to serve, boil up the rest with the cooking juices to make a good gravy.

Slice the meat, and serve it with plenty of gravy and smooth mashed potatoes, or if cooking the meat in the oven, bake a few jacket potatoes. You can thicken the sauce by sieving some of the cooked vegetables into it.

The pork skin will not, of course, crisp to crackling, as it is cooked in moist not dry heat, but it adds plenty of flavour and bastes the meat as it cooks.

barbecue sauce

serves 6 to 8

- 1 onion, peeled and grated
- 2 garlic cloves, finely chopped
- 1 jalapeno chilli pepper, seeded and sliced
- 1 tbsp olive oil or lard
- 2 tbsps tomato purée
- 4 tbsps strong black coffee
- 2 tbsps Worcestershire sauce
- 4 tbsps each cider and cider vinegar
- ½ tsp chilli powder, or more to taste
- 2 tbsps light or dark muscovado sugar

Fry the onion, garlic and pepper in the oil or lard until the onion is translucent, then stir in the remaining ingredients and cook gently for 5–10 minutes before serving with the meat.

Sharon's quick baked beans

See p.272.

potato loaf

As an accompaniment to a roast, or grilled meat, consider making a potato loaf, which can cook in the oven at the same time as the meat. It is particularly good with roast lamb or chicken.

serves 6

1kg (2lb) waxy potatoes

salt

freshly ground black pepper

a piece of Parmesan or other hard cheese

3 eggs

250ml (8fl oz) whipping or single cream

handful of herbs, such as chives, thyme and parsley

Peel, parboil and thinly slice the potatoes. Line a 1kg (2lb) terrine or loaf tin with greased foil, and then layer the potatoes, seasoning each layer and sprinkling with a little grated cheese. Beat the eggs with the cream and plenty of finely chopped herbs. Pour this over the potatoes, grate more cheese on top, and bake in a preheated oven at 180°C/350°F/gas mark 4 for an hour or so. Turn out, slice and serve.

grilled marshmallow fruit skewers

serves 12

- 3 very thick slices of white bread, crusts removed
- 2 tbsps rum
- 2 tbsps light muscovado sugar
- 1 egg, lightly beaten
- 2 large mangoes
- 1 pineapple
- 3–4 bananas
- juice of 1–2 lemons or limes
- 2–3 dozen marshmallows
- 12 wooden skewers, soaked in water for 30 minutes

Cut each slice of bread into four, giving you twelve cubes. Beat the rum, sugar and egg together, and dip the bread in this. Peel the fruit and cut into chunks, rubbing lemon or lime juice all over to stop them discolouring. Thread the bread cubes, fruit and marshmallows on the skewers and place under a hot grill, turning to brown them all over. Serve immediately.

soup 'n' sandwiches

One of my favourite casual meals is the one I make at home when Tom and I stop work in the middle of the day for a snack. As breakfast is unlikely to have been more than a piece of toast with coffee, the snack is substantial. If it is not a bowl of pasta, it will almost certainly be a sandwich, perhaps with a bowl of soup.

But what sort of sandwich? With luck, there will be one or two covered dishes of leftovers in the fridge, some roast chicken perhaps, and some coleslaw or cooked asparagus. Or some grilled vegetables. With those I'll add some mozzarella. If there's roast pork or meatloaf, I'll go and hunt for a jar of my homemade chutney.

It is difficult to improve on sandwiches as the ultimate casual meal, satisfying, comforting, easy to eat and relatively inexpensive. There are some fabulous ones on the market, but once you get started it is remarkably easy to come up with your own fillings and bread combinations. Here are ten meals in a bun to get you started. I particularly favour muffins, as they are quite sturdy, but ciabatta or a baguette will do just as well, as will wholemeal bread, rye, or what you will.

Bacon and egg – to be enjoyed at any time of day, take crisply cooked bacon rashers, thick grilled tomato slices, grilled black pudding slices or cooked sausage, and scrambled eggs or a one- or two-egg omelette folded to fit slices of granary bread or a muffin.

Chicken and avocado – take some diced or shredded chicken and mix with finely chopped, cooked spinach and slices of ripe avocado, season lightly and mix with a creamy lemon dressing, in wholemeal or granary bread, or in a split ciabatta bun or baguette.

Curry club – this is a club sandwich with a difference; devilled egg and curried chicken is layered with bread and greenery, spread with spicy mango chutney, lime pickle and butter.

Liguria – in a split ciabatta bun, spread with butter mixed with finely chopped dried tomatoes, layer sliced mozzarella, avocado and ripe tomatoes with plenty of fresh basil leaves.

The Mexican blanket – use roast beef with a subtle, fruity but not too hot salsa, and some guacamole and shredded lettuce, wrapped in a warmed floury tortilla, spread first with cream cheese.

The Oyster House fish sandwich – use a soft, large bun or bap, spread with tartare sauce, and in it place a freshly fried or grilled fillet of fish, trimmed to shape, sprinkled with Tabasco. A cold fish sandwich is also delicious, especially with the addition of thinly sliced marinated cucumber. Try it with cold grilled mackerel fillet.

Penang – sliced chicken breast rubbed with a little Thai curry paste, sandwiched in a muffin, spread with peanut butter mixed with finely chopped preserved ginger, some shredded iceberg lettuce and diced pineapple.

Roast lamb – left over from the Sunday joint, instead of a shepherd's pie, use pink slices of tender roast lamb and a spoonful or two of ratatouille, between slices of olive and herb bread, or tomato bread, spread with olive paste or tapenade.

Roast pork – use sliced roast pork, and stuffing if you have it, mixed salad leaves and fruit butter, apple sauce or chutney on a wholemeal muffin.

Topkapi – spread some pitta bread with hummus and fill with very thinly sliced roast lamb, watercress and a mixture of yoghurt, chopped dried apricots and flaked almonds. Roasted aubergine, peeled peppers and courgette slices can replace the lamb in a vegetarian version.

And here are some soups to mix and match with the sandwiches.

tomato and coriander soup

For a more sophisticated version, make a coriander cream to swirl into the soup. In a mortar, grind the coriander leaves with sea salt, pepper and nutmeg, and then gradually blend in the cream, a couple of tablespoons is plenty, once the coriander has been pounded to a paste. This is also extremely good with carrot or potato soup.

serves 2

300ml (½ pint) homemade tomato sauce

300ml (½ pint) stock, or the water in which you have cooked potatoes

1–2 tbsps fresh coriander leaves, chopped

salt

freshly ground black pepper

grated nutmeg

cream to finish (optional)

If like mine, your tomato sauce is chunky, sieve it into a saucepan. Add the stock, and bring to the boil. Stir in the coriander, simmer for 5 minutes, season and serve, with or without a swirl of cream.

cream of potato soup

serves 4

2 rashers streaky bacon

1 onion, peeled and finely chopped

1 carrot, peeled and finely chopped

1 celery stick, peeled and finely chopped

1 small turnip, peeled and finely chopped

1 leek, peeled and finely chopped

2 tbsps flour

1.25 litres (2 pints) stock

500g (1lb) potatoes, peeled and diced

salt

freshly ground pepper

good pinch cumin

150ml (¼ pint) soured cream

Discard the rind and dice the bacon. Fry it until the fat runs, then add the vegetables and fry gently. When soft, sprinkle on the flour, stir in, and gradually add the stock. Add the potatoes and a little seasoning, and cook until the potatoes are tender. Rub through a sieve. Stir in the cream, bring back to the boil, and add more seasoning if necessary.

curried cream of cauliflower soup

In summer, this makes a very good chilled soup.

serves 4

  1 onion, peeled and thinly sliced

  1tbsp sunflower oil

  1–2 tbsps mild or medium curry paste

  1 small cauliflower, separated into florets

  2 tbsps flour

  600ml (1 pint) vegetable or chicken stock

  200ml (7fl oz) coconut milk

  salt

  freshly ground black pepper

Gently fry the onion in the oil until wilted and transparent. Stir in the curry paste and the cauliflower. When this is well coated, sprinkle with the flour, stir until it is absorbed, then add the stock. Bring to the boil and simmer until the vegetables are soft.

Remove from the heat, and put in a blender with the coconut milk. Blend until smooth, then return the soup to the pan. Bring back to the boil and add salt and pepper as necessary.

minestrone

serves 6

250g (8oz) cannellini beans, soaked overnight

1.5 litres (3 pints) ham, chicken or vegetable stock

1 tbsp olive oil

1 onion

1 carrot

1 celery stick

1 leek

1 small white turnip

6 ripe tomatoes

garlic cloves, to taste, peeled and crushed or finely chopped

¼ cabbage, shredded

handful of green beans (optional)

salt

freshly ground black pepper

pesto (optional)

Place the beans in a heavy saucepan, cover with stock and simmer while you prepare the rest of the vegetables.

Heat the olive oil in a frying pan. Peel and finely chop the vegetables, removing the seeds from the tomatoes. Turn these in the olive oil, together with the garlic. When lightly browned, add them to the pot of beans, together with the rest of the stock. Bring to the boil, cover, and cook in a preheated oven at 170°C/325°F/gas mark 3 or on top of the stove on a low heat for 2–3 hours.

About 30 minutes before the end of the cooking time, add the cabbage and green beans, if using. Season to taste, and allow to cook until the green vegetables are just done. Stir in a spoonful of pesto sauce or some extra olive oil before serving, and hand round with it a chunk of Parmesan for grating. This is, if anything, even better the next day, reheated and poured over a thick slice of toasted wholemeal bread, a version of the Tuscan *ribollita*, which is why I always make more than I need for one meal.

lentil and bacon soup with wild mushrooms

serves 6

approx 1kg (2lb) knuckle of bacon, soaked for several hours

300g (10oz) green or Puy lentils

25–50g (1– 2oz) dried ceps, cut up small

2 litres (4 pints) water

approx 200g (7oz) finely chopped vegetables chosen according to preference:
    leeks, carrots, onions, celery and watercress

fresh parsley, chopped, for garnish

Put the bacon, lentils, ceps and water in a large stockpot. Bring to the boil, and skim the surface a few times. Partially cover, and simmer for an hour, until the lentils are tender. Add the vegetables, and cook for a further 30 minutes or so. Remove the knuckle of bacon, discard the skin and bone, chop some of the meat, and put it in the soup. Stir in some freshly chopped parsley before serving, if you wish.

dublin coddle

serves 6

500g (1lb) coarse pork sausages, with herbs and/or spices, if you like

350g (12oz) piece of bacon or gammon, diced

1.25 litres (2 pints) water

500g (1lb) leeks, sliced and rinsed

1kg (2lb) potatoes, peeled and sliced or diced

4 tbsps finely chopped parsley

freshly ground black pepper

Slip the sausages out of their skins and shape each into three or four small patties. Brown them and the bacon all over, and then put in a saucepan with the water, vegetables, parsley and pepper, and simmer for 45 minutes or so, until all are tender and the flavours well amalgamated. Serve in deep soup bowls, or from a tureen, with plenty of soda bread.

---

fresh pea soup

serves 6

50g (2oz) unsalted butter

bunch of spring onions, trimmed, sliced and rinsed

750g (1½lb) peas, shelled weight

1 tbsp flour

1.5 litres (3 pints) vegetable or chicken stock

salt

freshly ground black pepper

young sage or mint leaves

100ml (3½fl oz) whipping cream

Melt the butter in a heavy saucepan and in it gently cook the spring onions until wilted, but not coloured. Add the peas and cook, covered, for 5 minutes. Sprinkle on the flour and stir in. Add the stock, bring to the boil, and simmer for 5–8 minutes, or until the peas are just tender. Blend and sieve, and reheat to serve. Or cool and refrigerate to serve chilled. As a garnish, crush the herb leaves with salt, chop finely and fold into the whipped cream. Top each serving of soup with a heaped teaspoonful of herb cream. It makes a pleasant chilled soup in summer.

spiced carrot and seville orange soup

serves 4

  1 large onion, peeled and thinly sliced

  500g (1lb) carrots, peeled and sliced

  1 small to medium potato, peeled and diced

  2 tbsps extra virgin olive oil

  1 tbsp ground coriander

  1 tsp ground cumin

  grated zest of a Seville orange, and 4 tbsps juice

  1.25 litres (2 pints) vegetable or chicken stock

  salt

  freshly ground black pepper

  fresh coriander to garnish

Fry the onion, carrot and potato in the oil until the onion is wilted. Stir in the spices and cook for a few minutes. Add the orange zest and juice, then the stock. Bring to the boil and simmer until the vegetables are soft. Blend or sieve and return the mixture to the saucepan. Bring back to the boil, season with salt and pepper, and stir in the finely shredded coriander leaves before serving.

celeriac and chestnut soup

serves 4

> 1 onion, peeled and thinly sliced
>
> 2 leeks, trimmed, sliced and well rinsed
>
> 1 slender carrot, peeled and thinly sliced
>
> 1 tbsp extra virgin olive oil
>
> 1 litre (1¾ pints) chicken, turkey or goose stock
>
> 250g (8oz) piece of celeriac
>
> 150g (5oz) chestnut pieces, cooked
>
> handful of shredded cabbage
>
> 1 thick slice country bread, toasted on both sides
>
> salt
>
> freshly ground black pepper
>
> freshly grated Parmesan, to serve

Gently fry the onion, leeks and carrot in the olive oil until wilted, then add the stock and celeriac, and simmer for 15–20 minutes. Add the chestnut pieces and cook for a further 5 minutes, then add the cabbage and cook for a further 5 minutes, just until it loses its crispness. Dice the toast and place it in the hot soup plates. Season the soup to taste and ladle over the bread. Parmesan can be handed round to grate into the soup.

The following soup recipes are meals in themselves, as is Dublin Coddle (p.195), and crusty bread is all that is needed to accompany them.

mussel, bean and chorizo stew

If you cannot get whole chorizo, the sliced chorizo sold in supermarkets can be used, cut into shreds.

serves 2

- 1 small onion, peeled and sliced
- 2 celery sticks, trimmed and diced
- 1 tbsp extra virgin olive oil
- 300ml (½ pint) light chicken or fish stock
- 1 × 400g can cannellini, haricot or other white beans, drained
- 1 litre (2 pints) mussels
- 1 chorizo, diced
- 2 tbsps finely chopped parsley
- freshly ground pepper
- fresh mint, chopped (optional)

Fry the onion and celery in the oil until wilted, then add the stock, bring to the boil and cook until the vegetables are soft. Add the beans.

Meanwhile, prepare the mussels by scrubbing, cleaning, rinsing and steaming until they open. Strain the juices into the pan and, when cool enough to handle, remove the mussels from the shells. Sieve some of the beans to a purée and thus thicken the soup.

Add the chorizo and the parsley. Bring the soup back to the boil, season with pepper, and drop in the mussels. Allow them to heat through, then serve. A little chopped fresh mint is very good with this too.

chicken, prawn and coconut soup with rice noodles

This recipe is based on *laksa*, the fragrant hot and sour soup I first tasted in Malaysia. It is a meal in a bowl, which makes it a useful dish for a casual supper or lunch.

serves 6

for the sambal

    4 shallots or 1 medium onion, peeled and finely chopped

    8 garlic cloves, peeled and crushed

    6 tbsps groundnut oil

    4 dried chillies, soaked and chopped

    3 ripe tomatoes, roughly chopped

    1 tsp sugar

    1 tsp ground coriander seeds

    1 tsp ground cumin seeds

Gently fry the shallots and garlic in the oil until soft. Add the rest of the ingredients, bring to the boil, cook for a few minutes, then rub through a sieve. Put in a bowl, and cover until required.

for the soup

    300g (10oz) thin rice noodles or vermicelli

    300g (10oz) chicken breast

    600ml (1 pint) chicken stock

    600ml (1 pint) coconut milk

    15g (½ oz) tamarind paste or 2 tbsps lemon juice

    15g (½ oz) fresh ginger, grated

    4 lime leaves or 1 piece lemon grass

    3 tbsps shrimp paste

    300g (10oz) prawns

    75g (3oz) bean sprouts

    75g (3oz) cucumber, peeled, seeded and chopped

Blanch the noodles in boiling water for 3–4 minutes, then drain and refresh under cold water. Put to one side.

Poach the chicken breast for 8 minutes, remove and, when cool enough to handle, shred it and put to one side.

Pour the stock and coconut milk into a large saucepan, add the tamarind, ginger, lime leaves and shrimp paste. Bring to the boil and simmer for 5 minutes. Add the prawns, chicken, bean sprouts, cucumber and noodles. Bring back to the boil, then serve immediately, either in individual soup plates or in a large tureen, from which everyone can help themselves. Hand around separately a small dish of fried onion rings, one of sliced chillies, one of fresh coriander leaves and one containing the *sambal* or spicy sauce.

light entertainment

Sometimes, whether it is a particular time of year, or a particular place, one has a feeling of being over-entertained. For these circumstances, I offer suggestions and recipes for some simple, light suppers after too much feasting. My interpretation of light has nothing to do with 'lite', or with mean substitutes for the real thing, and everything to do with fabulously fresh and wholesome ingredients, served raw, or briefly cooked, to retain the taste, colour, texture and wholesomeness.

Home-grown vegetables are always welcome, sweet and nutty, and excellent candidates for the juicer or for a platter of crudités. As well as the usual carrots, celery and beetroot, look for fennel, mooli, also known as white radish, and celeriac. And supplement these with jicama, which is to be found in Asian and Caribbean markets, or in the exotic vegetable section of the supermarket. Shaped like a spinning top with a buff-coloured skin, the flesh is white, pleasingly sweet, with a juicy crispness. I have always used it raw. A real appetite sharpener is to dip the peeled slices in lime juice, and then, partially, in a little chilli powder, as they do in Mexico. Alternatively, it is excellent cut into batons and served with other raw vegetables.

Bagna cauda, the Piedmontese winter dish, is the perfect accompaniment to raw vegetables, and it makes an excellent dish for casual entertaining. In Piedmont, the vegetables will include strips of pepper, for dipping into the bubbling, pungent, communal pot of anchovy, garlic and olive oil.

Should your vegetables go into the juicer, do not waste the pulp, but make a vegetable broth to serve as a first course or a warming snack, perfect with rice cakes. Simply put the vegetable pulp in a large saucepan, cover with water and simmer for an hour, then strain, cool and refrigerate until required.

Fish, when you can buy it very fresh, is delicious raw. Thinly sliced, delicately seasoned and gently bathed in a little olive oil, it takes on a velvety, melt-in-the-mouth quality. For years, a favourite has been raw smoked haddock, brushed with olive or hazelnut oil and sprinkled with lime or lemon juice just before serving. I also prepare scallops in the same way, sometimes showering the fish with chopped chives and garlic chives.

When cooking fish, timing is crucial. Fillets cook in minutes, which makes them ideal for the notion of light suppers. I like to cook fish in its own juices, on a bed of vegetables. Use thinly sliced celery and cucumber with the watery core removed, diced or sliced; young spinach and oriental leaves; leeks thinly sliced or cut into strips; matchsticks of celeriac; in fact anything that will cook in the five minutes needed to cook the fish. Even traditional brassicas, such as cabbage, do well if finely shredded. Only after more than five minutes' cooking do they become sulphurous and disagreeable.

Any aromatics should be added to the fish or vegetables before you begin cooking, so that the flavours have time to develop. For me, certain combinations work particularly well: sliced monkfish rubbed with soy sauce and a little Chinese five spice powder on a bed of baby bok choi; organic salmon fillets seasoned with a little mace or nutmeg, salt and pepper, on a bed of spinach; smoked haddock on a bed of leeks or celeriac flavoured with grain mustard.

Citrus fruit, too, is perfect for tired palates, and since much of our entertaining falls in the winter months, the timing is perfect, for the best citrus fruit reaches us then. To round off such a delicious supper, it would be a pity to stray too far from this agreeable digestibility. Make a fresh ginger syrup and freeze it to a ginger sorbet. Use the juicer to create unusual tropical or citrus fruit combinations and freeze to a granita. A combination of English dessert and cooking apples makes a fabulous juice; freeze or make into a jelly. My dessert recipe below is slightly more ambitious, but hugely versatile, and adaptable through all the fruit seasons. But first, a vitamin-packed vegetable juice cocktail to kick-start jaded palates.

zinger martini

serves 4

1 cucumber
6 large celery sticks
handful of parsley
bunch of watercress
small piece of fresh ginger
1–2 lemon grass sticks
2 lime leaves, if available

Roughly chop the vegetables and juice them, together with the ginger, lemon grass and lime leaves. Pour into Martini glasses and serve with a cube of cucumber on a cocktail stick.

mulled vegetable broth

serves 4

800ml (28fl oz) vegetable broth – *see* p.202

slice of fresh ginger

8 green cardamom pods, crushed

6 cloves

1 stick cinnamon

to serve

salt

freshly ground black pepper

4 cinnamon sticks

Put all the ingredients in a saucepan, bring to the boil and infuse for 30 minutes. Scoop out the aromatics, bring back to the boil, season sparingly with salt and pepper and serve in tea glasses or cups, with a stick of cinnamon.

pink grapefruit and smoked salmon salad
with avocado and chicory

serves 4

2 ripe avocados

red chicory

2–3 pink grapefruit

200g (7oz) smoked salmon

for the dressing

grapefruit juice

walnut or olive oil

salt

freshly ground black pepper

Peel and slice the avocados, separate the chicory leaves and arrange on plates. Divide the grapefruit into slices or segments, as you prefer, removing the skin and as much pith as possible. Arrange on top of the avocado and chicory, alternating with folds of smoked salmon. Make a little dressing with grapefruit juice, walnut or olive oil, salt and pepper and spoon it over the salad just before serving.

ceviche

This makes a delicious and attractive appetizer when served in mussel shells. You can either use a single fish or, for a more elaborate dish, use a trio; smoked haddock, scallops and lemon sole make a pleasing combination.

serves 4

300–400g (10–14oz) freshest fish

1 shallot, peeled and finely chopped

zest and juice of ½ lime

2 tomatoes, seeded and diced

1 red and 1 green pepper, peeled, seeded and diced small

salt

freshly ground black pepper

Dice the fish very small, having removed any skin, bone, sinew and other unwanted bits. Mix with the remaining ingredients and spoon into shells, ramekins, Martini glasses or what you will.

bagna cauda

This olive oil, garlic and anchovy sauce is worth making in double quantities, if you like it, because it makes an excellent pasta sauce; you might want to add some chopped thyme or marjoram.

serves 4 to 6

   6–8 garlic cloves, peeled and chopped

   few grains of coarse sea salt

   2 × 40g cans anchovies, drained of their oil

   400ml (14fl oz) extra virgin olive oil

   approx 500g (1lb) prepared raw vegetable strips, including fennel, red and
      yellow peppers, carrots and celery

Crush the garlic on a board with the salt. Chop and then crush the anchovies into the garlic and transfer to a small saucepan on a low heat. Stir in the olive oil gradually, and raise the heat until the mixture is a bubbling mass. Transfer the saucepan to a small burner on the table and hand round the vegetables for each to dip into the *bagna cauda*.

smoked haddock with leeks and grain mustard

Chicken breasts, split horizontally, can be cooked in the same way, and go well with any of the vegetables I have suggested. Unlike the fish, the chicken will, of course, need to be thoroughly cooked.

serves 4

6–7 large leeks, trimmed, very thinly sliced and well rinsed

2 tbsps grain mustard

4 × 150–200g (5–7oz) pieces of undyed smoked haddock fillet, skin removed

freshly ground black pepper

Mix the leeks, while still wet, with the grain mustard and place in the bottom of a casserole with a tightly fitting lid. Place the fish fillets on top, season with pepper and cover with the lid or, in the absence of a lid, foil.

Set the casserole on a moderate to high heat and, once you can hear the pot beginning to seethe, or see it (if you have a saucepan or casserole with a glass lid), time the cooking for 4 minutes, then have a look at the fish. It may be cooked, or it may require another minute or so depending on thickness. The fish should still retain a slight translucence in the middle, as it will continue cooking once it is removed from the heat. (Cooking fish until it flakes is overcooking it, in my view.) Spoon the leeks and any juices into heated soup plates, and serve the fish on top.

yoghurt blancmange with orange and honey-poached cranberries

serves 4

500g carton thick Greek yoghurt

3 sheets leaf gelatine or 3 tsps gelatine granules

200g (7oz) cranberries, fresh or frozen

250ml (8fl oz) fresh orange juice

grated zest of 1 orange

1 cinnamon stick

honey or light muscovado sugar, to taste

Drain the whey from the carton. Spoon the yoghurt into a saucepan and clean the yoghurt container. Soften the gelatine in 2–3 tbsps of water, then heat gently until it is dissolved. Stir it into the yoghurt and gently heat to blood temperature. Stir until smooth, allow to cool somewhat, then pour the mixture back into the yoghurt pot. When cool, refrigerate it until set.

To prepare the cranberries, put them in a saucepan with the orange juice, zest and cinnamon and simmer gently until they just pop. Stir in sugar or honey to taste and, when ready to serve, remove the cinnamon stick. Turn the set yoghurt out on to a plate, pour a few of the cranberries on top, the rest around it. You can, of course, make the blancmange in individual pots or jelly moulds.

grapefruit and campari sorbet

serves 4

600ml (1 pint) pink or white grapefruit juice

200ml (7fl oz) sugar syrup made from an equal volume of sugar and water

175ml (6fl oz) Campari

Mix together all the ingredients, then freeze in a sorbetière or ice-cream maker. If you freeze it in a container in the freezer, it will need stirring from time to time to ensure a smoothly frozen mixture. If you can put the frozen mixture in the food processor for the last 'stirring', I find that gives very smooth results.

impromptu entertaining

Even the most organized host or hostess will sometimes be caught unawares. And how boring entertaining would be if that were never the case. Sometimes it will simply be a spur of the moment invitation. You're having drinks with friends in the Groucho and your better half says, 'Why don't you come back for dinner?' Thinks I, why can't we have dinner here? On another occasion, the two friends you've invited for dinner phone you just as they are about to get into a taxi to announce that they are bringing their neighbour with them, and 'You don't mind, do you?' Oh no. Quickly unset the table, pull out the extra leaf, and re-lay it while you think of how you are going to turn the four partridges into five. And if that worries you, multiply that to the larger scale of diplomatic entertaining, when the twenty invited for a sit-down dinner rapidly approaches thirty.

Clearly, in cases such as this, a well-planned store cupboard and/or a well-stocked freezer will solve the problem. Usually. How comforting to be able to take out an extra summer pudding and pack of smoked salmon. But a couple of fillets of beef buried deep in the back of the freezer are not much use if you need them NOW.

Pasta fits the bill perfectly for delicious food that can be speedily cooked at the end of a busy day, and it is as good to eat as it is enjoyable to cook. It is tempting to keep half a dozen types of pasta in the cupboard – thin for delicate sauces, thick for chunky sauces, short ones for baking. This is what I usually do, and then find myself with lots of packets containing no more than a handful or so of each. Then it's time to make minestrone, Tuscan bean and pasta soup, chickpea and pasta soup, or a mixed pasta salad. These are all very good, but if storage space is in short supply, the best all-purpose pasta is *spaghetti alla chitarra*. It is square cut, which helps it hold meat or fish sauce, but it is not too thick for a more delicate sauce. A good second choice is linguine, a flat, elliptical pasta, but not as broad as tagliatelle. I keep my pasta in an old-fashioned glass sweetie jar, which holds about 3kg.

There are many good brands of Italian-made dried pasta available, including supermarket own-label brands. I have cooked good Greek-made and Swiss-made pasta, which I also recommend. Fresh egg pasta cooks more quickly than dried pasta, but often is so stodgy that I much prefer to cook dried pasta and sacrifice the extra few minutes.

In case you do not know it, let me pass on the foolproof way of cooking dried pasta that I learned in Italy years ago. It saves on fuel too. Make a note of the cooking time given on the packet. Have your pan of water boiling and put in the pasta. Boil it for two minutes uncovered, three for very thick pasta, remove from the heat, put the lid on and leave for the full time stated on the packet. Drain and proceed in the usual way. The pasta is not off the heat long enough to cool it down.

All the Italian cooks I know are adamant about salting the water before you add the pasta, and will even taste the water to check it. I have become accustomed to cook my pasta in unsalted water and do not mind it at all.

No Italian cook of my acquaintance would dream of sullying their beautifully cooked pasta with the contents of a jar of sauce. The point of these sauces has quite passed me by. Carbonara is not a sauce. It is several ingredients tossed into freshly cooked pasta, namely bits of fried pancetta, cream and raw egg. What could be quicker than that? Or chopped fresh tomatoes wilted in a little olive oil and a small handful of shredded basil leaves, black pepper and coarse sea salt. Bottled pasta sauces are dull, flat and lifeless things, with preservatives, gums and stabilizers to keep them 'fresh' and bright.

Nothing could be simpler than to make a quick pasta sauce for two. While the pasta is cooking, halve three ripe tomatoes and squeeze out and discard the seeds. Trim, slice and thoroughly rinse two leeks, and drop these into the cooking pasta about three minutes before the end of cooking. Roughly cut up the tomato, and season it with salt and pepper. Dice some soft goat's cheese or mozzarella. Drain the pasta and leeks when the cooking time is up, tip them into a large warm bowl, or back into the saucepan, with some fruity olive oil. Turn the pasta in the oil, and stir in the tomato and cheese. Serve immediately, with more freshly ground black pepper and Parmesan.

This is a very good method for introducing vegetables to a pasta dish.

Instead of leeks, you can use broccoli florets, thin green beans, watercress, rocket, spinach, finely sliced fennel, asparagus tips in season, and match them with appropriate flavourings and ingredients to stir in with the oil; for example, anchovies and garlic with the broccoli, shredded ham with the asparagus, pesto with the beans, smoked salmon with the fennel, you get the idea.

And quicker still, if you have some good gravy or sauce left over from a Sunday roast, you can make a simple and very good sauce by reheating it thoroughly and stirring it into freshly cooked and drained pasta, which you also mix with fresh watercress or rocket.

You will note from the recipes below, with the exception of the macaroni cheese and the baked pasta dish, that I have not indicated quantities of pasta. In Italy, it is usually eaten before a main course of fish or meat, and possibly after a plate of *salumi* or antipasto. There, an amount of 50–115g (2–4oz) is usually judged sufficient, but even that allows for wide variation of appetite. In the Anglo-Saxon world, pasta has become the convenience food par excellence, and most of us eat it as the main course of a meal, probably with rather too much sauce for the Italian taste. Generally, when I cook for the two of us, I divide a 500g pack in two, keeping the remaining 250g for another day.

macaroni cheese

This first recipe has been part of the British culinary repertoire for so long, at least two hundred years, that it hardly counts as Italian any more. It is, nevertheless, absolutely delicious. Very grand versions are now served in posh restaurants, with the addition of crab, lobster and truffles. Certainly, a thread of white truffle oil added just before serving gives it a most appetizing scent.

serves 4 to 6

500g (1lb) ziti, macaroni, or penne
2 tbsps fresh breadcrumbs
50g (2oz) butter
300ml (½ pint) light cream or thin béchamel
125g (4oz) ricotta, crumbled
1 mozzarella cheese, sliced and diced
75g (3oz) freshly grated Parmesan
75g (3oz) Dolcelatte or Gorgonzola cheese
freshly ground black pepper
pinch of nutmeg

Cook the pasta for about 10 minutes in boiling water, then drain. Rinse and drain again. While the pasta is cooking, fry the breadcrumbs in half the butter, then put to one side. Heat the cream or sauce in a saucepan, and stir in the cheeses until melted. Season with pepper and nutmeg, then stir into the pasta, together with the remaining butter. Pour into a buttered, ovenproof dish, scatter the breadcrumbs on top, and bake in a preheated oven at 180°C/350°F/ gas mark 4 for 15–20 minutes.

Alternatively, you can cook the pasta fully, drain it, and immediately mix it with the cream and melted cheese and remaining butter. Scatter the bread-crumbs on top, and finish under a hot grill for a few minutes.

pasta with sage, ham and peas in cream

serves 2

enough pasta for 2 people – *see* p.213

150ml (¼ pint) double or whipping cream, or crème fraîche

good sprig of fresh sage, plus 2–3 leaves crushed with salt

small can or jar of petits pois

2–3 slices prosciutto, shredded (the cheaper ends and offcuts can be used)

While the pasta is cooking, scald the cream and sage sprig. Remove the sprig, and stir in the crushed leaves and the peas. Add the prosciutto, then fold the sauce into the cooked and drained pasta.

pasta with tomato, anchovy and caper sauce

serves 2

enough pasta for 2 people – *see* p.213

200g can chopped tomatoes in juice, drained

2–3 garlic cloves, peeled and sliced

½ × 40g can anchovies in oil, drained and chopped

1 tbsp capers, well rinsed

4 black olives, stoned and chopped

While the pasta is cooking, put the tomatoes in a sauté or small frying pan, preferably non-stick, and cook until they have lost much of their liquid. Add the rest of the ingredients, and cook together for a few minutes.

Freshly ground pepper and some torn-up basil can be stirred into the sauce when you mix it with the cooked and drained pasta.

pasta with prawns and fennel

serves 2

enough pasta for 2 people – *see* p.213

1 small fennel bulb, finely diced

1 tbsp butter

approx 125g (4–5oz) shell-off coldwater prawns

While the pasta is cooking, fry the fennel in the butter. When cooked, add the prawns and any juices and heat them through. Mix the prawns, fennel and any cooking juices with the cooked and drained pasta.

Parmesan is not usually served with shellfish, but fresh breadcrumbs fried in butter are a delicious alternative.

orecchiette with broccoli and peppers

serves 2

orecchiette pasta for 2, or other small chunky pasta, such as farfalle or fusille

200g (7oz) broccoli, broken into the smallest florets and the stalk peeled and
    thinly sliced

extra virgin olive oil

1 garlic clove, peeled and chopped

1 small red pepper (not too hot), seeded, or ¼ tsp dried chilli flakes

salt

pecorino cheese

Put the orecchiette in boiling water, and cook for about 8–10 minutes. Drop in the broccoli, and cook for a further 3–4 minutes. Drain, toss in a little oil, and transfer to a very hot bowl.

Meanwhile, crush the garlic, chilli and salt in a mortar, and work in about 3 tablespoons extra virgin olive oil. Stir this into the cooked and drained pasta, and serve with flakes of pecorino on top.

baked fish and pasta

This makes a very good weekend supper dish for friends and family. Serve a plate of salami and prosciutto first, follow the pasta with a salad and cheese, and finish with a fruit fool for a very easy feast.

serves 6

- 500g packet pasta, such as penne, rigatoni or penne rigate
- 500g (1lb) firm white fish, filleted and skinned
- 250g (8oz) prepared shelled shellfish, such as clams, prawns and/or mussels
- 25g (1oz) butter
- 25g (1oz) flour
- 450ml (¾ pint) milk, skimmed, semi-skimmed or whole
- 150ml (¼ pint) dry white wine, or fish stock, according to taste
- 1 tbsp chopped fresh chives
- generous grating of nutmeg
- salt
- freshly ground black pepper
- 2 tbsps breadcrumbs
- 2 tbsps ground almonds

Cook the pasta for three quarters of the time stated on the packet. Drain, rinse and toss in a little olive oil or butter to stop it sticking.

Dice the fish into 2.5cm (1 inch) chunks. Make a béchamel sauce with the butter, flour, milk and wine or stock. Cook for 10 minutes, then add the herbs and seasoning. Combine the fish, sauce and pasta and spoon into a greased ovenproof dish. Mix together the breadcrumbs and almonds, and sprinkle over the dish before baking in a preheated oven at 180°C/350°F/gas mark 4 for 20–25 minutes.

Here are a few more dishes that can be put together with minimum fuss after a foray through store cupboard or refrigerator.

prawns with salmon roe

serves 4 to 6

500g (1lb) peeled prawns

150g (5oz) crème fraîche

2–3 tbsps homemade mayonnaise

2 tbsps finely chopped fresh dill

salt

freshly ground black pepper

lemon juice

salad leaves

100g (4oz) salmon roe

Finely chop the prawns, then mix with the crème fraîche, mayonnaise and dill, and season to taste with salt, pepper and lemon juice. Arrange some salad leaves on plates, and spoon on the prawn mixture. Spoon the salmon roe on top, and serve with hot toast.

snails with potatoes, bacon and mushrooms

serves 4

2 large potatoes

8 rashers thinly sliced smoked bacon or pancetta

4 shallots, peeled and finely chopped

extra virgin olive oil

200g (7oz) fresh chanterelles, oyster mushrooms or other mushrooms, sliced

25–50g (1–2oz) dried wild mushrooms, soaked in hot water for several hours

freshly ground black pepper

2 garlic cloves, peeled and crushed

2 tbsps finely chopped parsley

24 canned snails, drained

wine, vermouth or stock – *see* recipe

salad leaves (optional)

Scrub and halve the potatoes, parboil, then, when cool enough to handle, hollow out to make a nice bowl. Grill the bacon until crisp.

Gently fry the shallots in olive oil until soft, then stir in the mushrooms. While these are cooking, brush the potatoes with olive oil, and roast until golden and tender. Season the mushroom mixture with black pepper, and add the garlic, most of the parsley and the snails. Cook for 5 minutes or so, adding a dash of wine, or vermouth, or stock, if you want more juice. Place the potatoes on plates, with or without salad leaves, spoon the snails and mushrooms into the potatoes, and some gravy around them, and top with the bacon and the remaining parsley. Serve immediately.

panforte ice cream

Note that this recipe contains raw egg.

serves 4 to 6

600ml (1 pint) single cream

125g (4oz) golden caster sugar

8 egg yolks

150g (5oz) *panforte di Siena*, crushed to fine crumbs in a food processor

Pour the cream into a saucepan and bring gently to the boil. In a bowl, mix together the sugar and egg yolks, then pour on the scalded cream, stirring well. Pour back into the saucepan and simmer gently for a couple of minutes, stirring continuously. Do not let the custard boil or it will curdle. Stir in the panforte crumbs, remove from the heat, and allow to cool before refrigerating. This will also allow the flavours to infuse. Cover the surface with a butter paper or cling film to stop a skin from forming. When the mixture is cold, simply freeze it in an ice-cream maker or sorbetière. Remember to ripen or soften the ice cream in the refrigerator before serving; 15–20 minutes is usually about right for this.

chocolate and orange 'risotto'

serves 6

    50g (2oz) unsalted butter
    150g (5oz) pudding rice
    1 cinnamon stick
    1 litre (1¾ pints) skimmed milk, hot
    50g (2oz) caster sugar
    100g bar each of best quality white and dark chocolate
    zest and juice of 1 orange

Melt the butter in a saucepan and stir in the rice until well coated. Add the cinnamon stick and about 200ml (7fl oz) of the hot milk. Stir in the usual way for risotto and, when the milk has been absorbed, add another helping and stir well. Continue until all the milk has been absorbed and the rice is creamy. Use more milk, if necessary. Alternatively, bake the rice slowly in a preheated oven at 150°/300°F/gas mark 2 for 3 hours, as you would for a traditional rice pudding.

Stir in the sugar, and remove the cinnamon. Divide the rice among three smaller saucepans, or bowls set in a roasting tin of hot water. Into one, stir the orange juice; into another, stir most of the white chocolate, broken into pieces, and into the last, most of the dark chocolate, again, broken into pieces. Serve immediately, one helping of each in shallow soup plates. Scatter the orange zest on the orange-flavoured rice, and grate the remaining chocolate on the appropriate rice.

drinks parties and cocktail time

The best drinks parties are those where the food is mainly hot, savoury and copious. Forget about little chilled indigestible things on sticks or on damp mattresses of toast. One solution is to opt for scaled-down versions of real food, set out on a table or passed round on trays at not too infrequent intervals. Coffee cups, or indeed tea cups of hot consommé with cheese straws, small bowls of chilli, risotto or paella, miniature batter puddings baked with sliced sausages for 'toad-in-the-hole' are all very successful. Miniature hamburgers and Cornish pasties also go down particularly well, I find.

These are all substantial items, not pretty, decorative mouthfuls. The common theme to many of the recipes below is that they consist of a bland staple and something savoury. The fillings are also, almost, interchangeable. The snails and snail butter or the oysters or the oriental vegetables can be baked in the savoury batter, for example. The batter pudding recipe can also be increased and baked in a larger container to allow you to cut it into wedges for individual servings. The large version is particularly good with mussels and lightly cooked sliced leeks. The savoury batter pudding is probably the favourite canapé at home, as it is non-crumbly and the only thing, apart from crudités, that I tend to serve not sitting at the table. The range of fillings and flavourings is endless.

There are many more versions of the staple-plus-savoury theme: blinis or griddle cakes with soured cream and caviar, pizzas, large or small, with traditional or unusual toppings (I like cream cheese and smoked salmon on mine; this goes on after the pizza has been baked), and small bread cases. Make the latter by stamping rounds out of sliced buttered bread, pressing them into buttered bun tins and baking them until crisp. A spoonful of mushroom ragoût, cheese fondue or scrambled eggs mixed with chopped ham, smoked salmon, herbs or cheese, for example, make good fillings.

On the subject of spoons, I suggest 'spoon food' to replace the notion of fork food. For food that is too wet, slippery, crumbly or otherwise difficult to eat with the fingers, such as miniature steak tartare, quenelles of pâté, herb cream cheese or steamed won tons, put them in Chinese soup spoons and arrange on a platter or tray. The food is eaten from the spoon no plates, no forks, and easy to manage with the spoon in one hand and the glass in the other. In these you can also consider serving food that you would not normally associate with 'cocktail' food; a spoonful of risotto, chilli or kedgeree, for example. Have an empty tray or receptacle nearby for the used spoons. Parma ham and smoked salmon slices can be wound round forks or breadsticks for similarly easy handling.

Another alternative is to look to the traditional British savoury, highly flavoured and very more-ish, such as stuffed prunes, bacon-wrapped chicken livers and devilled eggs. Or look to the Asian super-markets for ready-made snacks for you to cook at home, such as samosas and onion bhajis, or spring rolls and other dim sum.

Cheese straws, anchovy toast, won tons, quail's eggs in pastry barquettes, savoury popovers and puffs, curls of smoked salmon on rye bread, all of these are good to serve at drinks parties, together with stuffed prunes, miniature sausages and tiny skewers of satay with accompanying peanut sauce.

Because you cannot have too many recipes for food for drinks parties, I have been delving into my collection acquired over the years on my travels. Curiously, many started life as quite different things, but have adapted themselves to just the sort of food to accompany a glass of chilled fino, a champagne cocktail, a tequila sunrise or a glass of wine.

Nigerian street food, for example, in the form of *akara* or bean cakes, is supremely tasty, not to mention substantial, as well as being inex-pensive and a good, bland foil for drinks. I prepared some once for a pre-Christmas cookery demonstration and was reminded, however, how time-consuming they were. First soak the beans, then rub off their skins, and then swill and swirl the skins away before grinding and pounding (in a food processor, if you wish). This stage can be prepared in advance, but the final mixing, incorporating the egg and frying, needs to be done at the last moment; if the mixture is allowed to stand, it separates and will not fry in neat cakes.

Jamon de serrano, or other cured ham, especially a chunky end piece, cut into slivers can be used to flavour fritters, and these, too, are an apposite match for the wines and aperitifs of the Iberian peninsula, including fresh sparkling cava from Penedes in Spain.

For those who do not like deep-frying, I suggest an Ecuadorian recipe, *llapingachos*, a small potato cake, with cheese and onion buried in the middle, which is then shallow-fried. These are traditionally served 'meal-size', sometimes with a fried egg on top. I have adapted the recipe to make small cakes, which are easy to eat with the fingers, especially if served in paper cases. A fried quail's egg can replace the hen's egg. Both these and the bean cakes would be excellent with the more powerful spirit-based drinks, whether a Bloody Mary, or a Tequila Slammer.

It is quite a sound idea to plan complimentary food and drink. For example, you might consider offering a selection of iced vodkas. *Zakouski* are the perfect accompaniments. Morsels of smoked, cured and raw fish are the main ingredients, particularly herrings and salmon, but also caviar, salmon roe and smoked fish. Rye bread, blinis or pumpernickel can be the base.

To go with champagne or champagne cocktails, you may want to offer something more delicate. Prawns and saffron cream in chicory leaves or hollowed-out cucumber cups, devilled quail's eggs, oyster pasties, grilled chicken liver and mushroom skewers, for example. If tequila is your drink, offer a platter of *fajitas*, a pile of warm flour tortillas, a bowl of guacamole and one of salsa, and let your guests fold up their own parcels of food. Or simply offer tortilla chips and a selection of salsas and dips.

A selection of ciders suggests savoury galettes and sweet crêpes, Brittany style. Make small ones, as these will be easier to roll up and eat. Or for a really eclectic feast, if you have time, space and plenty of helpers, just do street food, from all over the world, and mix up a good punch. The samosas and spring rolls I have already suggested can be supplemented with hot dogs, bagels, miniature lamb kebabs, satay and peanut sauce, fish and chips, deep-fried bean cakes, spiced chicken wings or what you will.

sample menu

The following is the menu we planned when I was invited to cook at the British Embassy in Cairo. It was to be a very British occasion, so I chose miniatures of the following traditional dishes, which were well received.

- Glamorgan sausages, Miniature Cornish pasties, Toad-in-the-hole, Yorkshire puddings, Scotch eggs, Baked potatoes with filling (using new potatoes and mushrooms, shrimps, quail's eggs, devilled chicken liver, etc)

- Cheddar cheese, celery, bread and pickles and beer

- English wines with farmhouse cheeses

- English dessert buffet: Treacle tart, Bakewell tart, Taffety tart, Bread and butter pudding, Fruit crumble, English trifle, Strawberries and cream, and Gooseberry fool.

food quantities for a drinks party

Allow the equivalent of eight to twelve pieces for each person over a two-hour period. The larger the number of people, the more variety you will need to provide. And if weather is a factor, think about serving more cold bites in summer and more hot ones in winter. Personally, and I know not everyone agrees with me, I prefer to have more hot snacks whatever the weather or season.

For ten to twenty people, you need a minimum of six cold and two hot savouries in summer, and four of each in winter. For thirty to forty people, or more, plan on eight cold savouries in summer, and five hot and three cold in the winter. In addition, one or two sweet mouthfuls is a perfect way of indicating to your guests that they are on the last course, as it were, and the party is about to come to an end. This is a useful plan whatever the size of your drinks party.

fish and shellfish

olive and anchovy savouries

makes about 18

125g (approx 4oz) plain flour

1 egg

200ml (7fl oz) water

100g (4oz) black olives, stoned and quartered

12 anchovy fillets, chopped

½ tsp chopped fresh thyme

salt

freshly ground black pepper

This uses a classic Yorkshire pudding batter. Beat together the flour, egg and water to make a smooth batter. Mix in the rest of the ingredients. Lightly oil bun tins, or use a non-stick tin, pour in the batter, and bake in a preheated oven at 200°C/400°F/gas mark 6 for 30–35 minutes. They should be quite dark golden brown and puffed up when cooked, though will sink somewhat when removed from the oven. Serve warm.

hot anchovy toast

makes 24

2 × 40g cans anchovies

200g (7oz) unsalted butter, softened

6 medium thick slices of sandwich loaf

Drain the oil from the cans of anchovies and mash them with the butter. Toast the bread, remove the crusts, spread with the anchovy paste and cut into fingers or triangles.

oyster pasties

makes 12

12 oysters

125g (approx 4oz) cabbage, finely shredded and blanched

freshly ground black pepper

75g (3oz) butter, softened

good pinch of mace

grated zest of ½ lemon, and a dash of juice

250g (8oz) flaky or shortcrust pastry

egg yolk and water glaze (optional)

Remove the oysters from their shells (keeping the juice for another dish, oyster sauce, perhaps). Mix together the remaining ingredients. Roll out the pastry, and cut into 12 rounds. Place a spoonful of the cabbage mixture in the centre of each, and place an oyster on top. Moisten the edges of the pastry rounds and fold over to make half circles, pressing the edges to seal. Then crimp the edges as if you were making a Cornish pasty. Brush with an egg yolk and water glaze if you wish, and bake in a preheated oven at 200°C/400°F/gas mark 6 for 10–15 minutes. Serve either hot or warm.

baked oysters and horseradish in potatoes

makes 12

12 small potatoes, weighing about 50g (2oz) each

25g (1oz) unsalted butter, melted

salt

freshly ground black pepper

25g (1oz) creamed or grated horseradish

12 oysters in their shells

Wash and scrub the potatoes. With a melon baller, scoop out a hollow in each potato large enough to hold an oyster, and remove a very thin slice from the bottom to allow it to lie flat. Put the hollowed-out potatoes in a pan of salted water, bring to the boil, and boil briskly until just cooked. Drain.

Brush the potatoes inside and out with melted butter, season lightly, spoon a little horseradish into each and stand on an oiled baking sheet. Put an oyster into each potato. Place in the top half of a preheated oven at 180°C/350°F/gas mark 4 and bake for 5–8 minutes. Serve immediately, with lemon wedges and a pepper grinder.

oysters in overcoats

Fresh mussels or queen scallops can be substituted for the oysters, and the overcoat can be made with blanched lettuce leaves instead of spinach.

makes 12

3 sheets filo pastry

12 spinach leaves

12 fresh oysters, well-drained and dried

salt

freshly ground white pepper

juice of ½ lemon

25g (1oz) unsalted butter, melted

Cut each sheet of pastry into 4 strips, and pile them, one on top of the other, on a damp tea towel. Wrap the towel round the pastry to prevent it from drying out. Remove the central rib from the spinach leaves, and blanch them by draping them over a colander and pouring boiling water over them. Refresh under cold water, then dry them carefully. Wrap each oyster carefully in a spinach leaf, lightly seasoning with salt and pepper and a drop of lemon juice.

Unwrap the pastry, and brush the top strip with some of the melted butter. Place a wrapped oyster at the bottom right-hand corner of the strip, the edge nearest you. Fold the pastry over the oyster so that the bottom edge now meets the left-hand side, to form a triangular shape. Now fold that triangle over so that the parcel is sealed, and continue folding over until the strip completely encloses the oyster in a triangular parcel. Make the other parcels in the same way. Place them on a baking sheet and bake in a preheated oven at 200°C/ 400°F/gas mark 4 for 8–10 minutes.

little oyster pies

makes 10

10 oysters

freshly ground black pepper

10 blanched lettuce leaves

175g (6oz) puff or flaky pastry

75g (3oz) butter, softened

4 anchovy fillets, chopped

good pinch of mace

2 tbsps soft white breadcrumbs

grated zest of ½ lemon

egg and water glaze (optional)

Remove the oysters from their shells, keeping the juice. Season lightly with pepper, and wrap in the lettuce leaves. Roll out the pastry and use to line tart tins, reserving enough to make lids. Mix the remaining ingredients, together with a little lemon juice and the strained oyster juice. Spoon some of this mixture into the pastry cases, place a wrapped oyster in the middle of each, cover with the remaining butter mixture and top with pastry lids. Brush with an egg yolk and water glaze if you wish, and bake in a preheated oven at 200°C/400°F/gas mark 6 for 10 minutes. Serve either hot or warm.

entertaining

thai-style crab cakes

makes 10 to 12

> 1 bunch spring onions, trimmed and thinly sliced
>
> 2 tbsps sesame oil
>
> 500g (1lb) white crab meat
>
> 1 egg yolk and 1 whole egg, separated
>
> 2 heaped tbsps fresh white breadcrumbs
>
> 2 tbsps each chopped garlic, chives, basil, coriander and mint
>
> 1–2 tsps chilli sauce
>
> finely chopped green or red chillies, to taste (optional)
>
> salt
>
> freshly ground black pepper
>
> 2 tbsps mayonnaise
>
> groundnut oil for frying

To make the crab cakes, mix together all the ingredients, except for the egg white and mayonnaise. Whisk the egg white to firm peaks, then fold, together with the mayonnaise, into the crab mixture. Shape the mixture into cakes – small, medium or large, depending on how you plan to serve them. As the cakes are very fragile, and if you have time, you may prefer to chill them before frying.

Heat the oil, or use a non-stick pan, and shallow-fry the cakes until golden brown on both sides. Serve warm or hot.

prawn toasts

These are excellent served with chilled fino.

makes 24

    250g (8oz) peeled prawns

    3 spring onions, trimmed, rinsed and roughly chopped

    a few basil or coriander leaves

    small piece of orange zest

    pinch of ground Szechuan pepper or black pepper

    2 tsps rice wine or dry Amontillado sherry

    1 tsp grated fresh ginger

    1 egg white

    2 tsps cornflour

    6 slices from a good quality large white tin loaf, crusts removed

    1 tbsp sesame seeds

    groundnut or sunflower oil for frying

Place all the ingredients, except for the bread, sesame seeds and oil, in a food processor and blend until you have a not too fine paste. Spread on the bread.

Heat about 2.5cm (1 inch) oil in a frying pan and, when hot, fry the toasts for 1–2 minutes on each side until golden brown. Drain on paper towels, then cut each slice into triangles or fingers, and serve hot.

prawn and saffron griddle cakes

Clams, cockles, whitebait, oysters or mussels can all replace the prawns if you wish.

makes 12 to 16

pinch of saffron threads, soaked in hot water

125g (4oz) plain flour

1 egg

150ml (5oz) buttermilk or yoghurt thinned down with water

2 scant tsps baking powder

250g (8oz) peeled prawns

salt

freshly ground black pepper

4 tbsps snipped chives, chervil or parsley, to taste

oil or butter for frying, or use a non-stick frying pan or griddle

Beat together the saffron water, flour, egg and buttermilk to form a thick batter. Heat the frying pan or griddle and, just before you are ready to cook, sprinkle in the baking powder and beat the batter again thoroughly. Then stir in the prawns, seasoning and herbs.

Pour a small ladleful of batter on to the pan. Do not shake the pan to spread the mixture – these should be small, quite thick, cakes. When the top surface looks matt and full of holes, flip the cake over and cook the other side for 2–3 minutes. You will probably be able to cook them in batches of four. Serve hot or warm.

prawns in saffron cream

makes 20

1kg (2lb) shell-on prawns

good pinch of saffron threads

450ml (¾ pint) double cream

150ml (¼ pint) plain yoghurt, crème fraîche or soured cream

2 tbsps finely chopped chervil, chives or parsley

salt

freshly ground black pepper

1–2 tsps grated orange or tangerine zest

20 chicory or small lettuce leaves

Peel the prawns and place in about 300ml (½ pint) water. Simmer for 5–10 minutes, strain and reduce the liquid by half. Infuse the saffron in 2 tbsps of the shellfish stock. Whip the cream until stiff, fold in the yoghurt and the saffron liquid, and whisk once more. Stir in the herbs and prawns and season to taste with salt, pepper and orange zest. Spoon into chicory, Little Gem or radicchio leaves.

meat and charcuterie

parma ham, melon and cheese fingers

serves 4 to 6

1 ripe melon

225g (8oz) mild, nutty cheese such as Beaufort, Emmental, mature Gouda

175g (6oz) Parma ham, thinly sliced

Cut the melon and the cheese into narrow finger shapes. Place a piece of each on a slice of Parma ham and roll up. Secure each parcel with a cocktail stick, or tie with a chive or a ribbon of celery, and serve with fingers of granary bread and butter.

ham fritters

makes 30

2 eggs, separated

2 tbsps olive oil

pinch of salt

125g (4oz) flour

150ml (5oz) cold water

100g (3½oz) jamon serrano or prosciutto, cut into very small pieces

olive oil for frying

Place the egg yolks, oil and salt in a bowl, and mix. Add the flour and water alternately, mixing until you have a smooth batter. Leave to rest for 20 minutes, then fold in the two stiffly beaten egg whites and the pieces of ham.

Pour the oil into a frying pan to a depth of 5mm (¼ inch), and heat. Drop heaped teaspoons of the batter into the oil, and fry, a few at a time, until golden brown. Drain on crumpled paper towels. Serve hot.

minced meat pastries

With their sweet-and-savoury filling, incorporating meat, these little pastries are not unlike the precursor to the mince pie we know today. They are particularly nice when made with venison or pheasant.

makes 12

400g (14oz) puff pastry

250g (8oz) cooked minced or diced meat

2 tbsps olive oil

4 tbsps grated apple

2 tbsps finely chopped onion

2 tbsps dark muscovado or other unrefined sugar

¼ tsp each ground cardamom, cinnamon and cloves

freshly grated nutmeg

salt

freshly ground black pepper

milk and egg to glaze

Roll out the pastry and use to line twelve tartlet tins, reserving enough to cut out twelve pastry lids. Mix together the remaining ingredients, seasoning to taste with nutmeg, salt and pepper, then divide the mixture between the pastry cases. Cover with pastry lids and glaze. Bake in a preheated oven at 180°C/350°F/gas mark 4 for 15–18 minutes. Alternatively, make as pasties.

miniature venison burgers

makes 24

2–3 shallots, very finely chopped

2 celery sticks, trimmed and finely chopped

1 tbsp olive oil

1kg (2lb) lean venison, minced

freshly ground black pepper

grating of nutmeg

salt

small baps or cocktail pitta breads

Gently fry the shallots and celery in half the oil in a frying pan until transparent. Mix with the venison, and season with pepper and nutmeg. Form into small patties, about 5cm (2 inches) in diameter. Heat the remaining oil in the frying pan and fry the burgers on both sides, then salt lightly and slip between split small buns or pitta bread.

toad-in-the-hole

It is worth remembering that toad-in-the-hole started life as quite an elegant dish – in the 18th century Hannah Glasse gave a recipe for pigeons in a hole, and in the Victorian period Mrs Beeton suggested beefsteak baked in a batter pudding. You can return it to something of its former glory by experimenting with quail breasts, miniature truffled *boudin blanc* and slices of good quality black pudding, although I realize that not everyone likes black pudding as much as I, nor would consider it a luxury.

serves 20

750g (1½lb) plain or self-raising flour
good pinch of salt
3 eggs
1.5 litres (2¼ pints) semi-skimmed milk
1.5kg (3lb) sausages – beef, chicken or turkey can replace pork

Sift the flour and salt into a bowl, and make a well in the centre. Lightly beat the eggs, and pour into the well. Gradually draw in the flour, mixing with a spoon, and then gradually add the milk, stirring all the while to ensure a smooth, lump-free mixture. Once all the ingredients have been incorporated, beat vigorously until the mixture becomes noticeably lighter and bubbly, with the consistency of single cream. Cover, and put to one side.

Prick the sausages to prevent them from bursting, then fry them all over in a frying pan for 10 minutes, until the fat has run. Use some of the fat to grease a large baking or roasting tin, then put this in a preheated oven at 220°C/425°F, gas mark 7. (Alternatively, you can cook the sausages in the oven in the roasting tin for 10 minutes, and then drain away some of the fat.) Put the sausages in the hot roasting tin, and pour over the batter. Return it to the oven, and bake for about 40–45 minutes without opening the oven door until the batter is golden brown and well risen. Serve immediately.

cornish pasties

makes 30 small pasties

for the pastry

    750g (1½lb) plain flour

    300g (10oz) fat – use a mixture of lard and margarine

    good pinch of salt

for the filling

    500g (1lb) rump steak, cut in small thin pieces

    2–3 large potatoes

    1 onion (optional)

    piece of turnip (swede)

    salt

    freshly ground black pepper

Sift together the flour and salt. Rub in the fat, and mix to a pliable consistency with water. Leave to rest for 30 minutes or so in a cool place.

Divide the pastry into 30 portions. Take one of the portions and roll it into a round, not too thin. Peel and slice the potato finely, and place some on to the centre of the round, extending to each side to form a base. Slice the turnip on top of this, and then put a good layer of beef over the top, making sure that there is a good piece in each corner. Add a fringe of chopped onion. Season generously.

Dampen the edge of the top half-circle of pastry with water. Bring the bottom centre to top centre to seal firmly, and then enclose along right and left. The finer this sealed edge is, the neater will be the crimp. There should now be a neat, fat parcel with no bits poking through. If there are splits or holes, patch them with bits of pastry.

Now do the crimping, from one corner to the other. Make sure your hands are dry. Hold the edge with one hand, and follow on with a firm fold down with the other. Hold and fold alternately and swiftly along to the end. Place the pasty on a piece of butter paper and slit a hole in the top, to let out the steam. Brush the top with a little milk, and place on a baking sheet. Make the rest of the pasties in the same way.

Bake in a preheated oven at 400°F/200°C/gas mark 6 for 10 minutes, then reduce the heat to 190°C/375°F/gas mark 5 and cook for a further 15 minutes or so.

vegetarian cornish pasties

Two very good versions can be made, one using cooked leeks and blue cheese; another with cauliflower and Cheddar. Sliced potatoes and onion are still used in each.

snail puffs

makes 12
> 250g (8oz) puff pastry
> 100g (4oz) garlic butter – *see* recipe
> 12 medium-sized snails
> beaten egg yolk and water to glaze

Roll out the pastry, and cut into twelve 7.5cm (3 inch) squares. Place a snail in the centre of each, with a portion of garlic butter. This can be made by mashing crushed garlic into salted butter, seasoning with pepper, a little more salt if you wish, and adding finely chopped parsley. Dampen the edges of the pastry, fold the corners to the centre, and pinch to seal along the four edges, completely enclosing the snail and its butter. You can prepare to this point well in advance, in the morning or even the night before. Refrigerating the pastries does in fact help them to remain sealed tight during baking.

When ready to bake, brush with beaten egg yolk, and place in a preheated oven at 200°C/400°F/gas mark 6 for 12 minutes.

chicken tikka kebabs with masala sauce

makes 24

4 chicken breasts, cut into small cubes

for the marinade

1 onion, peeled, roughly chopped and pounded to a paste

2 garlic cloves, peeled and crushed

1 thumb-sized piece of fresh ginger, peeled and grated

2 tbsps lemon juice

1 tsp each ground coriander, cumin, salt and garam masala

2 tbsps chopped coriander or mint

3 tbsps plain yoghurt

24 small wooden skewers, soaked in water for 30 minutes

jar of mild, medium or hot curry sauce – *see* recipe

Mix together the ingredients for the marinade and marinate the chicken pieces for at least 2 hours, preferably overnight.

When ready to cook, remove the chicken from the marinade and thread two or three pieces on each of the skewers, then place the skewers under a hot grill or on the barbecue until thoroughly cooked through.

Arrange the skewers on a platter and in the middle offer a bowl of 'masala' sauce or dip, which is simply a curry sauce, of which there are many good commercial brands available, mild, medium or hot.

three satays with three sauces

This is also an excellent dish for a buffet or for a dinner party first course, or bar snacks.

makes 72

for the marinade

thumb-sized piece of fresh ginger, peeled and grated

200ml (7fl oz) groundnut oil

100ml (3½fl oz) fresh pineapple juice

2 tbsps toasted sesame oil

2 tbsps soy sauce

2 tbsps light, or dark, muscovado sugar

2 tbsps rice vinegar, or sherry vinegar

2 or 3 garlic cloves, peeled and crushed

for the satays

4 skinless chicken breasts

3 pork tenderloins

400g (14oz) tail-end piece of fillet steak

72 bamboo skewers

for the peanut sauce

250g (8oz) peanut butter, smooth or crunchy, according to taste

juice and zest of 1 lime

1 tbsp light or dark muscovado sugar

1 tbsp soy sauce

approx 250ml (8fl oz) warm water

for the herb sauce

2 good handfuls mint, basil and coriander, leaves only, finely chopped

2 lemon grass sticks, thinly sliced

3–4 lime leaves, snipped to fine shreds

juice and zest of 1 lime

2 garlic cloves, peeled and crushed

200ml (7fl oz) groundnut oil

200ml (7fl oz) warm water

for the chilli, ginger and garlic sauce

1–2 fresh red chillies, seeded and finely chopped

1 tbsp freshly grated ginger

4 garlic cloves, peeled and crushed

2 tsps Dijon mustard or 1 tsp wasabi paste

2 tbsps rice or sherry vinegar

1–2 tbsps light muscovado sugar

3 tbsps toasted sesame oil

200ml (7fl oz) groundnut oil

Mix together the ingredients for the marinade.

To make the satays, soak the skewers in water while you prepare the meats. (This is to prevent the wood from burning when the skewers are put under the grill.)

Cut each chicken breast into six strips, and thread these on to twenty-four skewers. Similarly, cut the tenderloins and steak into twenty-four strips each. Thread these on to skewers, too, and place all of them in a rectangular dish; something like a lasagne dish is ideal. Pour the marinade over the meat, cover, and leave overnight, or for at least 4 hours.

The ingredients for each of the sauces should be mixed together, either by hand or in a blender, and poured into serving bowls.

Remove the meat skewers from the marinade, allow any extra liquid to drip back, and then place under a hot grill for 10–15 minutes, turning as necessary. The marinade can be simmered for 5–10 minutes, sieved, and served as a dipping sauce.

cheese, eggs and vegetables

warm blue cheese and herb gougère

serves 4 to 6

for the choux paste
> 150ml (¼ pint) water
> 50g (2oz) butter
> pinch of salt
> 65g (2½oz) plain flour, sifted
> 2 eggs

Put the water, butter and salt in a saucepan. Bring to the boil, and add the flour all at once, beating vigorously and continuously as you cook the mixture, for 2–3 minutes, to obtain a thick firm paste. When it leaves the sides of the pan and has a shiny appearance, remove from the heat. Beat in the eggs, one at a time, making sure the first is fully incorporated before adding the second to obtain a soft, pliable, but not liquid, dough.

Because the absorbent quality of flour can change from batch to batch and can also vary with the day's humidity, it is a good idea not to add the whole of the second egg, as you may not need it all. On the other hand, if the flour is very dry, you may need to add a little more beaten egg.

for the gougère
> 175g (6oz) blue cheese, crumbled or diced quite small
> 1 tbsp finely chopped chervil, parsley, chives or tarragon

Stir these ingredients into the choux paste, then spoon or pipe the pastry into a ring on a greased baking sheet. To make it rise even more, create a steam-oven effect by inverting a deep roasting tin or cake tin over the pastry, and bake it in a preheated oven at 220°C/425°F/gas mark 7 for 15 minutes, then reduce the heat to 180°C/350°F/gas mark 4 for a further 12–15 minutes. Remove from the oven and serve while still warm.

Alternatively, place small heaps of the choux paste on the baking sheet – these will make excellent small bites to hand round with drinks.

---

entertaining

glamorgan sausages

These are particularly good with homemade tomato sauce, chutney or pickles.

makes 20

350g (12oz) fresh breadcrumbs

250g (8oz) grated hard cheese – *see* recipe

1 leek or 4 spring onions, trimmed and finely chopped

1 tbsp chopped fresh chives

1 tbsp chopped fresh parsley

1 tsp mustard powder

salt

freshly ground black pepper

grating of nutmeg

milk

2 eggs, plus 1 egg white

flour or breadcrumbs for coating

oil for deep frying

This is a good way to use up any and all kinds of leftover hard cheese. Traditionally, Caerphilly is used. Mix together the breadcrumbs, cheese, leek or spring onion, herbs and seasoning. Mix one whole egg and an egg yolk into the mixture, and as much milk as is needed to bind it together. Whisk the egg whites to a froth on a plate, and put the flour or breadcrumbs in another. Divide the mixture into twenty, and roll each piece on a floured board into a miniature sausage shape. Roll each one in the egg white and then in flour or bread-crumbs. Heat the oil in a deep pan, and fry for 4–5 minutes until golden brown. Serve hot, warm or cold.

quesadillas with mango salsa

Favourite bar food in America, *quesadillas* are easy to make at home for a cocktail snack or simple first course. If you cannot get tortillas, you can make a similar dish with two large crêpes or pancakes.

makes 18 to 24 portions

6 flour tortillas

250g (8oz) Gouda or Edam cheese, thinly sliced

for the salsa

1 mango, peeled and diced small

juice of 1 lime

juice of ½ orange

4 spring onions, trimmed and finely sliced

1 clove of garlic, peeled and crushed

1 tbsp light muscovado sugar

salt

freshly ground black pepper

1 tbsp freshly chopped coriander

Mix all the salsa ingredients together, cover, and allow to stand for at least 30 minutes to allow the flavours to develop. Sandwich two tortillas with cheese, and place on a baking sheet in a preheated oven at 150°C/300°F/gas mark 2 until the cheese is melted. Then cut into wedges, and serve with the salsa.

Alternatively, heat the *quesadillas* in a non-stick frying pan, set over a low heat and with a lid set slightly askew.

baked eggs in potato soufflés

makes 24

    12 potatoes, weighing approx 75–100g (3–4oz) each

    25g (1oz) butter, melted

    100g (4oz) cheese, grated; any type with a nice melting quality

    freshly ground black pepper

    2 eggs, separated

    salt

    24 quail's eggs

Scrub the potatoes, then bake them in the oven until soft. Remove from the oven and, when cool enough to handle, halve them, scoop out the centre, and sieve it into a basin. Mix with the melted butter, cheese and pepper.

Beat the egg yolks into the cheese and potato mixture. Add salt, if needed. Whisk the egg whites, then fold gently into the potato mixture. Crack a quail's egg into each potato hollow, then spoon a portion of the soufflé mixture on top, spreading it right to the edges of the potato and heaping it a little.

Return the potatoes to a preheated oven at 190°C/375°F/gas mark 5 for about 10 minutes or until the soufflés are risen and golden. Serve immediately.

devilled quail's eggs

makes 24

    24 quail's eggs

    1 tsp each celery salt, ground cumin, freshly ground black pepper, cayenne

    ½ tsp salt

Boil the quail's eggs for 5 minutes, partially shell them, and dip the ends in a spicy salt mixture, made by shaking together in a bag the spices and salts. Pile the eggs in a napkin-lined basket, shell end down.

hot cheese puffs

makes 18 to 24

  4 tbsps port or sweet oloroso sherry

  4 tbsps soft white breadcrumbs

  250g (8oz) hard cheese, grated

  75g (3oz) butter, softened

  4 eggs, separated

  freshly ground black pepper

Soak the breadcrumbs in the port for a few minutes. Drain, then mix with the cheese and softened butter. Mix in the egg yolks, season with pepper, and then fold in the stiffly whipped egg whites. Spoon into paper muffin or bun cases, and bake in a preheated oven at 180°C/350°C/gas mark 4 for about 15 minutes.

miniature pizzas

makes 12

  500g (1lb) bread dough

  extra virgin olive oil

  200g (7oz) tomato purée

  2 mozzarella cheeses, thinly sliced

Divide the dough into twelve pieces, or more if you want even smaller ones. Roll each piece out to a circle, place on a baking sheet and brush with olive oil. Spread with tomato purée, and top with slices of mozzarella cheese. This is the basic classic pizza, to which you can add all manner of toppings. For example, consider stoned olives, sliced mushrooms, sliced aubergine, pepperoni, spicy sausage meat, quartered artichokes, in any combination. For a delicious vegetarian version, spread the pizza with pesto, top with very thinly sliced potatoes, then slices of cheese and some black olives and capers. Bake in a preheated oven at 200°C/400°F/gas mark 6 for 15–20 minutes.

akara (black bean fritters)

makes 12 to 18

250g (8oz) black-eyed bean paste – *see* below

1 egg, separated

1 heaped tbsp finely chopped onion or shallot

1 small red chilli pepper, seeded and finely chopped, or ½ tsp dried chilli flakes

½ tsp salt

groundnut oil for deep-frying

To make the bean paste, soak the pulses overnight in a bowl of water, then rub handfuls of the beans between the palms of your hands several times to make sure that the skins are rubbed off all of them. Fill the bowl with water again, and scoop out the skins, which will float to the surface. Repeat the draining, rubbing and floating process until all the skins have been removed. Drain well, and grind or process them until smooth.

Put the bean paste in a bowl, and whisk in the egg yolk. Continue whisking, adding warm water until a light, thick batter of dropping consistency is obtained. Fold in the onion, chilli pepper and salt. Whisk the egg white, and fold into the mixture.

Heat the oil to 180°C/350°F, then drop in spoonfuls of the batter. When browned on the underside, turn the fritters over, and fry until uniformly golden brown. Remove and drain on crumpled paper towel to absorb excess oil. Serve while still very hot.

llapingachos (potato and cheese cakes)

Sliced avocados and a peanut sauce are the accompaniments if you make these 'meal-size' with an egg on top.

makes 16 to 20

1kg (2lb) floury potatoes

salt

freshly ground black pepper

75g (3oz) butter

1 onion, peeled and finely chopped

2 tbsps olive oil

150g (5oz) hard cheese, such as Jarlsberg, Gruyère or Cheddar, grated

Peel, boil and mash the potatoes with salt, pepper and half the butter. Fry the onion in half the olive oil until soft and golden. Allow to cool slightly, then mix with the cheese.

Form the potato into small patties, and bury some of the cheese and onion mixture in the centre. Heat the remaining butter and olive oil in a frying pan, and fry the potato cakes on both sides until golden brown.

stir-fried vegetables and toasted sesame tartlets

makes 24

24 thin slices of bread

2–3 tbsps groundnut oil, plus extra for frying

1 tbsp toasted sesame oil

2 tbsps sesame seeds

piece of fresh root ginger, peeled and sliced

2–3 star anise

cinnamon stick

500g (1lb) prepared vegetables, selected from thin slices of carrot,
   mushrooms, baby corn cobs, broccoli florets, mangetouts and spring onions

1 tbsp soy sauce

1 tbsp amontillado sherry or rice wine

1 tbsp sherry vinegar or rice vinegar

pinch of freshly ground black pepper or crushed Szechuan peppercorns

Cut the bread slices into twenty-four rounds with a pastry cutter. Brush twenty-four bun tins with some of the groundnut oil, and mix the remaining oil with half the sesame oil. Use this to brush the bread, then press each piece into a bun tin. Sprinkle a few sesame seeds into each. Lightly toast the rest of the sesame seeds in a small frying pan and set aside. Bake the tartlets in a preheated oven at 200°C/400°F/gas mark 6 for 10–15 minutes, until crisp and golden.

Meanwhile, heat the remaining groundnut oil in a frying pan or wok, and gently fry the ginger, star anise and cinnamon for 5 minutes. Remove the aromatics from the oil, then add the vegetables, starting with those that take longest to cook, and finishing with the mushrooms and spring onions. Stir continuously as the vegetables are frying, and when all have been added, splash in the soy sauce, sherry or wine vinegar and pepper, together with one or two tablespoons of cold water. Cover with the lid, and steam for a few minutes, shaking occasionally. When the vegetables are just cooked, but still crisp and vivid, stir in the remaining sesame oil, and spoon them into the hot tartlet cases. Sprinkle with toasted sesame seeds before serving.

vegetable spring rolls

makes 12

12 rice wrappers

150g (5oz) bean sprouts, blanched

1 cucumber, peeled, seeded and cut into juliennes

1 Little Gem lettuce, shredded

200g (7oz) fresh shiitake mushrooms, sliced and lightly fried in groundnut oil

3 carrots, peeled and cut into juliennes

2 celery sticks, strings removed and thinly sliced

bunch of spring onions, trimmed and rinsed, and cut into long strips

handful each of mint, coriander and basil leaves

50g (2oz) roasted, salted peanuts, crushed

for the dipping sauce

juice of 1 lime

2 tbsps dark muscovado sugar

4 tbsps rice or sherry vinegar

½ tsp fresh chilli paste or dried chilli flakes

Dip a rice wrapper in warm water until it is pliable. Place on a tea towel on a chopping board and, at the lower edge, place a little of each vegetable, some herbs and crushed peanuts, then roll tightly, away from you, tucking in the ends. Place seam-side down on a platter. Repeat for the remaining wrappers.

Put the sauce ingredients in a small saucepan and bring to the boil, then pour into a serving dish. To serve, cut each spring roll in half, on the diagonal, or, if serving as snacks, cut each into three or four pieces.

desserts

British puddings and desserts lend themselves just as well as the savouries to miniaturization, and I have suggested three here: Bakewell puddings, treacle tartlets and a syllabub. In addition, you might like to consider small wine glasses of trifle or fruit fool, or tiny ice creams sandwiched between homemade biscuits.

bakewell tarts or puddings

makes 24

400g (14oz) puff pastry
apricot or strawberry jam
200g (7oz) caster sugar
4 eggs
175g (6oz) butter, melted
175g (6oz) ground almonds
2 tsps lemon juice

Line twenty-four bun tins with the pastry, and spread them with a generous layer of jam. Whisk the eggs and sugar until thick and pale. Stir in the melted butter, then fold in the ground almonds and the lemon juice. Spread evenly over the jam. Bake in a preheated oven at 180°C/350°F/gas mark 4 for 20 minutes or until nicely browned on top.

treacle tartlets

makes 24

400g (14oz) shortcrust pastry

75g (2½oz) fresh breadcrumbs

freshly grated nutmeg

grated zest of 1 lemon

1 tbsp lemon juice

350g (12oz) golden syrup

Roll out the pastry, and use to line twenty-four greased bun tins. Mix the breadcrumbs with the nutmeg and lemon zest. Mix the lemon juice with the golden syrup, and spoon into the bun tins. Sprinkle the breadcrumbs over the top. Bake in a preheated oven at 190°C/375°F/gas mark 5 for 18–25 minutes.

cider syllabub

serves 25

75ml (3fl oz) English cider brandy

¼ nutmeg, grated

140g (5oz) golden caster sugar

450ml (¾ pint) English cider

1 litre (1¾ pints) double cream

Infuse the cider brandy with the nutmeg and sugar, and leave overnight. Stir in the cider or wine. In a large bowl, whip the cream, and then gradually incorporate the liquid. Serve in chilled port or liqueur glasses.

cocktails

Here are a few recipes to start you off. It is worth looking in secondhand book shops for cocktail manuals, which will have plenty of excellent recipes for cups and cobblers.

martini

serves 1

    1 part dry Martini
    4 parts (or more) Plymouth gin
    a slice of lemon cut in 2
    ice

Put everything in a cocktail shaker, shake vigorously until ice cold, then strain into chilled Martini glasses. Of course, in New York bars, they only show the Martini bottle to the gin, so vary the proportions to taste. And some like their Martini stirred, not shaken, and prefer a green olive to lemon.

cosmopolitan

serves 1

    cranberry juice
    Cointreau
    lime juice
    vodka
    ice

Mix in proportions to suit your taste, shake over ice, then strain into chilled Martini glasses.

citrus martini

serves 1 to 2

100ml (3½fl oz) lemon vodka

1 tbsp Cointreau

1 tbsp lemon juice

for the garnish

twist of lemon zest

Put the vodka, Cointreau and juice in a shaker with ice. Shake, then strain into a chilled glass, add the lemon zest, and serve. In Manhattan, this is a single serving. It will do two nicely. Then you can make another. They stay colder that way.

pina colada

serves 8 to 10

1 litre (1¾ pints) pineapple juice

1 × 400g can coconut cream or equivalent cartons, or a can of
   Coco Lopez coconut cream

300–400ml (10–14fl oz) white rum

sugar syrup, to taste (optional)

Put all the ingredients in a jug and whisk, or use a hand blender, until thoroughly mixed. Chill with ice, and serve, with a small wedge of pineapple on each glass, if you wish.

If you prefer the 1970s version, follow the instructions on the back of the Coco Lopez can.

champagne cocktail

serves 1

1 sugar lump
1 tsp cognac
Angostura bitters
champagne

The sugar lump is soaked in brandy and dropped in the bottom of a champagne flute, a few drops of Angostura bitters are splashed on top, and the glass is filled with chilled champagne; your local supermarket's own label will be fine.

champagne cup

serves 8

4 sugar lumps
1 orange, organic or unwaxed if possible
50ml (2fl oz) each brandy, amontillado sherry and orange liqueur
4–5 leaves of lemon verbena
2–3 apricots, halved and thinly sliced
1 bottle of ice-cold sparkling mineral water
1 bottle ice-cold champagne

Rub the lumps of sugar over the orange, and crumble into a large glass bowl or jug. Add the liqueurs and lemon verbena. Add the apricots, and leave to stand for 30 minutes before adding the mineral water and champagne. Serve before it gets too warm, preferably in chilled glasses.

mango margarita

serves 4

1 ripe mango

2 limes

2 measures Cointreau

4 measures tequila

fine salt for salting the glass (optional)

Have all the ingredients ice-cold. Peel, roughly chop the mango, and put the flesh in a blender. Take off four thin curls of lime zest, and reserve. Squeeze the juice into the blender. Add the spirits, and blend until smooth. Pour into chilled glasses, decorate with the lime zest, and serve. If you like, moisten the edge of the glass with the squeezed lime skin, and then dip it into salt.

mandarin margarita

serves 1

juice of ½ lime

1 measure Mandarine Napoleon liqueur

1 measure tequila

50ml (2fl oz) fresh mandarin juice (optional)

Chill, mix and serve, as above.

non-alcoholic party drinks

The following are useful ingredients to have for non-alcoholic drinks:

apple juices, such as James White for organic, and Brogdale and Jus
tonic water
sparkling mineral water
elderflower cordial, and all the other fruit and herb cordials
coconut milk
rice milk
almond milk

And both a juicer and a blender are indispensable pieces of equipment for the serious *barista*, whether making potent cocktails or non-alcoholic drinks.

nectarine lemonade

serves 6

6 ripe but unblemished nectarines, sliced
175g (6oz) golden icing or caster sugar
750ml (1¼ pints) chilled water
450ml (12fl oz) freshly squeezed lemon juice

Blend the nectarines, sugar and water, and then add the lemon juice. Strain into a jug, and serve with ice. Lemon verbena, lemon thyme, or lemon balm makes a perfect garnish. The drink is quite tart. If you wish, serve a small jug of sugar syrup with the lemonade.

Raspberries, blueberries, peaches, pineapples and many other fruits can be used to flavour lemonade. In each case, follow the same procedure by first blending fruit until smooth with sugar and water, and then adding the lemon juice and straining. You will want to experiment with the sugar levels. And you can, of course, have plain lemonade: fresh lemon juice, diluted with water, and sweetened with sugar or syrup, the *citron pressé* of the French café.

flowering cosmopolitan

serves 1

    1 tsp elderflower cordial

    2 tsps lime juice

    ½ glass cranberry juice

    ½ glass sparkling mineral water, chilled

Shake the cordial, lime juice and cranberry juice with ice, pour into a glass and top up with mineral water, adding more ice if you like.

- *Elderflower sparkler* elderflower cordial diluted with sparkling mineral water.

- *Sparkling apple mead* honey, apple juice and sparkling mineral water.

- *Raspberry shrub* puréed frozen raspberries mixed with equal quantities of tonic and sparkling mineral water.

- *Mango Bellini* mango juice or pure with apple juice and sparkling mineral water.

- *Tropical fruit crush* fruit purée, coconut milk and sparkling mineral water or apple juice.

- *Rock shandy* fresh lemon and lime juice, soda and plenty of Angostura bitters. Note, however, that like all extracts and essences, Angostura and other bitters contain alcohol.

outdoor eating
– barbecues and picnics

barbecues

There are barbecues and barbecues. In some places, it is a given that from May to September all entertaining will be done outside standing around the barbecue. In others, where the weather is more uncertain, a barbecue is an occasional summertime treat. In truth though, use of the barbecue need not be restricted to the summer. I have memories of Tom barbecuing oysters outside on our roof terrace in north London one cold February night, for the first course for our dinner party, much to our guests' astonishment. The idea came from friends in California who, living on Tomales Bay north of San Francisco, would hold an annual oyster barbecue on the Fourth of July, the oysters accompanied by plenty of chilled Sonoma chardonnay. It doesn't quite translate to an English winter. Nevertheless, the barbecue is one of the best ways of cooking oysters; the heat opens the 'hinge' and does not so much cook the mollusc as 'set' it to a juicy plumpness. This was a technique shown to the early settlers in Virginia and New England by the native Americans.

The good thing about barbecues is the wide variety of equipment now available, tailored to every need. If you happen to own a meadow, you can dig a pit for a stylish outdoor feast, a Bedouin-style lamb *mechoui*. For a city balcony, a disposable barbecue is the answer. I know people who use their elaborate barbecue/smoker all year round, and have it strategically placed on the deck outside their kitchen door as an extra oven. You can have a small oven in the garden, or build your own barbecue with bricks and grills. Gas or electric high speed, manoeuvrable barbecues are also available, which can be stored in the garage when not in use.

Good skewers are a worthwhile investment. They should be flat to prevent food swivelling, and long enough to avoid burns. A useful idea is to choose ones with different handles. I have a set with decorative ceramic vegetables on the end, so I know whose meat needs cooking longer, who likes it rare. Long chef's tongs, for turning food without piercing it, are useful, as are oven gloves. Add to these a plastic box or two for first marinating your ingredients and then carrying them out to the barbecue. Or consider using zip-lock bags. There is an interesting product from South Africa on the market, a marinade in a zip-lock bag. You add your pieces of fish or meat, zip up the bag, massage for a couple of minutes and then leave to marinate for 30 minutes or so. This is a simple principle to adapt to your own marinades.

Elegant French Laguiole knives, first devised by the shepherds of the Aubrac, are practical as well as pleasing to handle, and perfect for cutting through steaks and kebabs, as well as chunky grilled vegetables and crusty bread. Citronella candles are a must for keeping the area clear of midges, flies and other insects. You can find ones to stick in flower pots, as well as elegant ones for the table. Small weights or clips to secure the tablecloth from gusts of wind are useful, inexpensive gadgets. Kitchenware and hardware shops and departments, as well as the larger superstores will supply most of your barbecue needs, but probably the most comprehensive selection in the country, of the highest quality, is available mail order from Lakeland Limited (Tel: 015394 88100), or from any of their stores.

Having equipped yourself, or your partner, with all the above and a sturdy apron, and with a weather-eye out for rain clouds, what about the food?

Gone are the days of grilling everything in sight from aubergines to sardines. And anyone who barbecues chicken, other than split and flattened breasts, or boned portions, needs their heads looking at. If you cook thighs and drumsticks until 'the juices run clear', you will have a charred, dried-up piece of meat. And if you don't cook them long enough, you risk food poisoning, especially if the meat has been frozen and has not properly thawed out. The secret, as in the recipe for duckling which follows, is to start the cooking in a hot oven, or, as with the chicken thighs and drumsticks, to bone them first.

I buy beef that I am quite happy to eat raw, as steak tartar, let alone rare, so have no qualms about cooking it on the barbecue as a steak or a burger. For the latter, the risks are further minimized if you buy the meat in a piece and mince or chop it yourself. Meat that has already been minced and handled carries more risk of having bacteria seeded in it. Steaks and cutlets, whether beef, lamb or pork, are perfect candidates for the barbecue. Some sweetcorn cooked on the embers, and some small, foil-wrapped potatoes, if you have the space, are perfect accompaniments to the barbecued duckling.

To grill corn on the barbecue, carefully peel back the husk so that you can remove the silk, and then wrap the husk back around the ear, twisting, or tying, to secure it at the top. For this, clearly, it is better to buy loose ears of corn; the ready-packaged supermarket variety has had most of the husk removed. Soak the cobs in cold water for 10 minutes to stop them from drying out during cooking. Place the wrapped cobs on the grill, and cook for 15–20 minutes, turning them occasionally. You can, of course, also cook corn in the oven, wrapping it in foil, husks and silk removed, with a knob of butter, for 10–15 minutes or so.

I do not favour everything barbecued, so will always choose other food to top and tail my meal. Indeed, I like to think of the barbecue as just another cooking method, and will often take the barbecued food indoors to be enjoyed at the table as part of a civilized meal. Fresh goat's cheeses and green salad, strawberries in sparkling wine, peaches in elderflower syrup, sliced nectarines in a mixture of orange and lemon juice, a fruit tart, or a trifle all end a barbecue perfectly, as will a trio of good ice creams or sorbets.

A vegetable tart, a selection of charcuterie and chewy bread, smoked fish and brown bread, or crudités with mayonnaise are ideal for a first course, and can be prepared in advance.

For the main course, you might like to present a selection of food appropriately marinated, and let everyone make up their own skewers for barbecuing. Quartered chicken breasts, lamb neck fillet in cubes, diced rump steak, lamb's kidneys and squares of liver are all suitable, as are veal chops, duck breasts and quail. Or try scallops, prawns, chunks of monkfish, salmon, halibut, swordfish and tuna. Whole sardines, scaled and gutted by your fishmonger, can be lightly stuffed with herbs and couscous before barbecuing. If you barbecue fish often, a worthwhile investment will be a hinged heavy wire grill to hold the fish without the tender flesh falling on to the coals. Remember, too, to brush or spray with oil to stop the meat or fish sticking to the grill.

Or choose just one item to chargrill, for example a pair of spatchcocked ducklings, a couple of butterflied legs of lamb, a fillet of beef or a cured loin of pork. Not as impressive as a whole spit-roasted lamb perhaps, but more exciting than burgers, kebabs and chicken pieces. Plan it when you know the weather is going to remain good, invest in all the equipment, have your first course and pudding made in advance and serve large frosted jugs of strong, colourful drinks, well-chilled rosé cava and some equally chilled fino sherry. It will be a barbecue to remember.

roasted vegetable tart

serves 6 to 8

500g (1lb) bread dough

extra virgin olive oil

6 medium to large courgettes, blanched and sliced

1–2 aubergines, sliced and lightly grilled

2 red peppers, peeled and seeded

8–10 firm, ripe tomatoes, seeded and sliced thickly

coarse sea salt

freshly ground black pepper

fresh basil and mint

A tart tin some 45cm (18 inches) across, i.e. a good-sized paella pan, or a roasting tin can be used. A pizza tray, or stone, is, of course, ideal. Oil the tin and roll out the dough to fit. Brush the dough with olive oil, and arrange the vegetables on top. Dribble on a little more olive oil, and sprinkle with salt and pepper. Bake in the centre of a preheated oven at 200°C/400°F/gas mark 6 for 45–50 minutes. Serve warm or hot, with torn-up herbs scattered over it.

barbecued duckling

serves 8

2 × 2.3kg (5lb) ducklings

2 carrots, peeled and chopped

2 turnips, peeled and chopped

1 celeriac or celery heart, chopped

sprigs of thyme and rosemary

6–8 garlic cloves

4 bay leaves

freshly ground black pepper

1 bottle good full-bodied red wine

With heavy kitchen scissors or poultry shears, cut the backbone out of the ducklings. Then flatten them by pressing hard on their fronts to crack the breast bone and ribs. Put in a roasting tin on a bed of the root vegetables, herbs, the garlic, bay leaves and pepper, and pour over all the wine. Leave to marinate for 12–24 hours, turning the birds over after half the time, if you can remember.

Remove the ducks from the marinade, dry them, prick the skin in the fattiest parts, and roast in a preheated oven at 220°C/425°F/gas mark 7 for 15–20 minutes. Pour the marinade into a saucepan. Meanwhile, have your charcoal grill burning at medium low. When ready, remove the ducks from the oven, place on the grill, skin side down, and cook for 30–35 minutes or until the juices run clear when pricked with a skewer. At some point during cooking, turn the ducks over for 5–10 minutes to grill the carcass surface. Bring the marinade to the boil, and use to brush over the duck from time to time.

When the birds are cooked, transfer them to a carving board or platter, leave to rest for 10 minutes or so, then carve or cut up with poultry shears.

The same basic cooking method can be used for lamb or pork, with the following amendments:

Lamb: Have the leg, or legs, boned and the flesh opened out like a book, but keep the shank bone in as this provides a useful handle when carving the lamb. Baste from time to time during cooking.

Pork: The loin is a good cut for barbecuing but needs basting periodically. The chine bone should be removed and the thickest part of the meat and fat can be slashed between the ribs. A mustard and honey glaze, if liked, can be spread in the cuts.

Remember in all cases to bring the meat to room temperature before cooking.

The Perfect Strawberries

What better dessert than strawberries after a barbecue? Balsamic vinegar, black pepper, sherry vinegar, orange juice, verjuice, Beaujolais and claret are just some of the ingredients said to be *the* perfect accompaniment to strawberries. I have also tried them with the sweet-sour pomegranate syrup or molasses. All have their merits and are worth trying. I also like strawberries with a red wine syrup.

strawberries with red wine syrup

serves 6 to 8

1 bottle full-bodied red wine
stick of cinnamon
few cardamom pods
4 cloves
300g (10oz) golden granulated sugar
1.5kg (3lb) strawberries

Pour the wine into a saucepan, add the spices, bring to the boil and reduce by two thirds. Stir in the sugar, then allow the syrup to go cold.

Rinse, dry and hull the strawberries. Put them in a glass bowl, halving or slicing as necessary, then strain over the syrup. Chill until required, but do not prepare more than an hour or two in advance as the strawberries will go soggy.

---

entertaining

an american barbecue

One of my greatest pleasures one recent summer was to sit in a rocking chair in a screened porch under a fan during the American Midwest's sweltering summer sun and enjoy a barbecue prepared by my husband's relatives in Indianapolis.

They are a large family and everyone contributed to the barbecue so that our hosts, Maryellen and Mike, did not have to do all the work. Sisters and sisters-in-law brought desserts, salads and side dishes. Belinda made cherry and strawberry cheesecakes, chocolate brownies and a beautiful 'basket', carved from a large and long watermelon, which she filled with seedless red grapes, blueberries, strawberries and balls of watermelon, cool and refreshing throughout our long afternoon and evening.

They have a wonderful backyard, not just the porch where grandmother and great-aunt held court throughout, but a pool where a small bunch of noisy children swam and splashed for hours, looking like little frogs, and a wooden deck, where our host had set up a large gas-fired, two-tiered barbecue.

Lesson one in the art of barbecuing, I learned, is to have one person in charge. Cousin Walter set the hot dogs on foil, and cousin Mike removed the foil. He was the one person in charge.

It is a good plan, too, to have a table nearby for the equipment you may need – thick oven gloves, tongs, spatula, fish grills, something for brushing on the marinade, and platters to hold the cooked food.

Maryellen had planned a fine menu for our barbecue, fruit and nachos with a chilli cheese dip to nibble on, barbecued hot dogs for the kids, bratwurst for the adults, together with grilled chicken and homemade hamburgers for everyone. 'Sides', or side dishes, were mixed bean salads, coleslaw and extraordinarily good potato salad and baked beans. When I asked Sharon how long she had soaked the beans, she told me her quick and simple version of baked beans, which taste as though they have been simmering long hours in a crock pot.

And to drink? Ice-cold beer was just right, but if you have the time, space and inclination, I highly recommend Maryellen's 'slush', which she described as a 'summery backyardsy kind of drink'. I think it is the same as the drink referred to as Long Island tea. We drank it from one pint paper cups. One is quite enough. More might leave you legless for the rest of the barbecue. I have also included an unusual recipe for iced tea, and other summery drinks, together with a few of my favourite barbecue recipes. You'll find a recipe for mint julep on p.39 if the following do not appeal.

slush

makes about 3.5 litres (6 pints)
350ml (12fl oz) concentrated orange juice
juice of 4 lemons
600ml (1 pint) strong tea
600ml (1 pint) vodka, gin or white rum
1.75 litres (3 pints) water
sugar or sugar syrup to taste

Mix together all the ingredients. Pour into a large plastic bowl or container with a tight-fitting lid and freeze. It should freeze to a slush, the alcohol preventing total freezing. Serve in tall, chilled glasses, with, or without, a thick straw and whatever garnish appeals, such as slices of orange, lemon or lime, a sprig of borage or mint.

sun tea

This recipe requires a hot sunny day, and a porch, patio or window sill.

Put your favourite loose tea in a small muslin bundle, or staple it in a coffee filter paper, or use tea bags. Place in a large glass jug or jar, and fill with water. Stand it in the hot sun for several hours and, when infused to a rich golden brown, sweeten, if you like, and serve in ice-filled glasses with fresh mint leaves, sliced orange, lime or lemon, or enjoy the sharp, refreshing flavour on its own.

iced coffee

The best way to make this is simply to make coffee at least double strength, and pour it over a glass full of ice cubes, using syrup, rather than granulated sugar, to sweeten it.

fish kebabs with cajun cornmeal crust

If you plan to cook fish or shellfish on the barbecue, it is worth remembering how delicate it is. Prawns barbecue well because they have their own protective coat, but scallops and oysters, for example, if cooked out of their shell, need some protection; a piece of onion, a rasher of bacon, a piece of foil or a crust of some sort. Chunks of fish, too, are good with a crust, as they stay moist without the need for continual basting. Try this crisp, spicy, cornmeal coating with cod, haddock, monkfish, tuna, shark or swordfish.

serves 6 to 8
- 1kg (2lb) firm fish fillets, diced
- 300ml (½ pint) juice – tomato, vegetable or orange
- 250g (8oz) fine or medium cornmeal, well blended with 2 tbsps Cajun
  spice mixture or your own hot spice mixture

Use soaked wooden skewers, or flat metal skewers, and oil them. Dip the pieces of fish first in the juice, and then roll them in the spiced cornmeal mixture before threading them on to skewers. If you push food too tightly on to the skewers, in an attempt to be generous, all you will do is ensure that it will be undercooked in parts; heat must be able to circulate round the pieces of food. I prefer not to combine other ingredients, since there is little which cooks as quickly as fish. Skewers of vegetables can be put on to cook much earlier.

Place the kebabs on an oiled grill, and cook, turning gently, for 8–10 minutes, more if you like your fish well done.

---

maryellen's grilled chicken

To cook 'thick' food, such as chicken thighs, butterflied leg of lamb or whole fish, you need to make cuts through the thickest part. You lose some juice, but it allows for more even cooking. Alternatively bone the chicken and flatten it out before grilling

This marinade is also excellent with pork. Pineapple contains an enzyme which, amongst other things, tenderizes meat. Pork and chicken today scarcely need that, but do benefit from the good flavour of the marinade.

serves 12 to 16

> 6 boneless breasts
>
> 6 thighs
>
> 6 drumsticks
>
> 6 wings

for the marinade

> 600ml (1 pint) pineapple juice
>
> 6 tbsps soy sauce
>
> 3–4 tbsps light or dark muscovado sugar
>
> 4–6 garlic cloves, peeled and crushed
>
> 2 tsps freshly ground black pepper

Remove the skin from the chicken pieces, and bone the thighs and drumsticks. The wings will cook evenly enough without being boned. Mix together the marinade ingredients, add the chicken, and leave for 24 hours.

Remove the chicken from the marinade, and place on an oiled grill. Cook until the juices run clear. Baste the meat from time to time with the marinade as it grills.

---

entertaining

sides

marsha's potato salad

Use firm, waxy new potatoes. Scrub and boil until tender. When cool enough to handle, peel, dice and mix with finely chopped celery, onion or spring onion, hard-boiled egg, seasoning and mayonnaise.

no mayonnaise onion slaw

serves 12

- 1 carton soft tofu
- 2 heaped tbsps plain yoghurt
- 2 tbsps cider vinegar
- 2 tsps celery seed
- 1 tsp dill seed
- 1 tbsp Dijon mustard
- 2 garlic cloves, peeled and crushed
- 1 tbsp concentrated apple juice (available from health food shops)
- 2 large mild onions, peeled and finely chopped
- 1 head white cabbage, shredded
- 2 tbsps finely chopped parsley
- 1 tbsp chopped fresh dill

Using a blender, blend the tofu until smooth, then add everything except the onions, cabbage, parsley and dill. Once you have a smooth dressing, pour it over the vegetables and herbs, and mix thoroughly.

sharon's quick baked beans

serves 12

300g (10oz) smoked streaky bacon, in a piece

2 onions, peeled and thinly sliced

3–4 tbsps tomato purée

3 × 400g cans haricot or cannellini beans

2 tbsps molasses sugar, or more to taste

Fry the bacon in a large casserole until the fat runs, then add the onion and fry until it is a good golden brown, but not burnt. Add the tomato purée and cook for a few minutes, then add the canned beans and their liquid, and the molasses. Cook, uncovered, for about an hour or until the bacon can be pulled apart with two forks.

marshmallow fruit kebabs

For a sweet course, fruit such as chunks of mango, pineapple and bananas, interspersed with marshmallows and cubes of bread dipped in beaten egg and sugar, can be threaded on wooden skewers (that have previously been soaked in water for 30 minutes) and grilled, or you might have time to make a strawberry shortcake.

strawberry shortcake

This simple, scone-like cake is also very good with thinly sliced peaches or nectarines, a mixture of raspberries and strawberries or, later in the season, raspberries and blueberries.

serves 6 to 8

1kg (2lb) strawberries, rinsed, hulled and sliced

1–2 tsps rosewater

caster sugar to taste

250g (8oz) plain flour

1 tbsp baking powder

½ tsp salt

50g (2oz) butter, diced

3 tbsps plain yoghurt

1 egg

to serve

butter

cream

Put the strawberries in a bowl, sprinkle with the rosewater and sugar, and mash lightly with a fork.

Sift the flour, baking powder and salt, together with 25g (1oz) caster sugar, into a large bowl. Rub in the butter until it resembles coarse breadcrumbs. Beat the egg into the yoghurt, then gently fold into the flour mixture. Turn out on to a lightly floured board, knead for half a minute, then shape into a circle about 20cm (8 inches) in diameter.

Place on a baking sheet, and bake in a preheated oven at 200°C/400°F/gas mark 6 for 15–20 minutes or until golden brown. Allow to cool on a wire rack.

Split the cake, spread the bottom with butter, and cover with half the strawberries. Sandwich the other half of shortcake on top. Serve the remaining strawberries separately with some cream, or pile on top of the shortcake.

picnics

Some years ago, I was lucky enough to be invited to Glyndebourne with my husband, Tom. A once in a lifetime experience, we planned to make the most of it: the dressing up, the train ride from Victoria station and, of course, the picnic.

Even if an evening at Glyndebourne is not in the diary, there will be many other excuses for planning a glorious picnic, even if it is transported no further than the garden or balcony. Elegant cloths and cutlery, china rather than plastic, pretty baskets for fruit and vegetables can all be managed if you have plenty of helpers.

I often choose quite spicy, flavoursome food, which I like best for eating out of doors. The picnic menu which follows has a faintly Mediterranean/Moorish taste with the spices for the roast squabs and the fruit and nuts in the bulgar wheat salad.

Of course, you do not need to cook everything yourself. There are many other things you might like to buy for an elegant picnic, from dressed crabs to cooked lobsters. When gull's eggs are in season, in the spring, they will make a fine and easy starter. They can occasionally be bought, hard-boiled, from game-dealers, who may also have them fresh for you to cook yourself; pile them into a basket, let everyone shell their own, and dip into celery salt. A lemon tart, if you are lucky enough to live near a good pâtisserie would be welcome, as would some good quality chocolate. Rather than truffles, I would choose Green & Black's organic chocolate, Valrhona's Carrés de Guanaja or Michel Cluizel's chocolate squares in a flat box.

Other welcome extras might be olives, breadsticks and dried fruit and nuts. These would also be ideal for that other sort of picnic, the unplanned one, when a sunny day announces itself, and you look at the contents of your refrigerator and store cupboard to decide if you can make a meal with the contents. A packet of vine leaves? Rinse and blanch them and wrap around minced, leftover roast lamb, mixed with herbs and seasoning. A can of tuna fish? Dried tomatoes? Pasta? Cook the pasta, and mix in some snipped-up tomatoes, fresh herbs and the tuna fish for a satisfying pasta salad. A jar of olives? Rinse them of their brine, and toss in a little olive oil, with thyme, chopped rosemary and oregano, a pinch of chilli and grated lemon zest. A jar of homemade lemon curd? Make small triangular sandwiches and serve as dessert with fresh or marinated fruit. Eggs, potatoes and other vegetables? A thick omelette to cut into wedges. A can of consommé? Chilled or hot, as you wish, in a vacuum flask with black pepper and a shot of rum, if hot, and vodka, if chilled.

To drink, take champagne or young wines. Leave the old clarets and burgundies at home, as they should not be disturbed. Likewise, the vintage port, unless you have sent the butler on ahead, by some days, to find a place for it to rest. In which case, also plan to take along a decanter, funnel and candle. Full-bodied rather than thin wines might be more appreciated in the event that a mean little breeze steals across the meadows. At our Glyndebourne picnic, we included, with the dessert, a bottle of Lanson demi-sec champagne, not widely available, but worth looking for as a lovely ending to a festive meal. A good, full cava, such as Raventos i Blanc, an oak-aged Italian chardonnay, a cabernet sauvignon from Provence, and a demi-sweet sparkling Clairette de Die from the south-west of France make an alternative to the classic champagne, white burgundy, claret pattern. All very good in their own right, they should not be seen as the poor man's alternative. A bottle of homemade elderflower cordial, and one of lemon barley water will be welcome thirst-quenchers, when diluted with sparkling mineral water.

Here are some more quick recipe ideas for a planned picnic, and a couple of recipes for using what you might have in the refrigerator or store cupboard for a more impromptu one.

- *Strawberry and orange salad* Whole or quartered strawberries, peeled, sliced oranges in muscat wine. Carry in a glass preserving jar, and eat with elegant forks from the jar, or from a glass bowl.

- *Egg and asparagus pudding* Chopped, freshly hard-boiled eggs, mixed with softened butter and seasoning, and cooked green asparagus cut into small pieces. Pack firmly into a cling-film lined pudding basin.

Keep cold, and turn out on to a platter, plain or with salad leaves. Serve with wholemeal or granary bread.

- *Baby vegetables* Cherry tomatoes, button mushrooms, corn cobs, carrots, broccoli florets, radishes, baby turnips packed in and served from a basket lined with cabbage leaves, and with it a pot of home-made dip – fromage frais and crème fraîche, mixed with fresh horse-radish, chopped chives and parsley.

- *Strawberry basket* A leaf-lined basket piled high with strawberries interspersed with sprigs of mint. Carry, in two separate jars or pots, light muscovado sugar and crème fraîche for dipping.

- *Potato salad* A bowl or basket of boiled new potatoes, washed and brushed but not scraped or peeled. Do not dress them but carry separately sea salt, coarsely ground black pepper and a pot of home-made mayonnaise or herb and cream dressing.

savoury batter pudding

Good hot, warm or cold, these are excellent picnic food. As an alternative, I sometimes make them with grated courgettes and cheese instead of tomatoes, olives and anchovies.

makes 1 × 20cm (8 inch) pudding or 12 individual puddings

75g (3oz) flour

2 eggs

300ml (½ pint) milk or milk and water mixed

3 ripe tomatoes, peeled, seeded and chopped

2 tbsps black olives, stoned

1 garlic clove, crushed (optional)

2–3 spring onions, trimmed and sliced (optional)

6–8 anchovy fillets, chopped

freshly ground black pepper

Sift the flour into a large bowl, then add the eggs and milk, and beat until you have a smooth batter. Stir in the remaining ingredients and season with a little pepper. Pour into a lightly oiled flan dish or bun tins (or use non-stick baking equipment) and bake in a preheated oven at 200°C/400°F/gas mark 6 for 20–30 minutes for small puddings and 45–50 minutes for the large one. They should be quite dark golden brown and puffed up when cooked, though they will sink somewhat when removed from the oven. The texture will not be as light and crisp as a Yorkshire pudding.

quail's eggs in tarragon jelly

When I serve these at home, I unmould the jellies by briefly dipping the base of the ramekins in hot water, and turn out on to plates with some salad leaves. Alfresco, the jellies can be eaten with spoons.

serves 4 to 6
>   300ml (½ pint) good clear chicken stock
>   bunch of French tarragon
>   12 quail's eggs
>   4 sheets leaf gelatine or 4 tsps gelatine granules
>   salad leaves

Bring half the stock to the boil. Remove a dozen or so of the best tarragon leaves, roughly chop the rest, and add to the stock. Boil for 2 minutes, remove from the heat, and infuse for 15–20 minutes.

Bring a pan of water to the boil, gently slide in the quail's eggs and boil for 30 seconds. Remove the pan from the heat and leave for 2 minutes before plunging the eggs into cold water.

Soften the gelatine in the remaining stock, then heat gently until dissolved. Strain the tarragon stock into the gelatine stock, and mix thoroughly. Pour a little into the bottom of four or six small ramekins. Allow to set. Lay tarragon leaves on top. Shell the quail's eggs, and put two or three in each ramekin. Fill to the top with the rest of the cooled stock. Allow to set before serving with salad leaves.

entertaining

spiced lemon roasted squabs

This is a rather expensive bird but is delicious, quick to cook, and the carcasses make excellent stock afterwards. You could substitute quails, allowing for one or two per person, in which case the cooking time would be slightly less.

serves 6

- 6 squabs
- 1 large lemon
- 1–2 tbsps extra virgin olive oil
- scant tsp salt
- 1 tsp each freshly ground black pepper, ground coriander and cumin
- ½ tsp each ground cardamom, cloves and cinnamon
- 150ml (¼ pint) chicken stock, white wine or water

Cut the wing tips from the birds, and wipe them thoroughly, inside and out. Shave six spirals of lemon zest and put inside the birds. Halve the lemon and rub lemon juice all over the birds. Cut up the lemon and put a piece inside each bird. Brush with olive oil, then dust with the spice mixture, inside and out. Brown the birds all over in a lidded sauté pan or shallow casserole, then remove while you deglaze the pan with the stock, wine or water, scraping up any residue. Return the birds to the pan, cover, and cook on top of the stove or in a pre-heated oven at 180°C/350°F/gas mark 4 for 45 minutes. Allow to cool before wrapping. If you prefer, after the birds have been seasoned, you can put them, in pairs, in roasting bags and roast them.

bulgar wheat salad

This makes a substantial, and colourful, accompaniment to the squab. I use a measuring jug since it is a question of volume rather than weight in this recipe.

serves 6

600ml (1 pint) water or stock

200ml (7fl oz) bulgar wheat

extra virgin olive oil

spring onions or chives

black olives

dried apricots, chopped

toasted flaked almonds

fresh mint

fresh coriander

salt

freshly ground black pepper

Bring the water or stock to the boil, pour in the bulgar wheat, and remove from the heat. Allow to stand for 5 minutes or so, by which time the liquid will all be absorbed. Stir occasionally to break up any lumps. Pour into a large serving bowl, and allow to cool before adding the remaining ingredients, otherwise it will tend to cook them.

espresso coffee custards

serves 6

  450ml (¾ pint) full cream or semi-skimmed milk

  125g (4–5oz) freshly ground espresso coffee

  100–125g (4oz) golden caster sugar

  5 egg yolks

  scant pinch of salt

  whipping or double cream

Put the milk and coffee in a saucepan. Scald, remove from the heat, and leave to infuse for 5–10 minutes. In another saucepan, dissolve half the sugar in a tablespoon of water, then cook until it caramelizes, but do not let it burn or it will be bitter and you will have to start again. Remove from the heat immediately, and stir in a couple of tablespoons of water to make a thin caramel syrup.

Mix the egg yolks and remaining sugar in a bowl, stir in the caramel, and strain into it the coffee, through muslin or a jelly bag, squeezing to extract all the liquid. Add the salt, and then set the bowl over a pan of simmering water, or transfer the mixture to a bain marie. Cook gently until the custard thickens, stirring constantly. Remove from the heat, and pour into espresso cups, leaving about 2.5–5mm (¼–½ inch) at the top. Chill until set, then top with a layer of whipped cream, cover with cling film and carry to the picnic in a cool bag.

a boating picnic

There is a nautical, marine mood to the next menu, suitable for messing about in boats or at the seaside. Inspiration comes from the times we spent in Hong Kong in the late 1980s and early 1990s. In summer, one of the favourite forms of entertainment there, especially in the evening or on a Sunday, is to pack up a picnic and take a few friends for a ride on one of the large motorized junk boats to one of the outer islands for walking, swimming, sunbathing or simply feasting.

I remember one hot July night being invited by friends, who were off duty from the Mandarin Hotel, where I cooked as guest chef on a couple of occasions, for just such a trip. Our destination was, ultimately, a sea food restaurant on the waterfront of Lamma island. It was not a long journey, but a picnic was provided to be going on with. A box of petits fours from the pastry kitchen of the hotel was supplemented by cocktail sandwiches in a most ingenious presentation. A large loaf of bread had a 'lid' sliced off, and then the inner part, the crumb, was carefully removed in one piece with a very sharp knife. This crustless loaf was sliced, and small sandwiches were made which were then packed back into the loaf crust, and the lid replaced. This is such a good idea for picnic food; self-contained, easy to transport, keeps well, and can be eaten with the fingers. I commend it to you.

Smoked cod's roe is an excellent sandwich filling, and you can use it, not only as I have described in the following recipe, but also to fill small sandwiches to fit the cocktail loaf. For other fish fillings, consider smoked mackerel, smoked trout, flaked and mixed with a little horseradish, chopped prawns mixed with mayonnaise or soured cream flavoured with dill, and leftover cooked smoked haddock mixed with chopped hard-boiled eggs and mayonnaise.

Another lazy Hong Kong Sunday was spent on a friend's boat, moored in the New Territories, from where we took a short cruise in the South China Sea, swam from the boat, and ate mountains of sweet, freshly boiled tiger prawns, rice and a chicken curry. For me, spicy food, especially cold and curried, is the perfect food for a summer outing. My recipe for curried chicken and mango salad is a very easy one and can be served with a rice salad, mixed with chopped mint, coriander and basil. Suitable for picnics or boat trips, it makes an equally fine main course for a summer luncheon or supper. A sumptuous variation on this can be achieved by substituting lobster for chicken. Lobster does not get any cheaper than in the summer months, which is the best possible time to buy the large crustaceans.

Lobster and potato salad and lobster club sandwiches might also be considered for this nautical feast. For something more modest, try the prawns and avocado parcels, they are truly exquisite.

I like German wine with shellfish and smoked fish, and it is also a good accompaniment to lightly spiced food. Begin with a Mosel for aperitifs, and then move on to a Rheingau or Rheinpfalz with the prawns and the chicken salad. For those who like that sort of thing, here is a cocktail, which fits the nautical mood. I particularly like the colour.

deep blue

serves 1

1 measure vodka

1 measure blue curaçao

1 tsp syrup or icing sugar (optional)

sparkling mineral water

borage flowers

Pour the spirits into a chilled glass. Sweeten if you wish, top up with sparkling mineral water, and decorate with deep blue borage flowers, which you have taken on board, carefully wrapped in damp paper towel, and packed in a plastic box.

smoked cod's roe sandwiches

Buy about 200g (7oz) undyed smoked cod's roe. Scrape it out of the skin, and mix with a little unsalted butter. Spread on small rounds of pumpernickel, top with radishes, sliced paper-thin, and serve, with or without another slice of pumpernickel on top.

dressed crab

serves 6

1 large crab, freshly cooked

125g (4oz) unsalted butter, softened

1 shallot, peeled and finely chopped

pinch of mace

pinch of cayenne

sea salt

freshly ground black pepper

lemon juice

mayonnaise, crème fraîche or whipped cream

chopped herbs – *see* recipe

Remove the crab claws and legs. Separate the shell from the body. Remove the pale, feathery gills, the 'dead men's' fingers, and the stomach sac (which is like a tiny crumpled plastic bag). Scoop the pale, soft meat from the shell, and scrape away any sticking to the body part. Mix it with the butter, shallot, mace, cayenne, salt, pepper and lemon juice to taste. Use this as a spread for tiny crustless brown bread sandwiches, heaped on to a platter, in the centre of which should repose the clean and shiny crab shell, which you have filled with the white meat, lightly seasoned and eked out with mayonnaise, crème fraîche or whipped cream and chopped herbs. Chervil, tarragon or flat-leaf parsley are particularly good with crab.

prawn and avocado parcels

Large leaves of lettuce, spinach, Chinese cabbage or chard can replace the cabbage if you prefer.

serves 6

6 large cabbage leaves

350g (12oz) peeled prawns

2 ripe avocados, peeled and diced

2–3 tbsps homemade mayonnaise

crème fraîche or soured cream

1 tbsp chopped chives, plus 6 long chives for tying the parcels

freshly ground black pepper

1 green chilli, seeded and finely chopped (optional)

Boil the cabbage leaves until just tender. Drain and refresh under cold water. Dry on paper towels, and cut out the stem. Mix the prawns, avocado, mayonnaise and chopped chives, and season with pepper. If you like, a little chopped green chilli can also be added. Divide the mixture between the cabbage leaves, and enclose carefully, tying with a chive.

spiced chicken and mango salad

If you wish, you can toast and grind your own spices for this recipe, or buy a ready-made curry paste, of which there are some good ones available, in different strengths. Spices to toast are cumin, coriander and cardamom seeds, cloves, cinnamon and a little turmeric, together with black peppercorns.

serves 6 to 8

    2 tbsps medium curry paste
    4 chicken breasts, either sliced or diced
    150ml (¼ pint) thick coconut milk or crème fraîche
    salad leaves
    2 ripe mangoes, peeled and sliced or diced

Heat the curry paste in a dry frying pan over a medium heat for 3–4 minutes. Stir in the chicken, add the milk or crème fraîche, and simmer for about 15 minutes until the chicken is done. Remove from the heat, allow to cool, and then arrange on salad leaves, interspersed with slices of mango. Or dice the mango, mix with the chicken, and heap into a bowl lined with lettuce leaves.

a racing picnic

A day in the open air at a traditional British race meeting is something I rarely indulge in, and I forget what a great pleasure it is. In fact, I get so excited I can hardly eat.

Horse-racing is a delightfully all-embracing event. You don't have to be a toff with Jeeves serving you langoustines and foie gras sandwiches from the boot of the Bentley, although that is not to be sniffed at. Once we were invited to Ascot and our thoughtful hosts provided an amply filled hamper, which included chilled gazpacho with croûtons, poached salmon with homemade dill mayonnaise, chargrilled chicken breast with citrus dressing, a mixed leaf salad, couscous and roasted vegetable salad, and, to finish, pecan pie and cream, mixed summer berries, coffee and mints. Fortunately, a table and chairs were provided, too, as this was indeed a sit down, knife and fork lunch, and almost perfect. Nothing was forgotten, down to an ice bucket for the Veuve Clicquot and the Bordeaux rosé, and a corkscrew.

This was all a far cry from childhood visits to race meetings at Doncaster or Wetherby, which would be accompanied by my mother's bacon and egg pie, cheese and tomato sandwiches and fruit cake, washed down with a flask of tea.

If you are treating yourself to a day at the races, here are some ideas for substantial, yet unusual, and rather elegant, picnic food that can be prepared in advance and served and eaten with minimal equipment from a basket in the car boot. Like all my recipes in this chapter for picnics and outdoor eating, these will do equally well for an alfresco lunch at home. Quantities can be multiplied to furnish a buffet.

On the table, these dishes can be supplemented with bowls of green salad, potato and olive salad, and some mixed salads. In such circumstances I like to serve mixed fruit and vegetable salads with complementary flavours and colours. Try, for example, combinations of carrots and peaches, melon and cucumber, or steamed courgettes, sliced strawberries and jicama. By all means experiment with different oils and vinegars for dressings at home, but for a picnic, it is perhaps best to choose something such as a yoghurt or soured cream dip, which will be less likely to seep and leak over everything. Whatever food you choose for your picnic, there should be plenty of it; appetites sharpen in the open air.

In 1864, *The Times* had a long account of the Grand Prix at Longchamps, just outside Paris, saying it 'bids fair to rival the Derby', although the catering, apparently, was not up to the same standard, 'nothing like the excitement of luncheon on the hill at Epsom. If anybody wishes refreshment there are ice, lemonade, claret and every kind of pâtisserie provided for French tastes, and great fleets of tumblers, containing sherries and grogs, with piles of sandwiches for what are supposed to be the correct tastes of Englishmen and Anglomaniacs.'

Amongst the many English present on that day were two very knowledgeable racegoers. Isabella Beeton was the stepdaughter of the Clerk to Epsom racecourse, and her husband, Sam, was, according to their biographer and Mrs Beeton's great-niece, Nancy Spain, probably a heavy gambler. Isabella criticized the food too, as an 'imitation of English light foods which completely fails in its object'. Sam was less critical. His diary notes 'one refreshment booth, for all the crowd. Every body had just well breakfasted upon cotelletes, omelettes, Rognons and until the witching hour of dinner no one wanted anything for the inner Frenchman.'

Cold cutlets, provided they are well-seasoned, some spicy devilled kidneys and a thick multicoloured 'cake' of omelettes are easy to make, inexpensive, and taste as good cold as they do hot; they are the 'main courses' for today's racing picnic. I have also included a sandwich for the serious racegoer who, like the inventive Earl of Sandwich, cannot be doing with interruptions of the main business.

A rich tipsy cake is the perfect finale. This recipe is yet another adaptation of my tipsy cake recipe. My mother's further adaptation of it uses demerara sugar in the absence of dark muscovado, walnuts instead of pecans, and Irish Mist for the spirit.

silks

serves 2

> 2, 3 or 4 measures gin
> 2 measures elderflower cordial
> sparkling mineral water
> thin slices of lemon
> edible white flowers

Mix the gin and cordial in two tall, chilled glasses, top up with sparkling mineral water, decorate and serve.

omelette cake

serves 6 to 8

12 large eggs

1 bunch watercress, leaves only, or the equivalent amount of sorrel, spinach or rocket

4 firm ripe tomatoes, peeled, seeded and chopped

freshly ground black pepper

6 anchovies (canned)

50g (2oz) unsalted butter, softened, or sunflower margarine

Beat six eggs in one bowl and six in another. Blanch the watercress and chop it finely. (Do the same to the sorrel, spinach or rocket, if using.) Mix the tomatoes into one batch of eggs and the watercress into the other. Make two separate thick, open omelettes (like Spanish omelettes, not folded), and turn out on to racks to cool. Pound the anchovies with the butter, and use to sandwich the two omelettes when cold. Cut into wedges like a cake, then reassemble before wrapping.

parmesan lamb cutlets

makes 18 to 20

> 3 racks of lamb, chined, very well trimmed, and cut into cutlets
>
> 125g (4oz) white breadcrumbs, lightly toasted
>
> 25g (1oz) ground almonds
>
> 125g (4oz) freshly grated Parmesan
>
> 1 tbsp finely chopped thyme
>
> freshly ground black pepper
>
> 2 eggs, lightly beaten

The meat should be trimmed to give a clean rib bone with just the eye of the meat attached.

Mix the dry ingredients together very thoroughly. Dip the cutlets into the egg, and then into the crumb mixture, pressing it in well. Arrange on non-stick baking sheets, then roast in a preheated oven at 200°C/400°F/gas mark 6 for 8–15 minutes, depending on the thickness of the meat and how well done you like it. Allow to cool before wrapping.

devilled kidneys

An alternative way of cooking the kidneys to take to a picnic is to thread them on soaked wooden skewers, interspersed with mushrooms, then brush them with oil and grill them. Assuming, of course, that you have a portable barbecue or grill.

serves 6

8–12 lamb's kidneys

1 tbsp paprika

½ tsp chilli or cayenne

1 tbsp ground cumin

½ tsp freshly ground black pepper

2–3 tsps Madras curry powder (optional)

3 tbsps flour or cornmeal

butter or olive oil for frying

Halve the kidneys horizontally and snip out the white core. Put all the dry ingredients in a paper bag. Coat the kidneys in the seasoned flour by putting a few at a time in the bag and shaking it.

Heat the oil or butter in a frying pan until very hot, then add the kidneys and fry for a few minutes, turning them once, until just done, but still pink inside. It is important to cook kidneys fast on high heat if they are to remain tender; kidneys can also be made tender by cooking them very slowly for a long time.

bookies' sandwich

makes 2 to 3 large sandwiches

> 4cm (1½ inch) thick well-hung Aberdeen Angus sirloin steak,
>   weighing approx 350g (12–14oz)
> 1 ciabatta loaf
> unsalted butter, softened
> salt
> freshly ground black pepper

Grill the steak until done to your liking. Remove it from the heat, and allow to cool. Remove all the fat, and cut into small, thin rectangular slices. (It is much easier to eat a steak sandwich filled with small pieces of meat, rather than a large slice.) Split the ciabatta in half, and butter both sides. Fill the ciabatta with the meat, cut the loaf into two or three wedges and wrap tightly. By the time the sandwiches are eaten, the meat juices will have been absorbed by the bread. It is not a good idea to put lettuce between the bread and meat, as it will act as a moisture-proof barrier.

chocolate tipsy cake

serves 8 to 10

250g (8oz) unsalted butter

280g (10oz) light or dark muscovado sugar

400g (14oz) self-raising flour

pinch of salt

25g (1oz) cocoa powder

4 eggs, lightly beaten

125g (4oz) desiccated coconut

125g (4oz) pecans or walnuts, chopped

1 tsp pure vanilla essence

75–100ml (3–4fl oz) Plymouth gin

milk

Cream the butter and sugar until light and fluffy. Sift together the flour, salt and cocoa. Beat the eggs and flour alternately into the creamed mixture. Stir in the remaining ingredients, all except for half the spirit, adding enough milk to give a soft dropping consistency. Spoon the mixture into a greased and floured 1kg (2lb) loaf tin, and smooth the top. Bake in a preheated oven at 150°C/300°F/gas mark 3 for 2 hours. Remove and allow to cool in the tin. Prick the cake all over with a skewer or cocktail stick, then pour over the remaining gin. Cover the cake with foil, and allow to stand in a cool place for several hours until the spirit has been absorbed. Then remove the cake from the tin and wrap in grease-proof paper and foil. It will keep for several weeks.

an autumn picnic

The nearest I have ever been to live grouse was when we used to go picking bilberries amongst the heather on the north Yorkshire moors. However, I have friends who shoot, and I am a great fan of Edwardian novels with their shooting party set pieces, and these are the sources of inspiration for the recipes which follow.

An early, chill start to the day suggests that a flask of beef or game consommé with a shot of rum or sherry in it would be welcome. And if it stayed cold, then a wide-mouthed Thermos containing a casserole would be a good idea. Beef and pigeon or venison cooked in port, red wine and some herbs seem to me to fit the bill rather better than a pale casserole of chicken or rabbit in white wine.

Easily transportable food that does not crumble, go moist, limp or greasy is imperative. Sturdy fruit cakes and well-filled pies make excellent cold food. For this reason, I have suggested that the fruit cake is not made in a round tin. When cut into wedge shapes, fruit cake often crumbles in the centre, I find. A square tin, a ring or a loaf tin produces a cake that is much easier to slice.

Sandwiches remain one of my favourite foods for picnics and for snacks, and they will be perfect for any kind of autumn outing, whether foraging for wild mushrooms, stalking deer or simply taking the dog for a long walk. Cold roast meat or game is an obvious choice for filling, either sliced or potted. The recipe I have given below for spiced, pressed beef and grouse can be adapted to other game meats in season, or can be used for beef alone. I am also very fond of egg sandwiches, so would probably pack a round or two of those, however unorthodox, or some hard-boiled eggs.

Lettuce hearts, celery and firm, but ripe, tomatoes would help down all the starch and protein and be refreshingly crisp if the weather were warm. Ginger biscuits, shortbread and dark bitter chocolate would accompany the flask of coffee. I am not sure if cheese would be a good idea, too thirst-making perhaps. But the first job would be to find a fast-flowing stream or deep cold burn in which to chill the bottles of cider that I would also include in my picnic

spiced pressed beef with grouse

serves 10 as a starter, or use as a sandwich filling

1kg (2lb) rump steak in a thick piece

breasts of 2 young grouse

freshly ground black pepper

6 juniper berries

6 cloves

6 allspice berries

large blade of mace

75ml (3fl oz) port

75ml (3fl oz) beef or game stock made from the trimmings of
   grouse carcasses and beef

1 bay leaf

clarified butter

Slice the rump steak about 1cm (⅜ inch) thick. Remove the fillets from under the grouse breasts, and cut the breasts into strips or slices of a similar thickness as the beef. Layer the meat in a terrine. Season lightly with pepper, and scatter over the spices. Pour the port and stock over the meat, and place the bay leaf on top. Cover with foil, and cook in the bottom half of a preheated oven at 180°C/350°F/gas mark 4 until the meat is just cooked through and tender. Remove from the oven, and drain off the cooking juices, which can be reserved for another dish. Cover the meat with foil, weight down, cool and refrigerate for several hours. The meat can then be thinly sliced if using it immediately, or it can be covered with clarified butter for use in two or three days' time.

potted beef and grouse

The ingredients used in the previous recipe will also make potted meat. Prepare, season and cook the meat as above. When cooked, drain off the juices, and put the meat in a processor or mincer with about 125g (4oz) butter and a little of the cooking juice. Mince or process until smooth, pack into ramekins and cover with clarified butter, if it is to be served as a starter, or use as a spread for sandwiches.

---

little game pies

makes 24

- 500g (1lb) cooked meat off the bone, rabbit, grouse,
    pigeon or venison or mixture
- 75g (3oz) raisins
- 75g (3oz) sultanas
- 1 apple
- 75g (3oz) pine nuts or blanched almonds, chopped
- 75g (3oz) light muscovado sugar
- juice and grated zest of 1 lemon
- 300ml (½ pint) game stock, gravy or cooking juices
- 1 small onion, peeled and finely chopped
- 1 tbsp finely chopped parsley
- salt
- freshly ground black pepper
- ground mace or nutmeg
- ground allspice
- 350g (12oz) shortcrust pastry
- beaten egg and milk to glaze

Chop the meat very small, just coarser than mince, and put in a bowl with the fruit, nuts, sugar, lemon, stock, onion and parsley. Add salt, pepper and spices to taste, bearing in mind that dishes served cold often need a little more seasoning than those served hot.

Roll out the pastry, and use two thirds to line bun tins. Spoon in the filling, and cover with pastry lids, cut from the remaining pastry. Brush with the egg and milk glaze, and bake in a preheated oven at 180°C/350°F/gas mark 4 for 35–40 minutes.

herb and ham pie

If you prefer, chicken breasts that have been lightly poached can replace the ham.

serves 4 to 6

500g (1lb) shortcrust pastry

500g (1lb) gammon or bacon slices

250g (8oz) spinach, washed, blanched and dried

250g (8oz) tender leeks, washed, rinsed, thinly sliced and blanched

bunch of watercress, washed, dried and chopped

chervil

parsley

French tarragon

4 eggs

4 tbsps cream or stock

freshly ground black pepper

beaten egg and milk to glaze

Line a 25cm (10 inch) pie dish with half the pastry. Cut the ham or bacon into pieces, and scatter over the pastry. Chop the vegetables and herbs, mix with a couple of tablespoons of chervil and parsley and rather less of tarragon, and place on top of the ham. Beat together the eggs and cream or stock, season with a little pepper, and pour over the filling. Roll out the remaining pastry to make a lid. Seal the edges, and brush with the glaze. Place on a baking sheet, and bake in a preheated oven at 180°C/350°F/gas mark 4 for about 40 minutes.

berrichon meat pie

serves 6

for the pastry

    75g (3oz) fresh goat's cheese

    100g (4oz) unsalted butter, at warm room temperature

    300g (10oz) plain flour

for the filling

    250g (8oz) each boneless shoulder of pork, kid and lamb

    25g (1oz) butter

    1 small onion, peeled and finely chopped

    2 tbsps finely chopped parsley

    6 eggs

    salt

    freshly ground black pepper

    freshly grated nutmeg

Crumble the goat's cheese, and mix it with the butter. Chill it again before making a puff pastry with the flour and butter/cheese mixture, giving it six turns in all. If you are using commercial puff pastry, roll it out, and then dot with a mixture of 25g (1oz) butter and 25g (1oz) goat's cheese; fold the pastry in three, roll it, turn, and repeat with more butter and cheese. This will not only enrich what can sometimes be rather dull pastry, but it will also impart the goat's cheese flavour.

Dice the meat small, and fry it in the butter for 15–20 minutes. Mix in the onion, parsley and a lightly beaten egg yolk. Season lightly with nutmeg, salt and pepper. Allow the mixture to cool. Hard-boil four of the eggs, and shell them.

Heat the oven to 200°C/400°F/gas mark 6. Roll out two circles of pastry to a diameter of about 25cm (10 inches), one slightly thicker than the other, for the base. Place this on an oiled baking sheet. Pile the filling on to the base, leaving a margin of about 2.5cm (1 inch) around the edges. Cut the eggs in half lengthways, and arrange them, cut side down, petal fashion, on top of the meat, chopping any that won't fit and sprinkling amongst the meat. Beat the remaining egg with a little milk, or water, and brush it around the edge of the pie. Lay the second round of pastry on top, and seal it with the tines of a fork. Knock up the edges of the pastry with a knife. Brush the pie with beaten egg, and make a slit or two in the middle for the steam to escape. Bake in a preheated oven at 200°C/400°F/gas mark 6 for 15–20 minutes, then reduce the temperature to 170°C/325°F/gas mark 3 and bake for a further 20 minutes.

club sandwiches with fruit butter

The recipe is a most versatile one. Try it with blackberry, apple and prune butters, or with tropical fruits, such as mango, passion fruit and pineapple. If you are serving the sandwiches at home, the bread can be lightly toasted on one side and the sandwiches dusted with icing sugar.

makes 12

12 large slices of bread, crusts removed

3 peaches

125g (4oz) each strawberries and raspberries

250g (8oz) unsalted butter, at room temperature

75g (3oz) icing sugar

Halve, stone and roughly chop the peaches and hull the strawberries. Process each fruit separately with a third of the butter and sugar. Spread a slice of bread with strawberry butter, and top with another slice. Spread that one with peach butter and cover with another slice. Spread that with raspberry butter, and top with the last slice of bread. Cut into four triangles, and spear each with cocktail sticks. Prepare the other two rounds in the same way.

summer fruit and ginger cake

This cake is also very good with the addition of nuts and seeds, such as pistachios, almonds, pine nuts, pumpkin and sunflower.

serves 15 to 20

500g (1lb) butter

500g (1lb) sugar

8 eggs, beaten

500g (1lb) plain flour, sifted

250g (8oz) each sultanas, dried or crystallized pineapple and dried apricots

125g (4oz) each dried peaches or nectarines and dried pears

50g (2oz) crystallized ginger

juice and grated zest of 1 lemon

6 tbsps white rum

Double line and grease a square cake tin, ring tin or loaf tin, the equivalent volume of a 22–25cm (9–10 inch) round cake tin, and preheat the oven to 180°C/350°F/gas mark 4. Cream the butter and sugar until light and fluffy. Add the eggs and flour alternately, thoroughly mixing in each addition, but folding gently rather than beating. Stir in the fruit, ginger, juice and grated zest, and rum. Smooth the top, and bake in the middle of a preheated oven at 180°C/350°F/gas mark 4 for about 2–2½ hours. The cake is cooked when a skewer inserted in the middle comes out clean.

serial entertaining

I use the term serial entertaining as shorthand to describe the situation where two or three dinner parties, a drinks party and a buffet luncheon, for example, are fitted into a relatively short space of time, and accomplished with ease. Just the sort of situation in which many of us find ourselves, at least once or twice, whether during end-of-year festivities, a bout of housewarming celebrations or a major birthday or anniversary.

The thought of fitting so much into little more than the equivalent of a long weekend might seem terrifying, but it is not, I promise. It is easy and fun. In fact, it involves much less of the boring work than if you were to spread out your entertaining over several weeks. By boring, I mean cleaning the cutlery, dusting the house, scouring the bathroom, polishing the furniture, shining the windows, doing the flowers – all those little bourgeois habits that die hard. Have one big cleaning bash before you start, and the place will only need minor sprucing up in between.

With my plan of action, shopping can be kept to a minimum once you have decided on the main elements of the menu. This is where creative planning is balanced with careful economy. It might sound improbable, but with just three main ingredients, you can create at least four quite different menus that require the least possible preparation time, yet give the cook a great deal of pleasure. I have given several examples, and some recipes, one menu for spring and summer entertaining, one for autumn and winter, and one for a set of recipes suitable for all seasons. The first uses duckling, strawberries and salmon. The second uses pheasant, smoked haddock and pumpkin. The third uses chicken, salmon and apples.

These menu plans should be treated as no more than suggestions, however. You might want to use raspberries or apricots instead of strawberries, turkey or goose instead of pheasant, or base your puddings around pears or chestnuts instead of pumpkin; the same principles apply. Other ingredients readily suggest themselves for this treatment. For example, if you love chocolate, you might like to plan all your desserts *autour du chocolat*; mousses, truffles, individual warm chocolate cakes, pear and chocolate tart, chocolate sorbet and ice cream, for example. If you are someone who stocks the freezer with half carcasses of meat, this is the way to use it; elegant noisettes of lamb for one meal, a lamb cobbler or Irish stew for another, shepherd's pie for the buffet, spiced savoury lamb pasties or stuffed vine leaves for the drinks party. The possibilities are limitless. This is a blueprint for you to devise your own scheme.

With the three main ingredients I have suggested, you can produce two dinner parties for six to eight people, in which you either plate the main course or present it on a serving platter. The puddings can be made into individual servings or dished up family-style. The soups, too, can be served in individual bowls, or from a large tureen. The third menu forms a buffet or more casual meal, everyone helping themselves, and the fourth consists of small items to serve at a drinks party. Alternatively, these, too, could form part of a buffet.

You will find recipes in other parts of the book suitable for this style of entertaining, and certainly in my last book, *Modern Classics*, you will find a wealth of material to help you with serial entertaining.

spring and summer

Duck breasts, for a smart dinner for six, leaves you with legs for a richly flavoured casserole to be served at a more casual meal within the next few days. From the carcasses, you will be able to produce enough stock to make a large tureen of vichyssoise, borscht or other vegetable soup to be served hot, or chilled, depending on the weather. The birds might even yield enough leftovers to make potted duck, an excellent starter if packed into small ramekins, topped with clarified butter and served with hot toast.

A whole salmon produces a tail end with which to make gravadlax, as well as neat fillets to grill or fry. Leftover salmon can be potted, or you might have an alternative use for it. For example, I usually cut up any remaining gravadlax, and stir it into freshly cooked tagliatelle with a little mustard and dill sauce. It makes a delightful supper.

Strawberries, of course, lend themselves to a variety of different recipes, of which I have suggested four. And if in doubt, simply serve a huge basket of deliciously ripe but firm fruit, with, as accompaniments, a bowl of light muscovado sugar and one of cream. Even nicer, if you can arrange it, is for everyone to have their own basket of strawberries and small bowls of cream and sugar. This turns a very simple idea into an elegant treat.

The menu suggestions are:

for the first dinner party
    duck consommé
    with spring vegetables and miniature herb dumplings
    or
    duck and pistachio terrine

    salmon fillets with coriander chutney,
    served with olive oil mashed potatoes

    strawberry tart

for the next dinner
    salmon and dill broth under a pastry lid

    grilled marinated duck breasts with cherry and balsamic sauce,
    served with chive-mashed potatoes and grilled vegetables

    strawberry granita or ice cream
    with almond crisps

for the third meal, a buffet

    gravadlax or cured salmon

    duck and olive casserole with new potatoes

    strawberry and raspberry fool

With luck, you should also be able to make, some or all of the following:

for a drinks party

    miniature fish cakes

    cured salmon on pumpernickel

    chilled brandade of salmon on hot toast

    potted duck

    canapés topped with grilled vegetables

    individual strawberry tarts, strawberry fritters or tiny glasses of strawberry
       and raspberry fool

salmon fillets with coriander chutney

This recipe also works very well with cod or undyed smoked haddock fillets. It is worth cooking extra fish to make into fish cakes for another occasion. Cut the fillet into six pieces of similar shape and thickness.

serves 6

    6 × 150–170g (5–6oz) salmon fillets

    coriander chutney – *see* recipe below

    lemon or lime juice

    olive oil for cooking, or use a non-stick pan

Skin the fish, dry it thoroughly, and smear the chutney liberally all over it. Then let it marinate for at least an hour. Without lemon juice, the fish can be left for 4–5 hours, covered and refrigerated, which is why I leave the lemon or lime juice out of the chutney. Fish should not be left in an acid marinade for more than 10–15 minutes before cooking or the flesh will begin to soften.

Just before cooking, sprinkle the fish with lemon or lime juice. Heat a wide, heavy frying pan over a moderate heat. Place the fillets in a single layer, cover with a lid or foil, and let them sweat in their own juices. They will take about 8–10 minutes to cook, depending on the thickness and how well done you like your fish. Steaming is another suitable method for cooking the fillets. Again, it will take about 8–10 minutes. Alternatively, cook the fish in the oven *en papillote*.

coriander chutney

Use a large bunch of coriander. If you plan to serve very grand white burgundy with the salmon, you may prefer to leave out the chilli. Walnuts, pine nuts or almonds can be used. Sometimes I use a mixture of toasted nuts and seeds that I keep on hand, such as almonds, hazelnuts, pine nuts, pumpkin seeds and sunflower seeds. This is a flexible and versatile recipe, worth making even if you do not plan to use it with the fish. Mix it with mashed potatoes, or stir it into a risotto or pasta.

makes about 225 g (8 oz)
    1 large bunch coriander
    1 shallot, peeled and chopped
    2 garlic cloves, peeled and chopped
    1 green chilli, seeded and sliced
    75g (3oz) walnuts, pine nuts or almonds – *see* above
    extra virgin olive oil or walnut oil
    salt
    freshly ground black pepper

Shake the coriander. Rinse and dry it very thoroughly only if it needs it. Discard any wilted stems and most of the thicker stems. Roughly chop the rest, and place, together with the shallot, garlic, chilli, nuts and oil, in a food processor. Process until it has the texture you prefer, coarse or smooth. Season to taste, and refrigerate until required.

---

entertaining

cured salmon

serves 8

    1–1.25kg (2–2½ lb) boned and scaled tail fillets of salmon

    bunch of fresh dill or 3 tbsps dried dill seed or dill weed

    2 tbsps coarse sea salt

    1 tbsp granulated sugar

    1 tbsp coarsely ground black or white pepper

    1 tbsp cognac (optional)

Remove all the pin bones from the salmon. Spread a third of the dill on the bottom of the dish. Mix the salt, sugar and pepper, and sprinkle a third of it over the dill. Place one of the salmon fillets on top, skin side down. Sprinkle half the remaining seasoning over the fillet, and lay half the dill on top. Sprinkle on the cognac, if using. Place the other fillet on top. Sprinkle with the remaining seasoning, and put the rest of the dill on top. Cover with foil, and weigh down with tins. Refrigerate and keep for up to 4–5 days. The salmon is good to eat after just 12 hours or so.

    To serve it, wipe off the dill and seasoning, and slice into oblique or vertical slices. A sweet mustard mayonnaise is the traditional accompaniment.

duck and pistachio terrine

Apple juice can replace the cider and cider brandy. For an even more attractive presentation, you can wrap each of the strips of fillet in blanched, dried spinach, or roll them in finely chopped herbs. If you prefer, you can also substitute pork cuts for the veal.

makes 2 × 900g (2lb) terrines

> 350g (12oz) duck meat off the bone, plus 900g (2lb) fillets cut from
>> the skinned duck breasts
>
> 500g (1lb) breast or shoulder of veal or other fatty cut
>
> 225g (8oz) calves' or lamb's liver
>
> 2 tsps ground allspice
>
> 1 tsp ground cumin seeds
>
> 1 tsp celery seeds
>
> 2 tsps freshly ground black pepper
>
> 1–2 tsps sea salt
>
> 4 tbsps English cider brandy
>
> 300ml (½ pint) cider
>
> 150g (6oz) veal suet, or beef or vegetarian suet if unavailable, chilled
>
> flour
>
> 2 tbsps potato flour or cornflour
>
> 2 eggs
>
> 100g (4oz) soft breadcrumbs
>
> 100g (4oz) shelled, unsalted pistachios
>
> clarified butter

Coarsely mince or chop the 350g (12oz) of duck into 5mm (¼ inch) dice, removing any sinews. Mince the veal and the liver, and mix it with the minced duck, spices, seasonings, the cider brandy and all but two tablespoons of the cider, and marinate overnight, covered, in the refrigerator. Grate the suet and toss it lightly, a handful at a time, in a little flour in a paper bag. Put back in the refrigerator.

The following day, grease two 1kg (2lb) loaf tins, or terrines with similar capacity. Mix together the remaining cider and the potato flour, then beat in the eggs until thoroughly blended. Stir the egg mixture, breadcrumbs and the suet into the marinated minced meat and mix thoroughly. Layer the mince and duck fillets in each terrine, adding the pistachios at random. Push the meat well down, to expel any air bubbles, and heap up the top, as the mixture will shrink as it cooks. Cover with foil, and stand on a trivet or rack in a roasting tin deep enough to allow boiling water to be poured in, to come at least halfway up the loaf tin. Cook in the middle of a preheated oven at 180°C/350°F/gas mark 4 for 1½ –2 hours. The terrine is cooked when the juices released by a skewer inserted in the middle run clear. Remove from the heat, weigh down and allow to cool completely. Cover the surface with clarified butter to preserve it.

Serve sliced at room temperature, accompanied by pickled walnuts, Cumberland sauce and some rocket or watercress, as well as toast.

duck and olive casserole

This is very good with mashed potatoes, or potatoes sliced and baked in the oven in a layer, well seasoned and flavoured with stock or cream.

serves 6

6 duck legs
2 onions, peeled and sliced
piece of cinnamon
1 bay leaf
1 sprig of thyme
300ml (½ pint) full-bodied red wine
500g (1lb) small turnips, peeled
125g (4oz) olives, black or green, as you prefer
grated zest and juice of 1 orange

Divide the duck legs into thighs and drumsticks. In a casserole, fry the onions in a little duck fat, and then brown the meat. Add the cinnamon, herbs and wine. Bring to simmering point, add the turnips and olives, cover, and then cook in the middle of a preheated oven at 180°C/350°F/gas mark 4 for about 45–60 minutes or until the meat is tender. Add the orange juice and zest after 30 minutes.

grilled duck breasts
with cherry and balsamic sauce

Serve these with mashed potatoes mixed with plenty of chopped chives. In autumn this dish is very good adapted to cider, cider vinegar, cider brandy and, of course, apples instead of cherries. And try venison medallions in the same way, using pears.

serves 6

6 duck breasts

½ tsp each cinnamon, ground ginger, freshly ground black pepper

250ml (9fl oz) red wine

2 tbsps balsamic vinegar

sliver of fresh ginger

1 cinnamon stick

1 bay leaf

1 tsp black peppercorns

2–3 sprigs tarragon, plus extra for garnish

2 shallots, peeled and finely chopped

250g (9oz) cherries, Dukes or sours, ideally, or whatever you can get, stoned

75ml (3fl oz) extra virgin olive oil

Rub the duck breasts all over with the cinnamon, ground ginger and black pepper, having first scored the skin, then place them, skin side down, in a heavy frying pan over a moderate heat. When all the fat has melted, pour it off, and continue cooking the duck breasts, on both sides, until done to your liking.

Meanwhile, start the sauce. Put the wine, vinegar, fresh ginger, cinnamon stick, bay leaf, peppercorns, tarragon and shallots in a saucepan and simmer for 30 minutes or so, reducing by about half. Strain into a clean saucepan, add the cherries and simmer for 5–8 minutes. Remove from the heat and whisk in the olive oil, together with any further seasoning you wish to add.

To serve, cut the duck breasts simply in half, rather than slicing and fanning them, and place on top of the mashed potato at an angle, with the sauce spooned around. Some sprigs of watercress or rocket make a good, peppery contrast to the sweetness of the sauce.

strawberry ice cream

You can also make other fruit ice creams by cooking apricots with crushed cardamom seeds, cherries with cinnamon, and gooseberries with orange zest.

serves 6

300–400g (10–14oz) strawberries, rinsed and hulled
thinly pared zest of ½ lemon and ½ orange
200g (7oz) caster sugar
8 egg yolks
15g (½ oz) glucose (optional, for extra smoothness)
300ml (½ pint) milk
300ml (½ pint) single or double cream

Gently cook half the strawberries with the zest and half the sugar until they collapse, about 3–4 minutes only, in fact hardly enough to cook them, just to heat them through. Remove the zest, add the uncooked strawberries, and purée in a blender or food processor.

In a bowl, beat together the eggs and remaining sugar, adding the glucose, if using. Gently heat the milk and cream in a saucepan and, when warm, pour a quarter into the egg mixture, and thoroughly incorporate. Continue to heat the cream mixture and, when it boils, pour it over the egg mixture, beating continuously.

Sieve the mixture into a clean saucepan, and cook gently until thick enough to coat the back of a spoon. Cool, stir in the strawberry purée, then freeze either in an ice-cream maker or in a plastic container in the freezer. The former will turn the mixture and make it smooth without any further effort on your part. If freezing it in a plastic container, you will need to stir the mixture by hand (or in a food processor) when just frozen in order to get rid of ice particles and obtain a really smooth ice cream.

---

serial entertaining

strawberry and blueberry terrine
with strawberry sauce

serves 6 to 8

7 sheets leaf gelatine or 7 tsps gelatine granules

750ml (1¼ pints) clear apple, grape or pear juice

750g (1½lb) fresh strawberries, hulled and wiped

freshly ground black pepper

250g (8oz) blueberries

fresh herbs and flowers for garnish – such as mint, angelica,
sweet cicely, nasturtiums, rose petals

Soak the gelatine in a little water. Bring 200ml (7fl oz) of the juice to the boil, and stir in the softened gelatine. Stir until it has dissolved, then add another 400ml (14fl oz) juice. Allow to cool.

Take 200–250g (about 8oz) of the softest strawberries, and purée them with the remaining juice in a blender, adding a little freshly ground black pepper. Sieve into a jug, cover, and chill.

When the jelly is cool, start to assemble the terrine by first placing a layer of strawberries in the mould, a 1kg (2lb) terrine, covering them with jelly and chilling until set. Then add a layer of blueberries and jelly and, when this, too, has set, cover with another layer of strawberries and jelly. Continue in the same way until all the fruit and jelly have been used up. Chill until firm, turn out, slice, and arrange on plates. Spoon the strawberry sauce around the terrine, and decorate with flowers and herbs before serving.

entertaining

strawberry tart

An inner coating of thinly applied white chocolate makes the tart 'juice proof' and prevents the pastry getting soggy. It is a trick you can apply to all your fruit tarts.

serves 8 to10

250g (8oz) plain flour

100g (4oz) ground almonds

175g (6oz) unsalted butter, chilled and diced

50g (2oz) icing sugar, sifted

1 tsp pure vanilla essence

1 egg, lightly beaten

iced water, as necessary

200g (7oz) white chocolate

1kg (2lb) strawberries, rinsed and hulled

5 tbsps redcurrant jelly

600ml (1 pint) whipping cream (optional)

Sift the flour and ground almonds into a bowl. Rub in the butter, until you have a mixture resembling breadcrumbs, then stir in the sugar, vanilla essence and egg, and just enough water to bind to a smooth dough. Cover and chill for 30 minutes or so.

Roll out the pastry and use to line a greased and floured 25cm (10 inch) loose-bottomed flan tin or ring set on a prepared baking sheet. The ground almonds make this quite a fragile pastry, so if you find it difficult to roll it out, press it over the base and up the side of the prepared tin.Trim off the edges of the pastry, and prick all over with a fork. Line with foil or greaseproof paper, cover the base with ceramic baking 'beans' or dried beans, and bake blind in a preheated oven at 180°C/350°F/gas mark 4 for 20 minutes. Remove the beans and lining paper and return to the oven for a further 5–8 minutes, pricking it again if it has puffed up. Remove from the ring and cool on a wire rack.

Gently melt the white chocolate in a bowl set over hot water, then brush all over the inside of the cold pastry case. Once it has set, you can fill the tart, either with a single fruit, appropriately prepared, or with concentric circles of a variety of fruit. Melt the redcurrant jelly, allow to cool slightly but not set. Brush it over the fruit, and allow to set. Serve the whipped cream separately, or, if you prefer, pouring cream, crème fraîche, vanilla ice cream or Greek yoghurt.

eton mess

serves 6

250g (8oz) strawberries
250g (8oz) raspberries
75g (3oz) caster or icing sugar
1 tbsp rosewater, or to taste
600ml (1 pint) whipping or double cream

Put the fruit in a bowl, sprinkle on the sugar, and crush with the back of a fork. Stir in the rosewater. Whip the cream, then stir into the fruit. Pile into wine glasses or bowls to serve. If you are not going to serve the dessert for some time, keep the fruit and cream separate by spooning the fruit mixture into the glass and piping the whipped cream on top just before serving.

autumn and winter

Here the shopping list includes a couple of brace of pheasant, some whole fillets of undyed smoked haddock and a couple of Jack O' Lantern pumpkins. The pheasants are dismantled, and the breasts cooked for one meal, the legs for another. Again the carcasses can provide a clear, flavoursome broth.

Smoked haddock is a lovely, versatile ingredient, especially at home with rustic, English accompaniments, such as grain mustard, cheese, leeks and Savoy cabbage. It is also a very good addition to a substantial, chowder-like soup. On the other hand, the coriander chutney I suggested for the salmon on p.306 is just as good with the smoked haddock. And the leftovers can also be turned into excellent fish cakes and a very passable brandade, which you could serve on slices of grilled polenta. I love raw smoked haddock, thinly sliced and marinated in a little oil, lime juice and rum for 30 minutes before serving. Any left over from this is delicious finely chopped and mixed with a little mustard, shredded spring onions and capers, and served as tartare.

Pumpkin pie, pumpkin fritters, pumpkin ice cream and a pumpkin soufflé flavoured with mixed spices and almond liqueur are my suggestions for a small collection of autumn and winter desserts. Bear in mind that these recipes will all adapt to other seasonal fruit, with, obviously, minor adjustments in preparation and in cooking times.

Dinner for six

Pheasant consommé with herb dumplings

or

Tagliatelle with pheasant sauce

or

Pheasant risotto

Smoked haddock fillets with grain mustard and cider sauce,
served with Savoy cabbage and Lancashire cheese

Pumpkin soufflé

Casual supper for six

Smoked haddock and leek chowder

or

Smoked haddock tostadas

Stuffed pheasant breasts with their own hachis Parmentier

Pumpkin and pecan ice cream

Buffet

Marinated smoked haddock

Game crumble

Rum and pumpkin fool

Drinks party

Miniature fish cakes

Smoked haddock tartare on pumpernickel

Chilled brandade of smoked haddock on hot grilled polenta

Potted pheasant

Grilled polenta and mushroom canapés

Individual pumpkin tarts

or

Pumpkin fritters

---

entertaining

marinated smoked haddock

serves 6 to 8

    1 fillet undyed smoked haddock, weighing approx 800g (1¾lb)

    100ml (4fl oz) hazelnut oil

    Maldon salt or coarse sea salt

    freshly ground black pepper

    freshly squeezed lime juice

    aged rum or malt whisky (optional)

    salad leaves

Trim the fillet by removing the bones and then cutting away the thin side (belly side) of the fillet and the tail end so that you are left with a centre cut about 7.5cm (3 inches) wide and about 25cm (10 inches) long. (The trimmings can be used for other things – smoked haddock tartare, omelette filling or kedgeree.) Cut into vertical slices just under 5mm (¼ inch) thick and spread on a platter. Brush with hazelnut oil, sprinkle with a little sea salt and black pepper, and leave for 2–3 hours. Half an hour before serving, brush with lime juice and a little rum or whisky, if liked. Arrange 5–6 pieces on each plate with a few small salad leaves.

smoked haddock with grain mustard and cider sauce, and leeks and Lancashire cheese

serves 6

10 leeks, trimmed, very thinly sliced and well rinsed

2–3 tbsps grain mustard

6 × 150–200g (5–7oz) pieces of undyed smoked haddock fillet, skin removed

freshly ground black pepper

100ml (4fl oz) dry to medium cider

300g (10oz) Lancashire cheese

Mix the leeks, while still wet, with the grain mustard and place in the bottom of a casserole with a tightly fitting lid. Place the fish fillets on top, season with pepper, pour on the cider and cover with the lid, or foil in the absence of a lid.

Set the casserole on a moderate to high heat and, once you can hear the pot beginning to seethe (or see, if you have a saucepan or casserole with a glass lid), time the cooking for 4 minutes, then have a look at the fish. It may be cooked, or require another minute or so, depending on thickness. The fish should still retain a slight translucence in the middle, as it will continue cooking once removed from the heat. (Cooking fish until it flakes is overcooking it, in my view.) Spoon the leeks and any juices into warmed soup plates, top with most of the cheese, place the fish on top and sprinkle with the rest of the cheese. Quickly glaze with a blow torch or flash under a hot grill.

smoked haddock tostadas

sunflower or grapeseed oil for shallow frying

6 small tortillas

200g (7oz) crème fraîche or light cream cheese

8 spring onions, peeled or trimmed, and finely chopped

3 tomatoes, seeded and diced

2 tbsps fresh coriander, chopped, plus 6 sprigs for garnish

2–3 pickled jalapeno peppers, chopped

1 tbsp lime juice and grated zest of ½ lime

salt

freshly ground black pepper

350g (12oz) undyed smoked haddock fillet, skinned and cut into thin slivers

½ iceberg lettuce, shredded

1 ripe avocado, peeled and diced

Heat the oil in a frying pan, and in it fry the tortillas, one at a time, for about 2 minutes, until crisp. When cool, spread each of the tortillas with crème fraîche. Gently mix together, in the following order, the spring onions, tomato, coriander, jalapeno peppers, lime juice and zest, then add the smoked haddock and seasoning. Cover each tostada with shredded lettuce, heap the fish mixture on top, and spoon the diced avocado over it, finishing off with any remaining crème fraîche and sprig of coriander.

stuffed breasts of pheasant
with their own hachis parmentier

serves 6

legs and breasts of 3 pheasants, plus carcasses for stock

100g (4oz) black pudding

3 shallots, finely chopped

1 apple, peeled and grated

2 tbsps soft breadcrumbs

salt

freshly ground black pepper

a good pinch ground ginger

50g (2oz) butter

1 tsp finely chopped fresh thyme

4 tbsps dry white wine

500g (1lb) potatoes

freshly grated nutmeg

milk

Use the pheasant bones and carcasses to make about 500ml (16fl oz) of strong stock, some for this dish, and some to save.

Strip the meat from the legs and thighs, and mince, or finely chop it, together with the meat from the small fillet under each breast. Put to one side.

Crumble the black pudding, and mix it with half the shallots, the apple, breadcrumbs, salt, pepper and ginger. With a sharp knife, cut a pocket in each pheasant breast, and stuff with the black pudding mixture.

Melt half the butter in a sauté pan, and brown the stuffed breasts all over. Moisten with half the wine, partially cover, and cook for 35–40 minutes.

Meanwhile, fry the remaining shallots in the rest of the butter until soft. Stir in the minced pheasant, the thyme, the rest of the wine, and a little stock, and cook, partially covered, for 30 minutes or so. While this is cooking, boil, and mash the potatoes, adding seasoning, nutmeg and milk, together with more butter, or olive oil, if you wish, until you have a creamy purée.

Place six greased metal baking rings, about 7.5–10cm (3–4 inches) in diameter, on a baking sheet. Divide the mince among them, and then top with mash. Place in the top of a preheated oven at 230°C/450°F/gas mark 7 for 5 minutes or so.

To serve, transfer the *hachis* to hot dinner plates, using a palette knife, and remove the baking rings. Cut the stuffed breasts on the diagonal, and serve two halves on each plate. Boil up the pan juices with a little more stock and wine, if necessary, and pour over the meat. Fresh thyme for garnish, and a crisp salad to follow will be fine.

tagliatelle with pheasant ragoût

The meat sauce can be made a day or two in advance and refrigerated until required, when it makes a very quick dish, requiring just the time needed to cook the pasta and reheat the sauce. It also freezes well. Other game can be used in the recipe, such as hare, rabbit, pigeon or venison.

serves 6

500g (1lb) pheasant meat, off the bone

1 onion, peeled and chopped or sliced

1 tbsp extra virgin olive oil

1 pinch each of mace, cinnamon, ginger and cumin

grating of nutmeg

1 level tsp freshly ground black pepper

5g square of bitter chocolate

200ml (7fl oz) good dry red wine

150ml (¼ pint) pheasant or poultry stock

1 bay leaf

sprig of thyme

500g (1lb) tagliatelle or pappardelle

The meat should be diced into roughly even-sized small pieces, rather than minced, but the pieces should not be much larger than coarse mince.

Lightly brown the onion in a frying pan in the olive oil, then transfer it to a casserole. Brown the meat in batches, then transfer it also to the casserole.

Add the spices, chocolate and half the wine to the frying pan. Bring to the boil, scrape up any residues stuck to the bottom of the pan, and then add the remaining wine and stock. Bring to a full boil, pour it over the meat, tuck in the herbs, cover, and cook in a preheated oven at 150°C/300°F/gas mark 2 for about 2 hours or until the meat is tender. Alternatively, cook on top of the stove, on a low heat, whichever is more convenient.

Meanwhile, cook the pasta, drain it, return it to the pan and stir in the sauce. Spoon into warmed soup plates and serve immediately.

basic pumpkin mixture

makes about 1kg (2lb)

1kg (2lb) pumpkin, freshly cooked, well-drained and still hot

100g (4oz) light muscovado sugar

50g (2oz) dark muscovado sugar

2 tbsps honey

finely grated zest of 1 orange and 1 lemon

freshly grated nutmeg, ground cinnamon, ground cloves, ground ginger
    and ground cardamom, to taste

Mix together all the ingredients while the pumpkin is still hot. Cool and refrigerate until required.

for ice cream

Mix the purée with equal quantities of double cream, or a thick homemade custard, plus extra sugar to taste.

for pumpkin pie filling

Mix 500g (1lb) purée with about 250ml (8fl oz) milk or single cream and 5 beaten eggs, pour into a pastry lined tart dish or tin and bake.

rum and pumpkin fool

This is good garnished with crushed praline or caramelized pecans.

serves 6 to 8

350g (12oz) spiced pumpkin purée – *see* above

juice of ½ lemon

4 tbsps dark rum

150ml (¼ pint) homemade custard

300ml (½ pint) whipping or double cream, whipped

Mix the pumpkin purée with the lemon juice and rum, and leave for 30 minutes or so for the flavours to mellow. Stir in the custard, and then fold in the whipped cream. Spoon into glasses, chill and serve.

a blueprint for all seasons

Perhaps the best trio of ingredients to consider is chicken, salmon and apples. That way you need have no worries about seasonality. Granted, sometimes your apples might be Golden Russets rather than Bramleys, or imported Pink Lady. And you will need to look for organically farmed salmon when wild salmon is out of season or unavailable. But generally, the three ingredients are widely available in some form or another throughout the year.

You will bring seasonality to the menu through cooking methods and accompaniments rather than ingredients. In summer, make apple syllabubs and sorbets, in winter, pies and crumbles; cool chicken salad in summer, warming chicken soup in winter.

I have also included here a couple of useful techniques – smoking and curing – using tea as the flavouring.

For the four menus, I suggest the following combinations of recipes.

Formal dinner for six

Tea smoked salmon fillets

Chicken breasts stuffed with oysters

Apple sorbet

or

Apple, walnut and cinnamon soufflé

Casual supper for six

Tea cured salmon

Oven-baked chicken and potatoes

or

Chicken cobbler

Apple fritters

Buffet

Salmon tartare

or

Salmon in puff pastry

Chicken cobbler

or

Chicken and corn enchiladas

Apple and blackberry lattice tart

or

Vanilla baked apples

Drinks party

Espresso cups of velvety chicken and cucumber soup

or

Shot glasses of salmon and cucumber consommé

Chicken and vegetable spring rolls and dipping sauce

Mushrooms stuffed with potted chicken

Brandade of cured salmon on pumpernickel

or

Salmon or chicken won tons

Miniature apple tarts or turnovers

some notes on cooking salmon

To poach If you have a fish kettle large enough, put the salmon on the rack, lower it into the kettle, and just cover with water. Remove the fish and rack, and put to one side. Into the water put half a bottle or so of white wine, some aromatics such as lemon zest, a sliver of ginger, a piece of celery, one of onion, a few handfuls of parsley and watercress stalks, some peppercorns and a bayleaf. Bring the water to the boil and simmer for 45 minutes or so. Bring it to a full boil, and lower in the fish on its rack. The water temperature will drop immediately. Allow the water to come back to simmering point, which will take longer for a larger fish than for a smaller one.

The Canadian formula of 10 minutes per 2.5cm (1 inch) of thickness is a reasonable guide to cooking times. Time the poaching from when the water just comes back to the boil, not a full rolling boil, but just a few bubbles at the side of the pan.

To cook in foil Use extra strong or double thickness foil. Brush it all over with olive oil to stop the fish sticking. Season the fish inside and out with salt, freshly ground black pepper, and a little mace or nutmeg, and put a handful of herbs and lemon zest in its belly; lemon grass and ginger and lime leaves if you like, and a star anise or two, if you want a slightly oriental flavour. Put some herbs on the bottom of the foil, place the fish on top, add a little splash of white wine or dry vermouth, and then seal the parcel well. Place on a large baking sheet and put in a preheated oven at 180°C/350°F/gas mark 4. I would cook a 4kg (9lb) fish 45–60 minutes, again depending on the thickness, which should be measured at the shoulder, which is usually the thickest part. As it is all too easy to overcook fish, it is as well to check on it from time to time. Remember, though, that this will cool down both the fish and the oven and you may need to increase the cooking time as a result. Fish baked in foil will, when it is cooked, begin to give off clear juices; it will no longer have a bloody tinge at the backbone when you peer inside the belly cavity, and, rather like plucking a leaf from a pineapple crown, when the fish is cooked, you will be able to pull away quite easily a piece of fin from the back of the fish.

If the salmon is too big to fit your oven, divide it in two at the shoulder, wrap and cook each piece separately, then, when cool, reassemble on the platter and hide the join with a necklace of parsley and other herbs, perhaps even edible flowers, strung together like a daisy chain; pansies and flat-leaf parsley would look particularly good.

tea cured salmon

As an accompaniment, I suggest a homemade mayonnaise flavoured with lime juice and zest, a little wasabi paste (Japanese horseradish) and some shredded pickled ginger.

serves 8

- 1 tail of salmon, weighing about 1kg (2lb)
- 5 tbsps coarse sea salt
- 2 tbsps light muscovado sugar
- 1 tbsp freshly ground black pepper
- 1 tbsp Szechuan peppercorns, crushed
- 2–3 tbsps Mirin, saké or rice wine, or fino or dry amontillado sherry
- 4–5 tbsps Lapsang Souchong, Oolong, jasmine or other distinctive tea leaves

Have the fish scaled before dividing into two neat fillets. Remove as many bones from the fillets as possible.

Make the marinade by mixing together the salt, sugar, peppers and rice wine. Spread a tablespoon of the tea leaves in the bottom of a rectangular dish large enough to accommodate the fish. Spoon three tablespoons of the marinade over the leaves, then lay one piece of the fillets on top, skin side down. Spread some more of the marinade on the flesh side of each fillet, and sandwich the two together with plenty of tea leaves in between. The remaining marinade should be spread on the skin side of the top fillet, with the remaining tea leaves sprinkled on top. Cover with cling film, weight down and refrigerate for 2–3 days.

To serve, scrape off the curing ingredients, drain off the liquid, and slice the salmon.

fragrant tea smoked salmon fillets

These are particularly good served atop a bowl of noodles and stir-fried vegetables. Alternatively, serve them with mashed potatoes into which you have stirred plenty of chives or garlic chives. A lemon butter sauce is also a good accompaniment.

serves 6

6 × 150g (5oz) pieces salmon fillet

1 tbsp coarse sea salt

1 tbsp Szechuan peppercorns

1 tbsp black peppercorns

100g (4oz) uncooked rice

100g (4oz) sugar

handful of Lapsang Souchong, Oolong, Earl Grey
or other distinctive tea leaves

Crush the salt and spices, toast them lightly in a wok and, when cool, rub all over the salmon.

Line a wok with a double thickness of foil and put the rice, sugar and tea leaves in the bottom. Place a lightly greased rack on top, and lay the salmon fillets on it. Cover with the lid, sealing the join with foil or rolled up damp paper towel.

Place the wok on a medium high heat and, once the rice and sugar have begun to smoke, which you will smell rather than see, resist the temptation to open the lid, and instead leave for 10–15 minutes. Remove from the heat and, with the lid still on, leave for a further 15 minutes. Serve the fish either warm or cold.

salmon in puff pastry

serves 8 to 10

2 × 600g (1¼lb) salmon fillet or salmon trout,
    filleted, skinned and pin bones removed

sea salt

freshly ground black pepper

nutmeg

100g (4oz) butter, softened

1 tbsp finely chopped parsley

1 tbsp finely chopped chervil, fennel or tarragon

1 tbsp finely chopped chives

finely grated zest of 1 lemon

small glass of white wine

500g (1lb) puff pastry

egg and milk glaze

Lightly season the fish all over with salt, pepper and a grating of nutmeg, then place on a large platter. Mix the butter with the herbs and lemon zest, then use it to sandwich together the two fillets. Sprinkle the wine all over the fish, rubbing it well in, and leave for about an hour for the flavours to develop.

Roll out the pastry and use to enclose the salmon, carefully sealing the edges. Place, seam side down, on top of two folded strips of greaseproof paper on a wet baking sheet. The strips will help you lift the pastry-enclosed salmon off the baking sheet after it has been cooked. If you are artistic, you can decorate the pastry with fish scales and other salmon features. Brush the pastry with the egg and milk glaze and bake in a preheated oven at 220°C/425°F/gas mark 7 for 20 minutes, then reduce the heat to 180°C/350°F/gas mark 4 and cook for a further 25 minutes. Remove from the oven and carefully transfer to a serving platter. Serve with your chosen vegetables or green salad.

won tons

Hand these round with a dipping sauce made with soy sauce, rice or sherry vinegar, toasted sesame oil, and a little sugar and chilli if you like.

makes 24

  1 tbsp groundnut oil

  4 spring onions or a small leek, trimmed and finely chopped or sliced

  75g (3oz) bean sprouts, blanched and roughly chopped

  2 garlic cloves, peeled and crushed

  1 tsp freshly grated ginger

  2 tbsps soy sauce

  2 tsps clear honey

  1 tbsp rice vinegar

  150g (5oz) cooked chicken or salmon, chopped or shredded

  50g (2oz) peeled prawns, roughly chopped

  50g (2oz) shiitake or button mushrooms, finely chopped

  24 won ton wrappers

  oil for deep-frying (optional)

Mix the vegetables with the garlic and ginger, and then add the soy sauce, honey and vinegar, followed by the chicken or salmon, prawns and mushrooms. Taste to check the seasoning. Spoon a little of the mixture into the centre of a won ton wrapper, floury side up, dampen the edges, and pinch together to seal. Fill the rest of the wrappers in the same way. The won tons can then be deep-fried or steamed.

entertaining

chicken breasts stuffed with oysters

My favourite thing to serve with these, apart from mashed potatoes, is wilted spinach or cooked cucumber.

serves 6

6 chicken breasts

salt

freshly ground black pepper

ground mace or freshly grated nutmeg

2 shallots, peeled and finely chopped

2 celery sticks, trimmed and finely chopped

100ml (3½fl oz) milk

4 slices white bread, crusts removed

2–3 generous sprigs of tarragon, finely chopped

12 large fresh oysters, shucked, and the liquor reserved

seasoned flour

1 egg (optional)

breadcrumbs for coating (optional)

50g (2oz) butter

150ml (5fl oz) dry white wine or champagne

lemon slices for garnish

Remove the arrow-shaped fillet from under each breast and use in another dish – I find it the perfect amount of meat for chicken risotto. Cut a pocket in each chicken breast with the point of a sharp knife, then season lightly with salt, pepper and ground mace. Cover and refrigerate while you prepare the stuffing.

Simmer the shallot and celery in the milk until soft, then put to one side. Crumble the bread and put in a bowl with the drained vegetables, the chopped tarragon and enough milk to bind together. Divide the stuffing in 6, and fill each breast first with some stuffing, then 2 oysters, then some more stuffing. Secure closed with cocktail sticks, then dust with seasoned flour. You can also dip the breasts in beaten egg and coat with breadcrumbs, if you wish. Heat the butter in a sauté pan and fry the chicken until it is cooked through, and the outside is golden brown.

Make a gravy with the pan juices, wine or champagne and the reserved oyster liquid. Pour around the chicken, and garnish with lemon slices.

oven-baked chicken and potatoes

serves 6 to 8

    extra virgin olive oil

    6 chicken portions, thighs and drumsticks

    4 tbsps good white wine

    freshly ground black pepper

    ½ tsp paprika

    ½ tsp ground cardamom

    sprigs of rosemary or tarragon

    1kg (2lb) potatoes, scrubbed but not peeled, and cut into
        2.5cm (1 inch) chunks

Lightly oil an ovenproof dish. Skin the chicken, or not, as you prefer. Or as a compromise, remove the skin, and then place it over the chicken as it bakes to baste it, but remove it before serving. Rub the meat with the wine, and then rub in the spices. Put some of the herbs in the bottom of the dish, arrange the chicken in it, and tuck more herbs between them. Cover with foil, or chicken skin, and bake in the middle of a preheated oven at 180°C/350°F/gas mark 4 for about an hour.

At the same time, in a lightly oiled dish, put the potatoes, having first seasoned them with salt, pepper and a sprinkling of olive oil.

chicken, vegetable and herb cobbler

serves 6 to 8

2 tbsps sunflower oil

24 pickling onions or 12 shallots, peeled

1.35kg (3lb) boneless chicken, both dark and light meat, diced

1 tbsp flour

½ bottle dry white wine

150ml (¼ pint) chicken stock

1 bay leaf

vegetables

prepare a selection from amongst the following, about 675g (1½lb) in all:

green beans

small carrots

sweetcorn

courgettes

small potatoes

button mushrooms

for the herb cobbler

25g (1oz) fresh parsley, chervil and oregano

½ tsp coarse sea salt

300g (10oz) self-raising flour

1 tsp baking powder

75g (3oz) lard or butter, chilled and diced

150ml (¼ pint) buttermilk or plain yoghurt thinned with water to
the consistency of cream

Heat the oil in an ovenproof casserole, with a lid, and fry the onions and chicken to a golden brown. Sprinkle on the flour, and stir it in to absorb any extra oil. Add a quarter of the wine, and bring to the boil, scraping up any residues in the pan. Pour in the rest of the wine and the stock, add the bay leaf, return to the boil, cover, then lower the heat. Simmer gently for 20 minutes, then add the

serial entertaining

vegetables, and cook for a further 20–30 minutes, until the vegetables are tender. Courgettes, corn kernels and mushrooms will, of course, take much less cooking and should be added towards the end.

To make the cobbler, strip the leaves from the herb stalks, and crush them with the salt in a mortar. Sift the flour and baking powder into a bowl, cut in the fat, and then rub together. Add the herbs, and stir in just enough buttermilk to bind the mixture to a soft dough. Roll out to a thickness of about 2.5cm (1 inch), then cut into rounds.

Remove the lid from the casserole, arrange the scones round the top, and bake in a preheated oven at 180°C/350°F/gas mark 4 for about 15 minutes. Serve from the casserole.

chicken and corn enchiladas

Serve with shredded iceberg lettuce, refried beans, or cooked black beans, guacamole and a wedge of lime.

serves 6

3 corn cobs

6 flour tortillas

200g (7oz) crème fraîche or cream cheese

400g (14oz) chicken, off the bone

6 tbsps salsa

6 tbsps grated Gouda

2–3 tbsps finely chopped fresh coriander

Drop the corn into boiling water, and cook for 2 minutes. Remove and drain. When cool enough to handle, cut off the corn kernels.

Soften the tortillas in a frying pan, or steam over hot water. Spread each with crème fraîche, then put a layer of corn kernels in a band down the middle, and top this with a layer of chicken, followed by salsa, crème fraîche and herbs. Fold the tortillas in on two sides, and then roll them up. Place in a well-greased baking dish, cover with foil, and bake in a preheated oven at 180°C/350°F/gas mark 4 for 20–25 minutes.

velvet chicken and cucumber soup

makes 20 × 50ml (2fl oz) servings, or 6 normal ones

2 onions, peeled and sliced

25g (1oz) unsalted butter

1 level tbsp flour

1 large potato, peeled and diced

freshly ground nutmeg

pinch each of ground cloves, cardamon, mace or nutmeg, cinnamon
and freshly ground white pepper

150ml (¼ pint) semi-skimmed or skimmed milk

1 large cucumber, halved, half peeled, seeded and roughly chopped

1 litre (2¼ pints) chicken stock

salt to taste

3 heaped tbsps shredded cooked chicken

to finish

cream or herbs

In a large, heavy saucepan, sweat the onion in the butter until soft. Stir in the flour, potato and spices, then gradually add the milk. Bring to the boil, and simmer until the vegetables are soft. Remove from the heat and pour into a blender. Blend until smooth with the chopped cucumber and chicken stock. Return to the saucepan, bring back to the boil, adjust the seasoning, and stir in the chicken. Serve in warmed bowls with a swirl of cream or a sprinkling of herbs. Or cool, refrigerate and serve chilled.

apple sorbet

To prepare apples for sorbet, quarter, core and roughly chop them, then put in a food processor or blender with a couple of tablespoons of water and a teaspoon or two of lemon juice to prevent them discolouring. I like to keep a little of the peel on for the flecked effect it gives. Blend to a purée, then mix with the syrup as described.

for the syrup
   1kg (2¼lb) sugar
   575ml (1 pint) water

Dissolve the sugar in the water in a saucepan over a low heat, bring to the boil, allow to cool and then chill.

Dilute the syrup with an equal quantity of water and fruit purée. Stir in the juice of half a lemon. Blend thoroughly, then pour into a plastic container and freeze. As the mixture freezes, crystals will form, and it will need to be stirred from time to time. To ensure a smooth sorbet, it is a good idea to give it its final stir in a food processor before putting it back in the freezer. Alternatively, freeze in an ice-cream maker or sorbetière, according to the manufacturer's instructions.

I prefer to use raw apples, but interesting variations can be created with different apple varieties, cooked into a purée and then flavoured with cinnamon, cloves or cardamom. For another version, simply freeze cider into a sorbet for a coarser granita.

vanilla baked apples

Baked apples can be a delicious alternative to an apple pie or a crumble, especially when, as in this version, you flavour them with vanilla. Pears can be cooked in the same way.

serves 6

6 slices bread, brioche or panettone, cut into rounds

100g (3½oz) unsalted butter, softened

3 vanilla pods

6 apples, cored

75g (3oz) light muscovado sugar

1 orange

1 lemon

several tbsps Calvados or English apple brandy

Thickly butter the bread slices, then place them in a lightly buttered ovenproof dish. Cut the vanilla pods in half, and split them lengthways. Spike the pieces of vanilla into the apples, using a skewer to make the holes if necessary. Place an apple on each slice of bread. Smear the rest of the butter over them, and in the cavity, and sprinkle generously with sugar. Remove the zest from the orange and lemon in spirals, and wind this into the cavity. Bake in a preheated oven at 160°C/325°F/gas mark 3 for 50–60 minutes. Remove from the oven, pour on the Calvados, and serve when just warm, with crème fraîche, thick yoghurt, or if you are using English cider brandy, with clotted cream.

apple and blackberry lattice tart with walnut pastry

A quince or pear purée is equally delicious when combined with apples, if blackberries are unavailable. And you can replace the walnuts in the pastry with ground almonds.

serves 6

for the pastry
>   300g (10oz) plain flour
>   175g (6oz) butter, diced and chilled
>   50g (2oz) ground walnuts
>   25g (1oz) caster or icing sugar
>   1 egg yolk
>   iced water

Make a rich shortcrust with the pastry ingredients, using just enough iced water to bind to a dough. Cover and refrigerate for 30 minutes or so while you make the pie filling.

for the filling
>   500g (1lb) blackberries
>   sugar to taste
>   500g (1lb) Bramley apples, windfalls or other tart apples
>   lemon juice

Hull the blackberries, rinse, then stew gently for 10 minutes or so. Rub through a sieve or food mill, and sweeten to taste.

Peel, core and thinly slice the apples, sprinkling them with lemon juice to prevent discoloration.

Line a tart plate or tin with the pastry, keeping back a quarter for the lattice. Fill the pastry case with apples, then spread with the blackberry purée. Roll out the remaining pastry, cut into thin strips, and arrange across the top of the tart in a lattice pattern, securing each strip to the pastry edge by moistening it with water.

Bake in the middle of a preheated oven at 200°C/400°F/gas mark 6 for 10–15 minutes, then reduce the temperature to 180°C/350°F/gas mark 4, move the tart to a lower shelf, and bake for a further 15–20 minutes. Serve either hot or warm with custard, cream or yoghurt.

miniature apple turnovers

This is a very easy recipe to adapt to most fruit, and is especially good with plums, gooseberries, blueberries and apricots.

makes 20
500g (1lb) apples, peeled and diced or thinly sliced
200g (7oz) golden caster sugar
500g (1lb) puff pastry
milk

Put the apples in a bowl and mix in all but two tablespoons of the sugar. Roll out the pastry and cut out twenty rounds. Divide the filling, spooning it into the centre of each round. Brush the borders with milk, fold over and seal, crimping the edges. Brush with more milk, and sprinkle with the remaining sugar. Place on baking sheets and bake in a preheated oven at 200°C/400°F/gas mark 6 for 30 minutes or until golden brown.

special occasions and themed parties

Occasionally, perhaps just once, you may be called upon to cook a celebration meal for a Golden Wedding. Or you might be entertaining friends from abroad and want to give them a taste of Scotland. Perhaps you are abroad and are entertaining a Welsh VIP. You have planned a midsummer meal with a black and white theme. It is all here. Over the years I have devised menus and recipes to fit many themes and special occasions, from my parents' Golden Wedding to an Elizabethan dinner for a special jubilee newspaper feature. My suggestions will supplement your own repertoire and provide ideas for unusual party food.

food with a scottish flavour

From the Feast of St Andrew, in late November, to Burns' Night, in late January, we have open season for haggis. For two months these little dumpy beasties wing their way around the world, wherever there are homesick Scotsmen and women. The haggis will be cooked with great care, served with appropriate partners, and consumed with relish and nostalgia.

An Islay malt, taken with a little spring water is, for me, the ideal accompaniment to neat haggis, but if I turn it into a made dish, either with mash or in pastry, then an uncomplicated, fairly robust red wine partners it well, such as a Côtes du Rhône Village, a Gigondas, an Australian Cabernet Shiraz, or one of the newer Languedoc wines.

Haggis lends itself to made dishes, although I am sure the small part of me that is a Scot should not suggest this. A smooth creamy mash tempers some of its stronger flavours. For some years, I have used my haggis in a 'pie', lining the dish with either mashed potatoes, or a mixture of mashed potatoes and turnips, and topping it with the same mixture. In the middle, the haggis, having been partially cooked in its skin, is spooned out like mince.

Sometimes I have opted for baking haggis in pastry – in fact, treating it like a sausage, and producing a haggis roll. Make a long thin version, if you want small slices to serve as canapés, or make a sturdy short roll to serve sliced with mash and lentils, or split peas for a main course. A fruity chutney will be the only accompaniment you will need. Or you can try serving it with roasted root vegetables and a spicy salsa. This, I hasten to add, is not a dish that I would have served to my Scottish grandmother.

If you have a fishmonger nearby, or a wet fish counter in your local supermarket, buy some undyed smoked haddock, and make cullen skink, a very fine tasting fish soup, and traditional to the gaelic lands, where 'skink' means broth, as 'cawl' does in Welsh.

With a few ingredients from your store cupboard and refrigerator, you will be able to turn out a very presentable dessert with a real flavour of Scotland. Flour, butter and sugar are all you will need to make shortbread, unless you have a box of shortbread standing by. An egg or cream base and a flavouring of toasted oatmeal, marmalade, Drambuie, or malt whisky will make one of the various creams and custards attributed to the Hibernian culinary tradition. Marmalade and malt whisky combine in a delicious steamed pudding and custard.

Arbroath smokies, nettle kail, Scotch woodcock, lamb and barley broth with lamb sweetbreads, salmon cured in Islay malt, spiced cured Scottish beef and Scottish rarebit are some more of the dishes you might consider serving for a Burns' Night supper or other dinner full of Scottish flavours. Certainly, at home, Burns' Night is our annual excuse for a nosing, well, actually a tasting, of single malts, an occasion that demands substantial and flavoursome food.

Scotland is not short of this commodity. Its beef is arguably the best in the world, and its lamb superb. Fish and shellfish thrive in its cold clean waters – Scottish kippers, smoked haddock, oysters and scallops are second to none, and the better salmon farms produce fish in unstressed, uncrowded conditions. By the time Burns' Night rolls around, the raspberry canes are dormant, but there is a wealth of good potatoes and root vegetables about, and the dairy counter repays a visit, for there are excellent Scottish cheeses to be found.

Toasted bread spread with horseradish butter, Stichill or Orkney Cheddar grated and mixed with McKewan's and a drop of malt, gently heated through in a saucepan and poured over the toast makes the Scottish rarebit, fine as a savoury at the end of the meal or in place of the cheese course, but equally good served in small pieces with your malts.

Purists might not agree, but malt whisky is an excellent ingredient in the kitchen. A wide range of flavours is to be found, depending on where the malt is distilled, and one can match it, like olive oil, to the ingredient. With smoked salmon, smoked haddock and other smoked fish and meat such as venison, I would avoid Islay malts, with their peaty, smoky flavours and wild tang of the sea, as the food already has plenty of its own smokiness. Instead choose a softer Lowland malt or a fruity Speyside malt. Islay malts, however, are perfect with fresh fish, and I have developed a recipe for cured salmon using Islay malt, for which I would recommend Laphroaig, Lagavulin or the even smokier Ardbeg, the phenolic compounds matched by the distinctive essential oil, thymol, found in thyme, which I use in place of dill. Oatcakes or wholemeal bread go well with salmon prepared in this fashion, and if I want a sauce with it, I simply stir a little more malt, grain mustard and some heather honey into homemade mayonnaise, with a little fresh thyme and some chives, finely chopped.

For sweet dishes, or with game, I usually choose one of the malts that have been aged in sherry or port casks, such as Macallan, Balvenie and Glenmorangie. Add them to the sauce near the end of cooking, but leave enough time for the heat to evaporate the alcohol, leaving only the aromatic flavours. Alternatively, you can use the malt at the beginning of cooking, for example, flaming a pheasant before pot-roasting it on a bed of root vegetables, or a fillet of Aberdeen Angus before roasting it pink in a quick oven.

The recipes which follow will take you well beyond Burns' Night, and can be served as long as the weather has a nip to it. I would not suggest that you make all the dishes for a single meal whisky flavoured, but you could get away with the salmon and the pudding, separated by a sober main course.

In place of a hot soup for starters, before something as substantial as haggis, I have adapted the traditional cock-a-leekie of chicken, leeks and prunes, to produce a chilled jellied soup. It has the advantage of advance preparation, and you can either set the soup to jell in soup plates, pouring the liquid over some shredded or diced chicken, cooked leeks and prunes, or make it into a terrine, and serve slices of it.

jellied cock-a-leekie

serves 8

    4 sheets of leaf gelatine or 4 tsps gelatine granules
    500g (1lb) freshly poached chicken, off the bone
    8 thin leeks, cooked and split lengthways
    12 prunes, soaked
    600ml (1 pint) well-flavoured chicken stock

Soak the gelatine in a small amount of water, in a bowl large enough to accommodate all the stock. Cut the chicken into long strips, and layer with the leeks in a wet 1kg (2lb) loaf tin, placing a line of prunes down the middle. Boil 75ml (3fl oz) of the chicken stock, pour it over the gelatine, and stir until it has dissolved, then stir in the rest of the stock. Pour carefully over the chicken and leeks. Allow to cool, and then chill until set. Turn out on to a platter, slice and serve.

north sea fish chowder

A close relative of the traditional Cullen skink, this is a very quick and easy soup to make, which avoids having to bother with stock from fish bones. I do recommend making some stock with the prawn shells, however. The sweetness of the prawns nicely counterpoints the smokiness of the haddock and makes for an extremely flavoursome soup.

If you like, you could also add cooked white beans to the soup. And, if you want to warm up the colour, stir in a tablespoon or two of passata, or sieved tomatoes. As an alternative, you could add a few threads of saffron.

For a complete meal, serve the soup with oatcakes or wholemeal bread and unsalted butter, preceded by a salad of watercress and chicory, and followed by cheese and then a compote of dried fruit simmered in a fragrant tea.

serves 6

700g (1½lb) frozen, shell-on Greenland prawns

15g (½ oz) butter or 1 tbsp olive oil

1 onion, peeled and thinly sliced

2 leeks, trimmed, thinly sliced and well rinsed

1 large floury potato, peeled and diced

12 small waxy potatoes, such as Charlottes, peeled and sliced

6 inner leaves Savoy cabbage

300g (10oz) undyed smoked haddock fillet, skinned and cut into 6 pieces

freshly ground black pepper

1 tbsp finely chopped 'herbs for fish', such as dill, chervil, parsley,
    tarragon, chives – some, or all, of these

As soon as the prawns are soft enough to handle, peel them. Put the shells into a saucepan, cover with water, simmer for 20 minutes, then strain; you need 1.25 litres (2 pints) prawn stock for the soup, and can add extra water or white wine to make up the quantity. Meanwhile, heat the oil in a saucepan, and in it gently fry the onion until translucent. Add the leek and potato, and a couple of ladlefuls of the prawn cooking liquor.

Simmer until the potatoes are tender. Remove the centre ribs from the cabbage leaves, and shred them. Add them and the remaining stock to the pot. Bring to the boil, then turn down the heat. Add the smoked haddock, prawns, a little pepper, and the herbs. Simmer for 2–3 minutes, until the fish is cooked, and serve in warmed soup plates.

salmon cured with islay malt

serves 8, plus leftovers

1 tail of salmon, wild when available, weighing approx 1.5kg (3lb)

5 tbsps coarse sea salt

2 tbsps light muscovado sugar

2 tbsps freshly ground black pepper

2–3 tbsps Islay malt whisky

small bunch fresh thyme

Have the fish scaled before filleting, and remove as many bones from the fillets as possible. Make the marinade by mixing together the salt, sugar, pepper and malt.

Spread a few sprigs of thyme in the bottom of a rectangular dish, large enough to accommodate the piece of fish. Spoon three tablespoons of the marinade over the herbs, and lay one salmon fillet on top, skin side down. Spread the rest of the mixture on the flesh side of each fillet of salmon, and sandwich the two together with plenty of thyme in between. The remaining salt mixture should be spread on the skin side of the top fillet, which should then be scattered with the remaining thyme sprigs, covered with food wrap, weighted down and left for 2–3 days in the refrigerator.

To serve, scrape off the herbs and salt, drain off the liquid, slice thinly across the grain, or vertically in thicker slices, down to the skin.

baked haggis

The main protein ingredients of the haggis is the 'sheep's pluck', that is, the liver, lungs and heart. It involves a good deal of simmering with the wind pipe hanging over the pan, and the thorough washing of a sheep's bag, or stomach. But, by using lamb's liver and hearts, bought from your butcher or supermarket, you can make a 'pan haggis', which is steamed in a pudding basin, or, as I have suggested earlier, baked like a giant sausage roll.

serves 6 to 8

 200g (7 or 8oz) belly pork

 500g (1lb) lamb's liver

 2 lamb's hearts

 1 large onion, peeled and quartered

 4 cloves

 zest and juice of 1 lemon

 bay leaf

 sprig of rosemary

 75g (3oz) fine or medium oatmeal

 2 tbsps finely chopped parsley

 pinch of mace

 2 tbsps port or sherry (optional)

 salt

 freshly ground black pepper

 500g (1lb) puff pastry

 milk or egg and water glaze

Dice the belly pork, then brown it gently, cooking it until the fat runs. Remove from the pan. Trim all fat, piping and waste from the heart and liver, cut into large pieces, and brown in the pork fat.

Remove the meat. Deglaze the pan with a little water or wine, scraping up any bits stuck to the bottom. Put the meat back in the pan, cover with water, and add the quartered onions, stuck with cloves, the lemon juice and zest, and the herbs. Cover and simmer gently for 40 minutes.

Meanwhile, lightly toast the oatmeal in a heavy pan. Remove the meat and onion from the saucepan, and mince or finely chop it all. Mix in the oatmeal, parsley, mace, port or sherry, if using, and seasoning. Add enough cooking liquid to give a soft, sausage-like texture. Allow to cool.

Roll out the pastry to a thickness of about 5mm (¼ inch), and spoon the mixture into the middle in a rough sausage shape. Fold over the pastry, and seal along the longest edge. Place on a greased baking sheet, with the join underneath. Brush with milk, or an egg and water glaze, and bake in a pre-heated oven at 180°C/350°F/gas mark 4 for about 40 minutes.

Serve cold, as a first course, or hot, as a main course, with your chosen vegetable accompaniments.

haggis parmentier

Hachis Parmentier, a Parisian bistro favourite, is often made with black pudding and mashed potatoes. My version, made with haggis, is just as good. Serve your best malt whisky with it.

serves 4 to 6

1 × 500g haggis

1kg (2lb) good mashing potatoes, peeled

1 small turnip, peeled and diced (optional)

salt

freshly ground black pepper

freshly grated nutmeg

2 tbsps fresh breadcrumbs

25–50g (1–2oz) butter

Cook the haggis according to the instructions on its wrapper and, while it is cooking, boil the potatoes, and the turnip, if using. Drain, mash and season. Spread a layer of mash on the bottom and sides of an ovenproof dish. Halve the haggis, and scoop it over the mash. Top with the remaining mash, scatter with breadcrumbs, dot with butter, and bake in the top half of a preheated oven at 200°C/400°F/gas mark 6 for 25–30 minutes. Before covering the haggis with its layer of mash, you could sprinkle it with a little whisky or malt.

steamed marmalade pudding
with malt whisky custard

serves 6

    75g (3oz) unsalted butter or sunflower margarine

    75g (3oz) light muscovado sugar

    2 large eggs, lightly beaten

    75g (3oz) self-raising flour, sifted

    2 tbsps Dundee marmalade

Cream the butter and sugar, then add the eggs and flour alternately, folding them in rather than beating them, which gives a heavier mixture, until well mixed. Grease an 850ml (1¾ pint) pudding basin, spoon the marmalade into the bottom, then top with the pudding mixture. Cover and steam for an hour. Alternatively, cover with special perforated film and microwave on maximum power for 6 minutes. After cooking, allow the pudding to stand for a few minutes before turning it out and serving with the malt whisky custard.

malt whisky custard

serves 6

    600ml (1 pint) full cream milk

    ½ vanilla pod, split

    6 egg yolks

    100g (3½oz) caster sugar

    1 scant tsp potato flour, arrowroot or cornflour

    2–3 tbsps malt whisky

Scald the milk with the vanilla pod in a saucepan. Beat the egg yolks and sugar, then thoroughly mix in the potato flour. Pour the hot milk over the eggs, stirring continuously. Strain the custard back into the saucepan, and cook over a gentle heat, stirring just until the mixture thickens. Remove immediately from the heat, stir in the malt whisky and pour into a warmed jug. The custard can also be served cold, in which case it should be cooled, then chilled until required.

---

orange and whisky custard pots

serves 6

300ml (½ pint) full cream milk

150ml (¼ pint) double cream

spiral of orange zest

4 egg yolks

2 tbsps Highland malt whisky

3 tbsps orange marmalade, sieved

for the garnish

crystallized orange peel

toasted, flaked almonds

Scald the milk, cream and orange zest. Beat the egg yolks with the malt whisky and marmalade. Pour the hot milk on to the eggs, whisking continuously, then strain the custard into a double saucepan, or a bowl set over hot water, and cook until thickened. Pour into glasses, cups or ramekins, allow to cool, and then chill until set. Crystallized orange peel, or toasted flaked almonds can be used to garnish. Serve with shortbread.

shortbread

serves 6

125g (4oz) unsalted butter, at room temperature

75g (3oz) icing sugar, sifted

175g (6oz) plain flour, sifted

chilled water, to mix

unrefined caster sugar

Cream the butter and sugar, fold in the flour, then add just enough chilled water to make a firm dough. Roll out the dough to a square or circle, to a thickness of about 5mm (¼ inch), and place on a greased baking sheet. Prick all over with a fork, and cut into bars or wedges. Bake in a preheated oven at 160°C/325°F/ gas mark 3 for 30–40 minutes until a pale cream colour. Transfer to a wire rack to cool, dusting with caster sugar while still hot.

---

entertaining

the perfect oatcake

Whilst good commercial oatcakes are available, homemade ones are
infinitely superior, as well as very easy to make. You do need fine oatmeal, however, not the rolled oats used for quick porridge. Delicious
with cheese or served as an accompaniment to soup, they also make the
perfect canapé when spread with butter flavoured with lemon zest and
horseradish and topped with a fold of smoked salmon and a caper.

makes 20

1 tbsp melted lard or dripping

1 tsp of bicarbonate of soda

½ tsp salt

warm water

500g (1lb) fine oatmeal

Stir the lard, bicarbonate of soda and salt into the flour, then add just enough
warm water to make a firm but pliable dough. Roll out on a floured worktop to
the thickness of a £1 coin and cut into rounds or triangles. Bake on a hot griddle
for 5–6 minutes, carefully turning the oatcakes once. Transfer to baking sheets
and dry off in the middle of a preheated oven at 200°C/400°F/gas mark 6 for
4–5 minutes. Cool completely on wire racks before storing in an airtight
container.

food for st valentine's day

In February thoughts inevitably turn to food appropriate for
Valentine's Day. Mood food, aphrodisiac morsels, pink ingredients,
heart-shaped dishes form one strategy that I offer here.

Heart-shaped cutters, pierced heart-shaped moulds and a heart-
shaped baking tin would be a worthwhile investment to help emphasize
your message, and will be very useful for some of the dishes I have in
mind. For example, if time is no barrier, try a hearts and flowers soup –

edible blossoms in a chicken broth with a homemade, heart-shaped, chicken-filled ravioli. Or use the pierced ceramic moulds, used for *coeurs à la crème*, to make individual paprika cream cheese hearts, to be served with a smoked fish trio. The moulds can also be used for dessert, a sweetened cream cheese or a cream cheese mousse served with a compote of rhubarb, suitably pink, and perhaps flavoured with a little ginger for piquancy. The cake tin can be used to make a rhubarb or rose or red grape jelly, for serving with cream, or even custard, if your Valentine is a jelly and custard person. Or make a heart-shaped cheese-cake, topped with rhubarb and angelica or roses.

Others will decide that what is really needed is a practical plan in order to preserve the romance of the occasion. It is one thing to have prepared an elaborate and stupendous *diner à deux*, but if you have to disappear into the kitchen to turn out the heart-shaped pink jelly, and then feather its surrounding sauce with raspberry coulis, the mood of the moment risks disappearing for ever.

My practical solution here is food that can be prepared at the table. Not only is there a whole range of dishes that can be cooked on a variety of tabletop implements, some of them actually work quite well together as a meal. And some, of course, need no cooking.

Consider first a Caesar salad. Perhaps persuade your loved one to consider it. But whoever decides to make it should be left to get on with it, without interference. Even using the traditional ingredients for the Caesar salad, there are arguments about exactly how to prepare it. Do you use a raw or a coddled egg yolk? Should the anchovies be crushed in the dressing or rolled as a garnish? Are fried or baked croûtons best? Is the garlic whisked around the salad bowl on the prongs of a fork or crushed into the dressing? There is undoubtedly an air of theatre about preparing the salad at the table, and it is not difficult to do provided you have all the ingredients to hand, including the crisp lettuce, which should be a cos, torn across into pieces, definitely not cut. Torn-up iceberg lettuce is an adequate substitute, as are Little Gem lettuces, although purists might not agree with me. Take a tip from the professional kitchen and do a good *mise-en-place*. This simply means 'putting in place', or doing some advance preparation. If the lettuce needs washing and drying, then wash and dry it. Peel the garlic. Open the can of anchovies, drain them, and put them in a small dish. Coddle the egg or not, as you wish. Or leave out the egg if you do not eat raw eggs, and use instead a good quality, organic mayonnaise, made from pasteurized eggs. All you need is to have the ingredients ready to hand, on a tray, side table or sideboard, and the show can begin.

caesar salad

serves 2 to 4

1 garlic clove, peeled and halved

1 lettuce, trimmed and torn into pieces

extra virgin olive oil

sherry vinegar

lemon juice

1 egg yolk, raw or coddled (that is, cooked in the
    shell for 1–1½ minutes)

salt

freshly ground black pepper

dash of Worcestershire sauce

freshly grated Parmesan cheese

handful of croûtons per serving

Either rub the cut garlic around the salad bowl, or crush it with a little salt. Put the lettuce in the bowl, and pour a thin trickle of olive oil over the leaves. Add a little sherry vinegar and lemon juice, and then the egg yolk. Season with salt, pepper and Worcestershire sauce, and gently turn the leaves so that they are well coated with the dressing, adding the crushed garlic if you wish. Scatter on Parmesan, and add the croûtons. Fold once more and serve on individual plates.

What to serve next? Raclette and cheese fondue seem too hearty to be quite right for a romantic occasion, even though they are cooked at the table. Oriental dishes, such as the *da bin lo* or Mongolian hot pot, the 'steamboats', the dip-dips, and the *shabu-shabu* are all versions of the same thing, a broth into which you dip shellfish, meat, dumplings and vegetables. To cook them for a crowd of people is much more fun. And, as for *fondue à la bourguignonne*, you will have the smell of hot oil in your hair for days afterwards.

No, instead look to the dishes that the maitre d' in a fine grill room prepares at the side of your table, the steak tartare, the beef strogonoff, the steak Diane. Again, all that is needed is a careful *mise-en-place*, and none of these dishes will take more than a few minutes to cook, or in the case of the steak tartare, to prepare. Of course, to get the right tone of elegance, you might need a quick lesson by way of lunch in London. At the Savoy Grill, I have tasted a wonderful steak Diane, which, with the right equipment, such as a table-top burner, sturdy enough to hold a frying pan, could be accomplished at home.

Steak tartare is even easier to prepare, since no cooking is required. And for a non-meat version, I highly recommend my tuna tartare. In each case extremely fresh, good-quality produce is essential.

To finish a meal prepared at the table, you can continue in the same style, with some flamed fruit and ice cream. Crêpes Suzettes is perhaps too elaborate at this stage and is best served at the end of a very simple meal, where the other components have been cooked and served conventionally. To drink, it has to be pink champagne. If I were going to have red wine, it would be claret, a Château Calon Segur with the heart on its label. And if Calon Segur does not appeal to your taste or your budget, look for a St Amour Beaujolais.

tuna tartare with oriental aromatics

serves 2

250g (8oz) fresh tuna fillet

2 spring onions, trimmed and finely chopped

1 lemon grass stick, very finely chopped (optional)

½ tsp peeled and crushed fresh ginger

1 lime

pinch of five spice powder

pinch of Szechuan pepper

light soy sauce

rice or sherry vinegar

toasted sesame oil

Dice the tuna fish, and then, by hand, chop it very small. Using a food processor tends to turn the fish to a paste very rapidly, and I prefer a coarser texture. Put the fish in a large, shallow bowl and have the other ingredients to hand, ready chopped and crushed, as appropriate. Using two forks, stir in the spring onion, lemon grass, if using, and ginger. Grate in the zest of the lime, then halve it and squeeze in a little of the juice, stirring and blending thoroughly. Add the five spice powder and the Szechuan pepper. Then, from the bottles, add the soy, vinegar and oil, just a little at a time, until you have the level of seasoning you require. You should still be able to taste the fish, and not be overwhelmed either by the saltiness of the soy sauce or the flavour of toasted sesame oil.

classic steak tartare

For this I usually buy a tail-end piece of fillet steak, less expensive than the thick end of the fillet. Finely chop or mince it rather than using the food processor.

The meat is mixed with the yolk of an egg, and then, traditionally, with the following: shallots, parsley, capers and gherkins, all finely chopped. The mixture is then seasoned with freshly ground black pepper, salt and Worcestershire sauce. I prefer to leave out the gherkins, and I use a very light hand with the Worcestershire sauce. Fresh toast is the best accompaniment, although in Brussels and Paris, it is usually served with a heap of *frites*.

steak diane

Use the thick end of the tail-end of fillet, and slice off four pieces. Flatten them, and then, at the table, on a spirit stove, melt some butter in a heavy frying pan, and in it cook the steaks, turning them once. Season with a little Worcestershire sauce, anchovy essence, mushroom ketchup, Angostura bitters, or whichever of these old-fashioned condiments most appeals to you. Add salt, freshly ground black pepper and some finely chopped parsley, and serve.

steak stroganoff

Slice the tail-end of fillet steak, flatten the slices, and cut into finger-size pieces. A shallot, finely chopped, and a handful or two of button mushrooms will already have been prepared and put in place. Fry these in a little butter and, when soft, add the meat. Cook for 1–2 minutes, then add a spoonful or two of crème fraîche or soured cream. Season to taste and serve.

flamed fruit

Bananas with rum, bottled cherries with kirsch, soaked apricots with amaretto, prunes and Armagnac all work perfectly in this dish. Ripe or bottled fruit is essential, as the cooking time is minimal.

Melt a little unsalted butter in a frying pan, and add the drained fruit. Let it heat through, then add a little of its preserving syrup or, failing that, a couple of tablespoons or so of orange or apple juice. Allow it to become nice and syrupy, and then pour on a little spirit and light it, *standing or sitting well back*. Serve immediately with vanilla ice cream, clotted cream, crème fraîche, yoghurt or whatever you prefer.

Amongst first courses that you might try for the 'plan ahead' strategy are oysters or the best smoked salmon you can afford. One of my favourite oyster recipes has the oyster set in the half shell in a jelly made with the oyster liquor, a little lemon juice and plenty of finely grated zest. The whole is garnished with ruby red pomegranate seeds. This is not a new recipe, but dates from the seventeenth-century chef and writer, Robert May, whose *Accomplish't Cook* is published in facsimile paperback by Prospect Books. It remains one of my favourite cook books because the recipes are so lively and appealing.

Special, and expensive, cuts of smoked salmon are taken from the centre of the fillet, which gives a small, neat slice when taken vertically – perfect for arranging petal pattern on the plate, if such is your fancy. These cuts are variously called 'balik' or 'tsar' or some such, depending on what brand you buy. There is nothing to stop you buying a whole side and preparing it yourself, removing the pin bones and cutting away the thinner belly and tail parts. These will not be wasted, however. The offcuts can be used in pâtés, mousses and ramekins of potted smoked salmon. Alternatively, arrange traditional slices of smoked salmon in a rosette shape on the plate, and fill the centre with a horseradish and crème fraîche mixture topped with a spoonful of salmon roe. Serve with good toast, and you have a first course ready in minutes. A large tin of caviar is ready even more quickly.

oysters and leeks
with a champagne hollandaise

serves 2

12 fresh oysters

125g (4oz) unsalted butter

2 leeks, trimmed, thinly sliced and well rinsed

4–5 tbsps double cream

6 tbsps champagne

1 shallot, peeled and chopped

2 egg yolks

1–2 tsps lemon juice

Carefully open the oysters, and strain their juice into a small saucepan. Put the oysters to one side, reserving the deep shells.

Melt 25g (1oz) of the butter in a frying pan, add the leeks and sweat until soft, then stir in the cream and cook until somewhat reduced.

Add the champagne and chopped shallot to the oyster juice, reduce to two tablespoons, then put in a blender, together with the egg yolks and lemon juice. Melt the remaining butter and, when very hot, gradually add it, with the motor switched on, to the egg yolks. Alternatively, mix the hollandaise in the usual way in a bain marie.

To serve, spoon a little of the leek mixture into each shell, place an oyster on top, and coat with the sauce. Brown lightly under a hot grill. Alternatively, divide the leek mixture between two shallow dishes, place the oysters on top, spoon over the sauce and put under the grill.

the perfect oyster

For those who think it an abomination to cook oysters, however lightly, here is the way to get the most enjoyment out of raw oysters. You will need an implement with which to open the oysters, though you could try using a beer-can opener, which, according to my friend, Julia Child, is the method used by Yankee oystermen.

as many oysters as the appetite or pocket dictates
1 lemon, halved
freshly ground black pepper
freshly grated horseradish
shallots, finely chopped
red wine vinegar
Tabasco
brown bread spread with unsalted butter
rock salt or crushed ice

Open the oysters, taking care not to lose any juice, and, once the top shell has been discarded, loosen the flesh from the under shell. Arrange the oysters on a platter on a bed of rock salt or crushed ice (this will help keep the oysters stable) and serve with the condiments and bread and butter separately, rather than dictate what should accompany them. The shallots are mixed with the red wine vinegar to make the classic French accompaniment for oysters.

baked vanilla and rosewater cheesecake

This is the ideal recipe for the heart-shaped cake-tin that languishes in the cupboard from one February to the next. For extra flavour and texture, you can add 50g (2oz) ground almonds to the pastry, replacing an equal quantity of flour, and add some ground spice, such as cardamom, or some finely grated lemon zest.

serves 2, plus leftovers

250g (8oz) sweet shortcrust pastry

for the filling

250g (8oz) cream cheese or soft fresh cheese

75g (3oz) unrefined granulated, or caster sugar

4 medium-sized eggs

2 tbsps flour

½ tsp pure vanilla essence

1–2 tsps rosewater

juice of ½ lemon

200ml (7fl oz) single cream

150ml (¼ pint) milk

for decoration

crystallized rose petals or frosted grapes

Roll out the pastry and use to line a cake tin, baking dish, flan ring or other suitable container capable of holding a volume of about 600ml (1 pint). Place the container on a baking sheet, as this will conduct heat right through the pastry, which holds a rather dense mixture.

To make the filling, first cream the cheese and sugar, then beat in the eggs and flour, followed by the remaining ingredients. Pour into the pastry case, and bake in a preheated oven at 180°C/350°F/gas mark 4 for 45–75 minutes, depending on the depth of the filling, covering the top loosely with foil if it shows signs of browning. The cake is cooked when a skewer inserted in the middle comes out clean.

Allow the cheesecake to cool completely before decorating with rose petals and then slicing. Alternatively, use halved red seedless grapes or small bunches of grapes that have been 'frosted' by dipping first in whisked egg white then in icing sugar or caster sugar.

welsh food for sunday lunch

St David's Day, early daffodils and a hint of spring? The temptation is to cook dishes with a Welsh flavour, or plan a themed dinner. Fortunately, it comes at a dull time of year, when the idea of a series of themed dinners might not be unattractive. There are certainly plenty of opportunities, starting with Burns' Night, then St Valentine's, Chinese New Year about the same time, not to mention Shrove Tuesday and pancakes, followed by the Welsh and Irish saints, Mother's Day and Easter, in fairly rapid succession.

In fact, one can incorporate Welsh flavours and ideas into a fairly standard Sunday lunch, without going overboard for spurious themery. Leeks are good in early spring, and I like to use them, not only as vegetables to accompany poultry, meat and fish, but in soups, salads and tarts for first courses.

If you have chosen Welsh cheese for your cheese board, keep some for the leek tart to add another layer of flavour. An alternative first course or, indeed, you may serve them in place of the cheese, is Glamorgan sausages (p.245), a mixture of grated cheese and breadcrumbs, shaped into sausages and fried golden in butter. Miniature versions can be served with drinks, and it is a good dish to know about when you want to cook vegetarian food, as indeed is the leek tart. This recipe can, of course, be varied with the seasons, replacing the leeks with broccoli, courgettes, fresh peas and broadbeans, asparagus, chard, what you will.

In the greengrocer's early in the year, forced rhubarb, with its vivid pink colour and leafy yellow top, is the first thing that catches my eye. It makes the most wonderful ice creams, sorbets, compotes, tarts, fashionable fruit soups and sauces. I also like to use it with ginger wine in a soufflé. For a simpler version of this excellent flavour combination, cut the stalks into 5cm (2 inch) lengths, poach in a little syrup, with a bay leaf or sprig of rosemary, then flavour with ginger wine and serve with crème fraîche, yoghurt or custard.

And so to the main course; I have suggested three alternatives, lamb, mutton and duckling. I particularly recommend lamb that has over-wintered and fed on root vegetables. Sometimes called wether lamb or, if a year old, hogget, it has a full, sweet flavour and a fine-grained texture, just as good as new season's lamb.

A leg of lamb, roasted with potatoes and root vegetables, makes a homely centrepiece. But if you want something more elegant or fashionable, then a leg of lamb can be looked at in several ways, either as a whole, or the sum of its parts. Lamb is one of the ingredients that I use in seminars to illustrate different styles of entertaining, from formal to informal.

Roasted, served with a garnish of herbs, roasted garlic or onion sauce, potatoes and a green vegetable, lamb is suitable for a carving buffet, silver service or family-style weekend luncheon. Try it boned and diced for a casserole of lamb with herb dumplings and spring vegetables, or lamb cobbler for a buffet or family-style service. For plate service, cook and serve the casserole or cobbler in individual containers. If you have the joint seam butchered, that is, with all the muscles cut out separately, then cut into even pieces of approximately 140–200g (5–7oz), you can marinate, then grill or roast the pieces and serve as grilled rump of lamb, with appropriate garnishes. Lamb and barley broth, using the bones and trimmings, is excellent for a very informal lunch buffet or family supper. Sawn across into gigot steaks, try the lamb grilled and served with parsley butter, green beans and new potatoes. Mince and cook the lamb in a shepherd's pie for a casual lunch or supper, or dice and cook as a curry, to be served with all the accompaniments.

But lamb is also versatile in other ways. It is happily matched with a wide range of flavours. Use mustard, tarragon, sweet spices, lavender, rosemary, or citrus oils to flavour the meat. And sauce it with laver, onions, leeks, capers or anchovies, and serve it with sweet root vegetables, roasted, grilled, or mashed.

The lamb recipe I have suggested (on p.368) uses the less expensive shoulder of lamb, but you could just as well have your butcher bone a leg. Mutton, too, is well worth looking for, and is particularly good in slow-cooked dishes such as casseroles and cobblers.

I have also included my recipe for cured spring duckling, which is based on Lady Llanover's recipe. When you read the recipe it might sound like a French confit, but is, in fact, a traditional Welsh way with duck, curing it in salt. The whole duck used to be prepared this way, and served hot with onion sauce. This, too, is a fabulous dish for winter or early spring. Here I prefer to use the legs for another dish, the carcasses for stock and cure the breasts. The meat is delicious hot or cold. If I plan to serve it hot, I cook the breasts slowly, just in their own fat and juices, like a confit. For a cold dish, I poach the meat, cool it and then slice it thinly. A fruit chutney makes a most perfect accompaniment if served as a first course.

leek flan

serves 4

500g (1lb) prepared weight of trimmed, sliced and rinsed leeks
300ml (½ pint) milk
butter for greasing
125g (5oz) hard cheese, grated
3 eggs
freshly grated nutmeg
freshly ground black pepper

Gently simmer the leeks in the milk for 8–10 minutes, then strain them, reserving the milk.

Liberally grease a flan dish with butter, then line with alternate layers of leeks and cheese, finishing with a sprinkling of cheese.

Beat together the eggs and milk, and add a little nutmeg and pepper. Pour in the flan dish, and bake in a preheated oven at 180°C/350°F/gas mark 4 for 30 minutes. Serve warm.

mussels steamed in white wine with laver

Spring is a good time to enjoy shellfish, and I have combined my favourite, mussels, with laver, for a Welsh-flavoured version of *moules marinière*. The rich iodine flavour of the dark green seaweed marries beautifully with the sweet briny flesh of the mussel. If you do not like, or cannot find laver, shred two or three more leeks into the pot, a vegetable which partners shellfish extremely well.

serves 2 as a main course, 4 to 6 as a starter

2kg (4lb) mussels

1 small onion, peeled and finely chopped

2 celery sticks, trimmed and finely sliced

1 leek, trimmed and thinly sliced

freshly ground black pepper

generous splash (about ½ glass) good dry white wine

2 tbsps laver

Scrub the mussels well under cold running water, and remove the beards and any barnacles. Discard any open (dead) mussels.

Put the vegetables, pepper and wine in a heavy-lidded casserole, bring to the boil, cover, and simmer for a minute or two until the vegetables are no longer raw. Open the casserole, tip in the well-rinsed mussels and the laver, and put the lid back on. Give the casserole a vigorous shake or two to distribute the vegetables and seasoning, then let the mussels steam for 5 minutes or so. Serve from the pot with bread to mop up the juices.

cured spring duckling

serves 6

6 duck breasts

1 tbsp freshly ground black pepper

5 tbsps coarse sea salt

2 tsps light muscovado sugar

Score the skin in lozenges, and rub all over with the pepper, salt and sugar mixed together. Put the meat in a covered container, and keep for 1–2 days, rubbing the mixture into the duck every 12 hours or so.

When ready to cook, rinse the duck breasts under cold water and dry them very thoroughly with paper towel. Gently heat a heavy pan with a lid, and place the duck, skin side down, in a single layer. When some of the fat has been rendered, turn up the heat and sear the meat on the other side for 3 minutes. Turn the duck breasts skin side down once more, reduce the heat, partially cover, and cook for 30 minutes, or until the duck is done to your liking.

Serve the meat in wide, shallow soup plates on top of asparagus, small onions, quartered trimmed artichokes, fresh peas and new potatoes, all cooked in duck stock.

Garnish with fresh chervil or watercress.

mutton casserole with a laver and caerphilly cobbler topping

The casserole can be cooked in advance and refrigerated or frozen. The dry mixture for the scone topping can also be made in advance and refrigerated, but the final preparation, mixing the dough, topping the casserole and baking it, should be done no more than an hour or so in advance.

To replace laver, you can use very finely chopped parsley, which you have first briefly blanched in boiling water, and then a good quantity of chives or the green part of spring onions, also very finely chopped.

This topping recipe is extremely versatile, and can be used for making cheese and herb scones. The cheese can be varied to suit the theme and flavours of the meal you are serving, as can the herbs.

serves 6 to 8

1.5kg (3lb) diced mutton

1 tbsp flour

½ tsp each salt and freshly ground black pepper

3 tbsps olive oil

zest of 1 orange, plus its juice

½ bottle good, dry red wine

sprig of rosemary

for the cobbler

250g (8oz) self-raising flour

75g (3oz) butter or lard, diced

2 tbsps laver

75g (3oz) Caerphilly cheese, crumbled

freshly ground black pepper

2 tbsps plain yoghurt, mixed with 3 tbsps cold water

Toss the mutton, a few pieces at a time, in a bag with the flour and seasoning. Brown the meat in the olive oil in a casserole or flameproof dish, then add the zest, juice and red wine. Bring to the boil, tuck in the sprig of rosemary, cover, and cook in a preheated oven at 180°C/350°F/gas mark 4 for 1½–2 hours.

To make the cobbler, rub the flour and fat together in a bowl, then gently work in first the laver and then the cheese and pepper. Stir in just enough liquid to make a soft, pliable dough, then transfer to a floured board and knead lightly.

Roll out the dough to fit the top of whatever flameproof dish you are serving the cobbler from, using the lid as a template, cut into wedges and lay on top of the stew. Increase the temperature of the oven to 200°C/400°F/gas mark 6, and bake for 20 minutes. Alternatively, once you have rolled out the dough, use a scone cutter and arrange the pieces around the edge of the dish, slightly overlapping. When cooked, the under part will be soft like a dumpling, the top crisp and firm like a scone. It is an attractive way of decorating a casserole, as well as turning it into a one-pot meal. You will not need potatoes with it.

roast stuffed rosette of lamb with two sauces

Ask your butcher to remove the blade and thigh bones from the shoulder, but to leave in the leg bone. This makes for much easier carving. Remove as much fat as possible.

serves 4 to 6

  1 shoulder of lamb, boned as above, weighing approx 1.35–1.8kg (3–4lb)

for the stuffing

  100g (4oz) fresh soft breadcrumbs

  25g (1oz) butter, melted, or 2 tbsps extra virgin olive oil

  1 small onion, peeled and chopped

  2 tbsps chopped walnuts

  2–3 garlic cloves, crushed

  grated zest of 1 lemon and 1 orange

  1 tbsp finely chopped chervil or parsley or 1 tsp finely chopped tarragon

  4 large potatoes, peeled and sliced

  1 large mild onion, peeled and thinly sliced

Mix together all the stuffing ingredients, then place in the centre of the opened-out shoulder. Fold the edges of the meat over, then tie it three times round the middle to form a rosette shape, and place in a roasting tin. Roast in a pre-heated oven at 220°C/425°F/gas mark 7 for 20 minutes, then reduce the temperature to 150°C/300°F/gas mark 2 and continue to roast slowly for 2½–3 hours. Allow the meat to rest for at least 15 minutes in a warm place before carving.

for the laver sauce

  250g (8oz) laver

  40g (1½oz) butter

  grated zest of 1 orange and 1 lemon

  1 tsp each orange and lemon juice

  300ml (½ pint) lamb stock, made with the bones

salt

freshly ground black pepper

Heat the laver and butter in a saucepan. Add the zest and juice, then the stock. Bring to the boil, simmer for 5 minutes or so, then season and serve.

for the caper sauce
  15g (½ oz) butter
  15g (½ oz) flour
  250ml (8fl oz) lamb stock
  6 tbsps double cream
  2–3 tbsps capers, rinsed
  salt
  freshly ground black pepper

Make a roux with the butter and flour, and cook for 5 minutes. Gradually blend in the stock, and cook until smooth and the flour no longer tastes raw. Stir in the cream and capers. Bring to the boil, and season to taste.

rhubarb soufflés with ginger wine

serves 4 to 6

500g (1lb) rhubarb

2 tbsps water

100g (3½oz) unrefined granulated sugar

25g (1oz) butter, plus extra for greasing

1 tbsp unrefined caster sugar, plus extra for dusting

2 tbsps plain flour

150ml (¼ pint) skimmed milk

3 eggs, separated

icing sugar for dusting

for the sauce

3 tbsps orange juice

1 tbsp cornflour

6 tbsps ginger wine

Trim the tops from the rhubarb, cut into short lengths, place in a saucepan with the water and granulated sugar, and cook until soft. Then spoon the fruit into a sieve set over a bowl and let it drip.

Generously butter individual soufflé dishes, and dust the insides with caster sugar. Refrigerate until needed. Melt the butter in a saucepan, and stir in the flour to make a roux. Cook for a few minutes, then blend in equal quantities of the rhubarb syrup that has collected in the bowl and skimmed milk, no more than 300ml (½ pint) in total, until you have a smooth sauce. Cook for a few minutes until it thickens. Remove from the heat, and stir in the tablespoon of caster sugar, the cooked rhubarb and the egg yolks. Mix thoroughly.

Whisk the egg whites to firm peaks, and fold in carefully. Spoon the mixture into the prepared soufflé dishes, and place them in a roasting tin containing enough water to come a third of the way up the sides of the dishes. Bake in a preheated oven at 200°C/400°F/gas mark 6 for 12–15 minutes.

Meanwhile, make the sauce. Blend the orange juice and cornflour, then pour into a saucepan with the ginger wine. Bring to the boil, and cook for a few minutes until thickened slightly.

Remove the soufflés from the oven, dust with icing sugar and, as you serve each one, break open the top with a spoon and pour in a little sauce, which will cause the soufflé to rise in its dish.

coeurs à la crème with rhubarb and ginger sauce

This recipe, another variation on the rhubarb and ginger theme, uses uncooked egg white. When gooseberry season comes around, try the recipes with that fruit aromatized with elderflowers, elderflower syrup or muscat wine.

serves 6

500g (1lb) rhubarb
100ml (3½fl oz) water
100g (3½oz) sugar
1 bay leaf
4 tbsps ginger wine
250g (8oz) thick Greek-style plain yoghurt
250g (8oz) curd cheese or sieved cottage cheese
2 tsps rosewater
clear honey, or caster sugar, to taste
3 egg whites

Trim the tops from the rhubarb, cut into chunks and put to one side. Make a syrup with the water and sugar, adding the bay leaf, and in it poach the rhubarb. When cooked, allow to cool slightly before stirring in the ginger wine.

Blend the yoghurt and curd cheese, mix in the rosewater until smooth, then sweeten to taste. Whisk the egg whites to form peaks, and fold into the cheese mixture. Spoon into pierced moulds lined with cheesecloth or muslin, place on a plate, and refrigerate for about 12 hours to drain and firm up.

When ready to serve, turn out on to plates, and carefully peel the muslin from the cheese.

the perfect welsh griddle cakes

These are traditionally cooked for Sunday tea in the dripping from the Sunday roast. The cakes can be frozen once they have been cut out.

makes 12

125g (4oz) self-raising flour
pinch of bicarbonate soda
pinch of salt
50g (2oz) butter, melted
1 large egg, lightly beaten
50g (2oz) sugar
50g (2oz) currants

Sift the flour, bicarbonate of soda and salt into a bowl, stir in the butter and egg, then add the sugar and currants. Roll out, using a little extra flour if the mixture is sticky, and cut into rounds about 1cm (½ inch) thick. Gently fry in butter (or dripping) on a griddle or in a heavy frying pan until golden brown on both sides. Serve warm.

a taste of yorkshire

Yorkshire Day is 1 August, and, in celebration, I offer a handful of very easy recipes. Some, such as the kipper paste and the spicy cod steaks, are as much inspired by Yorkshire's rich local produce as by tradition. Sadly, with the decline of herring fishing generally, the herrings used in the Whitby smokehouses are no longer locally landed, but come instead from Iceland and Norway. And although Scarborough was noted for its cod, you can use cod from elsewhere for the recipe I give here.

Some of the recipes, such as the curd tart and the bilberry and mint pasties are familiar and favourite dishes from my childhood. Both are very representative of the long tradition of baking in rural Britain, and especially in Yorkshire, where we do have a tendency to claim most good things as our own. And indeed who could argue against apple pie with Wensleydale, sticky gingercake and crisp golden Yorkshire puddings.

For a few years, we lived very close to moorland, and every summer would see us children picking bilberries by the bucket, a much less back-breaking task for children than adults. My mother would turn the small, intensely flavoured berries into heavenly jam, as well as tarts and pies. Blueberries are but a pale shadow of the wild fruit. Mint is a typically local addition, and is well worth trying in combination with other fruit in season. And when fresh fruit used not to be available, similar pasties and pies were made with dried fruit and candied peel.

From these recipes, you can serve an entire Yorkshire meal, the full Monty as it were, or individual dishes can be added at any given point in the meal. Together, though, using the kipper paste on toast as an appetizer with drinks, they do make for a marvellous Sunday lunch. For a less copious lunch, use the kipper paste as a first course, serving it in individual ramekins, or scoop on to salad leaves. Then serve the cod or veal, as you prefer.

The recipes also adapt readily to greater numbers. For example, the main course of veal and oyster collops can be cooked as a whole fillet of veal for eight to ten people. In this case, cut the fillet horizontally and open out book fashion. Season the meat, adding some chopped chervil and tarragon if you wish, and arrange the shucked oysters along its length. Grate on lemon zest, close up the fillet and tie it in enough places to stop the filling from falling out. Brush with softened butter, place in a roasting bag and roast in a preheated oven at 180°C/350°F/gas mark 4 for an hour or so for a fillet weighing about 1.25kg (2½ lb). As with all large pieces of meat, the veal should be allowed to rest before carving.

I make the veal dish when I can get organic veal, which is not very often, I must admit. A similar recipe can be made with beef fillet, and the dish is then known as carpetbag steak. Organic beef or similarly high-welfare additive-free beef is more readily available. Make individual portions, or stuff the whole beef fillet as described above. Or, now that we are allowed to once more, simply roast a standing rib of beef and serve it with some light-as-air Yorkshire pud.

If I was serving a larger meal, perhaps a buffet, I would include my Yorkshire pork pie. You will find the recipe in the Buffet chapter on p.134.

whitby kipper paste

This is very good served with brown bread, either fresh or toasted.

serves 4 to 6

1 large kipper
2 bay leaves
100g (3½oz) unsalted butter, softened
yolks of 3 hard-boiled eggs
freshly ground black pepper
pinch of mace (optional)
clarified butter

Put the kipper and bay leaves in a large jug or bowl and cover with boiling water. Leave until cool enough to handle. Pour away the water, and remove the kipper flesh as carefully as you can – this is fiddly as the bones are very fine. In a food processor or with pestle and mortar, pound the fish with the softened butter and egg yolks, and add pepper to taste. If you like, and I generally do, you can also add a pinch of mace. Unless you are using it immediately, pack the kipper paste into a container or ramekins, smooth the top and cover with a layer of melted clarified butter.

devilled scarborough cod

This dish is lovely served with basmati rice scented and flavoured with plenty of grated lemon zest, coriander and cardamom seeds. If you wish to multiply quantities, simply calculate one steak per person, and increase the rest of the ingredients accordingly.

serves 4

4 cod steaks

2 tsps medium curry paste, or more to taste

2 tbsps good quality mango or other fruity chutney

1 tsp dry mustard

1 tsp anchovy paste

25g (1oz) butter, softened

Mix together the curry paste, chutney, mustard, anchovy paste and butter, then spread on top of each of the cod steaks. Place the fish in a buttered ovenproof dish and bake in a preheated oven at 180°C/350°F/gas mark 4 until the fish is just opaque, or done to your liking. You must check this, as timing will depend on whether you have broad, thin steaks, or small, thick ones. Cooking fish until it flakes is, in my view, overcooking it. The fish will continue to cook as you take it out of the oven, so when you do so, it should still have a slight resistance to the bone.

veal and oyster collops

serves 4

8 fresh oysters

4 × 200g (7oz) fillets veal

seasoned flour

1 egg, lightly beaten

breadcrumbs

25g (1oz) butter

lemon slices for garnish

Remove the oysters from their shells, and reserve the liquid. Using the point of a sharp knife, cut a slit in each piece of veal and stuff with two oysters. Dust with seasoned flour, brush with beaten egg, and coat with breadcrumbs. Fry in the butter until the meat is tender and the outside golden brown, about 15–20 minutes. Transfer the veal to warmed plates, then make a gravy with the pan juices and the reserved oyster liquid. Pour over the veal and garnish with lemon slices.

mint and bilberry pasties

serves 4

    400g (14oz) pastry – *see* recipe

    500g (1lb) bilberries

    2 tbsps light muscovado sugar

    pinch of ground cinnamon

    pinch of ground cloves

    25g (1oz) unsalted butter, chilled and diced

    1–2 tbsps chopped fresh mint leaves

Use puff or flaky pastry, or sweet or plain shortcrust pastry, roll it out and cut out four circles, about the size of tea plates. Mix the remaining ingredients in a bowl and spoon on to one half of each circle, leaving a border around the edge. Wet this, then fold over and seal the pastry, either by crimping it in the style of a Cornish pasty or by making regular cuts in the border and folding them up alternately to make a castellated pattern. For an optional glaze, brush with milk and sprinkle with sugar or with an egg and milk wash, before baking in a pre-heated oven at 180°C/350°F/gas mark 4 for about 15–20 minutes.

wilfra tart

Wilfra or St Wilfred's Day is celebrated in Ripon, Yorkshire, at the beginning of August, the original summer bank holiday in Britain, and probably the origin of Yorkshire Day. This rather plain almond tart is very good served with a compote of soft fruits as a pudding, and also cuts well cold at teatime or with coffee.

serves 6

  250g (8oz) sweet shortcrust pastry
  300ml (½ pint) full cream milk
  25g (1oz) soft white breadcrumbs
  50g (2oz) ground almonds
  25g (1oz) golden caster sugar
  grated zest of 1 lemon
  125g (4oz) unsalted butter
  3 eggs, separated

Roll out the pastry, and use to line a 20cm (8 inch) tart tin or quiche dish. Place on a baking sheet. Pour the milk into a saucepan, and bring to the boil. Remove from the heat, and stir in the breadcrumbs and ground almonds. Leave for 5–10 minutes, then stir in the zest, butter and egg yolks. Beat until smooth. Whisk the egg whites, fold them into the mixture, and spoon into the pastry case. Bake in a preheated oven at 180°C/350°F/gas mark 4 for 30–35 minutes until the filling is set and the top pale gold.

the perfect curd tart

This Yorkshire speciality is much nicer than many of the lurid cheese-cakes available commercially. Serve it as a dessert, or for Sunday tea.

serves 6 to 8

250g (8oz) rich shortcrust pastry

500g (1lb) smooth curd cheese

150ml (¼ pint) single cream

100g (3½oz) caster sugar

1–2 tbsps rosewater

grated zest of 1 lemon

4 eggs

100g (3½oz) sultanas

freshly grated nutmeg

Line a greased and floured tart tin or quiche dish with the pastry. Prick the bottom, and bake blind in a preheated oven at 200°C/400°F/gas mark 6 for 10–12 minutes. Allow the pastry to cool, and lower the oven temperature to 180°C/350°F/gas mark 4. Beat together the curd cheese, cream, sugar, rosewater, zest and eggs until smooth. Scatter the sultanas in the bottom of the pastry case. Pour over the curd mixture, and bake for about 40 minutes until set. The surface should not brown but remain pale. Serve warm or cold, lightly dusted with freshly grated nutmeg.

a golden celebration

When they celebrated their golden wedding anniversary, my parents gave me the perfect opportunity to indulge in cooking sybaritic dishes for golden feasts. I pass on some of these ideas, for I imagine many other people find themselves in this happy position. And the recipes are perfect too for a fiftieth birthday party or other jubilee.

Gold ingots, jewellery and objets d'art are beyond my means, but I can offer 24 carat gold in the form of edible gold leaf for use in this special menu. Some of it I use on top of a golden anniversary cake. A rich, dense fruit cake, its main ingredients are golden fruits, almonds, both bitter and sweet, orange flower water, orange zest and juice, and almond liqueur. It is just as sumptuous and fudgy as a traditional fruit cake, but paler, more golden in colour. Since part of my parents' celebrations were held in London, and the other part in Hong Kong, it also had to be a cake designed for travelling. Instead of an impractical three-tiered cake, I made a large round cake, and cut it in three – one half, and two quarters. Each piece I covered separately in marzipan, and then in gold leaf. I tied the whole together with gold ribbons and frills. We broached one quarter at home, packed a half for Hong Kong, and the last piece was kept for Christmas. You can use the Golden Christmas cake recipe on p.461, or the à la carte Christmas cake on p.462.

The cake travelled in good company, for with it was a bottle of 1945 Moulin Touchais, which Tom bought at a Christie's auction a few years ago. Such serendipitous purchasing is not always possible, but there are many golden wines available. We served a bottle of 1979 Roederer Crystal, elegant in its gold tissue, but an excellent substitute would be the Veuve Clicquot reserve with its gold label. Sauternes, Barsac and all the muscat wines are suitably festive, and, of course, make excellent presents too, as liquid gold. Do not forget either, the rare and unusual *vin Jaune* of the Jura.

Fortunately, there are many, many 'gold' ingredients around so that if you prefer, you do not have to rely on gold leaf. It works well in the ways I have suggested, but try it, too, crumbled into fruit salads, sparkling summer drinks, on risottos, and in sauces. Saffron will 'gild' many dishes, both sweet and savoury, adding the bonus of its unique, haunting flavour. A wash of egg yolk, milk and saffron will *endore* breads and roast chicken and other birds.

Petals of marigolds and yellow roses and nasturtium flowers will add the right note of colour to salads and desserts. All the golden fruits you can find will make a luscious fruit salad, and individually many of them will make mousses, ice creams, iced soufflés and granitas of the right colour.

For vegetable accompaniments, look to pumpkins, yellow squashes, carrots, yellow peppers and tomatoes, waxy potatoes, sweetcorn and chanterelles.

Here is another way of using saffron, with smoked haddock in an inexpensive and deeply satisfying dish.

saffron, garlic and smoked haddock soup

serves 6

12 garlic cloves, or more to taste, peeled

1 onion, peeled and sliced

500g (1lb) waxy potatoes, scrubbed and diced

good pinch of saffron threads

600ml (1 pint) water

handful of fresh dill

350g (12oz) undyed smoked haddock fillet, skinned

600ml (1 pint) milk, cold

salt

freshly ground black pepper

Simmer the garlic, onion, potatoes and saffron in the water, together with the dill stalks, saving some of the feathery tops for decoration. When the vegetables are soft, add the fish, cut into pieces, and let it steam on top of the vegetables for a minute or two only. Remove the dill stalks and put the fish and vegetables in a blender with half the milk to cool down the mixture before blending it. Sieve, and return to the pan. Add the rest of the milk, and bring to the boil. Season to taste, and serve.

If you prefer a chunkier soup, more of a chowder, do not blend the mixture. A grating of nutmeg adds a pleasing flavour to the soup. The smooth version is also very good served chilled, with the dill blended with a little cream and swirled in.

chilled almond soup

serves 4

    250g (8oz) blanched almonds, as fresh as you can find
    3 cloves new season's garlic
    pinch of sea salt
    450ml (¾ pint) boiling water
    50g (2oz) fresh white breadcrumbs
    1 tsp sherry vinegar

for the garnish

    gold leaf or peeled and seeded green grapes

Crush a few of the almonds with the garlic and salt, then place in a liquidizer
and blend with the rest of the almonds. Pour on the hot water. Allow to steep
for 30 minutes or so, then add the bread, and blend once more until smooth.
Push through a sieve, pour into tea or coffee cups and serve chilled with a piece
of gold leaf or a few grapes on top.

wild salmon fillets
with mostarda and horseradish sauce

Mostarda di frutta is an Italian preserve of crystallized fruits in mustard syrup which contains no vinegar. It is available in delicatessens and other shops, where it is sometimes sold under an English label, as hot fruit chutney.

serves 4

> 4 × 170g (6oz) wild salmon fillets, skin on
> salt
> freshly ground black pepper
> 50g (2oz) unsalted butter, chilled and diced
> 4 tbsps dry white wine
> 4 tbsps fish or chicken stock
> 3 pieces *mostarda di frutta*, chopped
> 1–2 tbsps creamed horseradish
> lemon juice to taste
> pinch of mace
> mint leaves for garnish

Lightly season the fish on both sides. Melt half the butter in a sauté or frying pan and, when it is hot, put in the fish, skin side up. After less than 30 seconds, turn over the fish, and cook on a high heat for a minute or two or until the skin is crisp and the fish is cooked to your liking.

Transfer the fish to a plate, cover, and keep warm. Add the wine, stock, *mostarda di frutta*, horseradish, lemon juice and mace to the frying pan and cook on a high heat until you have a well-amalgamated sauce. Stir in the remaining butter to gloss and thicken the sauce. Place the fish fillets on individual warmed plates, spoon over some sauce, and garnish with mint. Serve with Jersey Royal potatoes, or on a bed of small pasta, such as orzo.

gilded brandy snaps and golden fruit

For each serving, layer three brandy snap rounds with physalis and kumquats, halved and quartered, poached in syrup until semi-crystallized, or use ready-prepared crystallized fruit. Lay gold leaf on the top-most round and decorate with a physallis with its husk twisted back. This can be stuck to the biscuit with a little chocolate.

In the original dessert, the pastry chef had a hole cut in the middle biscuit and the centre was filled with a dense chocolate cream, surrounded by the golden fruit. To the side, place a scoop of mango sorbet and some slivers of fruit. The clear sauce is an infusion of saffron in Sauternes.

makes 12 biscuits

    40g (1½oz) butter
    25g (1oz) golden syrup
    25g (1oz) plain flour
    25g (1oz) caster sugar
    ½ tsp ground ginger
    1 tbsp brandy

Melt the butter and golden syrup in a saucepan. Then add the flour, caster sugar, ground ginger and brandy and stir until smooth. Drop four tablespoons of the mixture on a baking sheet lined with baking parchment, and spread to about 10cm (4 inches) leaving space in between. Bake in a preheated oven at 180°C/350°F/gas mark 4 for about 5 minutes, until a rich golden brown. Allow to cool for a few seconds on the sheet, which makes it easier to then transfer them to a rack to cool.

ivory and gold chocolate mousse

Twenty-four-carat gold leaf, which is the only one suitable for culinary use, is available from L. Cornelissen & Son Ltd, 105 Great Russell Street, London wc1 3ry, tel: 0207 636 1045, who also supply via mail order.

serves 6

25g (1oz) caster sugar
50ml (2fl oz) water
2 egg whites, beaten
200g (7oz) white chocolate, broken into pieces
200ml (7fl oz) whipping or double cream
grated zest of 3 oranges

Heat the sugar and water in a saucepan until the mixture reaches a temperature of 125°C. Pour over the egg whites, and whisk until stiff.

Melt the chocolate very gently in a bain marie or bowl set over hot water. Whip the cream to soft peaks, add a little of it to the melted chocolate, and mix thoroughly. Blend the chocolate with the whisked egg whites, then add the rest of the cream, blending lightly, but thoroughly, using a metal spoon so that the mousse does not collapse. Pour immediately into ramekins and, when cool, chill until set. Before serving, decorate with a piece of gold leaf or some crystallized lemon and orange zest.

golden crème brûlée

serves 10

- 1 litre (32 fl oz) double cream
- 1 vanilla pod
- 12 egg yolks
- 150g (5oz) caster sugar
- 4–5 squares of gold leaf (or silver, if you prefer)
- 250g (8oz) demerara sugar

Bring the cream and vanilla pod to the boil. Beat together the egg yolks and caster sugar, then pour over the scalded cream. Beat thoroughly, and strain either into a double boiler or into a bowl set over a pan of simmering water. Wash and dry the vanilla pod, split it, and scrape the seeds into the custard. Gently heat the custard, stirring continuously, until it thickens. Remove from the heat, and continue to stir for a few minutes. Stir in the gold leaf, which will break into flakes. Pour the custard into ramekins, and chill until set. Sprinkle the sugar evenly over the custards, then place under a hot grill just sufficiently long to melt and caramelize the sugar, or use a salamander. Place a little more gold leaf on top and chill once more until required.

almond meringues with banana ice cream and passion fruit sauce

serves 4 to 6

for the almond meringues

    4 egg whites

    300g (10oz) golden caster sugar

    1 tsp pure almond essence or 2 tsps almond liqueur

    pinch of salt

    350g (12oz) flaked or chopped almonds

Line four baking sheets with baking parchment or a non-stick professional baking mat such as Silpat. Whisk the egg whites until they stiffen. Add the sugar slowly, a tablespoon at a time, and continue whisking. Add the essence and salt, whisk until the meringue is stiff and glossy, then fold in the almonds.

Spread the mixture into six rounds on each baking sheet, and place in a preheated oven at 180°C/350°F/gas mark 4. Turn off the oven and leave the meringues overnight.

for the banana ice cream

    500ml (18fl oz) full cream milk

    1 vanilla pod

    6 egg yolks

    150g (5oz) golden caster sugar

    150ml (5fl oz) single, double or whipping cream

    2–3 ripe but unblemished bananas

Scald the milk with the vanilla pod. Beat together the egg yolks and sugar. Pour the hot milk over the eggs, then strain the mixture into a bowl, set over, but not touching, a pan of simmering water. Add the cream and stir until the custard thickens. Remove from the heat.

Rinse the vanilla pod, split it, and scrape the seeds into the custard. Rub the bananas through a sieve and also stir into the thickened custard. Once cool, freeze in a plastic container, stirring from time to time to ensure a smooth mixture. Alternatively, freeze the mixture in an ice cream maker or sorbetière, according to the manufacturer's instructions.

for the passion fruit sauce
    8 passion fruit
    sugar to taste

Halve the fruit, scoop out the pulp and cook gently with the sugar, to taste, until you have a still fresh-tasting sauce. I prefer not to sieve it as I like the appearance of the seeds; you may prefer the sauce without.

To assemble the dessert, layer three meringues with two scoops of banana ice cream, and place in a shallow soup plate, surrounded by a pool of passion fruit sauce. Continue until you have used up twelve or eighteen meringues. The rest will keep in an airtight container.

silver service

Having planned food, and devised recipes, for a golden wedding celebration in 1995, I should have been turning my attention to 'silver' food in December of the same year for our own twenty-fifth wedding anniversary. But instead of sitting down to an elegant *diner à deux*, candle-lit and refined, either at home or in some romantic restaurant, I was clearing up after one day's filming, and doing *mise en place* for the next, stepping over cables and lighting boxes. The mill dining room looks festive enough, indeed very pretty, but Christmassy, rather than suitably decorated for a silver wedding.

We were in Cornwall, filming my *West Country Christmas* series, and so were well-placed to buy much of the food I would plan for a silver wedding meal, but we finished up eating our favourite mill supper, bangers and mash, with the Reynolds' sausages from Swaddles Green Farm. I saved my ideas for the special silver dinner and cooked it instead on Christmas Eve.

Fish on Christmas Eve is traditional in many countries, and I decided to cook a lovely silver sea bass as the main course. There are many ways of cooking this prime fish, but it is all too easy to overcook it. The flesh has a marvellous flavour, but, unlike turbot or sole, the texture is soft, rather than firm. It is very good cooked in the way that it might be done for a Chinese banquet, left whole with some ginger, a piece of dried tangerine peel and some spring onions in the cavity, and steamed for about 8 minutes only for a 1kg (2¼lb) fish, with more ginger, spring onion, perhaps a star anise or two, and splashed with a little soy sauce and rice wine. Just before being brought to the table, it would be 'anointed' with a little hot toasted sesame oil.

I have also cooked sea bass off the bone, dipping the fillets in breadcrumbs, frying them in olive oil, and serving them with garlic mashed potatoes, into which I have stirred an olive or coriander 'pesto'; this is extremely good but perhaps not quite smart enough for a fancy dinner.

In the end I cooked my sea bass in a Provençal style, with fennel, olives and extra virgin olive oil for seasoning. A dash of Pernod might be added to enhance the flavour of the fennel, but I think I favour the more subtle addition of white wine or dry vermouth, as this is less likely to detract from the wine. I also include a twist of orange zest in the belly of the fish; orange is an excellent aromatic for fish, quite the equal of lemon. This dish is delicate enough to take a great white burgundy, if one goes easy on the fennel and orange. Alternatively, a fragrant and full-bodied Condrieu would be appropriate.

For the first course for a silver dinner, if money was no object, the finest, shiniest grey Beluga caviar would be very good, and I would hope that it would come in large enough quantity to eat on its own, with a mother-of-pearl spoon. Alternatively, with more 'ordinary' caviar, I would serve it in small, baked potatoes. And with it, perhaps a shot of vodka from a bottle kept permanently in the freezer, thus elegantly frosted, and bitingly cold, as it should be.

But perhaps even more appropriate than caviar are oysters. What could be more silvery? If you want something more elaborate than *au naturel*, I have prepared oysters in a number of ways over the years; baked with scallops, with potatoes in a pie, set in their shells in seawater jelly, and, one year, to a recipe from the seventeenth-century English cook, Robert May, set in a lemon jelly and garnished with pome-granates.

I once tasted oysters with a champagne granita on top. It was a lovely idea, but for me, the granita was too sweet, both for the oyster, and the simple white burgundy which accompanied it. I have adapted the idea, however, to seawater granita. And with that, I would drink either a Chablis Grand Cru with some bottle age, which has an almost identical mineral quality to that of the oyster, or an Alsace Riesling, Colette Faller's Domaine Weinbach, Cuvée Ste Catherine for preference.

As an alternative pair of starters, I might prepare what we enjoyed in Manhattan, one New Year's Eve. Having decided to stay 'home', in our nice cosy room at the Stanhope Hotel, we shopped for caviar in Macy's, bought exceedingly good Oscietra at bargain prices in New York's annual caviar 'war', and ordered, for two, from room service, oysters on the half shell and a bowl of fresh pasta, over which we spooned the caviar. I make a version of this at home, which is very good indeed, both with caviar and with salmon roe. If, like me, you are not keen on those little hard, silvery ball bearings, then puddings with a silver touch present problems. There are, of course, silvered chocolate dragees, nice but not very exciting. A granita of moscato d'Asti would be refreshing and appealing, but only if you serve the oysters without granita. Using Chinese teacups or miniature pudding basins, I might make individual *panna cotta*, turn them out, perhaps on to silver plates or doilies, and garnish with physallis dipped in white fondant, for a slightly frosted effect, and some silver-sugared almonds. I call it alabaster pudding. Alternatively, a soufflé with a thick frosting of icing sugar will also, just, look suitably silvery. And in it I would put some of last year's *marrons glacés*, now beginning to dry out, but perfect in ice creams, soufflés and the like. Moscato d'Asti would be the wine to serve with either pudding, or for something really grand, Veuve Clicquot's 1988 Rich Reserve, with its elegant silver label.

oysters with seawater granita

serves 2

6 fresh oysters

1 tbsp creamed horseradish (optional)

½ tsp finely grated lemon zest

1 tsp lemon juice

sparkling mineral water

salt

Open the oysters, and reserve and strain their juice. Place the oysters in the refrigerator. Clean out the deep shells, and put half a teaspoon of horseradish in the bottom of each, if using. Add the lemon zest and juice to the oyster juices, and make up to 150ml (¼ pint) with mineral water. Add more salt, if you think it necessary, and freeze. When frozen, fork it into crystals. Put an oyster in each prepared shell and spoon some granita on top. Serve at once.

caviar tagliatelle

serves 2

250g (8oz) fresh tagliatelle

1–2 ripe tomatoes, peeled, seeded and diced

generous measure of vodka

25g (1oz) unsalted butter

2 tbsps crème fraîche

50g (2oz) caviar, or more if your budget allows

Cook the tagliatelle and drain. Stir in the tomatoes, toss in the vodka, unsalted butter and crème fraîche. Serve in warmed bowls, topped with a scoop of caviar.

As you can imagine, once the pasta is cooked, it is a good idea to work as quickly as possible so that the pasta does not cool down. Usually, when I have drained the pasta I put it back in the still hot pan in which it was cooked, and sauce it there rather than in the serving bowl.

baked sea bass

Waxy potatoes, such as La Ratte, or Pink Fir Apple, scrubbed, thinly sliced, and baked in the oven, go particularly well with this.

serves 2

1 sea bass, weighing approx 1kg (2¼lb), scaled and gutted, but left whole
salt
freshly ground black pepper
twist of orange zest
1 fennel bulb, plus the feathery tops
2–3 shallots, peeled and thinly sliced
extra virgin olive oil
75ml (3fl oz) Pernod, Noilly Prat or good dry white wine
black olives

Season the sea bass, inside and out, with salt and pepper; put the orange zest and fennel tops in the fish cavity, and leave for 30 minutes before cooking. Trim and thinly slice the fennel, and put it with the shallots in an oiled ovenproof dish. Lay the fish on top, and pour on a little more olive oil and the Pernod, and tuck a few black olives around the fish.

Bake in a preheated oven at 180°C/350°F/gas mark 4 for about 30–35 minutes.

alabaster pudding

serves 2

1 sheet leaf gelatine or 1 tsp gelatine granules

150ml (¼ pint) double cream

75ml (3fl oz) single cream or full cream milk

1–2 tsps caster sugar (optional)

Soften the gelatine in a little water, then drain it. Heat the cream, and milk if you are using it, to blood heat, then add the sugar and drained gelatine. Stir until both have dissolved, then allow to cool. Before the mixture begins to set, pour it into two small wet pudding basins. Refrigerate overnight. Loosen the jelly by holding a hot cloth to the mould, and carefully easing it out on to a shallow dish.

marrons glacés soufflés

serves 2

150ml (¼ pint) milk

15g (½ oz) butter, plus extra for greasing

2 eggs, separated

25g (1oz) caster sugar, plus extra for greasing

25g (1oz) plain flour, sifted

2–3 *marrons glacés*

icing sugar for dusting

Generously butter individual soufflé dishes. Dust the insides with sugar, and refrigerate until needed.

Put three quarters of the milk and the butter in a saucepan, and bring to the boil. Whisk together the egg yolks and sugar. Mix the flour and remaining milk to a paste, then whisk into the egg yolks until well mixed. Stir this mixture into the boiling milk and butter, over a low heat, whisking all the time until the mixture thickens. Do not allow to curdle. Remove from the heat. Stir in the crumbled *marrons glacés*. Whisk the egg whites to stiff peaks, and fold into the mixture. Spoon into the prepared soufflé dishes. Place on a baking tray and bake in a preheated oven at 190°C/375°F/gas mark 5 for 30 minutes. Serve at once dusted with icing sugar.

variations on a black and white theme

Do you remember the Ascot scenes in the film version of *My Fair Lady*? The black and white set? There are many occasions for which a black and white dinner might be appropriate. An elegant dinner for the festive season might have a black and white theme, and I know people who have chosen black and white for their wedding.

With just a little thought, and with fairly readily available ingredients, this is perfectly achievable, and you will not have to resort to putting together ill-matched ingredients simply for the sake of sticking to a colour scheme.

Black truffles and caviar will enhance a black and white meal, albeit at considerable expense. Luckily, staple foods are white, or pale enough to pass for white. Bread, potatoes, rice, pasta, Chinese noodles made from bean flour (sometimes called glass noodles or cellophane noodles) can provide the background. In the vegetable rack look for fennel, onions, chicory, jicama, bean sprouts and water chestnuts.

A meat course might be chicken with truffles or, rather less expensive, black pudding. Or a creamy veal stew, *blanquette de veau*, with wild mushrooms, *trompettes de mort*, in the sauce, black against a pale background. Or choose fish as the centrepiece, an obvious choice, whether it is cod, monkfish, hake, sole or squid. Scallops, squid and monkfish can be partnered with rice or pasta, dyed black with squid ink. Salt cod, too, when soaked and mixed to a brandade, makes a lovely pale, creamy dish, as does undyed cod's roe. This makes a beautiful ivory taramasalata, which you will hardly recognize if you are used to the pink version. And do not forget quail's eggs, black olives and tapenade to add black and white notes right at the beginning of the meal.

And for dessert? *Panna cotta*, junket, syllabub, vanilla ice cream, pear sorbet, and anything else that you can match with a dark chocolate, coffee or, at a pinch, a blackcurrant sauce. Or consider a duo of angel's food and devil's food cake. White dessert will be either creamy or sugary, or both, since cream, sugar and egg whites will be the main ingredients for pavlovas, meringues, junkets, syllabubs, ice creams and sorbets. Lemon, apple and coconut will make suitably pale ices. Ricotta and mascarpone will also be suitable for creamy puddings.

We think of vanilla as a white dish, because of its association with ice cream, but the seeds of the vanilla pod are a black, sticky mass, and I use these to make a richly flavoured, black-flecked syrup to serve with a white pudding.

A few judiciously placed splashes of lipstick reds can be added to relieve the monochrome effect if you wish, with fuchsia pink radishes, small vermilion tomatoes, crimson cherries and scarlet strawberries on beds of shapely cabbage or vine leaves.

The full spectrum of white wines would be my choice to accompany this food. The black wines of Cahors are, after all, no longer black, but 'light, fruity reds', like so many others. Champagne, cava and Blanquette de Limoux for aperitifs, sauvignon blanc/semillon blends for the first wine, full-bodied chardonnays for the second, and Clairette de Die, Moscato d'Asti, or Asti Spumante for the puddings. Champagne cocktails and Black Velvet set the scene.

aubergine and smoked haddock salad

serves 8

2 large aubergines

150ml (5fl oz) extra virgin olive oil

sherry vinegar

coarse sea salt

freshly ground black pepper

8–10 garlic cloves, peeled

1 small potato, peeled and diced

100ml (3½fl oz) milk

500g (1lb) undyed smoked haddock fillet, skinned

flat-leaf parsley

Cut four or five slices, lengthways, about 5mm (¼ inch) thick, from all around the aubergines' circumference, which will leave a central core of aubergine without skin. Brush the slices with olive oil all over, and bake, grill or fry until tender. Dice the aubergine core, fry until soft and golden, then put to one side, after tossing in a little more oil, the sherry vinegar and a little seasoning.

Put the garlic and potato in a saucepan with the remaining olive oil and the milk, and gently cook until tender. Cut the fish into pieces, lay on top of the garlic and potato, cover, and cook for a few minutes until the fish is cooked. Remove from the heat and, either in a food processor or pestle and mortar, work the fish, garlic and potato to a cream with the cooking liquid. Heap this into the centre of a platter, and arrange the slices of grilled aubergine around it, folded if necessary. Fill in the gaps with diced aubergine, and decorate with flat-leaf parsley.

white asparagus with truffle and champagne vinaigrette

On the whole, I much prefer green asparagus to white, with the exception of fried or grilled white asparagus, which I first tasted in Arnaud and Veronique Daguin's restaurant, Les Platanes, in Biarritz. Because the asparagus is not boiled first, all the flavour is retained and the texture is firm. Use finger-thick white asparagus, and slice into four or five long strips, having first discarded the woody part of the stem.

Finely chopped black olives can replace the truffles, with a different, equally powerful flavour. The champagne can be replaced with a good quality dry sparkling wine. Adding wine to a vinaigrette in this way produces an extra and subtle layer of flavour without the vigorous acidity of a vinegar.

serves 8

750g (1½lb) white asparagus, prepared as described above

1– 2 tbsps extra virgin olive oil

for the dressing

1 tbsp finely chopped black truffle

8 tbsps extra virgin olive oil or walnut oil

freshly ground black pepper

sea salt

1 tbsp tarragon or champagne vinegar

2–3 tbsps freshly opened champagne

First make the dressing. Mix together the truffle, oil, seasoning and vinegar, and leave for at least 30 minutes, for the flavours to develop, or several hours in advance, if you prefer. Fry or grill the asparagus until just tender and without letting it char. Arrange on plates. Just before serving, whisk the champagne into the dressing and pour over the still warm asparagus.

mozzarella stuffed chicken breasts
with olive and thyme sauce

If you want to serve this dish cold, do not use mozzarella, whose soft elasticity, when freshly melted, will set into stringy rubber bands when cold. Use ricotta or, better still, a soft, fresh goat's cheese for extra flavour. On the other hand, you may prefer to save this for the cheese course, dusting it with coarsely ground black pepper to match the colour scheme.

serves 8

8 skinless, boneless chicken breasts

4 mozzarella cheeses, sliced

salt

freshly ground black pepper

25g (1oz) unsalted butter

75ml (3fl oz) good dry white wine

150ml (¼ pint) chicken stock

75ml (3fl oz) Noilly Prat or other dry white vermouth

1–2 tsps chopped fresh thyme leaves

12 black olives, stoned and chopped

With the tip of a sharp knife, cut pockets into the chicken breasts. Lightly season the slices of cheese, and insert in the chicken pockets. Close with cocktail sticks. Melt the butter in a large frying pan, and fry the meat gently for 8–10 minutes on each side, without colouring it. Transfer it to dinner plates, or a serving platter, and deglaze the pan with the white wine before adding the stock, Noilly Prat, thyme and olives. Cook for five minutes or so, over a relatively high heat, to reduce the liquid somewhat, then pour the sauce around the chicken breasts. Serve immediately.

If I had plenty of time and help, I would be tempted to make an ice bowl, and fill it with scoops of coconut ice cream, white peach ice cream, lemon sorbet and pear sorbet. If I had little time or inclination to make meringues, I would buy a box of meringue nests, which are made from pretty much the same ingredients I would use in meringues, and fill them with a white peach or pear fool, the fruit peeled and poached in syrup, made into a purée, and folded into whipped cream. With a little more time, I might make the following, both parts of which are best made the day before.

ricotta puddings with vanilla syrup

serves 8

    2 vanilla pods
    150ml (¼ pint) water
    350g (12oz) caster sugar
    juice and zest of ½ lemon
    250g (8oz) ricotta
    250g (8oz) mascarpone
    3 egg whites

Put the vanilla pods, water, 300g (10oz) of the sugar, plus the lemon zest and juice in a saucepan, and dissolve the sugar over a low heat. Bring to the boil, and simmer for 5 minutes. Remove from the heat, and allow to infuse until cold. Strain the syrup into a jug and refrigerate until ready to use. Discard the lemon zest, or snip it into shreds, and use to flavour a lemon sponge cake. Split the vanilla pods, and scrape the seeds carefully into the syrup. One half of the pods can be further split to use as a garnish. The rest can be used to flavour a jar of caster sugar.

To make the puddings, combine the ricotta and mascarpone to a smooth cream, and sweeten lightly with the remaining sugar. Whisk the egg whites, and fold into the cream. Spoon into pierced moulds, lined with wet muslin or cheesecloth. Place in a shallow dish, and chill for several hours or overnight. Turn out on to glass or white plates, and spoon the syrup around the cream, first stirring thoroughly to gather up all the vanilla seeds. Decorate with shards of vanilla pod if you wish.

teatime

On the rare occasion I treat myself to afternoon tea, it always induces a great sense of luxury. It is not, however, an intrinsically expensive treat. No great wines are called for, no rare and exotic foodstuffs. The luxury lies simply in having the time to sit down during the late afternoon and enjoy a contemplative cup of tea, served with a few traditional sandwiches and teatime delicacies. For afternoon tea is nothing if not traditional.

Originally a uniquely British institution, tea is to be enjoyed at home, with friends, or anywhere from a pretty tea-room in the West Country, to a grand country house hotel in the Cotswolds. If you are lucky enough to be on a train or airline which features afternoon tea, then there is no better way of whiling away the journey.

Tea from China and India was available in London by the 1660s, but it was not until some sixty years later that Thomas Twining opened his first tea shop for ladies. Tea was also served then in the home by the mistress of the house, for whom it was the perfect excuse to show off her prettiest china, or indeed acquire some more. It was also the ideal moment to catch up on the latest gossip. The singular feature about afternoon tea in the well-to-do household was that, unlike every other meal, which was served by the household staff, at teatime, the servants were dismissed and the mistress of the house served tea to her friends, and they could be as indiscreet as they liked. Indeed there are those who believe that afternoon tea was invented for the purpose of gossip. It also provided a good opportunity for manufacturers, who devised all the new appurtenances required for the tea ceremony, slop bowl, sugar tongs, sugar bowl, hot water jug, spirit lamp and stand for the tea pot, strainer and decorative tea caddy.

By Victorian times, afternoon tea had become a well-established meal, with its own particular foods, especially when the mistress of the house received callers on her 'At Home' day. Hot tea cakes, English muffins or scones, dainty savoury sandwiches, small cakes and biscuits, and one or two large cakes would be served.

Having imported tea, the beverage, to Britain, the British were not slow to export tea, the institution, a quintessentially British affair, throughout the empire, and anywhere else the British had influence. In recent years I have prepared and served afternoon tea in Paris and New York, but also in Bogota and Bangkok, in Colombo and Hong Kong.

A decent afternoon tea is quite worth spoiling one's appetite for, and my own indispensable teatime treats include small, but generously filled sandwiches, light scones and other tea breads, fruitcakes, Victoria sponges and some homemade preserves. For entertaining friends from abroad, there is really nothing better than afternoon tea. And, if you are entertaining abroad, it makes for a uniquely British occasion, where your guests can feel certain that they will be experiencing the real thing.

For several years, I spent much of February in New York, at The Mark Hotel, cooking and presenting an authentic British afternoon tea, at which a variety of my teatime recipes were offered, including finger sandwiches; tea breads such as scones, crumpets, and saffron buns, served with clotted cream and preserves; slices of fruit cakes and ginger cakes, as well as light sponge cakes, such as coffee and walnut cake; delicate tea pastries and biscuits.

tea, the beverage

On these occasions, I also like to present a selection of the finest single estate Ceylon teas. Such teas have an exquisitely refreshing, bright, pungent and fresh quality. This is real tea, as it should taste, and is always a pleasant surprise for the palates of those who are accustomed to the dull everyday tea made with tea bags or a loose-leaf commercial blend.

Unlike the familiar commercial blends, these are unblended teas, each one identifiably from an individual estate. In this the teas can be compared to the finest *grand cru* wines of Bordeaux; they are the Château Latour and Château Petrus of the discerning tea drinker. The character of the tea is formed by the height above sea level at which it is grown, its leaf size and whether it is harvested during the dry season or the monsoon. Indian single estate teas from Darjeeling and Assam are also available at different times of year from specialist tea purveyors.

These teas, which I also serve at home, are harvested using traditional methods, a delicate process, which allows much of the leaf's chemical makeup to remain intact in the leaf cells, thus preserving the flavour. This is especially noticeable in the larger leaf teas, the FBOP and OP (Flowery Broken Orange Pekoe and Orange Pekoe). Most Ceylon tea is grown in almost organic conditions, with only very low input of chemicals, which have, in any case, to be authorized. According to the European Tea Technical Committee, Sri Lanka produces the cleanest teas in the world. The level of pesticide residues are insignificant when compared with other tea producing countries.

It is also worth bearing in mind that whilst green tea was the first type of leaf to interest scientists looking into the effect of tea on cancer and heart disease, more recent research indicates that black teas, such as those described above, have similarly beneficial effects.

tea blending at home

In addition to serving the single estate teas, I also make my own special blend of tea, and in doing so, carry on one of the traditions of our grandmothers and great-grandmothers, when each household would have its own blends of tea made up by the tea-merchant. This always impresses people, but anyone can make up a tea blend, as long as one or two guidelines are adhered to.

Brewing time depends largely on leaf size. An OP, Orange Pekoe, which is the large, unbroken leaf, takes up to five minutes to release its full flavour into the water. A BOP, Broken Orange Pekoe, is, as its name suggests, a smaller leaf because it has been broken, and takes only a couple of minutes to brew. The BOPF, Broken Orange Pekoe Fannings, is smaller still, and brews even more quickly. So to create a blend of two or three different leaf sizes would produce an unbalanced tea; brewing it for five minutes to let the flavour come out of the largest leaf would be to allow the smaller leaf to stew. So choose leaves of the same size.

The altitude at which tea is grown affects both its colour and flavour. High-grown teas produce a pale brew, with a marked astringency, which is the refreshing signature of a fine tea. Low-grown teas produce a smooth, mellow brew, of a richer, coppery red colour, making them an ideal choice for those who like milk in their tea. Therefore, a suitable, all-purpose blend might be a low- or medium-grown tea, to which you add a proportion of high-grown tea. This is a blend you can serve with or without milk. It will brew to a warm coppery colour, to which milk can be added if liked, but the high-grown tea will give it a pleasantly refreshing astringency. My own special blend is just such a one, as good at breakfast time as teatime.

I would not recommend lemon as an addition to fine tea, as it distorts the flavour, both with its acid and its highly aromatic oil.

grades or leaf size

P – Pekoe. An unbroken leaf, and thus very large.

OP – Orange Pekoe. Another unbroken leaf, long and wiry.

FP and FOP – Flowery Pekoe and Flowery Orange Pekoe.

FBOP – Flowery Broken Orange Pekoe. A large leaf tea.

BOP – Broken Orange Pekoe. A broken grade, i.e. a smaller leaf tea, producing more colour, as in a breakfast-strength tea. Good for blending.

BOPF – Broken Orange Pekoe Fannings. This is, as the name suggests, broken leaf tea, the smaller size producing a stronger brew, and this is the grade used in blending, to add strength and colour.

Note that the term 'orange pekoe' has nothing to do with the variety, colour or flavour of the tea, it simply describes a large leaf size, as 'souchong' describes the large leaf size of China tea.

---

the perfect afternoon tea menu

My ideal afternoon tea would include exquisite sandwiches, of which more on pp.417–24, some meat, some fish and some vegetable. Then there would be freshly made scones. These are quick and easy to make, especially if you keep the dry mix in an airtight box in the refrigerator, and just mix it when required, with soured milk or water and yoghurt. When I cook at The Mark, I make up about 10 kg (22lb) of dry mix, which lasts me for a few days. This is a useful strategy for a large household where afternoon tea is popular.

With the scones, if I could not get clotted cream, I would simply use the best unsalted butter I could find. Crème fraîche and whipped cream are no substitutes, though mascarpone is often used as an alternative abroad. Whilst the thick, almost buttery texture is not much different, there is no flavour of West Country meadows and Jersey milk.

Strawberry jam is the classic accompaniment, but I love homemade lemon curd with scones, and then you do not need cream, or butter. But also try rose petal jelly, or my extraordinary tea jelly. And use the white nectarine jam recipe as a blueprint for other low pectin fruit jams.

If I was preparing tea on a large scale, I would also add one or two other traditional tea breads, such as crumpets, pikelets, Scotch pancakes, saffron buns, Fat Rascals and Sally Lunns. I would follow these with one or two large cakes, perhaps a fruit cake and a sponge cake, and probably my ginger cake, and then an assortment of tea pastries and biscuits, perhaps Maids of Honour and petticoat tails, or some rose and coconut macaroons.

high tea

Contrary to popular belief in America and elsewhere, high tea is not a supremely elegant version of afternoon tea. At high tea, there are no delicate cucumber sandwiches, no buttery scones topped with clotted cream and strawberry jam, no pretty china cake stands and silver sugar tongs. Of course, it is easy to understand how this misnomer came about. High table, High Mistress, high finance and high fashion all denote the *summum bonum*, the pinnacle.

Afternoon tea, taken between 3.30 and 5.30 pm in Britain, denotes, by its very timing, leisure, free time, and an insouciant attitude to the rigours of the daily grind. And indeed, afternoon tea began life as a pastime of the English aristocracy, when, according to tradition, in the 1840s, Anna, Duchess of Bedford used to take a cup of tea, or, more likely then, 'a dish of tay', and a little bread and butter, to ward off the hunger pangs which would strike between luncheon, taken at midday, and supper taken before bed, after an evening of dancing or card playing.

High tea, on the other hand, came into being somewhat later, with the coming of the Industrial Revolution. The class structure was no longer divided between those who worked on the land and those who owned it. A new working class and middle class developed, with bank clerks and bank managers, miners and mine supervisors, factory workers and overseers. They would go home for dinner at midday, or eat dinner in the canteen provided, and have another meal when they returned home about 6 pm. This meal would be accompanied by tea to drink, and was called tea or high tea, or sometimes hot tea. It was more robust than afternoon tea, designed to satisfy an appetite sharpened by hard work.

High tea has been forgotten in London and the more snobbish metropolitan regions, but it continues to thrive in the north of England, the West Country, Scotland and elsewhere where the good things of life are appreciated. I remember Sunday tea as a child in Yorkshire, which would include my mother's homemade bread, perhaps a salmon salad (made with canned salmon in those days), and a Madeira or ginger cake to finish. Ham and eggs, fish and chips, ham carved from the bone and served with chutney, smoked haddock and a poached egg, a raised game pie or pork pie, savoury tarts, Welsh rarebit are some of the dishes which feature at high tea, all of which are entirely in tune with today's eating habits. High tea food is homely and appetizing, just right for those occasions when you long, not for pan-seared foie gras with a

Zinfandel reduction and saffron-infused apples, but comfort food, macaroni cheese, perhaps, or bangers and mash with onion gravy.

For this is not the elaborate, subtle or expensive food served at dinner, but rather more casual food, exceedingly savoury and tasty, relying on eggs, cheese, ham, smoked fish and other well-defined flavours. And like any other meal, the food served at high tea can be seasonal. In the autumn, one might consider individual game pies or crumbles, or a ramekin of potted game served with hot toast. Salmon or crab salads and asparagus tarts are perfect for summer. Fruit tarts in autumn and winter, and ice cream for summer or special occasions will end the high tea on a sweet note.

I like Mrs Beeton's words of praise for high tea. 'In some houses', she wrote, 'it is a permanent institution, quite taking the place of late dinner, and to many it is a most enjoyable meal, young people preferring it to dinner, it being a moveable feast that can be partaken of at hours which will not interfere with tennis, boating or other amusements and but little formality is needed.' She goes on to suggest one or two small hot dishes, cold chickens or game, tongue or ham, salad, cakes of various kinds, 'sometimes cold fruit tart with cream or custard, and fresh fruit'. This is exactly the formula one would want to apply to a high tea menu today.

More substantial than afternoon tea, it is the perfect choice for a pre-theatre meal, or indeed to precede any evening event. Afternoon weddings are fashionable now, with a party later in the evening. High tea is the perfect refreshment, either as a sit-down meal or a buffet. But it is also a perfect meal choice to encourage different generations to sit down and eat together, when a later dinner might just be too late for the youngest and oldest members of the group.

For a summer menu, I might choose warm cheese scones filled with Coronation chicken salad, with jellied cock-a-leekie as an alternative, followed by cold poached salmon with asparagus and new potato salad and rice pudding ice cream with homemade tea biscuits; chocolate and almond, Scottish shortbread or rose and coconut macaroons. For high tea, there's always a 'big' cake, and for that I would serve my moist, sticky ginger cake or a classic Madeira cake.

My menu is loosely based on some of the dishes my mother used to prepare at home in Yorkshire for a summer Sunday tea, when our main meal, or dinner, was served at midday. Then, it was salad of tinned salmon; now fresh salmon, which with new potatoes and asparagus makes a fresh and appetizing dish. And the Coronation chicken comes from about the same period. It was a dish much served at parties and buffets in the 1950s and 1960s. Here it is turned into an elegant and tasty filling for savoury scones. The scones, a feature more usual at afternoon tea, here do the duty of vol-au-vents, but in a more British fashion.

As an alternative presentation, I sometimes use the melon that forms part of the salad ingredients, hollow it out and fill the shell with the chicken salad. The secret to producing a curry dressing for a salad is to use a good mayonnaise or yoghurt, and a curry paste, not raw curry powder. It shocks me to see curry powder being used in dishes that are not going to be cooked further, as the finished dish tastes unpleasantly of raw spices. In curry paste, of course, the spices have been cooked first.

For an autumn or winter high tea menu, I would suggest a selection from the following: macaroni cheese from the Supper section on p.214; individual pheasant pies, see p.411; Cornish pasties, see p.239; toad-in-the-hole, see p.238; kedgeree, see p.15; Glamorgan sausages with tomato chutney, see pp.245, 136; and the usual cakes and biscuits, as well as a fruit tart or crumble. For other suitable dishes, look to the repertoire of traditional savouries and supper dishes.

Tea is the perfect beverage at any time, and certainly is for high tea. This makes the meal ideally suitable for when you might be entertaining those who do not partake of alcohol. On the other hand, if you are arranging a festive high tea, a chilled glass or two of champagne will not go amiss.

cheese scones
filled with coronation chicken salad

These are best assembled shortly before they are required or they will become soggy and heavy. You can, of course, use leftovers from a roast chicken.

makes 12

for the scones

250g (8oz) self-raising flour

50g (2oz) butter, chilled and diced

50g (2oz) hard cheese, grated

approx100ml (3½fl oz) buttermilk or fresh milk soured with lemon juice

for the coronation chicken salad

2 skinless, boneless chicken breasts

½ ripe honeydew or other sweet melon, diced small

1 celery stick, trimmed and diced

200ml (7fl oz) homemade mayonnaise

1 tbsp mild or medium Indian curry paste

fresh basil or mint

Make the scones by rubbing together the flour and butter in a bowl. Stir in the cheese and add enough liquid to make a soft, pliable dough. Transfer to a floured board, and knead lightly. Roll out the dough to about 2cm (¾ inch) thick and cut out twelve scones. Bake in a preheated oven at 200°C/400°F/ gas mark 6 for about 15–20 minutes. Cool on a wire rack. Cut a thin slice from the top of each scone, and then hollow out the centre, leaving a case for you to fill with the salad.

Poach or steam the chicken for 8 minutes. When cool enough to handle, dice and mix with the melon and celery, then fold in the mayonnaise and curry paste. Spoon into the scones, decorate with basil or mint, and serve.

salmon, asparagus and new potato salad

A stunning presentation, which I have used in a photo shoot and on TV, was to use purple potatoes and garnish with pansies.

serves 6 to 8

500g (1lb) new potatoes

500g (1lb) asparagus, both green and white, if available

6–8 salmon fillets, weighing approx 150g (5oz), skinned

homemade vinaigrette or mayonnaise

grated zest of 1 lemon

salt

freshly ground black pepper

chopped chives or salad onions

fresh chervil or tarragon

salad leaves

Scrub and steam or boil the potatoes until tender. Snap the asparagus stalks and boil the tender parts in plenty of lightly salted water. Steam, poach or grill the salmon.

When cool enough to handle, skin or peel the potatoes, if you wish, and dice or slice them. Mix them with the asparagus and then with the dressing. If using mayonnaise, ensure the potatoes are not too hot, as this will cause the mayonnaise to split. Add the lemon zest, seasoning and herbs. Spoon the potato and asparagus on to the salad leaves, and place a fillet of salmon on top. Whole herbs can be used as a garnish.

pheasant pies

makes 4

    500g (1lb) pheasant fillets, from the breast and legs of 3−4 birds
    50g (2oz) butter
    1 onion, peeled and sliced
    225g (8oz) leeks or cabbage, finely shredded and blanched
    1 tsp each sea salt, juniper berries, allspice and black peppercorns, crushed
    2 tbsps chopped flat-leaf parsley or chervil
    450g (1lb) short or puff pastry
    2 hard-boiled eggs, shelled and chopped
    4 tbsps cooked wild or basmati rice
    milk and egg wash to glaze and seal the pastry
    100ml (4fl oz) game or pheasant stock

Fry the meat in the butter for a couple of minutes or so, remove, and put to one side. Add the onion and fry until soft, then stir in the leeks or cabbage and spices, and fry for a further 2−3 minutes. Remove from the heat, and stir in the herbs.

Roll out the pastry, and cut out eight circles − four large ones and four smaller ones, use a tea plate and saucer as the templates. Put the smaller circles on a baking sheet, lined with baking parchment. Heap the vegetables, pheasant, rice and chopped egg on each, leaving a 1cm (⅜ inch) border around the edge. Brush this with the milk and egg wash. Lay the larger pastry circles on top, and seal, pressing all the way round with the tines of a fork. Make a small hole in the centre of each pie, and keep it open with a roll of paper. Brush the pies all over with the glaze, and bake in a preheated oven at 200°C/400°F/gas mark 6 for 20 minutes. Reduce the oven temperature to 180°C/350°F/gas mark 4, and carefully pour in the stock through the hole in the top, having first removed the paper, and bake for a further 10−15 minutes.

rice pudding ice cream

It's best to use the cheapest short grain or pudding rice, rather than a good quality risotto rice. Arborio or carnaroli retain a firm centre, even when thoroughly cooked, and whilst this is perfection in a risotto, it is not at all what is wanted in this recipe.

serves 8 to 10

100g (3½oz) pudding rice

1 vanilla pod

600ml (1 pint) full cream milk

200g (7oz) caster sugar

300ml (½ pint) double cream, whipped

Cook the rice and vanilla pod in the milk until the grains are tender. Remove the vanilla pod, split it, and scrape the seeds into the rice and milk mixture. Blend or sieve this mixture until smooth. Stir in the sugar while it is still hot, then allow to cool. Bear in mind that the sweetness will diminish in intensity when the mixture is frozen. Fold the cream into the rice, then either freeze in a plastic container, in which case the mixture will need stirring from time to time, or in an ice cream maker, according to the manufacturer's instructions.

gouter à la française

Teatime in France, *le five-o-clock*, is certainly not the democratic meal that it is in Britain. It has really never moved beyond the *salons de thé* in Paris and the larger cities and elegant seaside resorts and spas. I have taken tea at Ladurée in the Champs Elysées and at the Crillon, and see many differences in the way the two cultures approach the ritual.

Essentially, the French afternoon tea is even more refined than the most elegant palm court tea in England. The sandwiches are even thinner and finer, the cakes and pastries more delicate. Airy nothings of choux pastry, fragile barquettes filled with fruit and whipped cream and, above all, macaroons. These bear as much resemblance to my rose and coconut macaroons as a ball gown does to a Barbour jacket.

The tea is sipped, usually without milk or sugar, although *un nuage de lait* is allowed, slowly and appreciatively, from exquisite Bernardaud porcelain. My host at Ladurée was, I now realize, shocked to see that I consumed tea as a refreshment, not as a spiritual experience.

But I was thrilled to learn how to make the macaroons, from pâtissier Laurent Carritie, in New York. They are not as difficult as they look when you see tray after expensive tray of these soft and light almond delicacies in Parisian pâtisserie windows. And when I was guest chef at the George V in Paris, doing a week of afternoon teas, I had time to learn how to make madeleines. They look very impressive, but could not be easier. The little shell-shaped moulds are important, however, to get the right shape. They are very shallow, hold little more than a tablespoon of batter, and it is the heat of the oven that causes that bump in the middle.

For a French afternoon tea, I would make cucumber sandwiches, see p.418, and perhaps peeled, seeded tomato, chopped and mixed with chopped chives or basil in a sandwich spread with cream cheese, in summer, and potted beef or pheasant, and smoked salmon with dill butter for winter. No crusts. Thin slices of bread. Finger sandwiches. Then a selection of macaroons, and some madeleines. Nothing else, apart from a pot of delicately refreshing high-grown single estate Ceylon tea. Or a pot of linden flower tea, of course, for those in search of a Proustian experience.

madeleines

The recipe multiplies well, certainly by up to ten; I learnt the recipe using 1kg (2¼lb) of flour. If you wish, you can add, with the eggs, lemon zest, or some vanilla seeds. I have also used a little orange flower water and grated orange zest. Alternatively, you can use vanilla sugar.

makes 24

- 100g (4oz) caster sugar
- 100g (4oz) self-raising flour
- pinch of salt, approx ½ coffeespoon
- 2 eggs, lightly beaten
- 130g (5oz) unsalted butter, melted

Butter and flour madeleine moulds or bun tins. Sift together the sugar, flour and salt. Beat in the eggs, and then mix in the melted butter. Pour the batter, and the mixture really is quite liquid, into the prepared moulds, and bake in the top half of a preheated oven at 220°C/450°F/gas mark 8 for 5–7 minutes. Remove from the oven once the madeleines are golden, well risen, and have the characteristic 'bump' in the middle.

raspberry macaroons

makes 20

125g (4oz) ground almonds

250g (8oz) icing sugar, plus 1 tbsp

100ml (3½fl oz) egg white (4−5)

1 tsp dried egg white (optional)

dash of cochineal or red food colouring

raspberry preserve

approx 200ml (7fl oz) double cream, whipped

Sift together the ground almonds and 250g (8oz) of icing sugar. Whisk the egg whites and, as they firm up, sprinkle in the powdered egg white and the extra tablespoon of icing sugar, continuing to whisk until the mixture is firm. Add some of the almond and sugar mixture to the egg white, together with the food colouring, and fold in gently, then gently fold in the remaining almonds and sugar, which should produce a mixture with the consistency of soft paste.

Pipe on to baking sheets, lined with non-stick baking parchment, into forty small mounds, about 2.5cm (1 inch) apart. Allow the macaroons to 'dry' for 20 minutes or so before baking in a preheated oven at 150°C/300°F/gas mark 2 for 4 minutes. Turn the tray around and bake for a further 4 minutes. Remove from the oven, allow to cool, then sandwich with raspberry jam and whipped cream.

white chocolate macaroons

makes 20

125g (4oz) ground almonds

225g (8oz) golden icing sugar, plus 1 tbsp

100ml (3½fl oz) egg white (4–5)

1 tsp dried egg white (optional)

100g (3½oz) Green & Black's organic white chocolate

100ml (3½fl oz) double cream

Sift together the ground almonds and the 225g (8oz) icing sugar. Whisk the egg whites and, as they firm up, sprinkle in the powdered egg white and the table-spoon of icing sugar, continuing to whisk until the mixture is firm. Add some of the almond and sugar mixture to the egg white, fold it in gently, and then gently fold in the remaining ground almonds and sugar, which should produce a mixture with the consistency of soft paste.

Pipe on to baking sheets, lined with non-stick baking parchment, into forty small mounds, about 2.5cm (1 inch) apart. Allow the macaroons to 'dry' for 20 minutes or so before baking in a preheated oven at 150°C/300°F/gas mark 2 for 4 minutes. Turn the tray around and cook for a further 4 minutes. Remove from the oven and cool on a wire rack.

Soften the white chocolate in a bowl set over hot water, then stir in the cream. Allow to firm somewhat in the refrigerator, then use to sandwich the macaroons.

chocolate macaroons

Make as above, but substitute 25g (1oz) cocoa for the 25g (1oz) ground almonds. A chocolate filling can be made as above, but substituting dark chocolate containing a minimum 70 per cent cocoa solids for the white.

Coffee, lemon and pistachio macaroons can also be made, using the same basic recipe.

sandwiches

The true teatime sandwich must be delicious, and irresistible, and must be easy to eat. Whether you cut it into small triangles or fingers, or stamp out fancy shapes for bridge parties and receptions, my sandwich will not embarrass you. You will not bite into it, and find a slice of rare roast beef hanging down your face, or a squirt of tomato seeds down your front. But it is still a generously filled sandwich.

The structure is simple. The main filling is chopped, potted, pounded, or grated, and mixed with a little cream, yoghurt, gravy or mayonnaise to bind it. An appropriately flavoured butter is made up, some pieces of greenery chosen. One slice of the bread is spread with filling, one with the butter, and the two are sandwiched together with the greenery in between. A richer sandwich can be made by buttering both slices of bread. Crusts are cut off, and the sandwich cut in half, quarters, fingers, or whatever.

You will quickly realize, as I did when first making tea for a hundred at The Mark hotel in New York, that if you are making teatime sandwiches in any quantity, it pays to have your loaf of bread sliced along its length. Spread with a palette knife, and use the knife blade as a guide if cutting the sandwich into fingers.

The principle I use can be applied to every possible sandwich filling that you can think of, and with a few of my ideas to get you started, you can make up your own unique sandwich collection. But first, that classic of the English tea table, the cucumber sandwich, which, in my opinion, is suitable only for summer. I do not understand why hotels and tea rooms persist in serving them for twelve months of the year. Cucumber and tomato are for the summer, so are poached salmon, crab, asparagus and cream cheese with herbs. Potted game, spiced beef, Stilton and roasted ham are for the winter. Seasonality makes sense in sandwiches, as it does for everything else on our table.

the perfect cucumber sandwich

On its own, cucumber has a refreshing texture and true flavour that is often swamped by other ingredients. If you use organic cucumber, you will find this recipe a perfect treat.

makes 4 rounds

1 cucumber

sea salt

8 slices good quality white sandwich loaf

unsalted butter, at room temperature

freshly ground black pepper

With a potato peeler, remove the thinnest layer of skin from the cucumber, in alternate strips. Halve, discard the seeds, and slice thinly. Salt lightly and drain in a colander for an hour. Rinse and dry the cucumber. Butter four slices of bread parsimoniously, but put a generous helping of cucumber on each of the other four slices and dust lightly with pepper. Place the buttered slices of bread on top of the slices spread with cucumber, press down firmly and, if you wish, cut off the crusts. Cut the sandwiches into fingers or triangles.

chicken and asparagus with lemon butter

serves 10

350g (12oz) cooked chicken

up to 100ml (3½fl oz) chicken gravy

a few sprigs of parsley or chives

freshly ground black pepper

salt

approx 200g (7oz) unsalted butter, at room temperature

2 tsps lemon juice

2 tsps grated lemon zest

20 slices bread

10 fresh asparagus stalks, cooked

Chop the chicken and mix it, by hand, or in a food processor, with the gravy, herbs and seasonings. Blend the butter with the lemon zest and juice and spread on half the slices of bread. Spread the filling on the remaining slices, and cut the asparagus stalks to fit. Place the buttered slices of bread on top and cut into triangles.

potted pheasant with pickled walnut butter and mustard and cress

serves 10

350g (12oz) cooked pheasant or other game, such as venison, or a mixture

up to 100ml (4fl oz) game gravy, sauce or stock

2 tsps redcurrant jelly

salt

freshly ground black pepper

approx 200g (7oz) unsalted butter, at room temperature

6 pickled walnuts, rinsed and drained

½ tsp mustard

20 slices bread

2 punnets of mustard and cress

Put the game in a food processor and process until mixed, then add the gravy and redcurrant jelly. Season to taste. Blend the butter with the walnuts and mustard until smooth, then spread on half of the slices of bread. Spread the potted game on the remaining slices, and cover with mustard and cress. Place the buttered slices on top and cut into triangles.

stilton with pears, walnut butter and watercress

To be doubly sure that the pears do not slide out of the sandwich, process them with the walnuts and butter if you prefer.

serves 10

350g (12oz) ripe Stilton, at room temperature

100–150g (3½–5oz) fromage frais

freshly ground black pepper

approx 200g (7oz) unsalted butter, at room temperature

12 walnuts, shelled and finely chopped

½ tsp mustard

2–3 ripe pears, peeled, quartered and thinly sliced

2 bunches watercress, trimmed, rinsed and dried

20 slices bread

Blend the Stilton and fromage frais until smooth, and season with pepper. Blend the butter with the walnuts and mustard until smooth, then spread on half the slices of bread. Spread the Stilton mixture on the remaining slices, and cover with watercress and sliced pears. Place the buttered slices on top and cut into triangles.

hot smoked salmon with horseradish butter and cucumber

serves 10

2 cucumbers

2 tbsps salt

350g (12oz) hot smoked salmon (sometimes labelled kippered salmon)

150ml (5fl oz) crème fraîche

¼ tsp ground allspice

¼ tsp dill seeds

approx 200g (7oz) unsalted butter, at room temperature

1 tbsp grated horseradish

finely grated zest of 1 lemon

freshly ground black pepper

20 slices bread

Halve the cucumbers lengthways, then scoop out and discard the seeds. Remove most of the outer skin with a swivel-head potato peeler, and finely slice. Put in a colander, sprinkle with salt, and leave to drain for an hour or two. Then rinse and towel dry.

Put the salmon, crème fraîche, allspice and dill seeds in a food processor and process until just combined. Blend the butter, horseradish and lemon zest. Season with pepper (the cured salmon will provide enough salt).

Spread half the slices of bread with the salmon mixture, the other half with the horseradish butter, and place a generous layer of cucumber in between.

entertaining

more sandwich suggestions

- turkey with cranberry butter and rocket
- goose with quince butter and radicchio
- lamb with olive butter and ratatouille
- smoked trout or mackerel with lemon butter and baby salad leaves
- smoked salmon butter and thinly sliced cucumber
- devilled egg mayonnaise (eggs, boiled, chopped and mixed with mild curry paste, butter mixed with mango chutney, and some cress for greenery)
- prawns with orange mayonnaise and shredded lettuce
- potted beef, horseradish butter and rocket
- potted ham with kumquat butter and lettuce
- cream cheese and watercress with hazelnut butter

thick sandwiches

For a more substantial tea, such as a high tea or picnic tea, I find that English muffins make excellent sandwiches. Warm them through, split them, remove a little of the inside crumb, and choose from among the following fillings.

Crab meat and asparagus: white crab meat mixed with mayonnaise and cooked asparagus tips.

Avocado and asparagus: combine diced avocado, asparagus tips, chopped spring onions and mayonnaise, flavoured with a little orange juice and grated orange zest. Suitable for vegetarians.

BLT: a muffin is the perfect vehicle for the classic bacon, lettuce and tomato sandwich, with a slick of mayonnaise.

Chicken liver: fry some trimmed rashers of bacon until crisp, then some sliced mushrooms and chicken liver. Roughly squash or mash together the mushrooms and chicken liver, crumble the bacon and fill the muffin with this mixture, together with some cress, shredded lettuce or other greenery. Serve warm or cold.

Tuna fish or salmon salad: flake the cooked fish, and mix with chopped celery, chopped spring onions, a little lemon juice and grated lemon zest and mayonnaise.

Prawn, mint, chilli and cucumber: chop cooked prawns and mint, and mix with prepared cucumber (see p.418), thick plain yoghurt and a little finely chopped chilli.

Smoked trout or mackerel: mash the smoked fish roughly with some horseradish, and mix with freshly ground pepper and soured cream. Good with prepared cucumber or lettuce hearts.

spiral sandwiches

Take a one-day-old tin loaf (either brown or white), and slice off the crust. Cut into horizontal slices, something less than 1cm (½ inch) thick. Spread each slice with butter, and then with your chosen filling and a little greenery. Sandwiches such as these are best filled, not with chunks or slices, but creams, pastes and mousses, as in the suggestions on pp.419–22. Greenery can include watercress, basil, young spinach, iceberg lettuce, rocket, purslane and mustard and cress. Larger leaves will be better chopped or shredded.

Roll up firmly from the short side, like a Swiss roll. Do the same with each slice. Put the rolls on a dish, seam side down, cover with cling film, and refrigerate for a few hours, until the sandwiches have firmed up. Cut into 1cm (½ inch) slices, arrange on a platter, and serve.

scones and teabreads

My arrangement of scones close together on the baking sheet has caused great scepticism in more than one professional kitchen, especially amongst French pastry chefs. However, they liked the results – well-risen scones, with tender edges. If you space the scones apart, they will bake with a uniformly harder crusty edge. My mother learnt this tip from her Scottish mother-in-law, and passed it on to me.

scones

makes 10

250g (8oz) self-raising flour

approx 50–60g (generous 2oz) butter, chilled and diced

approx 150ml (¼ pint) soured milk

Rub together the flour and fat in a bowl. Stir in enough milk to make a soft, pliable dough. Transfer to a floured board, and knead lightly. Roll out the dough to about 2cm (¾ inch) thick and cut out ten scones. Place on a lightly greased baking sheet, so they are just touching, but not squashed together, and bake in a preheated oven at 200°C/400°F/gas mark 6 for 15–20 minutes. Cool on a wire rack. Serve warm.

rich fruit and cardamom scones

makes 12

350g (12oz) self-raising flour

25g (1oz) caster sugar

crushed seeds of cardamom pods, chilled and diced

75g (3oz) unsalted butter, diced

75g (3oz) undyed candied mixed peel, chopped

up to 150ml (¼ pint) buttermilk

Sift together the flour, sugar and cardamom seeds, then rub in the butter. Stir in the peel, and add enough liquid to make a soft dough. Turn out on to a floured worktop, and pat or roll out to a thickness of about 2cm (¾ inch), then cut into rounds. Place on a lightly greased baking sheet, so they are just touching, but not squashed together, and bake in a preheated oven at 200°C/400°F/ gas mark 6 for 12–15 minutes. Cool on a wire rack. Serve warm.

saffron buns

makes about 20

few strands of saffron

150ml (¼ pint) boiling water

750g (1½lb) strong white bread flour

2 tsps salt

1 sachet (7g) fast action dried yeast

75g (3oz) unsalted butter, diced

75g (3oz) golden caster sugar

300ml (½ pint) cold water

250g (8oz) seedless raisins or sultanas

100g (3–4oz) undyed candied mixed peel

2 tbsps rosewater

Put the saffron in a bowl, and infuse in a little of the boiling water.

In a bowl (or food processor) mix together the flour, salt and dried yeast, then rub in the butter. Add the sugar and all the liquids, including the saffron liquor, then the dried fruit and peel, and mix together. When the dough is thoroughly mixed, knead it for 10 minutes on a floured surface until smooth and elastic.

Divide and shape into buns, and place on greased baking sheets. Cover with a damp cloth, and leave to rise until doubled in volume. Bake in a pre-heated oven at 200°C/400°F/gas mark 6 for about 15–20 minutes. Cool on a wire rack. Alternatively, bake as two loaves, in greased 500g (1lb) loaf tins, for about 40 minutes.

crumpets

If you do not have metal ones, crumpet rings can be made by folding baking parchment into strips of several thicknesses, about 2.5cm (1 inch) deep, and stapling them together.

makes 8 to 12

1 tsp dried yeast
450ml (¾ pint) water
pinch of sugar
300g (10oz) plain flour
scant tsp salt

Sprinkle the yeast on 300ml (½ pint) warm water, and add the sugar. When the yeast is bubbling, stir in the flour and salt, and mix until you have a smooth, firm batter. Cover with a damp cloth, and leave to rise in a warm, draught-free place for an hour or so.

Warm the rest of the water, and stir it into the mixture until you have a looser batter. Cover and let it prove for a further 10–15 minutes. Heat a greased griddle and have the greased crumpet rings in place. Pour in the batter to half fill the rings. Cook until holes appear on the top, the surface is dry and the underside nicely browned. Remove and keep warm in a cloth-lined basket until you have cooked the rest of the crumpets.

scotch pancakes

makes about 18

250g (8oz) plain flour

1 tbsp baking powder

pinch of salt

2 tbsps caster sugar

250ml (8fl oz) milk

1 egg, lightly beaten

2 tbsps melted butter

Sift the flour, baking powder, salt and sugar into a bowl, then stir in the milk, egg and melted butter. Beat until you have a thick batter of a dropping consistency. Heat a greased griddle or pan until hot. Drop tablespoonsful of the mixture on to the surface, cooking three or four pancakes at a time. When the underside is smoothly brown, and the top surface dry and bubbled, turn and cook on the other side. Remove and keep warm until you have cooked the rest of the pancakes.

yorkshire fat rascals

makes about 20

500g (1lb) self-raising flour

½ tsp salt

250g (8oz) butter, lard or vegetable shortening

50–75g (2–3oz) golden caster sugar

75g (3oz) seedless raisins, sultanas or mincemeat

1 heaped tbsp yoghurt

1 egg

150ml (¼ pint) milk

Sift together the flour and salt, then rub in the fat. Stir in the sugar and dried fruit. Beat together the yoghurt, egg and milk, and stir into the flour mixture until just bound together into a soft dough. Lightly flour a worktop, and quickly roll out the dough to a thickness of about 1cm (⅜ inch). Cut into rounds with a scone cutter, place on greased baking sheets, and bake in a preheated oven at 220°C/425°F/gas mark 7 for 10 minutes.

entertaining

sally lunn buns

Sally Lunn's are traditionally served hot, split and filled with whipped cream. I like to make smaller versions, too, shaping the dough into flattened balls about 7cm (3 inches) in diameter.

makes 6 to 8

500g (1lb) plain flour
1½ tsps salt
1 tsp fast-action dried yeast
50g (2oz) butter, lard or vegetable shortening
150ml (¼ pint) warm milk
2 egg yolks, lightly beaten
lightly beaten egg, to glaze
granulated sugar

Sift together the flour, salt and yeast. Rub in the fat, then mix in the milk and egg yolks. Knead until you have a smooth, soft dough, working with extra flour, as necessary, to absorb any excess moisture. The longer you knead, the better texture you will have. Shape the dough to fit greased baking rings about 15cm (6 inches) in diameter, or use greased sponge tins for larger teacakes. Leave to rise in a warm place until doubled in volume, then bake in a preheated oven at 220°C/425°F/gas mark 7 for 15–20 minutes. Halfway through baking, glaze with beaten egg, and sprinkle granulated sugar on top as soon as you take them out of the oven.

preserves

These are my own 'house preserves', particular favourites, and rather unusual flavours and combinations. The recipes can readily be adapted to other ingredients. Use the tea jelly recipe, for example, to make wine jellies. You can then embellish these by adding fruit, or even nuts. And a jelly made of Bramley apples, so full of pectin that you can use ordinary sugar and no setting agent, makes the perfect base for herb or spice jellies. Sage jelly and rosemary jelly are delicious, not only on toast or with scones, but as a glaze or accompaniment to roast pork and roast lamb respectively.

As well as teatime treats, the preserves are also perfect presents. As, indeed, are many of the cakes and biscuits in this chapter. And some are perfect for the school tuck-box, particularly the banana jam.

coffee jelly

makes 400 g (14 oz)

Filter coffee is the one to use for this, as it produces a clearer, cleaner brew than a cafetière. Make a pot of your favourite coffee, at usual strength, or perhaps a little stronger if you generally drink fairly weak coffee. The jelly should have a distinctive coffee flavour, not just a nebulous sweet hint. I have sometimes even added a shot of espresso to the filter coffee, allowing it, too, to drip through the filter.

Measure 400ml (14oz) filtered coffee into a saucepan, together with 400g (14oz) sugar with added pectin. Stir in 1 teaspoon lemon juice, and add a spiral of lemon zest. Bring the mixture to the boil, then boil for 4 minutes. Remove from the heat, remove the lemon zest and, if you think you will like the grainy texture, stir in a teaspoon of filter ground coffee. Pot and seal in the usual way.

damask rose and black muscat grape jelly

makes about 1kg (2lb)

1–2 large cooking apples

1 large bunch black muscat grapes

sugar – *see* recipe

500–600ml (1 pint) or more dark red, scented rose petals, measured in a jug

1 tbsp rosewater, if necessary

Wash and chop the apples, cores as well, and put in a saucepan. Add enough water to cover them by a couple of centimetres (an inch) or so. Cook until the apple is almost soft, then add the stemmed grapes, and cook until they are soft. Mash the fruit to extract as much juice and pectin as possible. Strain through a jelly bag for several hours or overnight.

Measure the volume of the liquid, and then measure out an equal volume of sugar. Pound half the rose petals in a small quantity of the sugar, and mix with the juice and the rest of the sugar. Put in a preserving pan or heavy saucepan and heat gently until the sugar has dissolved. Add the remaining rose petals, and bring the syrup to boiling point. Taste and add the rosewater if you think it necessary. Boil rapidly until setting point is reached, then pot in small, clean, hot jam jars. Seal and label.

tea jelly

makes 400 g (14 oz)

Make a pot of your favourite tea, at normal strength. Let the leaves infuse for 3–5 minutes, as usual, depending on leaf size.

Measure 400ml (14fl oz) brewed tea into a saucepan, and stir in 400g (14oz) sugar with added pectin (usually sold as 'jam sugar'), with 1 teaspoon lemon juice. Let the sugar dissolve, and then bring to the boil. Once it is at a full rolling boil, let the mixture boil for just 4 minutes. Remove from the heat, and pour into hot jars. Cover with waxed discs, and then seal, either with lids, or cellophane covers.

apple, green tea and almond jelly

makes about 2.5kg (5lb)

    1.5kg (3lb) cooking apples

    50g (2oz) green tea

    granulated or preserving sugar – *see* recipe

    75g (3oz) blanched almonds, flaked

    ½ tsp pure almond essence

Chop the apples, peel, core and all, and put in a large saucepan or preserving pan, together with half the tea wrapped in a muslin bag. Cover with water and cook until the fruit is tender, mashing to extract as much juice and flavour as possible. Suspend a jelly bag or large scalded muslin cloth over a bowl, and ladle in the fruit pulp. Let it drip through overnight.

Measure out the juice, and put it in a saucepan. Measure an equal volume of sugar, allowing 500g (1lb) to 600ml (1 pint) juice. Add the rest of the tea, in another muslin bag. Cook gently until the sugar has dissolved, and then bring to a rapid boil until setting point is reached. Skim the surface and allow to stand for a few minutes before stirring in the almonds and almond essence.

Pour into clean, hot jam jars, then cover with wax discs and cellophane.

strawberry preserve

Hull and rinse the strawberries and place in a bowl, adding, for each 500g (1lb) strawberries, 500g (1lb) granulated sugar and two tablespoons hot water. Leave overnight.

The following day, strain the syrup into a saucepan, add 75ml (⅛ pint) water to each 500ml syrup, and boil for 5–10 minutes. Add one tablespoon of fresh or thawed frozen cranberries, stapled into a damp coffee filter, and the strawberries, and boil until the fruit and syrup jell. Remove the packet of cranberries and spoon the jam into clean, hot, dry jars. Seal and label. If you prefer, you can add the cranberries to the jam, in which case, they should be cooked first with the small amount of water, crushed and then added to the syrup with the strawberries.

white nectarine jam

makes about 1.5 kg (3 lb)
1 Bramley or a few windfall apples
1kg (2lb) white nectarines
750g (1½lb) preserving sugar

Have your clean jars heating in the oven while you prepare the fruit. Peel and core the apples, and dice very small. Halve the nectarines and discard the stone. Chop the fruit very small. There is no need to remove the skin as this is soft. Put the apple in a saucepan with about 150–200ml (5–7fl oz) water and cook until soft, then add the nectarines. Cook until these, too, are soft, and the apple has disintegrated.

Strain the juices into a preserving pan or other suitable large pan, and add the sugar. Heat gently until the sugar has dissolved, boil the syrup for 2 minutes, then add the fruit. Stir well, bring back to the boil, skim any foam from the surface, then boil until setting point is reached. This will take 3–4 minutes.

Remove the pan from the heat, and fill the hot jars with the jam. Cover with waxed paper discs and screw-top lids or cellophane. Label and store in a cool dark place.

lemon curd

Seville oranges can also be used to make a very well-flavoured curd.

makes about 600 g (1¼ lb)

- 4 large lemons with good skins
- 8 egg yolks or 4 whole eggs, lightly beaten
- 150g (5oz) unsalted butter, cut into small cubes
- 350g (12oz) golden caster sugar

Grate the zest, and squeeze the juice from the lemons, and put in a double saucepan. Add the eggs, butter and sugar, and stir until the sugar has dissolved. Continue cooking, and stir until the mixture thickens. Pot in small, clean, dry jars, which you have warmed in the oven. Cover immediately. Allow to cool, then refrigerate and use within 3–4 weeks.

banana and pecan preserve

With a dark toffee-colour and flavour, banana and nut preserve is marvellous on toast or scones, perfect spooned over ice cream, or hidden away in a crêpe. It could not be simpler to make, and is a good way of using up bananas beginning to brown in the fruit bowl. To set the jam, I use a tart Bramley for its pectin, but you could also use cranberries, or in the summer, green gooseberries.

makes 2 × 200g (7oz) jars

    1 Bramley apple
    juice of 1 large lemon and any seeds
    4 ripe bananas
    400g (14oz) demerara, or light or dark muscovado sugar
    100g (3½oz) pecans, roughly chopped

Peel, core and chop the apple, and wrap the debris, together with any lemon seeds, in muslin. Put the chopped apple in a saucepan with two or three tablespoons of water, and add the lemon juice, the sugar and the muslin 'parcel'. Cook gently until the sugar has dissolved, then bring to the boil, add the bananas, which should be peeled and sliced just before using, and boil for 10–15 minutes, until the jam sets when dropped on a cold plate. Stir in the pecans. Pour into hot, clean jars, seal and label.

grapefruit and ginger marmalade

Perfect for those who prefer a sharper, more sophisticated flavour at teatime, this marmalade is also a delight for a leisurely breakfast.

makes 2 × 450g (1lb) jars

2 large grapefruits, scrubbed and rinsed

approx. 250ml (8fl oz) water

50g (2oz) fresh ginger, peeled, sliced and cut into shreds

1kg (2¼lb) demerara sugar

Put the grapefruit in a lidded saucepan with the water and ginger, and cook gently, covered, for 2 hours until soft. Remove from the heat, and allow to cool, overnight if this is convenient.

Halve the fruit, and scoop out the pulp and seeds into a sieve set over a wide pan. Rub through, and add the cooking liquid and the sugar. Heat gently and, when the sugar has dissolved, boil for a few minutes. Meanwhile, finely slice the grapefruit peel, or process for a few seconds in a food processor. Stir this into the boiling sugar syrup. Continue cooking just until the marmalade reaches setting point. Allow to stand for 5 minutes to distribute the peel evenly. Fill hot, clean jars right to the top. Cover with waxed discs and cellophane, label, and store when cool.

There is invariably a little marmalade left over. Serve it hot over vanilla ice cream, use it to flavour a homemade ice cream, or stir it into a freshly made rice pudding.

small tea pastries and biscuits

All biscuit dough freezes well. When I am preparing for a week of afternoon teas, or a large teatime event, I scale up the recipes for the chocolate and almond biscuits, Cornish fairings and Scottish short-bread, roll each mixture into cylinders, wrap in film and foil, and freeze. Then I simply slice off what I need. Thin slices will make thin, crisp biscuits, thick slices will give thicker biscuits and a chewier finish. You can also freeze biscuits once you have rolled out the dough and cut it into shapes. Pastry, of course, can also be made in advance and frozen.

I have included my mother's recipe for toffee cake, given to her by a neighbour when my brother and I were teenagers. It remains enormously popular in the family, particularly with small boys of all ages. I have to say that the cake is now better than ever because we can get such good chocolate. Use dark chocolate, containing at least 70 per cent cocoa solids, white chocolate or real milk chocolate, as you prefer. Or melt separately and swirl all three together before spreading on the cake; then it is known as millionaire's shortbread. It is best served in very small squares or fingers, as it is extremely rich.

toffee cake

makes 1 × 20 cm (8 inch) square cake

for the shortbread

    150g (5oz) unsalted butter, softened

    75g (3oz) caster sugar

    250g (8oz) plain flour

for the topping

    2 tbsps golden syrup

    395g can unsweetened condensed milk

    175g (6oz) good quality chocolate

Cream the butter and sugar together until pale and fluffy. Mix in the flour, and form into a ball. Press into a 20cm (8 inch) cake tin, about 4cm (1½ inches) deep, or a tin of roughly the same size. Bake in a preheated oven at 200°C/400°F/gas mark 6 for 12–15 minutes. Remove from the oven, and allow the shortbread to cool in the tin.

To make the toffee, put the golden syrup and condensed milk into a saucepan, bring to the boil, and boil for precisely 7 minutes, stirring all the time. Spread the mixture over the shortbread, and allow it to cool. Melt the chocolate in a bowl set over hot water, and spread it over the toffee, marking into small triangles, squares or fingers, as appropriate, before the chocolate has set. Cut when cold.

rose sablés

makes 20

250g (8oz) unsalted butter, chilled and diced

300g (10oz) plain flour

100g (4oz) granulated sugar

1 egg

to assemble

rose petal jelly

icing sugar

Use some of the butter to grease a baking sheet, and dust lightly with flour. Put the rest of the flour, the sugar and the egg in a bowl, electric mixer, or food processor, and mix for a few seconds, then add the butter, and mix until the dough forms a ball.

Roll out the pastry on a floured worktop to a little more than the thickness of a £1 coin. Cut out twenty-four biscuits with a pastry cutter, and then cut a hole out of the middle of twelve of them, about the size of a £1 coin. Place the biscuits on the baking sheet, and bake in a preheated oven at 180°C/350°F/gas mark 4 for about 10 minutes. Remove from the oven and cool on a wire rack.

Spread the whole biscuits with rose petal jelly, and thickly dust the others with icing sugar. Put the latter on top of the jelly covered ones, and spoon a little more jelly into the hole.

saffron curd tarts

makes 12

good pinch of saffron threads

250g (8oz) short pastry

300g (10oz) curd cheese

100g (4oz) unrefined granulated sugar

2 tbsps honey

4 tbsps milk

3 eggs

Soak the saffron threads for 20 minutes in 1 tablespoon of hot water. Roll out the pastry, and use to line tart tins.

Put the curd cheese in a bowl, and beat in the sugar. Mix the saffron liquid with the honey and milk, and add to the cheese. Beat in the eggs. Carefully pour the mixture into the tart cases, and bake in a preheated oven at 190°C/375°F/gas mark 5 for 8 minutes, then reduce the temperature to 160°C/325°F/gas mark 3 and bake for a further 5–8 minutes. Serve warm or cold.

chocolate and almond biscuits

makes 24

115g (4oz) unsalted butter

115g (4oz) golden caster sugar

1 small egg, beaten with 2 tbsps Amaretto

175g (6oz) plain flour

75g (3oz) good quality dark chocolate, chopped

75g (3oz) flaked almonds

Cream the butter and sugar, then beat in the egg and flour. Stir in the chocolate and almonds. With floured hands, scoop up balls weighing about 15g (½oz), and place, well spaced, on two greased baking sheets. Press down with your fingers, or a spatula, to a diameter of about 7.5cm (3 inches), and bake in a preheated oven at 180°C/350°F/gas mark 4 for 12–15 minutes. Remove from the oven, leave for a minute or so, and then cool on a wire rack.

maids of honour

serves 6 to 8

250g (8oz) shortcrust pastry

250g (8oz) curd or cream cheese

75g (3oz) caster sugar

2–3 tbsps rosewater

50g (2oz) seedless raisins

grated zest of 1 lemon

freshly grated nutmeg

4 egg yolks or 2 whole eggs

Roll out the pastry and use to line greased and floured tart tins. Mix the curd cheese with the rest of the ingredients until smooth, then pour into the pastry case. Bake in a preheated oven at 180°C/350°F/gas mark 4 for 15–20 minutes until set. The surface should not be brown but remain pale.

---

cornish fairings

makes 24

> 200g (7oz) plain flour
>
> 2 tsps ground ginger
>
> ½ tsp mixed spice
>
> pinch of saffron, rubbed to a powder
>
> pinch of salt
>
> 175g (6oz) golden caster sugar
>
> 175g (6oz) unsalted butter, softened

Sift together the flour, spices and salt, and cream the sugar and butter. Stir the two together, mixing thoroughly. Form the mixture into twenty-four balls. Place on greased, or lined, baking sheets, and press down with the base of a glass, a decorative one if you wish. Bake in a preheated oven at 180°C/350°F/gas mark 4 for 8–10 minutes until golden brown. Transfer to a wire rack to cool.

rose and coconut macaroons

makes about 20

> 125g (4oz) desiccated coconut
>
> 125g (4oz) caster sugar
>
> rosewater, to taste
>
> 1 egg white
>
> crystallized rose petals or small pieces of glacé cherry

Mix together the coconut and sugar, add a little rosewater, and enough egg white to bind together in a firm paste. Use teaspoons or dessertspoons, dipped in water, to shape small oval quenelles. Place them on a baking sheet, lined with rice paper, and bake in a preheated oven at 160°C/325°F/gas mark 3 for about 15–20 minutes until just pale gold. Remove from the oven, top each with a piece of crystallized rose petal, and cool on a wire rack.

---

entertaining

petticoat tails

makes about 30

    125g (4oz) unsalted butter

    75g (3oz) caster sugar, plus extra for dusting

    150g (5oz) plain flour, sifted

    25g (1oz) ground rice

    iced water

Cream the butter and sugar, stir in the flour and ground rice, and add just enough water to make a stiff pastry. Roll out to a thickness of about 1cm (⅜ inch). Cut out 10cm (4 inch) circles, and from the centre of each, cut a 1cm (⅜ inch) round. Mark each circle into six or eight wedges with a knife cut, and prick a design with fork or skewer. Bake in a preheated oven at 160°C/325°F/ gas mark 3 for 20–30 minutes, dusting with caster sugar 5 minutes before the end of the cooking time. Remove from the oven and cool on a wire rack. If preferred, the shortbread can instead be rolled into a square and marked into fingers before baking.

tea loaves, fruit cakes and spice cakes

date and walnut loaf

This moist loaf keeps well. Make one for eating and one for keeping.

makes 2

- 150g (5oz) butter, plus extra for greasing
- 150g (5oz) light or dark muscovado sugar
- 225g (8oz) plain flour
- 225g (8oz) self-raising flour
- ½ tsp salt
- 2 tsps ground allspice
- 2 tsps ground nutmeg
- 1 tsp powdered cinnamon
- 1½ tsps baking powder
- 225g (8oz) stoned chopped dates
- 225g (8oz) shelled chopped walnuts
- 3 eggs
- 12 tbsps milk

Cream the butter until soft. Beat in the sugar until the mixture is light and soft.

Sift together the flours, salt, spices and baking powder. Sprinkle a good tablespoon or so over the dates, then mix these, and the walnuts, into the creamed mixture. Beat the eggs, and stir them into the mixture, a little at a time, alternating with the remaining flour. Add the milk, and mix thoroughly.

Lightly butter two 1kg (1lb) loaf tins, and line the bottoms with greaseproof paper. Spoon in the loaf mixture, and smooth the surface. Bake in a preheated oven at 180°/350°F/gas mark 4 for 1–1¼ hours. The loaves are cooked when a knifepoint or skewer inserted into the centre comes out clean. Remove the loaves from the oven. Leave them to rest in their tins for 5 minutes, and then turn out on to a wire rack to cool. Peel off the greaseproof paper while still warm.

---

lardy cake

A traditional farmhouse yeast cake.

serves 12

1 tsp caster sugar

300ml (½ pint) warm water

1 tbsp dried yeast

500g (1lb) strong white bread flour

2 tsps salt

250g (8oz) lard, chilled

125g (4oz) mixed raisins and sultanas

125g (4oz) caster sugar

½ tsp ground nutmeg, cloves, cinnamon or allspice

Make a plain dough by mixing together the sugar and water and sprinkling the yeast on top. When it has begun to froth, mix it with the flour and salt and cut in 25g (1oz) of the lard. Knead until the dough is elastic and smooth. Place in an oiled bowl, and cover with cling film or a damp tea towel. Leave to rise in a warm place until doubled in size.

Knock it back, that is, punch all the air out of the dough, and, on a floured work surface, roll it out into a rectangle to a thickness of about 1cm (⅜ inch). Dot the surface at regular intervals with a third of the remaining lard, and sprinkle with a third of the fruit and sugar. Fold the bottom third of the dough up and the top third down, so that it is folded into three. Give the dough a turn so that the short edges are at the top and bottom.

Roll the dough out as before, dot with more lard, fruit and sugar, fold, and turn and repeat the process once more, this time dusting on the spice with the fruit and sugar. Roll out the dough for a final time to fit a 20 × 25cm (8 × 10 inch) greased cake tin. Score into squares or rectangles, cover with a damp tea towel or oiled cling film, and leave to prove for 20–30 minutes. Bake in a preheated oven at 220°C/425°F/gas mark 7 for 30–40 minutes or until golden brown. Remove from the tin, dust with sugar, and cool on a wire rack. Lardy cake is traditionally broken into pieces and not cut.

tennis cake

serves 12

> 6 tbsps rum or brandy
>
> 100g (3–4 oz) each dried peaches, apricots, cherries, mango, pineapple, sultanas and chopped mixed undyed citrus peel
>
> 200g (7oz) blanched almonds, chopped
>
> 1 tbsp finely chopped crystallized ginger
>
> 1–2 tsps freshly grated ginger
>
> 225g (8oz) unsalted butter, at room temperature
>
> 225g (8oz) light muscovado sugar or demerara sugar
>
> 4 eggs, lightly beaten
>
> 350g (12oz) self-raising flour, sifted with a pinch of salt
>
> milk

Pour half the rum over the dried fruit, almonds and ginger, and let them soak while you prepare the cake batter.

Cream the butter and sugar, then add the eggs and flour alternately, thoroughly mixing in each addition. Stir in the soaked fruit and nuts, and add enough milk to give a soft dropping consistency to the mixture. Grease and line a 20cm (8 inch) square cake tin 5cm (2 inches) deep, and spoon in the mixture. Smooth the top, and bake in a preheated oven at 150°C/300°F/gas mark 3 for about 1½ hours or until a skewer inserted in the centre comes out clean.

Allow to cool in the tin. Prick the cake all over with a skewer or cocktail stick, and pour over the remaining rum. Cover the cake with foil, and allow to stand in a cool place until the rum has been absorbed. Then wrap the cake in grease-proof paper and foil. It will keep for several weeks, but is also extremely good as soon as it is completely cold. If I want to serve it immediately, I leave out the last slug of rum, otherwise the alcohol does not have time to evaporate, and it rather overpowers the delicious fruitiness of the cake.

simnel cake

Make this for an Easter tea or, traditionally, for Mothering Sunday.

serves 12

150g (5oz) unsalted butter

150g (5oz) golden caster or light muscovado sugar

4 eggs, lightly beaten

200g (7oz) plain flour

pinch of salt

salt-spoon each of ground cardamom, mace, cinnamon and cloves

50g (2oz) diced mixed candied peel, undyed if possible

50g (2oz) each sultanas, chopped dried apricots, dried pears and dried
    peaches

grated zest of 1 lemon

redcurrant jelly or honey to glaze

for the marzipan

150g (5oz) ground almonds

150g (5oz) golden caster sugar

1 egg, separated and lightly beaten

dash of pure almond essence (optional)

First make the marzipan by mixing the almonds and sugar with the egg white, adding a little of the egg yolk if it needs more liquid to produce a soft consistency. The remaining egg yolk is beaten with a little milk or water for glazing the marzipan-topped cake. Add the almond essence if you think your ground almonds need a flavour boost. Knead the paste, then break off about a third and roll out to a circle with a diameter the same as the 20cm (8 inch) loose-bottomed cake tin in which you will cook the cake. Set aside. Grease and line the tin.

Cream the butter and sugar until light and fluffy, then gradually beat in the eggs. Sift together the flour, salt and spices, then add to the creamed mixture, alternating with the mixed fruit and peel. Spoon half the mixture into the cake tin, smooth it, and place the circle of marzipan on top. Spoon on the remaining cake mixture, smooth the surface, making a slight hollow in the centre. Bake in the centre of a preheated oven at 150°C/300°F/gas mark 3 for 1$\frac{1}{2}$–2 hours or until a warmed skewer inserted in the centre of the cake comes out clean.

Remove the cake from the oven, take it out of the tin, and allow to cool on a wire rack. When cold, brush the top of the cake with warmed honey or redcurrant jelly. Divide the remaining marzipan in half. Roll out one portion to a circle and cover the top of the cake. Make small balls with the remaining marzipan and use some more honey or jelly to stick them around the edge of the cake. Brush the top of the cake with the egg wash, and place under the grill to lightly brown the marzipan. Alternatively use a cook's blow torch.

sloe gin cake

serves 12

225g (8oz) unsalted butter
225g (8oz) dark muscovado sugar
4 eggs, lightly beaten
250g (9oz) self-raising flour, sifted with a pinch of salt
100g (4oz) each walnuts and undyed glacé cherries
150g (5oz) each sultanas and stoned prunes, chopped
1 tsp pure almond essence
75ml (3fl oz) sloe gin
milk

Cream the butter and sugar until light and fluffy. Beat in the eggs and flour alternately. Stir in the remaining ingredients, adding enough milk to give a soft dropping consistency to the mixture. Grease and line a 1kg (2lb) loaf tin, and spoon in the mixture. Smooth the top, and bake in a preheated oven at 150°C/300°F/gas mark 3 for 2–2½ hours or until a warmed skewer inserted in the centre comes out clean. Allow the cake to cool in the tin, then remove and wrap in greaseproof paper and foil. It will keep for several weeks.

entertaining

sponge cakes

At this point it might be worth remembering how to bake a sponge cake if you cannot get cake flour and have to make do with a general purpose flour more suitable for bread making. I write from the experience of having to bin a large batch of sponge cakes I had made for Afternoon Tea at The Mark in New York, using American All-Purpose Flour. I had assumed that by lightening the mix by adding more baking powder my problems would be solved. Not a good idea.

Later, lengthy experiments at home taught me that the underlying problem was too much gluten. Whilst gluten, or protein, is essential to give structure to a loaf of bread, it will make a cake coarse and heavy. The gluten needs to be reduced. If you only have strong bread flour, you can still make a wonderfully light cake by replacing 20–25 per cent of the flour called for in the recipe, with a flour that has no gluten, such as rice flour, potato flour or cornflour. You will still have sufficient starch and thus bulk, but less gluten.

I have come to the conclusion that this first recipe really is the easiest of all cake recipes, because the proportions are easy to remember, and they can be mixed altogether in a food processor. All you need to remember is that the recipe requires equal quantities of butter, sugar, eggs and flour. A large egg weighs about 60g (2oz), so that you need two eggs, for 125g (4oz) each of the other ingredients. For a chocolate version, substitute 25g (1oz) cocoa powder for the same amount of flour. For a lemon version, add the grated zest of one or two lemons, and the juice of about half. As long as your additional ingredients are modest, they are not going to upset the balance of the recipe. A couple of handfuls of dried fruit, or chopped nuts, can be added without any problem, as can a couple of tablespoons of coffee essence, if you want to make a coffee-flavoured pound cake.

plain pound cake

The cake will rise in baking to at least double the volume of the original mixture so that it is best to look for a loaf tin of approximately 1kg (2lb) capacity.

makes a cake that yields about 10 to 12 slices
- 125g (4oz) unsalted butter, very soft, but not melted
- 125g (4oz) golden caster sugar
- 125g (4oz) self-raising flour
- 1 tsp baking powder
- 2 large eggs, at room temperature
- icing sugar, for dusting

Put the butter and sugar in a food processor, and blend until smooth. Tip in the flour and baking powder, and the eggs, one by one, and process until you have a smooth batter. Spoon it into a greased and floured loaf tin, and bake in a preheated oven at 180°C/350°F/gas mark 4 for about 40 minutes or until a warmed skewer inserted in the centre comes out clean. Remove from the oven, turn out of the tin, and allow to cool on a wire rack. Dust with icing sugar before serving.

caramel and walnut cake

serves 10

- 170g (6oz) unsalted butter, softened
- 170g (6oz) unrefined sugar
- 3 eggs, separated
- 225g (8oz) self-raising flour, sifted
- 2 tbsps golden syrup
- 6 tbsps full cream milk
- pinch of salt

for the caramel filling and topping

- 350g (12oz) golden caster sugar
- 2 tbsps single cream
- 50g (2oz) unsalted butter
- 125g (4oz) walnuts, chopped
- walnut halves, to decorate

Butter two 20cm (8 inch) sandwich cake tins, and line the bases with grease-proof paper. Cream the butter and sugar until pale and fluffy. Beat in the egg yolks, one at a time, sprinkling on some of the flour, and mixing thoroughly after the addition to prevent curdling. Mix in the syrup and milk, and then fold in the remaining flour and the salt. Whisk the egg whites to stiff peaks, and then gently fold into the cake batter with a large metal spoon. Divide the mixture between the two cake tins, and level the surface with the back of a spoon.

Bake in a preheated oven at 180°C/350°F/gas mark 4 for 30–35 minutes or until a warmed skewer inserted in the centre of each cake comes out clean. Remove from the oven, turn out of the tins, and cool on wire racks. The cakes, when cold, can be stored in an airtight container and assembled the next day.

To make the caramel, put the sugar, cream and butter in a saucepan, and heat gently until the sugar has melted. Bring to the boil, stirring continuously, and boil for 7 minutes. Remove from the heat, and beat the caramel to thicken it. Sandwich the two sponges with some of the caramel and the chopped walnuts. Pour the rest of the caramel over the top of the cake, and decorate with walnut halves.

madeira cake

serves 10 to 12

225g (8oz) unsalted butter

170g (6oz) caster sugar

3 eggs

285g (10oz) self-raising flour, sifted

scant 140 ml (¼ pint) milk

candied lemon peel

Beat the butter to a cream. Add the sugar and cream thoroughly with the butter. Add the eggs, one at a time, alternating with a tablespoon of the flour, thoroughly beating in each addition before adding the next. Add the milk and the remaining flour, and incorporate well into the mixture.

Line a 20cm (8 inch) cake tin with two or three layers of greaseproof paper, pour in the cake mixture, and bake in a preheated oven at 180°C/350°F/gas mark 4 for about an hour. Halfway through the cooking time, lay strips of candied lemon peel on top of the cake, return it to the oven, and continue cooking for a further 30 minutes or until the cake is firm and golden brown.

victoria sponge

This is the classic English sponge cake, moist and light, with good keeping qualities.

serves 6 to 8

175g (6oz) unsalted butter

175g (6oz) golden caster sugar

3 large eggs, beaten

175g (6oz) self-raising flour, sifted

for the filling

jam and buttercream icing or lemon curd

icing sugar

Cream the butter and sugar until pale, light and fluffy, then gradually add the egg, a little at a time. Once the eggs have been incorporated, gently fold in the flour.

Spoon the batter into two 20cm (8 inch) greased and floured sandwich tins, smooth the tops, and bake in a preheated oven at 180°C/350°F/gas mark 4 for 20–25 minutes. Remove from the oven and allow to cool in the tins for a few minutes before easing the sponges out on to wire racks to cool.

To serve, sandwich with jam and buttercream or with lemon curd. Sift icing sugar over the top.

coffee and walnut cake

serves 6 to 8

Prepare as above, but add 2 tbsps coffee essence and 75g (3oz) chopped walnuts to the cake batter before spooning into the tins. When cooked, fill with a coffee buttercream, and glaze with coffee icing and decorate with walnut halves.

frances bissell's ginger cake

This recipe is based on the traditional Yorkshire ginger cake of my child-hood. It both keeps and freezes well.

serves 12

    125g (4½ oz) plain flour

    125g (4½ oz) self-raising flour

    ½ tsp bicarbonate of soda

    1 heaped tbsp dried ginger

    1 tsp each cinnamon and mixed spice

    100g (4oz) unsalted butter, chilled and diced

    75g (3oz) molasses or black treacle

    75g (3oz) corn syrup or golden syrup

    75g (3oz) honey

    100g (4oz) light or dark muscovado sugar

    300ml (½ pint) milk

    40g (1½ oz) chopped preserved stem ginger or 1 tbsp grated fresh ginger

    3 eggs, lightly beaten

Sift together the flours, bicarbonate of soda and spices, then rub in the butter. Melt the molasses, syrup and honey, then allow to cool. Put the sugar and milk in a saucepan, heat gently until the sugar dissolves, then also allow to cool. Add the liquids to the dry ingredients, then stir in the ginger and the eggs.

Pour the cake batter, and it is a *very* loose batter, into a lined and greased 1kg (2lb) loaf tin, leaving about 2.5cm (1 inch) for the cake to rise. Any extra mixture can be baked in a couple of small ramekins and served as a warm pudding. Bake in a preheated oven at 180°C/350°F/gas mark 4 for 45–60 minutes. Remove from the oven, allow to cool in the tin completely, then wrap in greaseproof paper and foil.

lemon, almond and pistachio cake

Here is a sponge cake, flavoured with ground almonds, pistachios and candied lemon peel which also makes an excellent pudding when served warm.

serves 6 to 8

    100g (4oz) unsalted butter, softened
    100g (4oz) caster sugar
    125g (5oz) self-raising flour, sifted with 1 tsp baking powder
    4 tbsps cream
    2 large eggs
    2 tbsps unsalted pistachios, lightly roasted
    2 heaped tbsps crushed or chopped blanched almonds
    2 tbsps chopped candied lemon peel
    1 tsp pure almond essence
    icing sugar, for dusting

In a food processor, cream the butter and sugar, then add the flour, cream and eggs. Rub the skin from the pistachios and crush them. Stir the nuts, lemon peel and almond essence into the cake batter, then pour it into a greased and floured 20–25cm (8–10 inch) cake tin, either round or square. Place in a pre-heated oven at 180°C/350°F/gas mark 4, no higher than the centre shelf, and bake for about 30 minutes or until a warmed skewer inserted in the middle comes out clean. Remove from the oven, turn out on to a wire rack, and allow to cool. Cut into squares or wedges, dust with icing sugar, and serve.

chocolate mousse cake

Note that the filling uses raw egg.

serves 8 to 10
>   4 eggs, separated
>   125g (generous 4oz) light muscovado or golden caster sugar
>   25g (1oz) cocoa powder
>   100g (3½oz) self-raising flour
>   1 tbsp strong coffee, rum or Tia Maria

for the chocolate filling
>   150g (5oz) good-quality dark chocolate, broken into pieces
>   1 tbsp strong coffee, rum or Tia Maria
>   25g (1oz) unsalted butter, softened
>   3 eggs, separated
>   25g (1oz) golden caster sugar
>   pinch of salt
>   icing sugar, for dusting

Put the egg yolks and three quarters of the sugar into a pudding basin set over a saucepan of barely simmering water and whisk together until pale, foamy and much increased in volume.

Sift together the cocoa powder and flour, then gently fold into the egg and sugar mixture. Stir in the coffee or liqueur. Whisk the egg whites with the remaining sugar and fold into the cake mixture. Pour the mixture into two greased and floured 20cm (8 inch) sandwich tins, smooth the tops, and bake in the top half of a preheated oven at 180°C/350°F/gas mark 4 for about 10 minutes. Remove from the oven, ease out of the tins on to a wire rack, and leave to cool.

To prepare the filling, put the chocolate and liqueur in a clean bowl set over very warm water, and melt the chocolate. Remove from the heat, cool slightly, then mix in the butter. Whisk the egg yolks and sugar until pale and ribbon-like. Whisk the egg whites with a pinch of salt until stiff, then fold both egg mixtures into the chocolate. Sandwich the sponge cakes with the mousse, leaving enough to spread over the top. Alternatively, slice each sponge in half, and use three layers of mousse to sandwich the four slices together. Dust the top with icing sugar.

sponge cake

This is the classic, fat-free whisked sponge. It does not keep well and is best eaten soon after baking.

serves 6 to 8

4 medium to small eggs, separated

125g (4oz) unrefined caster sugar

100g (scant 4oz) self-raising flour, sifted

for the filling

raspberry jam and buttercream icing or lemon curd

icing sugar

Beat the egg yolks with half the sugar until pale and thick. Whisk the egg whites with the remaining sugar, as for meringues. Fold the flour into the egg yolk mixture, and then 'cut' in the egg whites with a metal spoon. Divide the mixture between two greased and floured 20cm (8 inch) sandwich tins and bake in a preheated oven at 180°C/350°F/gas mark 4 for 12 minutes. Remove from the oven, ease the sponges out of the tins, and cool on wire racks before filling with raspberry jam and buttercream, or with lemon curd, and dusting with icing sugar.

christmas and other holiday entertaining

For most of us, this is the busiest time of year for entertaining, and the season seems to stretch further and further beyond the traditional twelve days of Christmas. This chapter tells you all you need to know in order to enjoy holiday entertaining, from what to serve for elevenses, as an alternative to mince pies when friends drop in, to how to produce delicious and elegant dishes from leftover goose and ham. Festive feasts from the store cupboard, and dishes to delight vegetarians are here, too, as well as food for presents and seasonal baking.

countdown to christmas

The best time to bake the cake and make the pudding is late October or November, when the pressure of the holidays is still far away, and certainly by Stir-Up Sunday, the Sunday before Advent. The bright colours of dried fruit, the heady scent of spices, and the fragrant warm smells escaping from the oven are an agreeable way to cheer up dark winter days. And while you have time, and the dried fruit, this is the moment to make a few jars of mincemeat to allow the flavours to mature nicely. One more thing you can make in advance is the brandy butter.

the cake

For some, traditional dark cakes and puddings are a must at Christmas, whilst others prefer lighter versions. This is my own preference, and I have developed several recipes over the years, including a Golden

Christmas cake and an 'à la carte' Christmas cake. For fans of the really traditional cake, however, I have included a recipe for a rich, dark Christmas cake. The first recipe is also very good for wedding, Christening and fiftieth anniversary celebrations.

golden christmas cake

400g (14oz) sultanas

175g (6oz) muscatel raisins

175g (6oz) currants

175g (6oz) chopped, dried apricots

75g (3oz) chopped, dried pears

125g (4oz) dried cherries

rich, dark christmas cake

400g (14oz) currants

175g (6oz) lexia raisins

175g (6oz) sultanas

175g (6oz) pitted prunes, chopped

75g (3oz) chopped dates

125g (4oz) dried blueberries

125g (4oz) flaked almonds

2 tsps grated orange zest

1 tsp ground allspice

1 tsp powdered mace or nutmeg

½ tsp powdered cinnamon

2 tbsps fresh orange juice

75ml (⅛ pint) brandy, whisky or orange liqueur

250g (8oz) unsalted butter, softened

250g (8oz) light muscovado sugar, or dark muscovado
sugar for the dark cake

4 free range eggs, lightly beaten

350g (12oz) plain flour, half white, half wholemeal, if liked

Line a 23cm (9 inch) round cake tin or a 20cm (8 inch) square cake tin with a double thickness of greased greaseproof paper, giving it a 5cm (2 inch) collar. Tie a double thickness of brown paper around the outside, and place the tin on a baking sheet.

Pick over the fruit, and mix it with the almonds, orange zest and spices. Stir in the orange juice and spirit, making sure that the fruit is well moistened, and leave to stand.

Cream the butter and sugar until pale and soft. Beat in the egg, a little at a time, adding a little flour after each addition to prevent the mixture curdling. When you have finished mixing in the flour and eggs, stir in the fruit. This is the time for everyone to give the cake a stir and make a wish. Spoon the cake batter into the prepared cake tin, smooth the surface with the back of a spoon, then make a slight hollow in the centre so that it will bake level.

Bake on the lowest shelf of a preheated oven at 150°C/300°F/gas mark 2 for 3–3½ hours. Lay a circle of foil or greaseproof paper lightly over the cake if it shows signs of browning too much, and turn the oven down a notch. The cake is cooked when a warmed skewer inserted in the centre comes out clean.

Remove the cake from the oven, and allow to cool completely in the tin. When cold, prick the top of the cake with a cocktail stick or skewer and pour over a little of the spirit you used to soak the dried fruit, then wrap it carefully first in greaseproof paper, then in foil. Store in a cool, dry place, 'feeding' it from time to time with a couple of spoons of spirit if you wish, but make sure that the cake is re-wrapped very carefully when you store it away again.

à la carte christmas cake

The next recipe, for another moist, golden cake is also a blueprint, which you can adapt to devise your own cake recipe for other festivities, such as Easter, a wedding or christening, a fiftieth birthday or golden wedding celebration. It uses all the exotic dried fruits our grandmothers and mothers would love to have used if they were available.

My most useful cake tin is the Silverwood, in which a large 30cm (12 inch) cake can be baked, or inserts can be used to give four 15cm (6 inch) cakes, or two 15 × 30cm (6 × 12 inch) cakes, or various permutations in between. I also use it for the small cakes I make for Christmas presents. I bake four square cakes and, when cold, divide each again into four, which I cover first with marzipan and then royal icing.

I have given quantities for three useful sizes, and suggest you might like to bake the cake in a divided cake tin, keeping one half plain, topped with a rich tapestry of nuts and undyed glacé cherries, and decorating the other with marzipan and icing in the traditional style. For different celebrations, of course, choose a different style of decoration, perhaps edible (24 carat) gold leaf for a fiftieth birthday, or golden wedding anniversary, edible silver leaf and silver almonds for a silver wedding celebration or twenty-fifth birthday.

The most important element of the cake, however, is the various combinations of flavours I have suggested, allowing you to choose the nuts, dried fruit and liqueur that appeal most.

cake tin size	15cm (6 inch)	23cm (9 inch)	30cm (12 inch)
approximate baking			
time in hours	3–3½	4½–5	6–7
ingredients			
dried fruit	500g (1lb)	1kg (2lb)	1.5kg (3lb)
nuts	250g (8oz)	500g (1lb)	750g (1½lb)
mixed ground spices	1 tbsp	2 tbsps	3 tbsps
spirits	100ml (3½fl oz)	150ml (5fl oz)	300ml (10fl oz)
rosewater or orange			
flower water	1 tbsp	2 tbsps	3 tbsps
unsalted butter	150g (5oz)	350g (12oz)	500g (1lb)
light muscovado			
sugar	125g (4oz)	300g (10oz)	400g (14oz)
eggs	3	6	8
flour	150g (5oz)	350g (12oz)	500g (1lb)

Line the cake tin with a double thickness of greased greaseproof paper, giving it a 5cm (2 inch) collar. Tie a double thickness of brown paper around the outside, and put the tin on a baking sheet. Have a sheet of folded brown paper (or foil) ready to put over the cake during baking, to stop it browning too much. Fruit cakes require long cooking and it is important to ensure that they do not dry up and burn, hence the careful preparation of the tin.

Mix the fruit with the nuts, spices, and spirits. Cream the butter and sugar until pale and soft. Beat in the eggs, a little at a time, adding a little flour after each addition to prevent the mixture curdling. When you have finished mixing in the flour and eggs, stir in the fruit, then the spirit and flower water. Spoon the cake batter into the prepared tin, smooth the surface with the back of a spoon, then make a slight hollow in the centre of the cake so that it will bake level.

Bake on the lowest shelf of a preheated oven at 150°C/300°F/gas mark 2 for 3–3½ hours. Lay a circle of foil or brown or greaseproof paper lightly over the cake if it shows signs of browning too much, and turn the oven down a notch. The cake is cooked when a warmed skewer inserted in the centre of the cake comes out clean.

Remove the cake from the oven, and let it cool completely in the tin. When cold, prick the top with a cocktail stick or skewer and spoon over a little of the spirit you have used in the cake, then wrap carefully, first in greaseproof paper, then in foil. Store in a cool, dry place, 'feeding' it from time to time with a couple of spoons of spirit if you wish, but make sure that the cake is re-wrapped very carefully when you store it away again.

flavour combinations

- Sultanas, dried apricots, dried peaches, dried pears (the larger fruit chopped sultana-size), almonds, pine nuts, candied orange and lemon peel, orange flower water, orange liqueur.

- Sultanas, dried cherries, dried cranberries, dried apple (chopped sultana-size), almonds, walnuts and hazelnuts, undyed glacé cherries (left whole), rosewater, kirsch.

- Sultanas, dried apricots, figs and dates (the larger fruit stoned and chopped sultana-size), whole, flaked and nibbed almonds, orange flower water, almond liqueur.

- Sultanas, dried pineapple, dried mango, dried peach (the larger fruit chopped sultana-size), angelica, desiccated coconut, cashew nuts, brazil nuts, rum.

- Sultanas, dried cranberries, dried blueberries, dried cherries, pecans and walnuts, maple syrup, bourbon (half and half of the liqueur quantity).

Note Where liqueur has been used rather than spirit, you can reduce the sugar by 50–85g (2–3oz). The dried fruit proportions should be about 50 per cent sultanas and 50 per cent the other fruit suggestions.

the pudding

frances bissell's christmas pudding

This is the recipe I gave year after year in *The Times*, having developed it as a result of readers' requests in 1987. It proved to be one of the most enduringly popular of all my recipes, and sufficiently different to appeal to those who claim not to like Christmas pudding.

The only fat comes from the egg yolks and almonds, and the only sugar from the dried fruits, the small amount of marmalade or candied peel and the fortified wine. The pudding is also high in fibre from the wholemeal breadcrumbs and the dried fruit. It is also absolutely delicious, full of flavour and very moist. Since it contains prunes, it can truly be called a plum pudding.

serves 8 to 10

250g (8oz) fresh wholemeal breadcrumbs

250g (8oz) moscatel raisins, roughly chopped

250g (8oz) sultanas, roughly chopped

250g (8oz) dried apricots, roughly chopped

170g (6oz) pitted prunes, chopped

50g (2oz) almond macaroons or Italian amaretti, crumbled

50g (2oz) almonds, chopped

50g (2oz) ground or flaked almonds

1 apple, grated

1 tbsp grated orange zest

1 tsp ground cinnamon

1 tsp ground mace

½ tsp ground cardamom

½ tsp cloves

½ tsp allspice

2 tbsps orange marmalade or candied orange peel

juice of 1 small orange

4 eggs

75ml (3fl oz) brandy or orange or almond liqueur

150ml (¼ pint) fortified muscat wine, port, marsala or oloroso sherry

Put the breadcrumbs, dried fruit, macaroons, nuts, apple, zest and spices in a large bowl and mix thoroughly, either using a large wooden spoon or your hands. Put the marmalade, orange juice, eggs, brandy and wine in another large bowl or in a blender or food processor, and beat until well blended and frothy. Pour over the breadcrumbs and dried fruit mixture. Mix thoroughly until everything is moist, then cover and let stand for a couple of hours at least, if possible overnight, to let the spice flavours develop.

Oil or butter a 1.75 litre (3 pint) pudding basin (or several smaller basins, if you prefer) and spoon in the mixture. As the pudding contains no raw flour, it is not going to expand very much during cooking, so you can fill the mixture to within 2cm (½ inch) of the rim. Take a large square of greaseproof paper, oil or butter it, and tie it over the top of the pudding basin with string. Place the basin in a saucepan, standing it on a long triple strip of foil to help you lift it out when cooked. Pour in boiling water to reach halfway up the pudding basin, cover the saucepan with a lid, and bring the water back to the boil. Lower the heat and, keeping the water at a steady simmer, steam the pudding for 5 hours. Make sure the water is kept topped up and does not run dry. When the pudding is cooked, remove it from the pan and allow it to cool completely before wrapping it, basin and all, in fresh greaseproof paper and foil.

When you want to serve it, steam for a further 2 hours. You can, for both stages of the cooking, use a pressure cooker, which will greatly reduce cooking times. Manufacturer's instructions should always be followed. As they should if you decide to re-heat the pudding in a microwave.

christmas pudding à la carte

One year I simplified my Christmas pudding, not in its making, for it is already extremely easy to make, but in its contents. It is the least prescriptive recipe imaginable, hardly a recipe at all, in fact, and I call it Christmas pudding 'à la carte'. It allows you to mix and match flavours and ingredients to create your own pudding. Thus, you can opt for a traditional flavour, using the usual dried vine fruits, or go for an American version, with cranberries and pecans dominating. Kumquat marmalade, mandarin liqueur, orange oil, dates, apricots and figs will give a Mediterranean flavour; whilst rum, ginger, coconut, pineapple and mango will produce a Christmas pudding from the tropics.

Like most good things, this recipe came about by accident. I had puddings left over from previous years and was not planning to make a Christmas pudding. In mid December my niece and nephew stopped off in London, on their way back to Hong Kong, for some Christmas food shopping. I decided to make Christmas puddings for them to take back, and it was a question of what was available in my store cupboard. I emptied out all my hoarded small cellophane packs of dried cranberries, cherries and blueberries, some bought here, some in America, and with a bag of dried apricots, I found I had enough dried fruit. Pecans, cashews, almonds and hazelnuts went in and that emptied a few more bags and jars. Kumquat jam, candied orange peel, mandarin liqueur and orange oil, together with a few spoonfuls of light muscovado sugar went in, as did some extra virgin sunflower oil. For dry ingredients, I did not have enough fresh breadcrumbs, so I made up the quantity with oatflakes and a portion of crumble topping that I had in the fridge. I added more rum for good measure, since some of the fruit was very dry; and thank goodness I had four eggs left.

750g (1½lb) dried fruit, such as currants, raisins, figs, dates, sultanas, peaches, pears, apricots, apples, cranberries, blueberries, cherries, mangoes, pineapple, prunes

1 generous tbsp ground spices, such as cloves, cinnamon, ginger, cardamom,
  mace, nutmeg, allspice
250g (8oz) shelled nuts, such as walnuts, pecans, cashews, hazelnuts, Brazil
  nuts, almonds
150g (5oz) fat, such as beef or vegetarian suet, butter, creamed coconut,
  sunflower oil, polyunsaturated margarine
250g (8oz) dry ingredients, such as fresh wholemeal breadcrumbs, flour,
  oatflakes, desiccated coconut, crumble topping
100g (3–4oz) sweet ingredients, such as sugar, marmalade, candied peel,
  crystallized ginger
250ml (8fl oz) spirits, or equal quantities, i.e. 100ml (4fl oz) each, spirits and
  fortified wine, such as rum, brandy, oloroso sherry, cream sherry, Pedro
  Ximenez sherry, Amaretto, mandarin liqueur, kirsch
4 eggs
1 tbsp citrus zest or 1 grated apple or 1 grated carrot or 1–2 tsps orange or
  other citrus oil (optional)

Put the dried fruit, spices, nuts, fat, dry ingredients and sweet ingredients in a
large bowl and mix thoroughly, either using a large wooden spoon or your
hands. Put the spirits and egg, together with optional ingredients, in another
large bowl or in a blender or food processor, and beat until well blended and
frothy. Pour the liquid over the dried fruit mixture. Mix thoroughly until everything is moist. Cover and let it stand for a couple of hours at least, and, if
possible, overnight to let the spice flavours develop.

   Oil or butter a 1.75 litre (3 pint) pudding basin (or several smaller basins, if
you prefer) and spoon in the mixture. Fill the mixture to within 2cm (1 inch) of
the rim. Take a large square of greaseproof paper, oil or butter it, and secure it
over the top of the pudding basin with string or a thick rubber band – the kind
that are dropped all over the front step by the postman. Place the basin in a
saucepan, standing it on a long triple strip of foil to help you lift it out of the
saucepan once cooked. Pour in boiling water to reach halfway up the pudding
basin, cover the saucepan with a lid, and bring the water back to the boil. Lower
the heat and, keeping the water at a steady simmer, steam the pudding for 5
hours. Make sure the water is kept topped up and do not allow to run dry. When
the pudding is cooked, remove it from the pan, and allow it to cool completely

before wrapping it, basin and all, in fresh greaseproof paper and foil.

When you want to serve it, steam for a further 2 hours. You can, for both stages of the cooking, use a pressure cooker, which will greatly reduce cooking times. Manufacturer's instructions should always be followed. As they should if you decide to re-heat the pudding in a microwave.

mincemeat

Homemade mincemeat is a delight and extraordinarily easy to make. Over the years, I have made rich vegetarian mincemeat (which is every bit as luxurious as the suet version), and 'à la carte mincemeat', where you make up a basic recipe, and then add extra ingredients each time you want to use it. I have also created a tropical fruit mincemeat, which is not only rich and luxurious, but also suitable for vegetarians, since it uses not suet but grated coconut cream. Make some for yourself, and some for your friends.

Small, traditional mince pies, dusted with icing sugar, are a welcome offering to callers with a glass of fine amontillado or oloroso sherry or Madeira. A large mincemeat tart with a lattice top looks good on a holiday buffet table. A hot mincemeat sauce is marvellous with good vanilla ice cream. You can also use mincemeat in soufflés and batter puddings.

Here is a basic mincemeat recipe, which, since it doesn't contain raw apple, is in little danger of fermenting. I then dress it up, when I want to use it, with the addition of nuts, other dried fruit, or exotic fresh fruit combinations. With the abundance of tropical fruit in our shops at this time of the year, now is a good time to experiment with your own combinations.

à la carte mincemeat

makes about 2 kg (4 lb)

250g (8oz) dried apricots or stoned prunes

250g (8oz) raisins

250g (8oz) dates

250g (8oz) sultanas

250g (8oz) currants

250g (8oz) shredded beef or vegetarian suet or grated coconut cream,
 or 8 tbsps ground nut oil

125g (4oz) demerara sugar

125g (4oz) chopped mixed peel

grated zest and juice of 1 lemon and 1 orange

1 tsp ground mixed spice

½ tsp ground cardamom

150ml (¼ pint) rum or brandy

150ml (¼ pint) oloroso or cream sherry, or port

Chop or mince the dried fruit, then, in a large bowl, mix with all the other ingredients and leave, covered, for 2–3 days before potting and labelling.

When you wish to use the mincemeat, spoon out about 250g (8oz) into a bowl. That, together with one of the following, will fill twelve to eighteen mince pies: 1 Bramley or russet apple, peeled, cored and grated, and mixed with 75g (3oz) flaked almonds; 1–2 Conference pears, peeled, cored and grated, and mixed with 15g (½oz) fresh, grated ginger or stem ginger; 75g (3oz) dried cranberries, cherries or blueberries; ½ a medium pineapple, peeled, cored and chopped, and mixed with a handful of pine nuts, finely chopped Brazil nuts or desiccated coconut; 100g (3–4oz) dried mango, chopped, and mixed with a handful of chopped cashew nuts; 100g (3–4oz) fresh cranberries, cooked in a little orange juice until they pop, and mixed with chopped mandarin segments and grated mandarin zest or chopped kumquats.

tropical fruit mincemeat

Suitable for vegetarians.

makes 2 × 500g (1 lb) jars

grated zest and juice of 1 lime or 1 lemon

200g (7oz) dark muscovado sugar

500g (1lb) dried fruit chosen from the following and chopped small:

mango, papaya, banana, dates, figs and pineapple

250g (8oz) fresh fruit, finely chopped, chosen from the following:

pineapple, physalis, guava

100g (3½oz) creamed coconut, grated

50g (2oz) blanched almonds, chopped

½ tsp each ground cardamom, cinnamon, cloves and mace

2–3 tbsps dark rum (optional)

Thoroughly mix all the ingredients in a large bowl, and leave overnight for the flavours to blend before potting, sealing and labelling.

flavoured butters and hard sauces

These, too, make excellent presents, but they are really designed to accompany the Christmas pudding. You can also slip a little under the lids of your mince pies before serving them.

mandarin butter

250g (8oz) unsalted butter

175g (6oz) icing sugar, sifted

pinch of ground mace

4 tbsps Mandarine Napoleon

2 tbsps cognac

sherry butter

250g (8oz) unsalted butter

200g (7oz) icing sugar, sifted

pinch of cinnamon

4 tbsps old oloroso sherry

2 tbsps Brandy de Jerez

quince butter

250g (8oz) unsalted butter

4 tbsps quince jelly

4 tbsps *eau de vie de coing* (quince eau de vie)

2 tbsps brandy

In each case, have all the ingredients at room temperature. Blend until smooth, pack into pots or jars, seal, label and refrigerate until required. They will keep for 4–6 weeks.

holiday baking

When friends come calling before lunch, serve them spiced wine bread and mulled wine for elevenses as an alternative to mince pies and sherry, or a glass of rich egg-nog with a piece of poppy seed roll.

There are those who admit to no variations on a so-called traditional recipe. Some years ago, I gave a recipe for stollen and suggested that, as a yeast bread, it was also rather good to eat at breakfast, as one might a Danish pastry. A reader wrote to me with her recipe, which she had used for years, which was totally authentic, was not made with yeast, and was certainly not a breakfast bread. In the same post, I received a letter from Claire Clark, then head pastry teacher at Le Cordon Bleu School in London, with her stollen recipe. Like mine, it was a yeast-based recipe. Both versions are very good. The non-yeast version improves with keeping.

One winter's day, a few weeks before Christmas, we were leaving our friends the Lancellottis in Soliera, in northern Italy, for Bologna airport. Signora Lancellotti sat me down with a cappuccino, and gave me the *pane di natale* recipe, which she had learned in her mother-in-law's kitchen. Not nearly as rich as our own Christmas cakes and puddings, it is made with the ingredients that would be found in most larders in the village. Concentrated grape juice is used in Soliera but, as it is not available here, I suggest using prune juice, which is quite concentrated, or ordinary red grape juice, enriching it with a little of the thick, raisiny sweet Pedro Ximenez sherry.

stollen

serves 8 to 10

1 tbsp dried yeast

200ml (7fl oz) warm milk, plus a pinch of sugar

500g (1lb) strong plain flour

½ tsp salt

125g (4oz) unsalted butter, chilled and diced

grated zest of 1 lemon

250–300g (8–10oz) mixed, dried fruit, chopped to an even size

75g (3oz) almonds, chopped

1 egg, beaten

250g (8oz) marzipan or almond paste made with 115g (4oz) ground almonds,
125g (4oz) caster sugar, 25g (1oz) melted butter and sufficient egg white to
bind together

to finish

50g (2oz) unsalted butter, melted

50g (2oz) icing sugar

Sprinkle the yeast on the milk and leave until it froths. Sift the flour and salt into a bowl and rub in the butter. Add the lemon zest, dried fruit and nuts, then the yeast mixture and egg. Mix to a dough, and knead for 10 minutes. Cover and leave to rise somewhere warm until doubled in size. Knock back, knead for a few minutes, then roll into a long oval. Roll the marzipan into a cylinder, and place down the length of the dough slightly to one side. Fold over the dough, and pinch down to seal. Place on a greased baking sheet, cover with a clean, damp cloth, and leave to rise again somewhere warm for 40 minutes or until doubled in size.

Bake in preheated oven at 200°C/400°F/gas mark 6 for 30–35 minutes until well risen and golden brown. Transfer to a wire rack to cool. Dust with icing sugar before serving. The top can be glazed before baking, if you like, with beaten egg and milk. An alternative presentation is to dip the loaf in melted butter while still hot, and then dredge with caster sugar.

non-yeast stollen

Here is a non-yeast version, based on the recipe sent to me by a reader in Cambridge.

serves 8 to 10

- 500g (generous 1lb) self-raising flour
- 200g (7oz) unrefined caster sugar
- pinch of salt
- few drops of pure almond essence
- 4 tbsps rum
- grated zest of 1 lemon
- 1 tsp each of ground cardamom and nutmeg
- 2 eggs
- 200g (7oz) unsalted butter, diced
- 250g (8oz) curd cheese or Quark
- 125g (4oz) each currants, raisins and chopped almonds
- 40g (1½ oz) mixed candied peel

to finish

- 50g (2oz) unsalted butter, melted
- 50g (2oz) icing sugar

Sift the flour into a bowl. Make a well in the centre and in it put the sugar, salt, essence, rum, zest, spices and eggs, and mix thoroughly. Add the remaining ingredients. Knead thoroughly, shape into a loaf, and place on a greased baking sheet. Bake in a preheated oven at 150°C/300°F/gas mark 3 for about 75 minutes. When still hot, brush with the melted butter, and dredge with icing sugar. Allow to cool completely before storing in a tin.

pane di natale

makes 4 loaves or cakes

> 1kg (2lb) dried fruit and nuts, including walnuts, hazelnuts, almonds,
> pine nuts, raisins and figs
>
> 1 x 1 litre carton red grape or prune juice
>
> 4 tbsps Pedro Ximenez sherry (unless you can get concentrated grape juice
> or *mosto*)
>
> 1kg (2lb) strong plain bread flour
>
> 25g (1oz) dried yeast
>
> 4 tbsps mincemeat (optional)

Prepare the fruit and nuts the day before you plan to bake the *pane di natale*. Chop the larger nuts and the figs, and put in a bowl. Add enough juice to cover, and stir in the sherry. Leave for 24 hours, stirring the mixture occasionally.

The following day, mix together the flour and yeast in a bowl, then stir in the fruit and nuts, and enough liquid to make a dough. Add the mincemeat, if using. You can now, if you wish, let the dough rise slowly, covered, for 24 hours, in a cool place, or, if you prefer, let it prove somewhere warm for a shorter time. In other words, treat it as you would bread, and let it work to your timetable rather than the other way round.

When the dough has doubled in size, shape into four loaves, and place in greased and floured 450g (1lb) loaf tins, or shape into four round cakes about 13cm (5 inches) in diameter, and place on baking sheets. Allow to prove for an hour or so, covered with a light, damp cloth. Bake in a preheated oven at 180°C/350°F/gas mark 4 for 20 minutes, then reduce the heat to 150°/300°F/ gas mark 2, and continue to bake for a further 20–25 minutes or until the loaves sound hollow when tapped. The crust will be very hard, and traditionally the cakes are stored for eight days in the larder before being eaten, covered with a cloth moistened with *saba* or thick grape juice, which 'feeds' and moistens them. Alternatively, as it was done in Camillo's mother's house, you can brush the loaves with a goose feather, dipped in the liquid.

panforte

This is another traditional holiday speciality, full of spices, dried fruit and nuts, this time from Siena and Perugia in northern Italy.

serves 8 to 10

75g (3oz) plain wholemeal flour

100g (4oz) plain flour

1 tbsp ground mixed spice

1 tsp ground cardamom

½ tsp ground cumin

175g (6oz) undyed mixed candied citrus peel, not ready cut,
   but in whole chunks

75g (3oz) undyed glacé cherries

200g (7oz) whole blanched almonds, lightly toasted and chopped

300g (10oz) clear honey

cornflour

icing sugar

cinnamon

Sift the flour and spices into a large bowl and mix well, then add the candied peel, cherries and nuts, having first chopped the peel into not too small chunks. In a saucepan, gently heat the honey for 2 minutes, then pour it over the mixture in the bowl, stirring thoroughly to blend the sticky mass. Spoon the mixture into a 20cm (8 inch) sandwich tin lined with rice paper or greased baking parchment, and, with oiled fingers, pack the mixture well down. Dust the top with a mixture of cornflour, icing sugar and a little cinnamon, and bake in the centre of a preheated oven at 180°C/350°F/gas mark 4 for about 35 minutes. Lift on to a wire rack and do not cut until the *panforte* is completely cold.

poppyseed roll

makes 1 loaf

150ml (¼ pint) warm milk or water

2 heaped tsps dried yeast

250g (8oz) strong plain bread flour

½ tsp salt

for the filling

150g (5oz) poppy seeds

50g (2oz) raisins

2 tbsps each warm milk and butter

100g (3½oz) sugar

Sprinkle the yeast on the milk, then leave for about 10 minutes to froth. Sift the flour and salt into a bowl, make a well in the centre, pour in the yeasty liquid, and mix the flour into it. Knead the dough until elastic and smooth, using a little more flour if necessary. Place the dough in an oiled bowl, cover with a clean, damp cloth, and let the dough rise for 1–2 hours, until at least doubled in size. Knock back the dough, knead for few minutes, then roll out on a floured work surface to form a rectangle about 0.25cm (¼ inch) thick.

Spread the poppy seed mixture all over, leaving a border of 2.5cm (1 inch) around the edge. Roll up from one of the short edges, and place, seam side down, on an oiled and floured baking sheet. Curve the roll slightly to form a crescent. Cover with the damp cloth again, and allow to rise for 40–60 minutes. Bake in the top half of a preheated oven at 180°C/350°F/gas mark 4 for 35–40 minutes.

twelfth night cakes

In the south and south-west of France, a *fouace*, or *fougasse*, is served on Twelfth Night. Like the Italian foccacia, *fouace* is a hearth bread, cooked on a bake stone or in the bottom of the oven. The bread is shaped into a flattish round, baked until it has risen, and then turned over to bake the top crust. Trencher bread was the same bread, halved between two people as plates. Further north in France, the cake is likely to be a *galette*, filled with a perfumed almond mixture.

galette

Traditionally, the finder of the bean hidden in this cake becomes king or queen of the Twelfth Night festivities.

serves 6

150g (5oz) ground almonds
75g (3oz) unsalted butter, softened
75g (3oz) caster sugar
2 tsps orange flower water
300g (10oz) puff pastry
1 china bean or dried haricot bean
egg and milk wash, to glaze

Mix together the almonds, butter, sugar and orange flower water. Roll out the pastry in two circles about 20–23cm (8–9 inches) in diameter. Place one circle on a baking sheet lined with greaseproof paper, and spread the almond mixture over it, leaving a border of a 2cm (I inch) around the edge. Push the bean into the almond mixture, and smooth over it. Brush the border with a little of the egg and milk glaze, and lay the second circle of pastry on top. Press down lightly with the prongs of a fork to seal. Prick the top in one or two places, and decorate either with pastry trimmings, or by marking it decoratively with a sharp knife. Brush with the glaze. Bake in a preheated oven at 200°C/400°F/gas mark 6 for 15–20 minutes until well risen and golden brown.

fouace

Candied peel can be added to the dough, if you wish, and the crust can be brushed with the scented water again after baking.

serves 4 to 6

- 1 tbsp fermipan yeast or dried active yeast
- 3 tbsps warm water
- 4 eggs, lightly beaten
- 2 tsps salt
- 25g (1oz) caster sugar
- 1 tbsp orange flower water or rosewater
- 500g (1lb) plain flour, sifted
- 150g (5oz) unsalted butter, softened

In a bowl mix the yeast and warm water. Add the eggs, salt, sugar and scented water. Add half the flour, and work the mixture thoroughly for 5 minutes or so, gradually adding the butter, which should be soft and creamy but not oily. Finally, add the remaining flour, and knead or work with a spatula until you have an elastic mixture which sticks to itself rather than to your hands. Cover with cling film and let the dough prove all day.

Knock back the dough, cover again, and leave in the refrigerator overnight. Turn it out on to a floured worktop, knead again simply to expel all the air, and then roll it out to resemble a large oval pitta bread of similar thickness. Nick the edges with scissors at intervals, and transfer it to a baking sheet. Cover with a clean damp cloth. Leave to double in size before baking in a preheated oven at 230°C/450°F/gas mark 8 for 20 minutes. Allow to cool before serving.

spiced wine bread

makes 1 × 1kg (2 lb) loaf

350g (12oz) plain flour

½ tsp each ground allspice, cloves, cardamom, freshly grated nutmeg and
　　ground ginger

pinch of salt

200g (7oz) butter

200g (7oz) light muscovado sugar

2 tsps baking powder

2 tsps dried active yeast

500g (1lb) mixed dried fruit

3 eggs, lightly beaten

approx 200ml (7fl oz) warm wine, a full bodied red or an amontillado sherry

Sift the flour, spices and salt into a bowl. Cut in the fat, and then rub it in. Add the sugar, baking powder and yeast, and then the dried fruit. Mix in the eggs and wine. Spoon into a greased and lined 1kg (2lb) loaf tin, or two 500g (1lb) tins, allow to rise and double in volume, then bake in a preheated oven at 150°C/300°F/gas mark 2 for about 3 hours for the large loaf, and for 1½–2 hours for the smaller loaves.

Allow to cool in the tin before removing, then wrap in greaseproof paper and foil and store. Serve sliced and buttered with a mug of mulled wine or a glass of rich, velvety egg-nog.

mulled wine

makes 1.5 litres (2¾ pints)

1 litre (1¾ pints) full-bodied red wine

500ml (16fl oz) red grape juice

thinly peeled zest of 2 tangerines

1 cinnamon stick

6 crushed cardamom pods

freshly grated nutmeg

1–2 measures brandy

Put all the ingredients except the brandy in a saucepan and bring just to the boil. Immediately remove from the heat, stir in the brandy and serve in hot glasses.

the perfect egg-nog

Note that this contains raw egg. Pasteurized liquid eggs, if available, or dried pasteurized egg can be used instead, if preferred. If you are lactose-intolerant, substitute the milk and cream with the soya products.

serves 8 to 10

1 litre carton rice milk, soya milk or fresh milk

200ml (7fl oz) single cream or soya cream substitute

1 tbsp honey

100ml (3–4fl oz) cognac or rum

3 eggs

copious grating of nutmeg

Put the milk, cream, honey, cognac and eggs in a blender, and blend until smooth and thick. Pour into glasses, and serve with grated nutmeg on top.

---

other ways with seasonal food

Most people plan the main Christmas meal well in advance, but with the holidays now lasting for a week or so, there are many other opportunities for feasts and festivities. Because I like to cook food in season, I'm happy to have an overflowing fruit bowl and a kitchen full of turkey, dried fruit, chestnuts and all the usual Christmas food. But I do not always choose to cook it in a traditional fashion.

And we might look beyond the traditional vinous accompaniments. As an alternative to indifferent cheap champagne, I suggest a fino sherry, such as Valdespino's 'Inocente', or Barbadillo's Manzanilla Vieja 'Solear', both appealing, dry wines with some weight and character. Good as aperitifs, they are also excellent with fish, shellfish and poultry. For a white wine, I would look for Condrieu, or its younger cousins from the Languedoc made with the viognier grape, and as a change from our usual claret, Tom might be persuaded to open a bottle of Tignanello.

Instead of Christmas cake and pudding, I sometimes like to serve chilled fruit desserts, such as ices, sorbets and fools. A mango fool is one of the easiest things to make, requiring only the blending of ripe mango flesh with cream, yoghurt or custard, and spooning it into large wine glasses to serve it. With only a little extra effort, you can make a very good mousse. And I recommend the richly textured almond ice cream. You will find more alternatives to the Christmas pud in the dessert section from p.522.

Smoked salmon or oysters on the half shell are traditional starters, but perhaps save some to serve in another way. Shred smoked salmon, and stir it into some creamy pasta for a holiday supper. Use oysters to make a large tureen of exquisite velvety soup for a lunch party.

Instead of the Christmas roast or Boxing Day ham, try the following suggestions.

a christmas grill

This can be such a flexible arrangement that a recipe is less helpful, I feel, than a selection of suggestions. A grill such as this can produce an extremely glamorous and festive main course for meat eaters and vegetarians alike; it works best in multiples of two. Use the breasts from chicken, turkey, pigeon, quail, pheasant, partridge or duckling in whatever combination pleases. Field or flat mushrooms and thick slices of aubergine, brushed with oil and dipped in breadcrumbs will grill very well too, as will fennel wedges and slices of haloumi cheese and tofu. Soft or grilled polenta would make an appropriate accompaniment, but so, too, would a garlic and potato mash. And if cranberries are a must, try them in a lively salsa.

preparation

I strongly advise preparing the birds the day before required. I remember one Christmas at a friend's home, where we were preparing pheasant breasts for lunch and we were sixteen at table. Our host had been instructed to buy eight brace of birds, but as we tipped them on to the kitchen table, it was clear that sixteen brace had been delivered. We spent a long time dismantling them. Fortunately, the dish itself was quick to cook. For the grill, too, you need to dismantle the birds. Remove the breasts and the legs. Use the carcasses for a very good stock, and casserole the legs, on, or off the bone, with plenty of good wine and aromatics, and serve it on its own, or use it as the base of a Boxing Day pie or cobbler.

Turkey thighs and drumsticks make a particularly good casserole with green or dark olives, white wine, a little thyme and a small amount of orange zest. The breasts can be marinated and refrigerated overnight, and, if you wish, different meats can be given different marinades. A simple one of red wine and olives is very good for dark meat, but it stains pale meats. For these, I would use white wine with the oil. But these are not the only suitable marinades. In the past I have marinated turkey breasts in walnut oil and the juice, squeezed by hand, from pomegranates; pheasant breasts in hazelnut oil with mandarin juice; and duck breasts in soy sauce, rice wine or sherry, and toasted sesame oil.

cooking

It is difficult to give even approximate cooking times, for although chicken and turkey breasts should be thoroughly cooked, thickness will dictate how long. Juices should run clear when the meat is pierced with a skewer. Pheasant and duck are often preferred more on the medium side, and I prefer to cook pigeon breasts fast to keep them medium rare to rare, as any more cooking tends to toughen them. But if you do not like rare game, then there is much else to choose from. Different cooking times and temperatures need not be a problem. I use my rectangular cast-iron griddle across two plates of the hob. That way one end of the griddle can cook slowly and steadily, the other end fast and furious.

As with all meat, it is a good idea to let the grilled breasts rest on a warm serving platter for 10 minutes or more. They will be far easier to cut.

The grill, the top of the oven and seasoned cast-iron frying pans on the hob can also be used for cooking the meat. High, dry heat is what is needed and, for this reason, it is important when you have removed the meat from the marinade to dry it well on paper towel before cooking it, otherwise it will steam.

quick cranberry and kumquat salsa

Serve with grilled meats, game or vegetables. It is also excellent with leftovers of roasts, particularly ham and turkey.

makes 500g (1lb)

175g (6oz) kumquats

1 onion, peeled and chopped

3–4 garlic cloves, peeled and crushed

250g (8oz) fresh cranberries

juice of 2–3 mandarins

175g (6oz) light muscovado or demerara sugar

1 or more green chillies, seeded and finely chopped

salt

freshly ground black pepper

Halve the kumquats, discard the seeds, and quarter the fruit. Cook the onion, garlic, kumquats and cranberries in the mandarin juice until the cranberries have popped. Stir in the sugar and chillies, and, once the sugar has dissolved, boil until the mixture thickens. Allow to cool.

entertaining

turkey and oyster chowder

If you have cartons of homemade stock piling up in freezer and refrigerator, here is something good to make with it. Call it goose and oyster chowder or chicken and oyster chowder, if more appropriate.

In place of oysters, you can use shelled shrimps or lightly steamed mussels, but the oyster and turkey combination is a delicious one.

serves 6 to 8

    2 shallots or 1 onion, peeled and chopped

    50g (2oz) butter

    50g (2oz) flour

    600ml (1 pint) full cream milk, hot

    1.15 litres (2 pints) strong turkey stock

    500g (1lb) waxy potatoes, peeled and diced

    2 tbsps chopped dill

    pinch of mace

    salt

    freshly ground black pepper

    12 oysters, freshly shucked, with the juice reserved

Sweat the shallots in the butter until translucent. Stir in the flour, and cook for a few minutes until golden. Gradually add the milk, stirring continually, and cook until smooth and creamy. Blend in the stock, and then add the potatoes, dill, mace and seasoning, and cook until the potatoes are tender.

Strain the oyster juice into the soup, bring to the boil, then remove from the heat. Place the oysters in warmed soup plates, and ladle over the soup. The heat of the soup is sufficient to just plump up the oysters. They should not be overcooked.

provençal-style casserole

Here is what to make with the other parts of the bird you did not grill. Duck, chicken, goose and turkey are all worth cooking this way, but not the smaller birds. It is particularly good served with brown rice or wholewheat noodles.

serves 6 to 8

    1kg (2lb) meat, off the bone, diced, or about 1.8kg (4lb) poultry
        and game thighs
    1 bay leaf
    6 firm ripe tomatoes, peeled, seeded and cut into strips
    125g (4oz) green or black olives
    zest of 1 orange

for the marinade

    600ml (1 pint) good dry white wine
    1 carrot, thinly sliced
    1 onion, thinly sliced
    1 leek, thinly sliced
    1 celery stick, thinly sliced
    2 thin slices fresh ginger (optional)
    4 garlic cloves, crushed
    2 tbsps extra virgin olive oil

First, make the marinade. Put the wine in a saucepan with the carrot, onion, leek, celery and ginger, and most of the olive oil. Bring to the boil, then allow to cool. Stir in the garlic, and leave overnight.

Put the meat in a bowl, and strain the marinade over it. (The vegetables can be chopped and used in stock or soup.) Leave the meat to marinate for half a day, then remove it and dry on paper towels.

Heat the remaining olive oil and, when it is hot, add the meat and sear it all over. Pour the marinade over the meat, add the bay leaf, tomatoes, olives and orange zest, allow to bubble once or twice, then turn down the heat very low.

Cook for 45 minutes or until the meat is tender. Timing will depend on the size of the joints if using meat on the bone.

marinated grilled turkey escalopes with pomegranates and hazelnut sauce

If your Christmas would not be Christmas without a turkey, but you do not relish wrestling with a mammoth and dealing with the inevitable leftovers, take a lateral look at the bird. Regard it as a collection of joints, and dismantle it into its separate parts.

Pomegranates and hazelnuts may not appeal as much to you as they do to me. But I have also marinated turkey breast in white wine and extra virgin olive oil and grilled it as described. This, too, is good, but I like the garnish of deep, red pomegranate seeds and the sweet yet slightly acidic note that the juice imparts to the sauce in a way which does not interfere with the wine. This is an important consideration since one wants to bring out the best bottles at Christmas.

serves 4

4–8 escalopes cut from the turkey breast, approx 750g (1½lb) altogether

2 ripe red pomegranates

75ml (3fl oz) hazelnut oil

7.5cm (3 inch) twist of lemon zest

7.5cm (3 inch) piece of cinnamon stick

4–5 cloves

crushed seeds of 8 cardamom pods

freshly ground black pepper

150ml (¼ pint) turkey stock

1 tbsp ground hazelnuts

sumac, if available, or freshly grated lemon zest

toasted blanched, lightly crushed hazelnuts

Cut the pomegranates in half, and squeeze out the juice, reserving the seeds of one half for decoration. Whisk the juice with the hazelnut oil until blended,

---

then pour over the meat. Add the lemon zest and spices, including the pepper. Cover and marinate for several hours, or overnight if more convenient.

Remove the meat from the marinade, and dry on paper towels. Pour the marinade into a saucepan, bring to the boil, skim the foam from the surface, and simmer for 5 minutes. Strain into a clean saucepan, add the stock, bring to the boil, then turn down the heat and simmer while you grill the turkey, placing it on an oiled rack under a hot grill, or on a well-seasoned or oiled cast-iron grill or griddle. Turn once only, and do not overcook the meat. Cooking time will depend on the thickness of the escalopes, but the juices should run clear and not pink. Once cooked, put the meat to one side, and finish the sauce by reducing it to a well-flavoured gravy. Stir in the ground hazelnuts, and add salt to taste, if you wish, or allow guests to add their own. Put the turkey on a serving platter. Scatter the pomegranate seeds and crushed hazelnuts on top, and spoon over the sauce.

This slightly spicy, slightly sweet turkey goes well with couscous, bulgar wheat, mashed potatoes or a number of rice dishes, including wild rice, a white risotto, or a fluffy pilaff of basmati rice. For vegetables, I would serve stewed celery hearts.

turkey burgers with
avocado and roasted red pepper salsa

serves 4

    500g (1lb) minced raw turkey meat

    4 heaped tbsps soft white breadcrumbs

    100g (3oz) feta cheese, crumbled

    freshly ground black pepper

for the salsa

    2 red peppers, roasted, peeled, seeded and diced

    1 red tomato, quartered, roasted and chopped

    2 plum tomatoes, roasted, seeded and chopped

    2 tbsps fresh cranberries, poached until soft

    grated zest of 1 lime

    1–2 tbsps unrefined sugar

    1 ripe avocado, peeled and diced

    finely chopped green or red chilli, to taste

First make the salsa by mixing all the ingredients together in a bowl. Put to one side while you make the burgers.

Mix all the ingredients together, shape into burgers, then grill, bake or fry. Serve on toasted split wholemeal muffins with lettuce, pickle and the salsa. If you like, you can add other seasoning, such as chopped fresh herbs, dried herbs or spices, to the turkey.

spiced minced meat pie

A pie is a very welcoming sight on a lunch table, handsome and burnished in a crisp crust, promising intriguing flavours and a succulent filling.

serves 8 to 10

- 500g (1lb) puff or short pastry
- 500g (1lb) pork, preferably belly pork
- 500g (1lb) lean beef, such as rump, tail end of fillet or blade steak
- ½ tsp each ground cumin, cinnamon, cardamon, allspice and mace
- 50g (2oz) each chopped dates, prunes, dried cranberries and raisins
- 50g (2oz) mixed candied peel, chopped
- 100g (3–4oz) almonds or pine nuts, chopped
- 150ml (¼ pint) stock, made with gelatine-rich ingredients, such as the pork skin
- 2 tsps cornflour
- egg and milk glaze

Use about half the pastry to line a 22–25cm (8–10 inch) pie dish or spring-form cake tin. Mince or finely dice the meat and fry until it loses its rawness, stirring in half the spice mixture. Mix the rest of the spices with the dried fruit and nuts. When the meat is cool, spread a layer on the bottom of the pastry case, scatter with the fruit and nuts, and then cover with more meat. Repeat, finishing with a layer of meat.

Bring the stock to the boil, thicken with the cornflour, then pour over the meat. Roll out the remaining pastry to a circle large enough to cover the pie. Seal the edges well, decorate with pastry trimmings, if you wish, and brush with an egg and milk glaze. Bake in a preheated oven at 180°C/350°F/gas mark 4 for about 40 minutes. Serve hot, warm or cold, with salads and chutneys, or with a green vegetable.

entertaining

almond ice cream

This ice cream is excellent served with a hot chocolate sauce, a fruit coulis (try one made with dried apricots), or as one ingredient in a white dessert. Note that it contains raw egg.

serves 6 to 8

125g (4oz) ground almonds
150ml (¼ pint) skimmed or semi-skimmed milk
450ml (¾ pint) water
5 heaped tbsps skimmed milk powder
3 egg yolks
1 tsp arrowroot or cornflour (optional)
2–3 tbsps double cream
3 tbsps almond liqueur or 1 tsp pure almond essence
icing sugar or sweetener to taste

Bring the milk to the boil with the almonds, remove from the heat and leave to infuse overnight. When cool, chill.

Make a custard with the water, skimmed milk powder and egg yolks. For extra stability, stir in a teaspoon of arrowroot or cornflour, slaked in a little water, before you start cooking the custard. When the custard cools, stir in the cream and almond essence. Combine the custard and infused almonds, and then sweeten to taste, remembering that freezing a mixture dulls the sweetness. Freeze either in an ice-cream maker, according to the manufacturer's instructions, or in a plastic container, in which case you will need to stir the mixture from time to time in order to prevent ice crystals forming.

mango mousse

Note that this recipe uses raw egg.

serves 4

2 sheets leaf gelatine or 2 tsps gelatine granules

300ml (½ pint) mango, apple or apple and mango juice

150g (5oz) cottage cheese

1 ripe fragrant mango

sugar to taste

2 egg whites

for the garnish

toasted flaked almonds

Soften the gelatine in a little of the juice. Heat 150ml (¼ pint) of the juice, add the gelatine, and stir until it has dissolved. Sieve the cottage cheese, and put it in a blender. Peel the mango over the blender to catch as much of the juice as possible, put in the fruit pulp, the gelatine mixture, and the remaining juice. Blend until smooth, and add sugar, if necessary. Whisk the egg whites until stiff, then fold into the mango mixture. Pour into a dish, chill and set. Garnish with toasted flaked almonds.

the main thing – traditional holiday centrepieces

Shall it be a turkey or a goose this year, a wild boar or a suckling pig, or a majestic English ham with all the trimmings?

Over the years, I have cooked and written about wild boar, free range turkey and goose for Christmas. I would recommend these again; the wild boar from Barrow Boar (01963 440315), a truly free range turkey from Pipers Farm (01392 881380) or Richard Guy's Real Meat Company

(01985 840562), or an organic turkey from Swaddles Green Farm (01460 234387). Judy Goodman (01299 896272) is the farmer from whom I would buy the goose. In addition, a fine rib of beef from Donald Russell (01467 629666) makes a majestic centrepiece for one of the holiday meals. From Anne Petch at Heal Farm (01769 574341), I buy the best hams I have ever eaten, and that is my recommendation for at least one main meal over the holidays, perhaps a large family lunch or buffet party on Boxing Day.

On the whole, I advise making your own accompaniments. Many of the establishments selling by mail order also sell all the trimmings, stuffings, sauces and what you will. My limited experience of these has not been good. One year we sat down to Christmas dinner with friends who had ordered a goose from a company I have not used. The goose was delicious, but the stuffing did nothing for the goose, nor the company's reputation. Most mail order companies will send with your order cooking instructions as well as recipes for accompaniments and serving suggestions.

With such substantial main courses, I would serve the simplest of cold dishes as a first course – a smoked trout, pomegranate and fennel salad; a platter of smoked salmon; some oysters; or simply some anchovy toast with crudités. Your pre-prandial champagne or fino sherry will easily take you through any of these.

Alternative desserts and puddings can be found from p.523, as well as a recipe for small Stilton soufflés, if you like to serve a savoury. In our house we serve the cheese before the pudding, and I might serve the soufflés as an alternative to the cheese course, or as an addition. They are also very good as appetizers and with drinks before dinner or lunch. And they can be made in the miniature paper cases used for sweets.

a holiday ham

I prefer to bake, not boil, my ham, wrapping it in several layers of foil. This is safer than manoeuvring a huge pot of boiling water and a heavy ham, and not everyone has catering-size pots. As with all large joints and birds, however, it is a good idea to check your oven size before ordering a giant.

Cumberland, or other sharp fruit sauce is perfect with ham. Shallots, orange and lemon zest and juice, mustard, redcurrants, port, salt and pepper, cooked together will make a good Cumberland sauce. Orange zest, kumquats and watercress make a lively garnish, both in flavour and colour.

The glaze needs sweet, sour, sharp and spicy, flavours. You could replace the lemon juice with balsamic or sherry vinegar, the honey or cordial with a fruit cordial or syrup, and you might include cinnamon and cardamom. Use some of the glaze on the ham before cooking it. There will be plenty of cooking liquid collected in the foil, and this, carefully drained into a saucepan, together with the soft onions, can be rubbed through a sieve to provide one of the accompaniments, a flavoursome onion sauce.

I cut off a small piece of ham before cooking it and use it, and some of the ham skin, to make a broth in which I cook pease pudding.

serves 12

    1 uncooked ham, weighing approx 4.5–5kg (10lb)
    5–6 onions, peeled and quartered
    butter
    freshly ground black pepper
    3tsps mustard
    1tbsp lemon juice
    2tbsps ginger cordial
    cloves

Soak the ham overnight, or according to the retailer's instructions.

Wrap the ham in a triple thickness of buttered foil, on a bed of quartered onions, place in a roasting tin, and bake in a preheated oven at 150°C/300°F/ gas mark 3 for 4 hours. Then increase the temperature to 180°C/350°F/ gas mark 4 for 1 hour. Alternatively, allow 50 minutes per kg at 180°C/350°F/ gas mark 4. The ham is cooked when the 'mustard spoon' bone at the shank end waggles quite freely.

When cool enough to handle, take the ham out of the foil, making sure you retain the juices and the by now soft onions. Remove the skin, keeping only a thin layer of fat. Score this in lozenges, and rub with a mixture of mustard, lemon juice and ginger cordial (or honey and fresh or ground ginger), and nail cloves in a decorative pattern over the ham's surface. Bake in a preheated oven at 220°C/425°F/gas mark 7 for 20 minutes. Remove from the oven and let stand for 10–15 minutes before carving.

Serve the ham with parsley sauce, pease pudding, boiled or baked pota- toes, roasted parsnips or celeriac, a crisp green vegetable such as broccoli or crisply stir-fried cabbage, but not mangetout or Brussels sprouts.

pease pudding

serves 6 to 8

500g (1lb) split peas
1 litre (1¾ pints) ham stock
freshly ground black pepper
fresh mint

Boil the peas in the stock until soft. They need no initial soaking. Add more liquid if necessary, and, when ready to serve, season with pepper, and stir in a good helping of chopped mint or sage.

split pea and ham soup

If you make extra pease pudding, rub it through a sieve, add to ham stock, bring to the boil, and stir in some shredded or diced ham, and top with homemade croûtons. A very warming soup for a winter's day.

parsley sauce

serves 6 to 8
- 50g (2oz) butter
- 50g (2oz) flour
- 600ml (1 pint) milk, hot
- 50g (2oz) parsley purée, made by blanching 1 large bunch of parsley, blending it with a few tbsps of boiling water, and then sieving it

Melt the butter, stir in the flour, and cook for a few minutes. Remove from the heat, and stir in about a quarter of the milk until smooth. Put on the heat again, stirring continuously, and, as the mixture begins to thicken, remove again from the heat. Gradually add another quarter of the milk, stirring until smooth, thickening it again over the heat, and so on, until you have a smooth thick sauce. Cook it for 5 minutes, stir in the parsley purée, and cook for a further 5 minutes.

tortellini in brodo

A baked ham, when cold and thinly sliced, makes the best sandwiches I have ever eaten, and I am quite happy to use up all the leftovers this way. However, it also makes a fine risotto, together with the stock, or excellent *tortellini in brodo*, especially if you add some cooked goose, duck, turkey or chicken.

This is the way our friends in Modena, the Lancellottis, taught me to make *tortellini in brodo*. I have taken liberties with it, using boiled English ham instead of dry-cured Parma ham, and goose instead of pork and mortadella. Making filled pasta is a most agreeable occupation on a cold, dry winter's day. Although time-consuming, it is not difficult, and time passes quickly if there are two of you in the kitchen.

serves 6 to 7

for the filling
175g (6oz) cooked ham, including some fat
175g (6oz) cooked goose, including some fat
1 egg
½ tsp salt
½ tsp freshly grated nutmeg
125g (4½ oz) freshly grated Parmesan cheese
50g (2oz) fine fresh soft breadcrumbs

for the broth
2.8 litres (5 pints) stock made from a goose carcass and ham bone
fresh chervil
half a celery stick
1 small onion, peeled and halved
1 garlic clove

for the pasta
generous 300g (10oz) flour
3 eggs

Chop the meat finely, then mix in the egg, salt, nutmeg and Parmesan, and finally the breadcrumbs. Mix by hand, kneading and working it for 5 minutes, until the mixture is thoroughly bound together, adding more breadcrumbs if the mixture is too soft. Put the mixture in a bowl, cover, and keep until required, but use the same day.

To make the broth, put all the ingredients in a large saucepan, bring just to the boil, skim off the foam, and simmer for 30 minutes while you make the pasta.

To make the pasta, pile the flour on to a work surface, make a well in the centre, and slide in the whole eggs. Working with your fingertips, draw flour from the edges to the centre, gradually blending the eggs and flour together by hand until a dough is formed. Sprinkle with some flour if the mixture is sticky, which it may well be if you are working in a humid atmosphere, and knead for 5–10 minutes until the dough is smooth and elastic. Cover and let it rest for 15 minutes at room temperature.

Roll out the dough on a floured work surface to the thickness of a 20p piece, stretching and rolling it over the rolling pin. (A long narrow pin, or *matarella*, is used in Italy.) With a fluted cutting wheel, cut out squares of dough. Place a small pea-sized ball of filling in the centre. Fold one corner over to the opposite corner, and pinch together the two edges of the resulting triangle really hard to seal them. Bend the central point of the triangle up and over, drawing the other two points together round the top of the same finger, and pinch together to seal. Set aside on a cloth until you have made all the tortellini. Leave covered until you are ready to cook them.

Remove the flavourings from the broth, return to the boil, and put in the freshly made tortellini. Simmer for 2–3 minutes, and then ladle into a warmed soup tureen. The pasta will continue cooking in the hot broth and will be just right by the time you serve it.

Here is a quicker pasta recipe for using your leftover ham, which I learned when helping to cook family lunch at the Lancellottis'. There they use pancetta instead of the cooked ham in this thick bean and pasta soup.

maltagliati con fagioli

serves 8

1 medium onion, finely chopped or minced

2–3 garlic cloves, peeled and finely chopped

handful of parsley, chopped

2 tbsps extra virgin olive oil

800g can peeled plum tomatoes

1kg (2lb) cooked beans, borlotti or other, plus their cooking liquid

300g (10oz) cooked ham, finely chopped or minced

400g (14oz) dried pasta – small pieces of broken tagliatelle

    or pappardelle will do

extra stock or water, as necessary

Gently cook the onion, garlic and parsley in the olive oil until light brown, then add the tomatoes, beans and cooking liquid. Simmer for 30 minutes, uncovered, then add the ham and pasta. Cook until the pasta is al dente and serve. You might need to add more liquid if the soup is too thick.

goose for two

Goose for Christmas for two people seems extravagant. But my solution is an economical one; I dismantle the goose, leaving the breast intact and on the bone. This is a very handsome piece of meat when roasted, like a golden brown cushion. The legs, thighs and carcass produce all manner of good dishes, as does the leftover breast meat.

There is, of course, a whole range of basting (flavouring) combinations you might like to try in place of the one I suggest here, such as cider and honey, soy sauce and mirin or rice wine, mandarin or lemon juice and herbs, or you may prefer to leave it unflavoured. A handful of herbs, such as sage under the ribcage, as it roasts, will flavour the goose delicately.

As with any traditional roast, potatoes can be cooked around the meat and will absorb some of the lovely goose fat. Baked onions also go well with goose. As for other accompanying vegetables, I am much more partial to a green salad afterwards, or a vegetable course to begin with, such as a celery and chestnut soup.

Goose fat stored in the refrigerator is excellent in pastry and bread-making. I use it to make excellent ciabatta-style bread, substituting the fat for olive oil.

Use the carcass to make stock, and preserve the wings and drumsticks in a confit for use in the future.

1 whole goose breast, or 'crown', weighing about 1.5–1.75kg (3–4lb)

2 tbsps honey

2 tbsps fino or amontillado sherry

1 tbsp sherry or cider vinegar

1 tsp freshly ground black pepper

Line the roasting tin with foil to come up the sides. Prick the skin of the breast all over, down through the thickness of the fat, but without piercing the flesh too much. Melt the honey in a saucepan, then mix in the rest of the ingredients. Brush over the breast, and place on the middle shelf of a preheated oven at

180°C/350°F/gas mark 4 and roast for about 20 minutes per 500g (1lb). Periodically, drain off the fat, and baste the bird with the honey mixture. This gives it a nice glaze and a subtle flavour.

goose confit

Confit, whether of duck or goose, is easy to make and well worth doing because you then have on hand a luxurious instant meal. It makes a fine addition to a cassoulet, but it is good on its own, gently reheated in a frying pan to crisp up the skin, and served with potatoes fried in a little of the fat, perhaps some lentils, or red cabbage, or a crisp salad of fennel.

Duck confit is made in the same way. You can also preserve the heart and gizzard in fat, and use them later in a warm salad with potatoes and salad leaves.

serves 4 to 6
    wings, thighs and drumsticks
    coarse sea salt – 25g (1oz) per 500g (1lb) meat
    raw fat from the goose
    1 bay leaf
    a few black peppercorns

Rub the joints all over with salt, cover, and refrigerate for 24 hours. Wipe off the salt, and put the meat, fat and seasoning in a heavy pan or casserole. Melt the fat on top of the stove, bring it to the boil, cover, and then transfer to a preheated oven at 150°C/300°F/gas mark 3 and cook very slowly for about 2–2½ hours.

Transfer the pieces of goose to a sterilized preserving jar, boil up the fat, and then strain it over the goose. The fat must cover the meat by about a couple of centimetres (an inch or so) to ensure that it is airtight. Even so, I keep it refrigerated until I need it, as I live in a centrally heated flat, not a farmhouse with a larder.

goose pasties

Served with the barley broth these are a homely, yet festive dish, that makes marvellous use of leftovers, such as bits of goose left over from the confit or roast, and the stock made with the carcass. Turkey can produce similarly good leftovers, and I would make this dish the main feature of a lunch buffet over the holidays. I like to experiment with sweet and savoury mixtures, something like the traditional mince pies, when meat was added to the fruit mixture.

makes 12 to 18

250g (8oz) puff pastry

250g (8oz) cooked goose, diced or shredded

2 tbsps olive oil

2 tbsps grated apple

1 tbsp finely chopped onion

1 tbsp dark muscovado or other unrefined sugar

¼ tsp ground cardamom

¼ tsp ground cinnamon

freshly grated nutmeg

salt

freshly ground black pepper

milk, to glaze

Roll out the pastry, and use it to line tartlet tins, reserving enough to cut out pastry lids. Mix together the goose, oil, apple, onion, sugar and spices, season to taste with nutmeg, salt and pepper, and then spoon the mixture into the pastry cases. Cover with the pastry lids, and brush with milk to glaze. Bake in a preheated oven at 180°C/350°F/gas mark 4 for 15–18 minutes. Alternatively, fill the pastry rounds and shape like Cornish pasties.

barley broth

serves 6 to 8

1 tbsp goose fat

1 large onion, peeled and thinly sliced

1 carrot, peeled and thinly sliced

1 celery stick, trimmed and thinly sliced

1 leek, trimmed and thinly sliced

wedge of shredded white cabbage

100g (3–4oz) pearl barley

3 garlic cloves, crushed

½ tsp dill seeds or chopped fresh dill

1.75 litres (3 pints)goose stock

150ml (¼ pint) good white wine

Melt the fat in a large saucepan, and stir in the onion, carrot, celery and leek. Cook until light brown. Add the cabbage, barley, garlic and dill. Pour in the stock and wine, bring to the boil, and simmer gently for an hour or so, or until the barley is tender.

rillettes d'oie

Belly pork is the cut traditionally used for this rustic French speciality, with as much fat as lean. It is becoming increasingly difficult to make such dishes, however, with modern breeds of slim-line pigs. The whole point of rillettes is the texture and flavour supplied by the fat. No one says you have to eat the whole pot in one go. Rillettes keep well in the refrigerator for a week or so, and make a good sandwich filling. A scoop of rillettes with lettuce salad, a pickle or two, bread and a glass of wine makes for a good lunch; spread on fingers of hot toast it is an excellent appetizer to serve with drinks. If you are serving goose over the holidays, save some to make rillettes. Duck and pork or rabbit and pork can also be used.

makes about 1kg (2 lb)

500g (1lb) fat belly pork

meat from the uncooked goose legs and wings

approx 200g (7oz) raw goose fat

150ml (¼ pint) water

½ tsp salt

freshly ground black pepper

1 bay leaf

1 sprig of thyme

1 sage leaf, if you like the flavour

pinch each of nutmeg or mace, cloves and cinnamon

Cut the meat into 2.5cm (1 inch) chunks, and put in an earthenware casserole or other ovenproof dish. Add the rest of the ingredients, and put in the bottom of a preheated oven at 120°/250°/gas mark ½ for at least 4 hours or overnight if you prefer. After this time the meat will be cooked, swimming in fat, and the water will have evaporated.

Pour into a large sieve set over a bowl. Remove any bones and the herbs, and shred the meat with two forks. Pack the meat, but not too tightly, into straight-sided pots or jam jars, and pour on the fat so that it seeps around the meat and covers the surface. Cool, cover, and then refrigerate.

It is worth making double quantities of the recipe for presents, and for buffet lunches. Goose rillettes can also be used in a risotto. This is exceedingly rich and luxurious, and quite one of the best ways I know for using the rillettes.

goose risotto

serves 4

    2 shallots, or 1 small onion, peeled and thinly sliced
    1 tbsp goose fat
    400g (14oz) arborio, vialone or other risotto rice
    1.25 litres (2 pints) goose stock, boiling
    sprig of rosemary
    freshly grated nutmeg
    salt
    freshly ground black pepper
    4 scoops of goose rillettes, at room temperature
    freshly grated Parmesan

Gently cook the onion in the goose fat, and then stir in the rice. When well-coated with fat, add a ladle of hot stock, and cook the rice, stirring continuously. When the stock has been absorbed, add a little more, continuing to stir, and then add the rosemary, nutmeg and a light seasoning of salt and pepper. Continue adding the stock, stirring continuously, and waiting until it has all been absorbed before adding more. If you find you need more liquid, use a little white wine or water. If you prefer a drier risotto, you may find you do not need all the liquid. Once it is cooked to your liking, remove the rosemary, stir in the rillettes, and, when heated through and well mixed, grate on a generous amount of Parmesan and serve.

Alternatively, stir in the cheese and put a scoop of rillettes on each serving before it goes to the table. This looks very good, but it does cool down the risotto somewhat.

cold goose chiu chow-style

As there are usually only two of us to eat roast goose, leftovers go on for some time, as you can see. The cold goose Chiu Chow-style is truly delicious, and based on some of the dishes I have eaten in restaurants in Hong Kong. The secret is to marinate the goose when freshly cooked and still warm. Ideally, remove a whole goose breast, after, of course, serving your family and friends.

serves 6 to 8 as a first course, or as part of a Chinese meal
- 1 goose breast, cooked and still warm
- 2 tsps five spice powder
- 100ml (3–4fl oz) strong brewed tea, Ti Kuan Yin, Bo Lih or Oolong for preference
- 2 tbsps soy sauce
- 2 tbsps toasted sesame oil
- 2 tbsps rice wine or sherry
- 1 tbsp grated fresh ginger
- 3 spring onions or leeks, washed, trimmed and shredded

Rub the meat all over with five spice powder, and put in a bowl. Mix together the rest of the ingredients, and pour over the goose. Leave to marinate for at least 24 hours, preferably 48–72 hours.

Remove the meat from the marinade, slice thinly, and serve on a bed of cooked noodles dressed in groundnut oil with the marinade poured over it. Alternatively, serve the goose on a bed of crisp salad that includes blanched bean sprouts, white radish and shredded Chinese leaves.

goose and sauerkraut salad

If you are prepared to wait three days, you can easily make your own sauerkraut. You need a large, white winter cabbage. Remove any damaged outer leaves, and then quarter and remove the hard core. Shred the cabbage very finely, and then mix it in a bowl with about 100g (3–4oz) salt per 1kg (2lb) cabbage, a few crushed juniper berries, fresh or dried dill, if you have it, crushed black peppercorns and two or three cloves. Add hot water to about two thirds depth. To encourage fermentation, place a slice of good yeasty bread on top and weight down with a plate. Put to one side in a cool place until the cabbage is lightly fermented. It can be kept in an airtight box in the refrigerator. Use some for this salad. Or buy a vacuum pack or jar of sauerkraut.

serves 4 to 6

500g (1lb) drained sauerkraut, rinsed, if you prefer

75ml (3fl oz) walnut oil

1 tbsp cider vinegar

1 tbsp grated horseradish, horseradish cream, or rather less mustard

75g (3oz) chopped walnuts

1 red skinned apple, cored and diced or coarsely grated

1–2 sticks from a celery heart, sliced

1 tbsp chopped fresh dill or 1 tsp dried dill weed

cooked goose, including liver and heart, if available, sliced

Mix together all the ingredients except the meat. Place the sauerkraut on plates, and arrange slices of meat on top. Crisp, fried goose skin provides a good additional texture. If you prefer, sauerkraut can be replaced with shredded Chinese leaves, dressed with the same ingredients.

foie gras

Foie gras is more of a holiday classic in France than in Britain. Indeed, no New Year's Eve *Réveillon* table is complete without it. But it is a relatively costly treat. However, ever since I visited a small factory in Alsace, where they were preparing foie gras for cooking and preserving, I have quite got over my fear of dealing with such an expensive ingredient, and do occasionally buy some to cook for a special occasion.

My other worry was overcome when I visited an organic farm in the south-west of France. The farmer had a few ducks which he force-fed for two or three weeks in late October and early November for the *marché au gras*. I watched him doing it, and took a close look and feel at a duck's mouth and throat to see how it copes. A duck does not have a glottal stop, so does not gag on the food. And the throat and mouth is not soft tissue, but more of a chitin-like substance, like the carapace of a prawn or shrimp, which is not damaged by the funnel.

Fresh, raw duck foie gras from France comes whole, vacuum-packed in amounts weighing 500–800g. The larger amount will feed up to ten people. Because it is so rich, 50–75g (2–3oz) is sufficient for a serving. Once cooked, it can be kept, if refrigerated, for two or three days. I am also surprised at how well a cooked terrine freezes, certainly for a month and probably longer.

If you do not want to serve it cold as a terrine, another very good, and easy, way of preparing foie gras is to slice the raw liver into short pieces, i.e. across rather than along the lobe, about 1cm (⅜ inch) thick, season them, and fry them for a minute or so on each side in a non-stick, or well-seasoned, frying pan set over a moderate heat.

It is a curious thing, but all these luxury foods taste best of all with the plainest of accompaniments – brown bread, toasted brioche, and also potatoes. I have come across terrines and gâteaux, in which foie gras is layered with potatoes. Fried slices of foie gras also go very well with crisp potato cakes.

to prepare foie gras en conserve

You need a preserving jar, with a seal, somewhat larger than the foie gras that you are about to prepare. So for a 500–650g liver, use a 750g jar. The foie gras will be vacuum-packed, almost certainly. Remove it from its packaging, cut away any green parts, rinse gently under the cold tap, pat dry with paper towel, and let it come to room temperature for 20 minutes or so. Some chefs advocate soaking it in warm, not hot, water for 20 minutes or so.

It is best to work on a marble surface, but any cold, smooth worktop will do. Without separating the lobes, and pressing on the liver with the heel of your hand, soften it a little, flatten and open it out, and gradually disclose the network of veins, which should carefully be removed with a knife point.

To season the foie gras, mix on a plate a generous teaspoon of sea salt, a scant teaspoon each of unrefined caster sugar and freshly ground black pepper, and a grinding of nutmeg. Rub this mixture over the foie gras, and baptize it liberally with a small glass of good tawny port, Madeira, Armagnac, English apple liqueur or Sauternes.

Put the foie gras into the jar, bending it as necessary. Seal the jar, wrap it in muslin, or an old table napkin, put it in a saucepan and cover with warm water. Bring to the boil, simmer very gently for 40 minutes, then remove the pan from the heat. When the water is no more than hand hot, remove the jar from the pan. Allow to cool, and keep for at least two weeks before serving.

If you wish to cook the foie gras in a simple terrine, prepare and season it as described above, and then put back into a terrine or loaf tin, cover with a sheet of greaseproof paper, and place in a bain marie. Cook in a preheated oven at 100°C/210°F/gas mark ¼ for 35–40 minutes. Remove from the oven and, as soon as the fat has solidified, cover the surface with greaseproof paper and weight down the foie gras. Refrigerate overnight. Scrape off all the fat, melt it, and pour it over the terrine for an even coating. When it is set once more, cover, refrigerate, and let it mature for a couple of days before serving.

And may I suggest that you serve your terrine or conserve of foie gras after the main course, instead of cheese, and accompany it with a first glass of your best dessert wine before going on to the dessert itself. It is a revelation. This is how it used to be done, which partly explains the present anomaly of serving sweet wine before dry at the beginning of the meal, because foie gras is now served at the beginning of the meal.

a smaller bird

An organic chicken or duckling, or pheasant, wild duck or a brace of partridges is a more manageable alternative for a festive meal for two, or multiples thereof. Braising is a particularly good method for keeping pheasant juicy.

truffled chicken

serves 4

1.85kg (4lb) very fresh chicken
50g (2oz) butter
1 black truffle, thinly sliced
1 tsp each freshly ground black pepper and sea salt
1 lemon

Remove any visible fat from the chicken cavity. Ease the skin away from the flesh by gradually inserting your fingers between the skin and the breast. Continue working your way around the bird until the skin is loose around the legs and back. Spread butter over the flesh and then place the slices of truffle all over the breast and thighs. This is all much easier than it sounds.

Rub the salt and pepper over the chicken and season inside. Prick the lemon all over with a skewer and put it into the cavity. Cover the bird loosely, but carefully, with foil, or plastic film, and refrigerate for 24 hours, to let the truffle scent permeate the chicken. When you are ready to cook, bring it back to room temperature, and roast in a preheated oven at 200°C/400°F/gas mark 6 for about 1¼ hours. With this I would serve, as well as a good red burgundy, braised fennel or celery hearts and roast potatoes.

braised pheasant with root vegetables, flavoured with sage and clementines

serves 2

1 pheasant

1 tbsp sunflower oil

1 tbsp flour

1 medium celeriac root

2 carrots, peeled

½ swede or 3 small turnips, peeled

sage leaves

juice and thinly peeled zest of 2 clementines

150ml (¼ pint) white wine

150ml (¼ pint) pheasant stock

salt

freshly ground black pepper

Remove the breasts from the carcass, and cut each in half. Take off the legs, and divide in two. Use the lower drumsticks and the carcass to make stock. You should be able to make about 1 litre (1¾ pints); reduce, cool, and, after keeping back enough for this recipe, freeze the rest.

Brown the meat all over in a frying pan, and dust with the flour. Cut the vegetables into even chunks, about the size of a wine cork. Put them in the bottom of a greased ovenproof dish, and place the pheasant on top. Tuck in the sage leaves. Squeeze the clementine juice into the frying pan to deglaze it, and pour in the white wine and stock. Add a little salt and pepper and a few shreds of clementine peel, from which you have removed the membrane. Pour over the meat, cover with foil, and cook in a preheated oven at 180°C/350°F/ gas mark 4 for 40 minutes. Remove the foil, baste the meat and vegetables with the juice, and cook, uncovered, for a further 10 minutes.

The dish needs no more vegetables to accompany it, though perhaps a green salad to follow.

pheasant consommé with wild mushrooms under a golden dome

This glamorous dish is adapted from a Paul Bocuse recipe, which I have taken the liberty of simplifying. Follow it with a plain dish, such as a baked fish, or a roast. And for pudding, something chilled and fruity, such as a fruit fool.

serves 6

    pheasant carcass (optional)

    1.25 litres (2 pints) game stock

    150g (5oz) chicken, off the bone, minced

    400g (14oz) pheasant, off the bone, minced

    125g (4oz) mushroom stalks and trimmings, diced

    several parsley stalks

    2 garlic cloves

    6 juniper berries, lightly crushed

    ½ tsp black peppercorns

    1 bay leaf and a sprig of thyme

    1 coffeespoon salt

    2 egg whites

for the garnish

    40g (1½ oz) julienne of pheasant breast

    40g (1½ oz) julienne of wild mushrooms

    400g (14oz) puff pastry

    milk and egg glaze (optional)

If you have it, chop up and brown the pheasant carcass. Put all the ingredients, except for the garnish, into a stockpot, and mix well. Put the stockpot on a low heat and, stirring continuously, bring the contents to the boil, then reduce the heat, and cook for 45 minutes. Strain the consommé, and check the seasoning.

Place the julienne of pheasant and mushrooms in ovenproof soup bowls, and pour on the boiling consommé. Allow to cool slightly. Roll out the pastry and cover each soup bowl with a thin layer, about the thickness of a £1 coin. Trim off any excess pastry and use it, if you wish, to decorate the pastry lids. Brush with a milk and egg yolk glaze, if you wish, and seal the edges tightly. Cook in a preheated oven at 220°C/425°F/gas mark 7 for 5 minutes or so, for the pastry to puff up, then lower the heat to 190°F/375°F/gas mark 5, and cook for a further 13–15 minutes in all. Serve immediately.

to roast a turkey

As a once-a-year treat, an organic turkey is a lovely thing to cook for a large gathering round the table, producing not only the deliciously moist, flavoursome meat, but all the good leftovers, such as giblets and carcass for stock. The best advice I can give for cooking a turkey is to follow the instructions which accompany it from the producer. There is a world of difference between a turkey that has had plenty of exercise outside and a varied diet, including grubs and gravel, and one that has been kept in a shed and fed on poultry formula.

Other factors that need to be taken into account are the size of the bird, whether and where you stuff it, how many times you take it out of the oven to baste it, the accuracy of your oven, and whether or not you are cooking other things in the oven at the same time. All affect either the temperature of the bird or the temperature of the oven, and thus the length of time needed to cook the bird.

Weigh the stuffed bird and, as a rough guide, calculate 30 minutes cooking time per 1kg (2¼lb) for a bird weighing up to 6 kg (13lb), and 25 minutes per 1kg for larger birds.

Season the bird lightly inside and out. Rub it with lemon juice and a little spice, if you wish, and plenty of softened butter. Place the bird breast down on the roasting rack, and put in a preheated oven at 200°C/400°F/gas mark 6. After 20 minutes, reduce the temperature to 180°C/350°F/gas mark 4. Halfway through cooking, increase the temperature to 200°C/400°F/gas mark 6 again. Remove the bird from the oven, turn it breast up, and return it to the oven. After another 20 minutes, lower the temperature again to 180°C/350°F/gas mark 4, and cover loosely with foil.

Continue cooking and testing the bird until the juices run clear when you prick it in the thickest part of the thigh. The drumstick will also feel loose when you 'shake hands' with it. Please note that these tests are every bit as important as the 'x minutes per kg' rule. Remove from the oven, transfer to a serving platter, or carving board, cover loosely with foil, and let it rest for 15–20 minutes while you make the gravy by boiling up the cooking juices with a splash of wine. The resting makes the bird much easier to carve, and allows the juices to spread throughout the meat.

elegant leftovers

It is interesting that the French refer to *l'art d'accommoder les restes*. In Britain, I am not sure that we have ever regarded using up leftovers as an art, more a way of feeding the family on odds and ends after feast days. But turkey sandwiches, turkey rissoles, and turkey and chips begin to pall after a few days. Here are some more ideas for dressing cooked leftovers in an appetizing enough guise to set before the most discerning palate. Some recipes will lend themselves to larger scale entertaining, and the quantities can be doubled, or more, if you have copious leftovers.

For those who have uncooked turkey portions left over or other poultry or game, I have included a recipe for game sausage, which can also be made in a terrine if you do not have access to a butcher who makes his or her own sausages and who might be willing to let you have a length of sausage casing.

Fruity, sharp accompaniments go well with cooked meat, from cranberries to pickled cabbage. The former is ideal with white meats, such as pork and turkey, whilst the richer duck and goose are well matched with pickled cabbage, or even better, with sauerkraut. If I haven't made sauerkraut (see p.509), I usually keep a jar or vacuum pack in the store cupboard, as it makes such excellent instant meals

with a grilled pork chop, smoked pork loin or sausages and boiled potatoes. It is not expensive and is available in most supermarkets and
delicatessens.

Cooked meat from dark game, such as venison, hare or wild duck,
will mix with left over gravy or rich stock, some fried mushrooms and
a flavouring of herbs and spices, to make a good sauce for pasta. One
year's Christmas goose leftovers became a goose lasagne, but with a
slight difference. One of our guests was allergic to gluten, and instead of
sheets of wheat lasagne, I sliced thinly peeled celeriac root, and
blanched the slices before layering them with the rich goose sauce. It
was an excellent combination of flavours and certainly looked like a
dish of baked pasta. Large slices of celeriac can also be substituted for
crêpes or cannelloni. Fill them with a mixture of chopped, cooked
game, poultry or ham and plenty of sauce or gravy, top them with a
grating of cheese, and bake them.

Christmas pudding sliced, fried in butter, dusted with icing sugar,
and served with ice cream or brandy butter is the easiest way of using it
up afterwards. But there are other ways of serving it the second time
around, which disguises it even more successfully, if disguise is what
you are after.

game sausage

If you can get caul fat, the mixture can also be used to make game faggots. Whilst this recipe is best made with a mixture of meat, a single meat, such as turkey, can be used. In this case, I would add a little extra in the way of texture with some unsalted pistachios or walnuts, and flavour it with extra spices and herbs.

serves 8 to 10

2 pheasant legs and thighs

2 rabbit hindquarters, chicken thighs and drumsticks, or turkey thighs or drumsticks

2 wild duck legs

250g (8oz) chicken livers

250g (8oz) belly pork

2 shallots or 1 onion, peeled and finely chopped

2 egg yolks

1 tbsp finely chopped fresh herbs, such as sage, pennyroyal, hyssop, chives

50g (2oz) fresh breadcrumbs

salt

freshly ground black pepper

to finish

sausage casing and game stock for poaching

or

unsmoked bacon, rinds removed

1 bay leaf

Remove all the meat from the bones, and use the latter for stock. Pick out some neater pieces of meat, about 115g (4oz) in all, to dice small. Put to one side with two of the chicken livers, trimmed and diced. Chop the belly pork, and fry until the fat runs. Add to the pan the remaining chicken livers and the undiced meat, and cook through. Remove from the heat, and allow to cool slightly. Put in a food processor with the shallots, egg yolks, herbs and breadcrumbs, together with a little seasoning, and blend until smooth. Mix with the diced meat and chicken livers. Spoon or pipe the mixture into sausage casings, tying and cutting at regular intervals.

Poach the sausages gently in game stock for 12–15 minutes. Remove, and put to one side to cool. Serve on individual plates with salad leaves and relish or fruit jelly.

Alternatively, line a loaf tin with thin, rindless slices of unsmoked bacon, pack in the mixture, top with a bay leaf, and cook in a bain marie in a preheated oven at 200°C/400°F/gas mark 6 for 20–25 minutes. Remove, weight down, allow to cool, then serve in slices. If you can get caul fat, the mixture can also be used to make game faggots.

hachis de la saint-sylvestre

This is based on a dish we ate in Paris one New Year's Eve, a superior shepherd's pie. It is excellent served with a watercress, rocket or chicory salad.

serves 6 to 8

1.5kg (3lb) potatoes – see below
100g (4oz) Gruyère, grated
1kg (2lb) cooked goose, beef or ham
2 tbsps blanched and chopped parsley
salt
freshly ground black pepper
½ tsp ground allspice
450ml (¾ pint) gravy or rich stock
unsalted butter, melted

Peel and dice all the potatoes, except one or two, which should be sliced paper-thin and put in a bowl of lightly salted water. Boil the rest of the potatoes, drain, and mash them. Use butter, olive oil, milk or potato water to mash to the texture you prefer. Stir in the cheese. If you use waxy potatoes, you will get a creamy, French-style purée, especially if you use an electric beater. Floury potatoes will give you a fluffier mash.

While the potatoes are cooking, shred or mince the cooked meat, and mix with the parsley, seasoning, spice and gravy. Spoon into a greased ovenproof dish, flatten the top, and cover with the mash. Smooth the surface, and arrange the thin slices of potato on top. Brush with melted butter, and bake in a pre-heated oven at 200°C/400°F/gas mark 6 for 30 minutes.

christmas salad

If poultry was your choice for a main course, here is a way of using up the livers in a very colourful and appealing salad. It can be served as individual starters, but also makes an excellent dish for a Boxing Day lunch buffet. A liver from a large bird could be used in a pâté, either with or without a pastry crust. I would mince fat pork and the rest of the farce, and leave the liver whole or in slices so that, when cooked, there is some variation in texture. You can also use the gizzard and heart of the bird, cooked in the same way as the liver, although the gizzard is best sliced first and then cooked.

serves 6 to 8

1 turkey, duck or goose liver

250g (8oz) chicken livers

2 tbsps groundnut or sunflower oil

250g (8oz) oyster or white button mushrooms

100g (3–4oz) cranberries

1 round fennel bulb

juice of 1 lemon

salad leaves

fresh herbs, such as chervil or chives

250g (8oz) peeled prawns

1 pomegranate

2–3 tbsps raspberry or balsamic vinegar

75ml (3fl oz) extra virgin olive oil

Trim the livers, removing any green bile-stained parts and sinews. Fry them in the oil until just cooked but still pink inside. Transfer to a plate. Slice the mushrooms, and fry very briefly in the same pan until just wilted. Poach the cranberries for 2–3 minutes and then drain. Trim the fennel, and slice into rings or slivers, and sprinkle with the lemon juice. Arrange salad leaves and fresh herbs on a large platter or individual plates. Arrange the fennel around the outer edge, followed by the mushrooms. Place the prawns on top. Slice the livers, and arrange these on top of the prawns before garnishing with cranberries and pomegranate seeds. Deglaze the frying pan with the vinegar, then mix with the olive oil and spoon over the salad.

christmas desserts

In Provence, *les treize desserts* are a traditional Christmas sweet, including all manner of dried fruit, nuts, nougat and baked goods. To make something similar at home, choose a shallow, circular basket, lined with a piece of Provençal fabric, or a large, decorative platter, and fill with a variety of sweetmeats, such as nougat, halva, honey-dipped figs, Medjool dates, crystallized fruit, moscatel raisins, dried apricots, and a selection of nuts, shelled or not, as you prefer. Make or buy marzipan petits fours and spice biscuits. Cut ginger cake into individual squares, and wrap in colourful paper. Treat yourself to Elvas plums, the 'sugar plums' of legend. In fact greengages not plums, these sweetmeats came to England in the early days of the port trade, but for a long while were no longer imported. A few years ago, I visited Conservas Rainha Santa, near Estremoz, where the fruit was being prepared in traditional fashion, first being harvested from old, unsprayed orchards, soaked in syrup, and then sun-dried before being packed in wooden boxes or ceramic bowls. I am pleased that they have reappeared. Many good shops sell them, as well as specialist mail-order companies.

When looking for nuts for your dessert basket, and indeed for your Christmas baking, I recommend the range available in Oxfam. Pecans, cashews and Brazil nuts are fresh and good. Whilst there, I highly recommend, for after dinner, Café-direct coffee, which comes from fair trade sources, as does the unrefined sugar, tea and Bolivian cocoa. You could make up a very appealing gift hamper with these edibles.

pears in white wine and orange

Make a bowlful of these pears for a buffet lunch, or do them as individual servings. It is a light, easy, undemanding dessert, yet elegant to look at, and subtle in flavour, every bit as good as pears in red wine. I have made it most successfully with the small, firm, sweet, neatly shaped Rocha pears from Portugal, available in some supermarkets, but Conference or Williams can also be used. It is a perfect alternative to the Christmas pud and will follow any rich main course very well. Not too sweet to fight with a pudding wine, the pears can be accompanied by a moscato d'Asti, or picking up the second fruit flavour, one of the orange muscat wines, such as Essencia. Portugal's moscatel de Setubal is also a good accompaniment.

12 firm, slightly under-ripe pears
1 bottle good white wine
zest and juice of 3 oranges
6 cardamom pods
1 small cinnamon stick
sugar or honey to sweeten

to garnish
toasted flaked almonds or gold leaf (optional)

Carefully peel the pears, leaving on the stalk. Place in a large saucepan, along with the peel for extra flavour, and pour on the wine. Add the orange zest, juice and spices, and poach for 20–30 minutes until the pears are just tender. Riper pears may only take 15 minutes. Transfer the pears to a glass bowl or other serving dish. Strain the cooking juices into a clean saucepan, and reduce until you have about 300ml (½ pint) liquid. Sweeten to taste, then pour the syrup over the pears. For extra effect, you can decorate with gold leaf or toasted flaked almonds.

mandarin and almond tart

Here is an elegant, entirely seasonal way to finish a dinner. It uses my favourite amongst the orange liqueurs, the Belgian Mandarine Napoleon.

serves 6 to 8

for the pastry

    150g (5oz) unsalted butter, softened

    125g (4oz) icing sugar

    25g (1oz) ground almonds

    pinch of salt

    drop of pure vanilla essence

    250g (8oz) plain flour, sifted

    1 large egg, lightly beaten

for the filling

    125g (4oz) unsalted butter

    125g (4oz) caster sugar

    75g (3oz) ground almonds

    25g (1oz) plain flour, sifted

    4 egg yolks, lightly beaten

    juice and grated zest of 2 mandarin oranges

    2 tbsps mandarin liqueur

to garnish

    flaked almonds or crystallized orange peel

Make the pastry by mixing together the butter, icing sugar, ground almonds and seasoning until you have a soft mass. Work in the flour and egg, then let the pastry rest in the refrigerator whilst you make the filling.

Cream the butter and sugar, then beat in the remaining ingredients. Roll out the pastry, and use to line a 23–25cm (9–10 inch) flan dish or tart ring. Prick the base all over with a fork, line with foil or greaseproof paper, scatter with baking beans, and bake blind in a preheated oven at 180°C/350°F/gas mark 4 for 15 minutes.

Take out of the oven, remove the baking beans and foil or greaseproof paper, and allow to cool slightly before spooning in the filling. (Indeed, if you prefer, the tart shell can be baked blind the day before it is required.) Smooth the surface, then return to the oven and bake for 35–40 minutes or until the filling is just set and golden. About 10 minutes before the end of baking, scatter flaked almonds on top, or pieces of crystallized orange peel.

This is best served warm with crème fraîche, custard, mascarpone or one of the flavoured butters that you will probably have on hand over Christmas. About 10 minutes before the end of baking, scatter flaked almonds on top, or pieces of crystallized orange peel.

caramel and walnut ice cream

This is a good ice cream, easy to make, as it does not require an ice-cream machine and is based, not on an egg custard, which you first have to make, but mascarpone, syrup and that incredibly moreish store cupboard standby, Dulce de Leche. This speciality from Argentina – slow-cooked, caramelized milk – has never been off my shelves since it was introduced a few years ago. *Cajeta* is the Mexican version, made with goat's milk.

serves 8 to 10

jar of Dulce de Leche (also called Luxury Caramel Spread)
200ml (7fl oz) corn syrup or golden syrup
500g (1lb) mascarpone
100g (3½oz) double cream, clotted cream, Greek yoghurt or extra mascarpone
100g (3½oz) broken walnuts, lightly toasted

Mix all the ingredients, except for the walnuts, in a food processor, then spoon into a plastic container, stir in the walnuts, and freeze.

marzipan mince tart

For a make-ahead dessert, which could be served after any of my suggested main courses, I have developed this recipe for a large mince tart, with rich orange and marzipan flavours. A little goes a long way. Less fiddly than individual mince pies, this makes a very attractive tray bake. Make it in a Swiss roll tin, and top with a lattice of pastry if you wish. The layer of marzipan under the mincemeat makes this an even richer than usual mince tart. Cut into squares or fingers for serving, dusted with icing sugar. If you use bought mincemeat, you can dress it up by pouring a miniature of Grand Marnier or Cointreau into the jar before you start making the pastry, and preferably the day before you plan to use it. For a chilled fruit dessert to serve with or instead of the tart, make a mixed orange salad, of mandarins, clementines, navel and Valencia oranges with roasted flaked almonds, rosewater and orange flower water.

serves 10 to 12

    400g (14oz) plain flour, sifted

    200g (7oz) butter, chilled and diced

    2 tbsps caster sugar

    grated zest and juice of 2 chilled oranges

    250g (8oz) marzipan

    milk

    400g (14oz) mincemeat

Crumble the flour and butter together, by hand or in a food processor. Stir in the sugar, zest and enough juice to bind, adding iced water if necessary. Line a standard Swiss roll tin with greased baking parchment, long enough for you to use it to ease the baked tart out of the tin. Divide the pastry in half and roll out one piece to fit the tin. Roll out the marzipan as thinly as possible to fit on top of the pastry, cutting and patching if necessary, but leave a border of about 5mm (¼ inch) around the edge to allow the mixture to spread. Brush the border with milk.

Spoon the mincemeat on top, spreading it to the edge of the border. Roll out the second piece of pastry to fit, and press it down to seal the edges. Decorate the edges using a fork or spoon handle if you wish. Prick the pastry all over with a fork and bake in a preheated oven at 180°C/350°F/gas mark 4 for about 25 minutes until the pastry is crisp and pale golden. Remove from the oven and, after about 5 minutes, carefully transfer from the tin to a wire rack.

Serve warm as a pudding with custard, ice cream, yoghurt or cream, or cold, cut in smaller pieces, at teatime.

grilled fruit skewers

serves 2

1 sharon fruit

6 dried apricots, soaked overnight in juice or white wine

8 kumquats

10 physalis, minus their husks

icing sugar

Cut the sharon fruit into eight wedges, and then thread with the rest of the fruit on to two wooden skewers, which have previously been soaked in cold water for 30 minutes.

Spread a thin layer of icing sugar on a piece of greaseproof paper, or on a plate, and roll the fruit skewers in it until well coated.

Heat the grill until it is very hot, and put the skewers under it for a few minutes, just until the edges of the fruit begin to caramelize.

Serve on their own, as an accompaniment to dark or white chocolate mousse, or alongside a wedge of ricotta or a dollop of mascarpone. A syrup flavoured with rum or mandarin liqueur also goes well with them.

almond and amaretto crown
with caramel and mascarpone

serves 6

    50g (2oz) self-raising flour

    50g (2oz) ground almonds

    100g (4oz) caster sugar

    100g (4oz) unsalted butter, softened

    3 eggs, separated

    2 tbsps Amaretto

for the topping

    150ml (5fl oz) mascarpone or whipped double cream

    3 tbsps Dulce de Leche or other caramel cream

    2 tbsps toasted, flaked almonds

    a dozen physalis fruits (optional)

Butter and flour a 25cm (10 inch) diameter non-stick ring mould. Sift together the flour and ground almonds. Cream the sugar and butter until pale and light. Beat in two eggs yolks and one whole egg, one at a time, alternating with the flour and almond mixture.

Whisk the remaining egg whites, and fold into the cake batter. Spoon into the ring mould, smoothing the surface, and bake in a preheated oven at 180°C/350°F/gas mark 4 for 40–45 minutes. Turn out on to a wire rack, and cool for 10–15 minutes. Prick the cake all over with a cocktail stick or skewer, then pour over the Amaretto.

Top the ring with a cream made by mixing two thirds mascarpone or whipped, double cream, and one third Dulce de Leche or other milk caramel cream. Decorate with toasted flaked almonds, or squirt zig-zags of caramel over the cream. Serve warm or cold. The centre can be filled, if you wish, with physallis, some plain, some dipped in fondant icing.

christmas pudding surprise

serves 6

6 × 1cm (½ inch) slices of Christmas pudding,
   cut to fit the base of an individual ramekin
rum, brandy or other liqueur
500g (1lb) best quality vanilla ice cream, just slightly softened
2 egg whites
75g (3oz) caster sugar

Place the pieces of pudding in the bottom of ramekins. Moisten with rum, brandy or liqueur. Spoon in the ice cream, leaving 5mm (¼ inch) space at the top. Smooth the surface, and freeze the ramekins until the ice cream is hard. Whisk the egg whites with half the sugar to firm peaks, fold in the remaining sugar, and whisk until fully incorporated. Remove the ramekins from the freezer, place on a baking tray, and top each with a heap of meringue, which should meet the edge of the ramekin. Bake in the middle of a preheated oven at 180°C/350°F/gas mark 4 for 8–10 minutes. Serve immediately.

christmas pudding truffles

These are very easy to make. Take a tablespoon of leftover pudding, place it on a square of cling film, draw the edges to the centre, and twist tightly until the pudding forms a round ball. It should be moist enough to do this without crumbling, but, if not, add a little extra spirit or liqueur. Remove the cling film and finish the truffles by rolling in cocoa, icing sugar, caster sugar mixed with grated orange zest or melted chocolate, either white or dark.

Oranges and all their easy-peel cousins are at their best in winter. In the following recipes, clementines, mandarins or satsumas can replace the tangerines, according to availability.

tangerine granita

serves 4 to 6

1 tbsp fresh lemon juice

600ml (1 pint) fresh tangerine juice

75ml (3fl oz) water

Mix all the ingredients together, pour into a plastic container, and freeze, stirring from time to time until the mixture has a grainy, coarse texture. Serve at once.

tangerine sorbet

serves 6 to 8

1 tbsp fresh lemon juice

75ml (3fl oz) water

300g (10oz) icing sugar, sifted

600ml (1 pint) fresh tangerine juice

Mix together the lemon juice, water and icing sugar, and stir until the sugar has dissolved. Add the tangerine juice, and freeze in a sorbetière or ice-cream maker, or in a container placed in the freezer or ice-making compartment of the refrigerator. If using the latter method, stir the mixture from time to time as it freezes to ensure a smooth sorbet. The last stirring, when the mixture is almost hard, can be done in a food processor.

tangerine ice cream

This, like all ices and sorbets, is best made for immediate eating, as the flavour and texture deteriorates with keeping.

serves 6

500ml (18fl oz) single cream

175g (6oz) caster sugar

1 tbsp grated tangerine zest

3 egg yolks

450ml (¾ pint) tangerine juice, chilled

In a saucepan, bring the cream, sugar and tangerine zest to the boil, then pour it over the egg yolks, whisking continuously. Return the mixture to the saucepan, and cook over a very low heat, without boiling or curdling the mixture, until the custard thickens and coats the back of a spoon. Remove from the heat, pour into a bowl, cool, then cover and refrigerate overnight to allow the flavour to develop. The following day, mix with the tangerine juice, and freeze as described in the sorbet recipe.

stilton and port soufflés in paper cases

These are delicious either as savouries or as appetizers.

serves 6 to 8

- 4 tbsps soft white breadcrumbs
- 4 tbsps port or sweet oloroso sherry
- 250g (8oz) Blue Stilton, crumbled
- 75g (3oz) butter, softened
- 4 eggs, separated
- freshly ground black pepper

Soak the breadcrumbs in the port for a few minutes. Drain them and mix with the cheese and butter. Mix in the egg yolks, season with black pepper, and then fold in the stiffly whipped egg whites. Spoon into buttered paper cases and bake in a preheated oven at 180°C/350°F/gas mark 4 for about 8–10 minutes.

---

christmas without meat

If you do not want to cook and serve meat, there are wonderful alternatives, which make quite spectacular centrepieces; majestic pasta pies based on Renaissance recipes from Emilia Romagna; a pyramid of stuffed pancakes; a crisp jacket of filo pastry filled with lentils and quinoa and served with a sharp, fruity sauce of cranberries and kumquats.

Quinoa is a tiny grass seed, originally from the Andes, now cultivated elsewhere, and available in healthfood shops. It absorbs three to four times its volume of water and has a very good flavour. If you cannot find it, cooked wild rice or brown rice can be substituted.

At this time of year I also make a rich, red risotto, which, with a few amendments, makes an excellent party dish for vegetarians. I always hope vegetarians make similar plans for their carnivorous guests.

The risotto is a glorious colour, given depth by red wine and beetroot. Often in the past, when I have cooked sauces and risottos with red wine, they have tasted wonderful but the ruby colour has faded into a purplish brown. Then I discovered the colouring powers of betacarotene, naturally present in carrots. From then on my vegetable stock was made from the fibre left over after juicing carrots and celery, and the juice itself was sufficient to maintain a clear, bright red in the risotto. Chestnuts, pine nuts, wild or cultivated mushrooms, and dried cranberries are suitably festive ingredients for the risotto, but you can, of course, vary these at will.

If I was serving the risotto as the centrepiece of a vegetarian meal, I would, to start with, serve a pumpkin and almond soup, a celery and apple soup with saffron cream and cheese biscuits, or a pressed vegetable terrine with a chickpea and sesame seed sauce. Pomegranate seeds garnishing a green leafy salad with a walnut oil dressing would follow the risotto very well. For pudding, a tangerine granita and crisp biscuits, perhaps. Alternatively, I might make a beetroot soup with a swirl of saffron cream, and for a main course a potato soufflé tart with glazed golden vegetables and onion sauce – a pastry case in which I bake

---

a soufflé potato mix and top it with glazed, almost caramelized wedges of swede, pumpkin, carrot and sweet potato.

Even meat eaters might like a day or two of vegetarian food over the holidays, although my husband, Tom, draws the line at tofu. To test these recipes, I tried to sneak some into the refrigerator without him noticing, but he found it. Eeeeuuuuuggggghhh! Toe-foo! was the reaction. In fact, some of the recipes here are every bit as rich and luxurious as the dishes in a carnivore's diet. I do not favour the approach which tries to make the vegetarian Christmas dinner look like a traditional one, complete with Brussels sprouts and roast potatoes. These, for me, need to meld into the background of a juicy and succulent goose or turkey. With the more subtle vegetable- and grain-based dishes, they dominate, unless perhaps doused in a racy, oriental dressing, with liberal adjuncts of soy. Rather like the dressing I have chosen for my second tofu dish.

Whenever I think about vegetarian dishes, I cannot now persuade myself to develop recipes using meat substitutes. I have done so in the past, but I found the results deeply unsatisfactory and the whole notion absurd. Unsatisfactory, not because I am a bad cook, but because the end product was so dull in texture compared to what I could create with grains, pulses and vegetables. And absurd because I'm convinced that most vegetarians do not want to be reminded of the taste and texture of meat in so-called vegetarian burgers, sausages and other travesties. And whilst most meat-eaters would readily eat these dishes, they would not, I feel, be happy with the meat look-alikes.

The recipes which follow reflect either Mediterranean or oriental flavours, with a classic dessert, a small rich piece of deliciousness in the form of a chocolate tart. No one says vegetarians have to be abstemious. The tomato soup, warm leek salad and the two tofu recipes can also be served to vegans. And since not everyone is as fond of dark chocolate as I am, a large bowl of tropical and Mediterranean fruit salad, enlivened with a splash of Moscato d'Asti or other floral, sweet muscat wine, is a must.

Careful shopping and planning will ensure that you have plenty of fresh food over the holidays. The bonus with vegetarian food is that grains, flour and pulses do not need to take up valuable wine chilling space in the refrigerator. Salad greens, as well as fennel, endive, celery and radicchio should be well rinsed, but any roots left on, and everything put in a bowl of water, roots down, to which you add a few ice cubes from time to time. Keep this in a cool place, and the vegetables will stay fresh and crisp for a few days, although they will lose some vitamins.

If you peel, halve, seed and slice two or three cucumbers, salt them lightly, drain for an hour or so, then rinse and dry, they will keep in the refrigerator for two to three days. Serve with chopped dill and vinaigrette for a simple salad, mix with chopped shallots, herbs and yoghurt or soured cream as an accompaniment to smoked fish, or fry briefly in olive oil for a hot vegetable accompaniment. Most soups can be made a day or two in advance, and the garnish, such as cream, sherry, croûtons, herbs or what you will, can be added on reheating.

Fish is also an option, not for vegetarians of course, but for non-meat eaters. Many countries with a Catholic heritage serve fish on Christmas Eve, often a whole baked fish in a salt crust. I suggest something a little smaller and more manageable, perhaps a fish pie, or some fresh salmon, which you can now buy from organic salmon farms.

salmon and scallop cutlets

For a lighter sauce, reduce the wine and wine vinegar as described, then whisk in fruity extra virgin olive oil instead of the egg yolks and butter. This is very good served on a nest of deep fried leeks, see p.550.

serves 6

> 1 × 25cm (10 inch) long strip of salmon, weighing approx 400g (14oz) and cut from the centre of the fillet
> 12 scallops, trimmed with roe removed
> 6 wooden skewers, soaked in water for 30 minutes
> salt
> freshly ground white pepper
> 2 shallots, finely chopped
> blade of mace
> 150ml (¼ pint) dry white wine
> 1 tbsp white wine vinegar
> 2 egg yolks
> 125g (4oz) butter, chilled and diced

to garnish

> 3 ripe tomatoes, peeled, seeded and chopped
> sprigs of chervil, chives or dill

Skin the fish, and slice it into six long equal strips. Wrap each strip around two scallops to form the letter 'B'. Secure with a wooden skewer pierced through the centre. Lightly season, and put to one side while you make the sauce.

Put the shallots, mace, wine and wine vinegar in a saucepan, and reduce by two thirds. Remove the mace and, off the heat, whisk in the egg yolks, as for a sabayon sauce. Whisk in the butter, a piece at a time, and, when well incorporated, season lightly with a little white pepper.

Heat a grill, griddle or heavy frying pan, and quickly cook the fish on both sides. Serve on warm plates with some of the sauce and the diced tomatoes or herbs.

---

salt cod and cranberry pie

I love the sweet and savoury combinations found in dishes where there has been Arabic influence in the kitchen. In Lisbon we have often eaten a marvellous warm salt cod tart at the restaurant Conventual and I have made several versions of it at home. It is a perfect Christmas Eve dish, but also very useful later on during the holiday week when fresh fish might be scarce.

Now that our dried fruit stock includes cranberries from America, I have used them to good effect in this fish pie. If you can get salt cod, choose a thick centre piece, and soak it for 48 hours with several changes of water. Alternatively, take a thick-skinned fillet of fresh cod and skin it. Scatter a couple of handfuls of coarse sea salt in a shallow dish, and place the fish in it. Sprinkle on a similar amount of salt, cover, and refrigerate, or leave in a cold place for 3–4 hours. Rinse the fish thoroughly. If you want to salt it for several days, you will then need to soak it to get rid of the excess salt.

serves 4 to 6

8 sheets filo pastry

750g (1½lb) salt cod, prepared as above

1 onion, peeled and very thinly sliced

100g (4oz) unsalted butter

2 tbsps ground almonds

150ml (¼ pint) single cream

1 egg, lightly beaten

good pinch each of ground mace, cloves and cinnamon

100g (3–4oz) pine nuts

100g (3–4oz) dried cranberries

Keep the filo wrapped until ready to use it. Put the fish in a shallow pan, cover with water, bring slowly to simmering point, then remove the fish from the heat and leave for 10–15 minutes. Drain the fish.

Meanwhile, gently fry the onion in about half the butter until soft and golden.

Remove from the heat, and stir in the almonds, cream, egg and spices.

Melt the remaining butter, and with it, brush the filo pastry, a sheet at a time. Use six sheets to line a buttered rectangular dish, leaving the edges over-hanging. Flake the fish into the lined pie dish, and scatter on the pine nuts and cranberries. Pour over the 'custard' mixture. Cut the remaining two sheets of dough to fit the pie, and bring the overhanging sides over the top to seal it. Tear up any remaining pieces of pastry to cover the top like a patchwork. Bake in a preheated oven at 180°C/350°F/gas mark 4 for 30–40 minutes.

This is best followed by a green salad, rather than served with vegetables.

spiced tomato and lentil soup

serves 6 to 8

2 tbsps sunflower, grapeseed or groundnut oil

approx 900g (2lb) ripe tomatoes or canned plum tomatoes

1 tsp each ground cardamom and coriander

1.66 litres (2¾ pints) vegetable stock

200g (7oz) red lentils

½ tsp freshly grated ginger or a pinch of powdered ginger

salt

freshly ground black pepper

Heat the oil in a heavy saucepan, stir in the tomatoes and spices, and cook until the juices begin to evaporate slightly. Add half the stock, the lentils and the ginger, and cook until the lentils are soft. Allow to cool slightly, blend and sieve, then return the liquid to the saucepan. Stir in the remaining stock, reheat, and season to taste. Serve with chunky bread, or these delicate crisp biscuits.

cumin and almond crisps

makes 18

1 egg white

pinch of salt

50g (2oz) ground almonds

1 tsp cumin seeds

½ tsp turmeric

1 tsp grated lemon zest

1 tsp cornflour

1 tbsp finely grated hard, dry cheese (optional)

Stir together all the ingredients, then put heaped teaspoonfuls on to lined baking sheets. Bake in a preheated oven at 150°C/300°F/gas mark 3 for 15–20 minutes until just set and golden. Remove from the oven and cool on a wire rack. They will keep fresh for a few days in an airtight tin, and can, if necessary, be re-crisped in the oven.

cheese crisps

For as many cheese crisps as you want, cut 2.5cm (1 inch) cubes of Gruyère, Jarlsberg, Comté or other similar hard cheese. Place on a lined baking sheet with plenty of space between to allow for spreading, and bake in the top half of a preheated oven at 200°C/400°F/gas mark 6 for 3–5 minutes. The cheese will first melt and then harden as it cools on emerging from the oven and is lifted off the baking sheet. Plain, these make very good snacks with drinks. Prepared in the following way, you can turn them into a very impressive cheese course, which could not be simpler.

goat's cheese crisps and salad

If you prefer, the goat's cheese can be replaced with cream cheese or curd cheese mixed with herbs and black pepper.

serves 4

200g (7oz) goat's cheese log

16 cheese crisps, see recipe above

small salad leaves, such as rocket, mâche (lamb's lettuce),
    baby spinach, herbs and watercress

walnut oil and sherry vinegar dressing

Take the ends and rind off the goat's cheese, and divide into eight slices. Put one slice between two cheese crisps, and arrange two of these on each plate with a little dressed salad.

warm baby leeks with orange, almond and olive oil dressing

The leeks are best eaten while still slightly warm. Preparing them in advance and refrigerating them never seems quite as successful. The leeks begin to look dull, and their flavour is not improved.

serves 4

12–16 thin leeks

2 tbsps black olives

2 tbsps flaked almonds, lightly toasted

grated zest and juice of 1 mandarin

4–5 tbsps extra virgin olive oil

sea salt

freshly ground black pepper

Trim and clean the leeks carefully. Split lengthways down towards the base, but without cutting right through. Rinse and drain. Drop into boiling, lightly salted water, and cook until quite tender, 5–10 minutes, depending on size. Alternatively, you can steam them.

Drain, and arrange in a shallow dish. While still warm, scatter on the olives, almonds and zest, and pour over a dressing made by mixing together the oil, juice and seasoning. Serve immediately.

christmas risotto

The risotto will be creamy if you use the Italian rice, much more chewy if you use the red rice.

serves 4

    1 pink shallot, peeled and chopped

    2 tbsps olive oil

    250g (8oz) arborio, carnaroli or red Camargue rice

    1 beetroot, cooked and grated

    2–3 dried porcini, broken into pieces and soaked

    100ml (3fl oz) good dry red wine, hot

    up to 500ml (18fl oz) vegetable stock, hot

    200ml (7fl oz) carrot juice

    salt

    freshly ground black pepper

    handful of chives, chopped (optional)

    freshly grated Parmesan

Fry the shallot in the oil, and then stir in the rice until coated with oil. Add a handful of the beetroot, the porcini and their soaking water, and the red wine. Simmer, stirring continuously, until the liquid is absorbed. Continue to stir, add a ladle of stock, and again let the rice absorb all the liquid before adding more. Once you have added half the stock, stir in the remaining beetroot and the carrot juice. Continue to cook, stirring, until all the stock has been used. If you find you need more liquid, add boiling water.

    Serve the risotto in warmed bowls, sprinkled with chopped chives, if you like. You can either stir in some grated Parmesan cheese before serving the risotto, or pass it round separately.

tea smoked tofu with bean sprouts and shiitake in a lime and soy vinaigrette

For a more substantial meal, serve the tofu, bean sprouts and shiitake with rice, and a condiment made by mixing plenty of freshly grated ginger, salt, a dash of chilli, some toasted sesame oil, and a little vinegar made from rice wine or sherry. It is also very good with Japanese pickled ginger.

serves 4

1 packet firm tofu

1 tbsp coarse sea salt

1 tbsp Szechuan peppercorns

4 star anise

1 cinnamon stick

3–4 tbsps fermented soy sauce

100g (4oz) uncooked rice

100g (4oz) sugar

2 tbsps fragrant black tea

150g (5oz) bean sprouts

150g (5oz) fresh shiitake mushrooms

1 lime

1 tsp or more grated ginger

2 tbsps toasted sesame oil

Crush the salt and spices, and toast them in a wok. Allow to cool, then rub them gently all over the tofu, having first brushed it with soy sauce.

Prepare the wok for smoking. Line it with a double thickness of foil. Mix the rice, sugar and tea, and spread over the bottom of the wok. Place the rack on top, and on it lay the tofu. Put the lid on, and seal the rim, either with a strip of foil, or with moistened paper towels. Place the wok on a medium high heat and, once it has begun to smoke, which you will be able to smell rather than see, resist the temptation to have a look, and leave the wok on the heat for 10–15 minutes. Remove from the heat, and leave for a further 15 minutes before removing and serving.

Slice the tofu thinly, and serve it with a warm salad of stir-fried bean sprouts and sliced shiitake mushrooms, with a dressing of soy, lime juice, grated ginger and toasted sesame oil.

terrine of grilled tofu, aubergine and red pepper

A nice salad with this is mâche (lamb's lettuce), one of the best winter leaves, with an olive or walnut oil vinaigrette, some pine nuts or walnuts, and some sultanas, chopped apricots or dried cranberries. For a more substantial dish, serve with couscous.

serves 6

1 × 200g packet firm tofu, sliced not too thinly
1 aubergine, sliced
2–3 red peppers, quartered
salt
freshly ground black pepper

Grill the tofu briefly on each side on an oiled griddle, followed by the aubergine, just until it is turning soft, but do not let the slices blacken. Grill the red peppers until the skin is well blistered, then, when cool enough to handle, peel.

Oil a 500g (1lb) loaf tin, or terrine, and layer the tofu, aubergine and peppers, trying to catch and use as much of the juice from the peppers as possible, and lightly seasoning at intervals. Fill to within 2.5cm (1 inch) of the top, cover with foil, and bake in a preheated oven at 180°C/350°F/gas mark 4 for 15–20 minutes. Remove from the oven, weight down very heavily, which will make for easier slicing, and leave for 15–20 minutes before serving.

vegetable and tofu creams served with tomato and basil vinaigrette

The vegetable cream recipe can be adapted as a filling for a flan. Perhaps in this case, add diced smoked tofu to make a more substantial dish. It is important that the creams, which are really egg custards, cook gently so that the egg protein does not harden and separate.

Although not suitable for vegans, the recipe can be served to vegetarians.

serves 6 to 8

- 1 onion, peeled and finely chopped
- 1 tbsp sunflower oil
- 1 small fennel bulb, trimmed and finely chopped
- 125g (4oz) celeriac or 1 celery stick, trimmed and finely chopped
- 2 carrots, peeled and finely chopped
- 2 courgettes, finely chopped
- 1 small aubergine, diced
- 1 small turnip, peeled and finely chopped
- 1–2 tbsps chopped parsley
- 200g (7oz) silken tofu
- 3 eggs
- 75ml (3fl oz) cream or soya cream
- salt
- freshly ground black pepper

for the tomato and basil vinaigrette

- 2–3 ripe tomatoes, roughly chopped
- 75ml (3fl oz) extra virgin olive oil
- 2 tbsps sherry vinegar
- sprigs of fresh basil
- salt
- freshly ground black pepper

Sweat the onion in the oil in a pan until soft, then add the rest of the vegetables. Moisten with two or three tablespoons of water (or dry white wine if you have a bottle opened), cover, and cook until the vegetables are soft, then add the parsley.

Put the vegetables in a blender with the tofu, eggs and cream, and blend until smooth. Rub through a sieve, and season to taste. Oil or butter dariole moulds or ramekins, and spoon in the vegetable cream. Steam over a low heat, or cook in a bain marie in a preheated oven at 150°C/300°F/gas mark 2 for 30 minutes. The creams are set when a knife point inserted in the middle of them comes out clean. Allow to cool a little before turning out on to plates.

To make the dressing, put the tomatoes in a blender or food processor with the olive oil, vinegar and a few of the basil leaves. Process until smooth, then sieve. Spoon around the vegetable creams, and garnish with basil leaves, shredded or left whole.

celeriac, pumpkin and walnut crumble

serves 8

500g (1lb) celeriac, peeled and trimmed

500g (1lb) pumpkin, peeled

2 onions, peeled and finely chopped

25g (1oz) butter or 2 tbsps olive oil

2 tbsps finely chopped parsley

for the crumble

250g (8oz) button mushrooms, wiped then sliced

150g (5oz) butter

50g (2oz) fresh breadcrumbs

3 tbsps finely chopped chives

75g (3oz) walnuts, chopped small

Slice the celeriac and pumpkin into pieces about the thickness of a 20p coin and about 5cm (2 inches) broad. Blanch the celeriac immediately in lightly acidulated water. Drain. Sweat the onions in the butter or oil until soft, then add the other vegetables. Cover with a lid, and let the vegetables 'steam' on top of the onions until tender. Transfer to a buttered baking dish, sprinkling each layer with parsley.

To make the crumble, fry the mushrooms in a little of the butter until soft. This should be done over a high heat to evaporate the liquid. When cooked, finely chop the mushrooms. Mix them with the remaining ingredients, and spoon over the vegetables. Bake on the top shelf of a preheated oven at 230°C/450°F/gas mark 8 for 10–12 minutes, or finish off under the grill.

winter vegetable gratin

serves 6 to 8

> 250g (8oz) each celeriac, onions, potatoes, leeks and pumpkin
>
> 1 fennel bulb
>
> 300ml (½ pint) vegetable stock
>
> 1 bay leaf
>
> 2 cloves
>
> blade of mace or piece of nutmeg
>
> 50g (2oz) black olives, stoned and chopped
>
> 50g (2oz) dried tomatoes, snipped into small pieces
>
> 300ml (½ pint) thick béchamel sauce – see p.163
>
> 175g (6oz) hard cheese
>
> 50g (2oz) ground hazelnuts
>
> 50g (2oz) mixed chopped nuts
>
> 50g (2oz) fresh breadcrumbs

Peel and slice all the vegetables, the tougher ones about the thickness of a £1 coin, the leeks and pumpkin somewhat thicker. Bring the stock and spices to the boil, add the vegetables, and cook for 8–10 minutes, adding boiling water if necessary.

Drain, reserving the cooking liquid, and transfer the vegetables to a lightly oiled or buttered baking dish, mixing in the olives and tomatoes. Reduce the stock to about 150ml (¼ pint), removing the spices and bay leaf first, stir in the béchamel, and cook for 2–3 minutes before pouring it over the vegetables.

Mix together the cheese, ground hazelnuts, chopped nuts and breadcrumbs, and scatter over the top. Bake in a preheated oven at 180°C/350°F/gas mark 4 for 20 minutes or so, until bubbling and golden.

quinoa and lentil strudel

serves 4 to 6

- 75g (3oz) fresh breadcrumbs
- 75g (3oz) almonds, finely chopped but not ground
- 50g (2oz) butter
- 4 tbsps extra virgin olive oil
- 2 leeks, white parts only, peeled, trimmed and sliced
- 2–3 garlic cloves, peeled and crushed
- 125g (4oz) ceps, oyster or other tasty mushrooms, sliced
- 3 ripe tomatoes, peeled, seeded and chopped
- 12 ripe black olives, stoned and chopped
- 2 tsps green peppercorns
- 2 tbsps fresh parsley, finely chopped
- 2 tbsps fresh basil, chervil or coriander, finely chopped
- handful of chives, finely chopped (optional)
- 200g (7oz) green or Puy lentils, cooked until tender and cooled
- 200g (7oz) quinoa, cooked and cooled
- 6 large sheets filo pastry
- 1 mozzarella cheese, diced
- 75g (3oz) pine nuts, toasted

Fry the breadcrumbs and almonds in half the butter and a spoonful of olive oil. Put to one side. In half the remaining olive oil, sweat the leeks until soft, then stir in the garlic and mushrooms. When the mushrooms are almost cooked, stir in the tomatoes. Stir in the olives, together with the peppercorns and herbs. Chives, too, can be added if you have them.

Melt the remaining butter, and mix with the rest of the olive oil. Brush the sheets of filo pastry with it and, between each of them, scatter a little almond and breadcrumb mixture. Leaving a 2.5cm (1 inch) border around the edge, spread the quinoa over the pastry, followed by the vegetable mixture, the lentils and finally the diced mozzarella and toasted pine nuts. Roll up and carefully transfer to a baking sheet. Alternatively, spoon the fillings into a rectangular heap in the middle of the pastry and fold it like a parcel. Brush all over with melted butter and olive oil, and bake in a preheated oven at 200°C/400°F/gas mark 6 for 10 minutes, then reduce the temperature to 180°C/350°F/gas mark 4 and bake for a further 10–15 minutes.

Serve the strudel with glazed chestnuts, deep-fried or creamed leeks, and the cranberry and kumquat sauce.

glazed chestnuts

serves 8

500g (1lb) chestnuts, peeled
600ml (1 pint) vegetable stock or fruity white wine
50g (2oz) butter
50g (2oz) light muscovado sugar

Cook the chestnuts in the stock until tender, then drain, reserving the cooking liquid for soup or stock for another dish. Add the butter and sugar to the pan, and set it over a low heat until the sugar has dissolved. Shake with the lid on to glaze the chestnuts.

deep-fried leeks

serves 4 to 6

750g (1½ lb) fresh leeks
groundnut or sunflower oil for frying

Trim the leeks, and remove the coarse tops and outer skin. Cut into 7.5cm (3 inch) lengths, slice in half lengthways, then shred into long thin strips. Rinse and dry thoroughly.

Pour the oil into a wok or deep frying pan to a depth of about 7.5cm (3 inches) and heat until hot. Test by dropping in a cube of bread; if it sizzles, the oil is hot enough. Fry the leeks in batches, draining on paper towels before serving. Shredded so finely, they will cook in about 20 seconds.

creamed leeks

Use the same quantity of leeks. Trim, slice and wash them thoroughly. Put in a heavy saucepan with a nut of butter, cover with a lid, and cook gently until tender. Fork to a purée with a little more butter, cream or crème fraîche and a grating of nutmeg. Brussels sprouts can be prepared in the same way.

cranberry, kumquat and juniper salsa

makes about 1kg (2lb)
   2 medium to large onions, peeled and chopped
   1 tbsp groundnut oil
   25g (1oz) butter
   200g (7oz) kumquats
   250g (8oz) cranberries
   1 tsp juniper berries, lightly crushed
   1 bay leaf
   2 cloves
   75g (3oz) light muscovado sugar
   2–3 tbsps sherry vinegar

Cook the onion very gently in the oil and butter until soft and beginning to slightly caramelize. Allow 30–40 minutes for this, and stir from time to time to prevent the onions from burning.

Meanwhile, halve the kumquats, discard the seeds, and roughly chop. Simmer in two or three tablespoons of water until the fruit is tender.

When the onion is soft, stir in the kumquats and their cooking liquid, the cranberries, juniper berries and the bay leaf, into which you have pinned the cloves. Cover with a lid, and cook over a gentle heat until the cranberries have popped. Remove the lid, raise the heat, and let the cooking liquid evaporate. Stir in the sugar, and add the vinegar. Cook until thick and glossy. Remove the bay leaf and cloves, allow to cool, then pot and refrigerate.

double chocolate tarts

makes 4

for the pastry
75g (3oz) plain flour
25g (1oz) cocoa
50g (2oz) unsalted butter
1 tbsp caster sugar
1 egg yolk
iced water

for the filling
2 egg yolks, plus 1 whole egg
caster sugar
150g (5oz) dark chocolate, at least 70 per cent cocoa solids, broken into pieces
50g (2oz) unsalted butter

to decorate
icing sugar
gold leaf (optional)
thinly cut crystallized orange peel

Sift together the flour and cocoa, rub in the butter, then stir in the sugar and egg yolk. Add iced water, if necessary, to bind to a pastry. Leave to rest for 30 minutes, then roll out, and use to line four 12cm (5 inch) tart tins. Bake blind in a preheated oven at 180°C/350°F/gas mark 4 for 6–8 minutes, remove from the oven, and allow to cool. You can make these a day or so in advance, if you wish.

Make the filling by whisking the eggs and sugar until pale and much increased in volume. In a bowl set over a pan of hot water, melt the chocolate and butter. Remove from the heat, and fold into the egg mixture. Leave to cool, then spoon into the pastry cases, and bake in a preheated oven at 150°C/300°F/gas mark 2 for 5 minutes.

Serve, dusted with icing sugar, or decorated with a small piece of gold leaf or thinly cut crystallized orange peel.

---

appendix 1: kitchen counsel

alcohol
Too much in sorbets and ice creams will stop the mixture from freezing; 75–100ml (3–4fl oz) alcohol per 575–700ml (1–1¼ pints) syrup or cream mixture will freeze, and is sufficient to give flavour.

aloe vera
This is a very good plant to have on the kitchen window sill. The gel in the succulent leaves is excellent for kitchen burns. It is also highly recommended for sunburn.

apples
Unripe mangoes make a very good substitute for apples in apple pies, crumbles and charlottes. Christophene (cho cho) can be used in the same way, but needs a good helping of lemon juice, or, even better, concentrated apple juice.

arrowroot
This is good for a clear glaze on sweet or savoury food, as well as for thickening sauce. However, unlike cornflour, it thins if you reheat or overcook it.

artichokes
If you treat them like flowers, which they are, they will keep better. Buy them with stalks, and put them in a deep bowl of water with a sugar lump. Change the water every day, and cut off a slice of stalk.

aubergines
To salt or not to salt? Indoor-grown hybrids from Holland and elsewhere are not bitter, indeed have very little flavour, and do not need salting. Outdoor-grown aubergines, like most outdoor-grown produce, have a distinctive flavour, a tough skin and retain many of their original characteristics, which,

in the case of the aubergine, includes bitterness. They will thus benefit from salting. Use about two teaspoons for each large sliced or diced aubergine, and leave to drain in a colander. Rinse and dry thoroughly before cooking. Instead of frying them in oil, brush with just a little oil and grill or bake in the oven.

avocados
To ripen them, put in a fruit bowl with other fruit, especially bananas, the ethylene gas from which tends to ripen anything near it. Avocados can also be ripened in a paper bag put in a warm place. They are also said to ripen when buried in self-raising flour. Once ripe, provided they have no blemishes, they will keep for a few days in the salad drawer in the refrigerator.

bananas
Store separately from other fruit unless you want the fruit to ripen quickly. You can slow down their ripening in the refrigerator, and putting them in a paper bag prevents the gases ripening other food.

batter
A self-raising flour batter must be used immediately; a plain flour batter can be left for up to 12 hours, after which it begins to ferment.

cabbage
To avoid cabbage smells (hydrogen sulphide), cook it for less than 5 minutes; steaming or stir-frying are good methods. Alternatively, cover and cook for a very long time to disperse the smell. A thick piece of coarse country bread put in the pot with the cabbage is said to help get rid of the smell.

cakes
The Victoria sponge is an indispensable recipe (see p.455) and can be adapted to a multitude of flavours and fillings. Baked, cooled and tightly wrapped in cling film and foil it will freeze for two months. As well as a filled and iced cake for the tea table, it can be used for trifles, steamed puddings and desserts when served with a syrup or fruit sauce.

cake tins
A 20cm (8 inch) diameter tin has the same volume as an 18cm (7 inch) square tin.

---

candles

To stop them dripping, soak new candles in very salty water for an hour. Remove and let them dry on their own before lighting. In hot climates, they are best stored in the freezer.

cheese

How much to serve? Allow 60g (a generous 2oz) per person, and two more cheeses than there are guests according to Pierre Androuet, the French cheese expert. I disagree. I would serve five cheeses, at most seven, and possibly just three for an informal occasion – unless, of course, it was a cheese tasting. A hard, a blue and a soft would be sufficient.

cheese biscuits

The 3/3/3 + cayenne cheese biscuits are very good kept and served from the freezer: three parts each of flour, butter and grated hard cheese.

clotted cream

Indispensable for afternoon tea, but often unavailable. Mascarpone is a reasonable substitute, much more stable, and closer in taste and texture than either crème fraîche or whipped cream. However, I would opt for simply serving my scones with really good quality unsalted butter if I could not get clotted cream.

coffee

This is best kept sealed in the freezer. The refrigerator dries it out, as it does with bread, cheese and other products.

Ground coffee mixed to a paste with lemon juice is said to cure a particular tummy bug prevalent in Greece, Turkey and, no doubt, elsewhere.

cream

If you wish to add cream to sweet and savoury dishes that have been frozen, thaw them, reheat, and then add the cream, rather than putting in the cream before freezing. This prevents curdling, and also freshens the dish, as does the addition of any ingredient at this stage, whether herbs, a dash of lemon juice or a splash of spirit.

To freeze cream, you need one of at least 35 per cent butter fat. The best results are achieved by whipping the cream and then freezing it in a large container to provide for expansion. Before freezing, you can pipe the cream into rosettes and then open-freeze them on sheets of greaseproof paper, before packing in freezer boxes, layered with greaseproof to avoid damage. Cream will keep in the freezer for three months, and should be defrosted overnight in the refrigerator.

eggs
If you are uncertain about making mayonnaise with raw eggs, try the old-fashioned salad cream recipes, using the yolks of hard-boiled eggs, mixed with seasoning, mustard, a little lemon juice or wine vinegar, then the slow, careful addition of oil.

Egg yolks can be frozen, but to prevent them from hardening, they should be mixed first with half a teaspoon of salt or sugar for every two yolks. It is a good idea to freeze some sweet and some savoury. They will keep for three months.

Egg whites, which are best frozen individually in ice-cube trays, will keep for six months. Yolks and whites, once thawed, should be used on the same day.

energizer
Make an infusion of fresh mint leaves, a lot of leaves and a little water. Chill and mix with tomato juice, add ice cubes and a wedge of lime.

flour
Hard wheat produces strong flour, for bread making, with a protein content up to 14–15 per cent. Soft wheat produces soft flour, for cake and pastry making; the protein content is about 8–9 per cent. American all-purpose flour is still too strong for sponge cakes; look for specifically designated cake flour. If you can only get strong flour, 'dilute' the protein, i.e. gluten, content by replacing about 20 per cent of the strong flour with rice flour, potato flour or cornflour which has virtually no gluten, but still the requisite amount of bulk. Do not compensate by increasing the amount of baking powder.

gelatine
Alternatives to gelatine from animal products include agar-agar, carrageen, gelozone and a kosher fish gelatine called Aqua-gel.

ginger
Peel and preserve in a jar of amontillado sherry, or peel and freeze it in thumb-size pieces, well wrapped in foil. The flavoured sherry makes an excellent ingredient for marinades, sauces for oriental dishes and salad dressings.

ham

For ease of handling, bake in the oven in a triple thickness of foil rather than boiling it, after soaking overnight.

hard water

Put a cleaned oyster shell in your kettle and the deposit will stick to the shell, and not the element. Boiling potato peelings in them for 30 minutes then rubbing with a not-too-abrasive scouring pad is said to get rid of hard water deposits from saucepans and non-electric kettles.

lemon curd

This freezes well as it is so rich, and is worth making when you can get good lemons. Curd can be made in the microwave in 4–5 minutes.

lobster

Canadian/Atlantic lobsters require slightly less cooking time than their harder shelled Scottish/European cousins. Add 50g (2oz) salt to each 1 litre (1¾ pints) water and boil for 12 minutes for the first 450g (1lb), then about 4 minutes for each 450g (1lb) after that. Thus:

12 minutes for 375g (12oz)
13 minutes for 500g (1¼lb)
15 minutes for 750g (1¾lb)
18 minutes for 1kg (2¼lb)

melba toast

This is worth making in batches, as it keeps well in an airtight tin. If it goes slightly soft, crisp it in the oven for a minute.

nuts

Store these well wrapped in the freezer for much longer keeping, otherwise they go rancid.

pancakes

Very useful as a standby for sweet and savoury dishes. Make in different sizes and thickness, and pack separated between sheets of greaseproof paper. They freeze well and will keep for three months.

papaya

As well as being useful as a meat tenderizer, it is very good for removing the spines of sea-urchins once embedded in the foot. The papain 'dissolves' the spines.

pineapple

As well as being a good meat tenderizer, see also below, pineapple skins are rich in vitamins and can be used as a tea or tisane.

soya 'milk' and 'cream'

These are useful UHT long-life products. The first makes good 'milk shakes' and smoothies, and the 'cream' excellent desserts when mixed with other good quality ingredients, as in the following recipe. Rice milk and oat milk are even more palatable in drinks. Soya 'cream' is a useful replacement for thick coconut cream, without the flavour of course.

chocolate creams

The texture of these is very smooth and creamy, and the good quality chocolate quite masks any soya flavour. As well as being suitable for those who cannot eat milk products, they are also low in sugar and fat. The chocolate cream can also be used as a filling for a fatless sponge cake, or to make excellent chocolate truffles; when it has set hard, scoop it with a teaspoon, roll into balls and dust with cocoa powder.

serves 6 to 8

200g (7oz) Soya Dream or other cream substitute made from soya beans
200g (7oz) dark chocolate, broken into pieces, at least 70 per cent cocoa solids

Heat the soya 'cream' and, when hot, but not near boiling, pour it over the chocolate pieces in a bowl. Vigorously beat the mixture until cold, then spoon into small ramekins or espresso coffee cups. Cover with cling film, refrigerate until set, and then serve.

tough meat

Papaya skins and leaves can be used to wrap around tough meat for an hour or

---

so to tenderize it. Papain is a powerful tenderising agent, and it should not be left in contact with the meat too long. A similar enzyme is to be found in pineapple, and the skin can be used in the same way. Beef marinated in pineapple juice is good, and the marinade can be boiled up to make a sauce or added to the cooking juices.

Tough meat can also be tenderized by coating with a paste of two table-spoons water, and one teaspoon each of salt, pepper, sugar and bicarbonate of soda, then wrapping in foil and roasting slowly.

yoghurt
Even high fat Greek yoghurt will curdle when boiled, unless stabilized first. To stabilize yoghurt, which can then be cooked in a sauce or soup, slake one teaspoon cornflour in one tablespoon water, stir into 500g yoghurt, bring to the boil and simmer for a few minutes.

Yoghurt can be frozen. Full fat yoghurt freezes better than low fat, and sweet better than plain.

yorkshire puddings
Use 100g (3½oz) plain flour, not self-raising, 300ml (½ pint) water and milk mixed, 2 eggs and a pinch of salt. A thin roasting tin should be used in pre-ference to enamelled cast iron.

appendix 2: notes on cooking for special needs

vegan

No animal products are eaten. Grains, pulses, nuts, fruit and vegetables and their by-products, such as seeds, sprouts, oils and juices, form this diet. A good source of recipes will be found in books covering the Mediterranean and oriental diets, as well as, of course, a wide range of books aimed specifically for vegans.

coeliac

This is caused by intolerance to gluten, thus wheat products are to be avoided, plus, in some cases, other grain consumption is also restricted. In principle, bread, cakes, pasta, flour-based sauces and many commercial products should be avoided. In practice, it is now possible to find gluten-free flour for baking and pasta made with rice flour.

lactose intolerant

Dairy products are banned from this diet. Soya milk and soya milk products can be substituted, to replace milk, cheese, yoghurt, cream. In addition, rice milk and oat milk can also be used.

low-fat, low-cholesterol and low-sugar diets

Some useful ingredients include olive oil sprays, and oil and water sprays, including make-your-own. Soya milk and cream, rice milk and oat milk. Fruit and vegetable juices and stocks instead of flour and butter sauces. Fructose instead of sugar (sucrose), because the former is sweeter, so less is required. Try fragrant infusions of herbs and teas instead of syrups; sweeten them lightly to make granitas, or use very diluted cordials. The soya bean in all its forms, including flour, and Quorn are useful store cupboard stand-bys.

some ideas for people who are over-entertained

Light, appetizing food, including chilled fruit and vegetable soups, tomato pudding and similar, jellied terrines, steamed dishes, fish en papillote, consommé. Serve vegetable-based first courses instead of protein, for example warm salads, vegetable terrines, stuffed vegetables, baby vegetables in a well-flavoured broth, and fruit-based desserts, such as sorbets, fools with yoghurt not cream or custard, compotes of dried fruit and nuts in fragrant tea, terrines and jellies. Or small intense chocolate desserts. Steam or grill main courses instead of roasting, braising or casseroling.

some remedies to assist jet-lag

Fresh vegetable juices and raw fruit and vegetables. Rice and pasta based dishes, including those combining meat or fish. Fish and potato pie. Potato-based soups.

vegetarian

Some professed vegetarians also eat fish; others will eat eggs and dairy produce, but cheese must be made with vegetable based rennet. Quorn is not approved by the Vegetarian Society, as egg whites from battery eggs are used in its production.

meat substitutes

TVP – a textured vegetable protein. It is available in ready-made meals, or as an ingredient to make into casseroles, for example.

Quorn – a mycological (fungus) product, available in ready-made meals and as an ingredient to turn into casseroles, stir-fries and sauces. It cooks quickly, and is highly absorbent of flavours.

Soya bean curd – available plain and smoked, firm and soft. It is also available as ready-made meals.

Tempeh – a dense, chewy, fermented soya bean product originally from southeast Asia, but now produced in the west and available in healthfood shops.

On the whole, when cooking for vegetarians, I favour recipe ideas using vegetables, pulses and grains rather than meat substitutes. Most vegetarians I know have given up meat and fish because they do not like the taste and texture, so would not welcome a substitute. These are some of the recipes I cook:

• savoury quire of pancakes

• crêpes filled with cooked vegetables, a matching sauce and topped with flaked, toasted nuts

• small, one-egg omelettes, three to a serving, with different fillings and herb garnishes

• mixed vegetable casseroles with pasta shapes or cooked pulses, topped with crumble, cobbler or gratin

• layered vegetable terrines – chunky or smooth

• grilled vegetable platters with good dressing as a starter; for a main course, put the vegetables on top of couscous or a fried potato, leek and apple cake

• warm single vegetable tarts – ripe tomato, onion, cauliflower cheese, spiced carrot, sweet and sour beetroot

useful recipe sources
Vegetarian Society publications. Books by Rose Elliot, Deborah Madison, Alice Waters and Sarah Brown. My last book, *Modern Classics*, and my earlier *Times Cook Book*, both have extensive chapters on grains, pasta, pulses, fruit and vegetables with recipes suitable for vegetarians. See also my *Times Vegetarian Cook Book*.

Glossary

acidulate to add vinegar or lemon juice to water in which you put slices of fruit or vegetable as you peel them. The acid prevents oxidation and discolouring. Note, however, that if you are making apple or quince jelly, that you do not add lemon juice as you want the lovely rich pink/red colour, which is caused by oxidation, to develop.

al dente used to describe pasta and vegetables which are cooked to retain a slight resistance 'to the tooth', i.e. not cooked until soft.

bain marie a water bath which is used on top of the stove or in the oven to give a particularly gentle method of cooking dishes such as custards and mousses. Typically, a roasting tin is half filled with water, the filled ramekins put in it, and the whole thing placed in the oven. This method can also be used for keeping pans of sauce warm on top of the stove, without over cooking them.

bake blind to bake an unfilled pastry case, the pastry is lined with greaseproof paper and a layer of baking beans or some other small weights are spread in the bottom to prevent the pastry from rising. Instead of buying baking beans, small ceramic or metal weights, you can improvise with chick peas, and then, when cool, store them for similar use in the future.

baste a term usually used in connection with roasts, when the cooking juices or oil or butter are spooned back over the meat from time to time during cooking, to prevent drying out.

blanch literally to whiten, but the term is used to describe food having brief contact with boiling water. The effect depends upon the foodstuff blanched. Cabbage leaves are blanched to soften them and make them pliable for stuffing. Bean sprouts are blanched to remove any surface toxins. Raw chicken breasts are blanched to whiten them.

caramel the stage reached by cooking sugar, sometimes with a little water until it reaches 176°C, when it becomes a rich golden brown, and sets hard when cool.

clarified butter this is butter from which the liquid and other deposits are removed, leaving nothing but pure fat, which is an excellent cooking medium because it has a high smoke point, and is also used for sealing terrines and pâtés, as well as in baking, and in Indian cooking, known as ghee.

cream the creaming of butter and sugar is one of the main techniques used in cake-making (the other is the rubbing-in method) and produces a light, airy cake. In a food processor, mixer or by hand with a wooden spoon, caster sugar and butter, at room temperature or softer, are worked together until a homogenous creamy mixture is achieved.

curdle usually used of milk, the term denotes a separation of liquid and solid, as when acid causes milk to turn sour, and the effect is to separate the curds, or solids, and the whey, or liquid.

cut in this is another way of combining fat into a pastry or, occasionally, a cake mixture. The fat is cut up with a knife in the flour, into smaller and smaller pieces, after which the liquid is added, or further worked in by hand. A food processor, with its sharp blades, makes quick work of this, on the 'pulse' button.

double boiler see also bain marie. Sometimes called a porringer, this utensil is essentially a small saucepan sitting inside a larger one, with water in between, which is kept at simmering point. It is used particularly for delicate mixtures such as egg-based sauces and custards which require extremely gentle cooking to prevent the egg from hardening.

en papillote food cooked 'en papillote' is food cooked in a paper parcel, either foil or parchment, which is baked in the oven, thus retaining all the juices and flavours. The paper is best cut into a heart shape, which is then folded down the middle, and the edges folded together to seal the parcel. A good method for small neat pieces of fish or meat, such as salmon cutlets or steaks or chicken breasts.

glaze to brush the surface of food to give it a glossy finish. This might be a fruit tart glazed with redcurrant jelly, or a cold salmon brushed with aspic. Vegetables can also be glazed by finishing them off, after cooking and draining, by tossing in a little butter.

---

julienne one of the classic French cookery terms used to denote how vegetables or other food stuffs are prepared. In this case they are cut into fine strips. Brunoise are finely diced vegetables.

knock back used in bread baking, this term refers to punching the air out of dough once it has been given its first rising, or proving.

mise en place another term from the professional kitchen to describe the whole of the basic preparations prior to cooking a dish, including the making of any stock, pastry or dough required, chopping of all the vegetables, for a soup for example, the boning and portioning of meat, filleting of fish, preparation of garnishes.

poach to cook gently in water or other liquid at a temperature just below boiling point.

prove used in bread-making, this term means the period after mixing when the dough is covered and left to rise, or prove, until doubled in volume.

quenelle a small, neat oval, shaped with two teaspoons, or dessertspoons for a larger portion; quenelles of ice cream, pâté or other soft mixture are often considered more appealing than the round shape produced by an ice-cream scoop. Quenelles are also a classic mixture, of fish or meat, pounded with cream and bound with beaten egg white, made into the traditional shape and then poached in stock, such as the famous 'quenelles de brochet', for which pike dumplings is much too solid a translation.

reduce to diminish the volume, and thus concentrate the flavour, by boiling.

render to gently cook a fatty piece of meat until the fat melts off, or is rendered, after which it can be discarded or used for another purpose, and the meat can then be prepared according to the recipe.

rest this is the short period in which you leave well alone. It might be pastry that you rest after making it, in order for it to relax and become easier to roll out. It might be a joint of beef you allow to rest after roasting. This causes the juices to distribute throughout the meat and the fibres to lose their tautness, making the meat easier to carve.

roux this is a thickening of cooked fat and flour, used in sauces, soups and casseroles. In a classic roux, the fat is allowed to brown and the flour cooked in it. This is used in meat casseroles, and most notably in Creole dishes such as gumbo and jambalaya, the recipes for which invariably begin, 'make a roux . . .' In a white roux, the fat is not browned and the sauce remains pale.

rub in see also, cut in. This is the technique employed in pastry-making where you use your fingertips to work the fat lightly into the flour until it resembles fine breadcrumbs.

sabayon egg yolks and water, wine, liqueur or spirit, whisked in a bowl over hot water, or in a bain marie, until thick, pale and fluffy. The Italian zabaglione is the same preparation.

scald to bring just to boiling point, as in the case of milk being used for making custard.

sear using a hot pan to brown the surface of a piece of meat. This is what ultimately produces a tasty, well-coloured gravy.

slake to dampen a dry substance such as flour or cornflour with water or other liquid, and then work it to a paste with more liquid, before adding it to a hot stock or sauce.

spatchcock to cut a chicken or other bird down the back and open it out flat, skin side up, for grilling or roasting.

split this is a chef's term which means much the same as curdled.

strain sieve.

sweat to cook something in its own juices or a little fat in a lidded pan, without browning.

sugar syrup a mixture of sugar and water, boiled together. The addition of glucose will prevent crystallizing.

toast (nuts) use a frying pan over a moderate heat to lightly cook flaked almonds, walnut halves, hazel nuts or what you will. When cool, the nuts take on an agreeable crispness and an enhanced flavour. Take care, however, as nuts burn easily.

wash (egg and milk) a mixture of egg yolk and milk can be beaten together and brushed over bread, for example, before baking. This will give it a shiny, golden finish when it comes out of the oven.

Index

index